Yale Agrarian Studies Series
James C. Scott, Series Editor

Frontiers of Fear

Tigers and People in the Malay World, 1600–1950

Peter Boomgaard

Yale University Press
New Haven & London

Designed by Mary Valencia
Set in Meridien Roman type by The Composing Room of Michigan, Inc.,
Grand Rapids, Michigan.
Printed in the United States of America by Sheridan Books,
Ann Arbor, Michigan.

Library of Congress Cataloging-in-Publication Data
Boomgaard, P., 1946–
Frontiers of fear : tigers and people in the Malay world, 1600–1950 / Peter Boomgaard.
p. cm. — (Yale agrarian studies series)
(Includes bibliographical references and index.)
ISBN 0-300-08539-7 (alk. paper)
1. Tigers—Asia, Southeastern—History.   2. Human-animal relationships—Asia,
Southeastern—History.   I. Title.   II. Yale agrarian studies.
QL737.C23 B658   2001
599.756'0959—dc21   2001026536

A catalogue record for this book is available from the British Library.

♾ The paper in this book meets the guidelines for permanence and durability
of the Committee on Production Guidelines for Book Longevity
of the Council on Library Resources.

10 9 8 7 6 5 4 3 2 1

To the memory of my father

Contents

Preface

It took me more than ten years to do the research for this book and to write it all down. Research started in September 1988, when I was invited to spend some time at the Netherlands Institute for Advanced Study in the Humanities and Social Sciences (NIAS), at Wassenaar. My plan was to write an article on people being killed by tigers in comparison with tigers being killed by people in Java between the 1850s and 1900. Annual numerical data were available on the number of people killed by tigers from the late 1860s up to 1905, and there were occasional figures for the number of tigers captured or killed by people.

I had barely started my research when I discovered that there was also quite some information about tigers for the period between 1600 and 1850, even if most of it was more qualitative than quantitative. It was the fortuitous discovery of H. J. V. Sody's study on the Javan rhinoceros in historical perspective (Sody 1959) that pointed me in the right direction. Following in Sody's tracks, I found so much material on tigers prior to 1850 that I decided to expand the period to be covered.

Another expansion occurred after I had read Robert Wessing's booklet on tiger beliefs in Indonesia (Wessing 1986). As an economic and social historian, I was not familiar with the anthropological literature on tigers. Having read Wessing's monograph, I decided to include the rituals and beliefs and added the study of the supernatural tiger to that of the natural one.

By then, I had come across so many references to real and imagined tigers in Sumatra that I felt obliged to include Sumatra. Not much later I decided if I was going to write about Javan and Sumatran tigers, I might as well include the ones from Bali and the Malayan Peninsula. Thus I would cover all the tigers of what is often called the Malay world, an area with many historical, cultural, and natural similarities.

Around the same time I must have substituted the idea of a book for that of an article, as it was clearly impossible to put all this information in just one article of 25 to 30 pages at the most. In the end I produced nine chapters of more or less that size, plus an introductory and a concluding chapter. It took me also ten times as long as I had thought that the initial plan would. What had started out as a fairly limited project turned into a serious undertaking.

The beginning of my research in 1988 was not the beginning of the project. The seed was sown in the summer of 1976 when I visited the Sukamade-Bandealit area, adjacent to the Meru Betiri nature reserve in eastern Java, together with a biologist friend, Henk Lof, who had heard that this was the last refuge of the Javan tiger. We did not see a tiger (after all I have read about the Javan tiger, I am tempted to add "of course"), but the notion of the Javan tiger, perhaps already extinct (if not, at least on the verge of extinction), got stuck in my subconscious. I started to follow the rather scarce information on the status of this subspecies in the media.

At the same time I was doing research for my dissertation, and occasionally I would come across references to tigers. It was not until another biologist friend, Wouter van der Weijden, urged me to systematically make notes of such remarks that I became professionally interested in the topic.

As a warning to those who wish to do similar research (elephants and crocodiles would be excellent candidates) I should point out that, in fact, it can only be done as a sideline. I have read hundreds of books in which a few lines on tigers would have been my only reward if I had not been looking at a whole range of other data as well. The tiger (or the leopard and the clouded leopard) is rarely the main protagonist of a book, and in libraries and archives "tiger" is very seldom a key word or a search category.

According to Alain Delon, in the movie *Samourai* (1967)—but I quote from memory and may have got it wrong—only the tiger in the jungle is as lonely as the samurai. I would like to add: or the person who tries to write a book on the history of tigers and people in the Malay world, no matter how many people shower him with information and support.

Acknowledgments

This kind of research can hardly be done without the help of many people who come across references to tigers. The main procurers of useful information about tigers were the following: Jet Bakels, P. J. H. van Bree, J. G. de Casparis, Robert Cohen (deceased), Robert Cribb, Michael Dove, Th. van den End, Erwiza Erman, Marianne Fluitsma, Louise Fresco, Ramachandra Guha, Vincent Houben, Frans Hüsken, Wouter Hugenholtz, Peter Jackson, Bernice de Jong Boers, Huub de Jonge, Han Knapen, Willem Korthals Altes, Denys Lombard (deceased), Machfudi Mangkudilaga (deceased), Harry Poeze, Peter Post, J. J. Quarles van Ufford, Mahesh Rangarajan, Rosemary Robson, Jan van Rosmalen, Ticia Rueb, Willem van Schendel, Ann Stoler, Paul Storm, Heather Sutherland, Thommy Svensson, Gerard Termorshuizen, Tundjung, Karel Voous, Wouter van der Weijden, and Annemarijke Winkel.

Most of my research was carried out in the archives in Jakarta (Arsip Nasional) and in The Hague (Algemeen Rijksarchief), and in the libraries of the Koninklijk Instituut voor de Tropen (KIT; Royal Tropical Institute) in Amsterdam, and of the Koninklijk Instituut voor Taal Land-en Volkenkunde (KITLV; Royal Institute for Linguistics and Anthropology) in Leiden. It was the personnel of the latter library (Rini Hogewoning, Nico van Rooyen, Josephine Schrama, Alfred Schipper) who had to bear the brunt of my research activities. Not only did they do so without complaint, they even managed not to lose their good humor when I ordered yet another pile of dusty and heavy volumes.

I also owe a debt of gratitude to the people who ran the marvelous library service that is offered by NIAS.

ACKNOWLEDGMENTS

I am grateful to Ian Brown (School of Oriental and African Studies, London), John Knight (International Institute for Asian Studies, Leiden), and Michael Parnwell (Association of South-East Asian Studies in the United Kingdom, London) for inviting me to give talks on a topic of my own choice, and for not trying to wriggle out of it when that topic turned out to be tigers.

I had the good fortune of discussing ideas, problems, and shorter and longer pieces of text with a number of friends and colleagues. Wouter van der Weijden and Jet Bakels, who read various chapters, were my most important sparring partners. I would like to mention Erwiza Erman, Henk Lof, and Karel Voous as people with whom I could always discuss my tiger problems.

Moreover, I could swap experiences with the members of the so-called EDEN team, Freek Colombijn, David Henley, Bernice de Jong Boers, and Han Knapen. EDEN, an acronym for Ecology, Demography, and Economy in Nusantara (another word for Indonesia), is a project of the KITLV, my employer since 1991. Tigers were not and are not one of the main concerns of the members of this team, but we shared an interest in environmental history. Although my interest in tigers predated the EDEN project, my book can be seen as part of it, as my research was decidedly stimulated by debates with the team members.

I owe a debt of gratitude to Jolanda Leemburg–den Hollander and Hagar Visser (both, KITLV) for their assistance in getting the various drafts of the book in good shape, and to Marjan Groen (also KITLV), who produced the maps. The book I had started 12 years earlier at NIAS also underwent its finishing touch there, and I wish to thank Petry Kievit-Tyson, Yves de Roo, Kathy van Vliet-Leigh, and Willem van der Wal, who assisted me with the final version, and the executive director of NIAS, Wouter Hugenholtz, who kindly managed to find me a place there at short notice.

Finally, I am grateful to James Scott, who suggested that I submit my manuscript to Yale University Press, and to Jean Thomson Black, Heidi Downey, Judy Sacks, and Vivian Wheeler, the Yale editors who guided me through the publishing process.

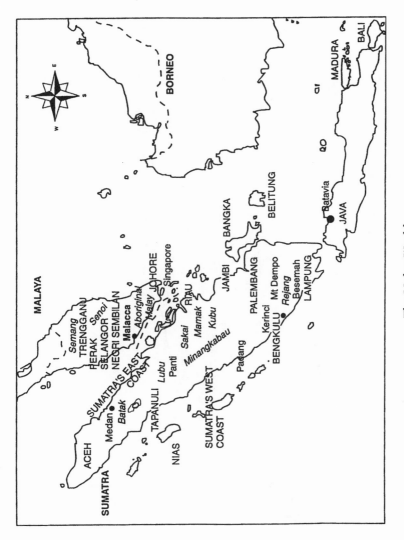

The Malay World

The Island of Java

1

Introduction

This book is about the relation between humans and the three big cats of the Malay world: the tiger, the leopard, and the clouded leopard. Above all, however, it is about the tiger.

It is difficult to be neutral about tigers. They seem to elicit either strongly positive or strongly negative sentiments, and it is even possible (and far from rare) that one person has both positive and negative feelings about tigers. Indeed, many Westerners clearly have regarded the tiger as a beautiful animal but at the same time as a terrible force of nature and a cruel brute, as the following remarks illustrate: "If it is the lion who rules Africa, it is undoubtedly the tiger who is the tyrant of the Indian jungles and forests. It is a beautiful animal—black stripes against a yellow and white background—graceful in his movements, but of a mean, cruel disposition, so that one could compare him with a Nero or a Philip the Second" (Hartwig 1860, 61).

Almost 70 years later the American tourist and big-game hunter Mary Bradley held similar opinions, although she stated them more lyrically:

Never in my life had I seen such a picture. Elephants by moonlight, lions at dawn, gorillas at blazing noon I had seen, but nothing was ever so beautiful and so glorious to me as that tiger walking out of his jungle. He was everything that was wild and savage, lordly and sinister.

The tiger was there, to the right of the [dead] buffalo, a picture of savage life and death. So he must have stood many times, over his kills, wary, yet arrogant in his great strength, lording it over the jungle, inspiring terror in every living thing—superb and terrible.

The tiger was lying stretched out, about fifty yards away from the buffalo. As we came up he roared with fury, dying as he was—dying by vio-
lence as he had lived. Every night of his life he had been nourished on
the blood and pain of some defenseless creature and now a sudden,
sharp destruction had struck him down. He had been terrible in life and
he was terrible in death (Bradley 1929, 212–15).

A great many travelogues of Western visitors to the Malay world contained
tiger stories, mostly popular hunting stories. It has been argued that such stories prepared readers for their role as tiger-hunting rulers over the Orient. The
following quotation is an explicit illustration of this argument: "I have devoted
considerable space in this book to the tiger. For, to my mind there is a romance
and a devilishness about a tiger possessed by no other Indian animal. To meet
and overcome a tiger is probably the first great ambition of every young big
game hunter" (Wardrop and Morris 1923, 4).

However, in the eyes of the people of the Malay world the tiger was not always the enemy. He could be a friend as well.

History behind the Scenes

This book is also a study of what normally remains hidden—a history of the
invisible, in more than one sense.

Not so long ago, historians were mainly interested in kings, wars, diplo-
macy, and "high" culture. A minority studied economies of the past, which
brought agriculture, industry, and commerce into view. The "common people"
as a popular research topic arrived later on the scene. So did "the people without history" (Wolf 1982), the non-European societies who had often left no
written records, and so did women. Courts and the cities around them are being studied, as are the countryside, its villages and its people, and the arable
lands around these villages. Most history writing, however, stops there.

My book not only deals with kings, courts, and villages, but also focuses on
what lies beyond the edge of the arable lands, namely the "wild," uncultivated
areas and their inhabitants. It is, among other things, a history of forests and
other wildernesses. It is also a history in which several kinds of animals are
among the protagonists. Therefore, this study leaves the realm of human history from time to time. However, it stops short of being the history of the tiger
only, let alone the history of this animal written from his point of view.[1] Crossing the species boundary seems to be one step too far, although occasionally I
will present interpretations of observed tiger behavior, from which one can try
to infer the tiger's mentality.

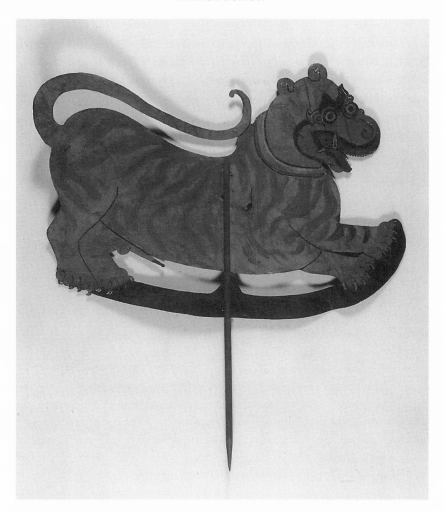

Among the many deities, princes, and other people to be found in the Javanese and Balinese shadow play, the tiger is one of the few animals represented by a *wayang kulit* puppet. Author's collection

The book is also a history of the invisible because by now tigers have disappeared from some of the areas dealt with here and have become rare in other regions. Even when tiger populations were large, few Europeans ever saw a tiger in the wild. Nor did most indigenous inhabitants of towns and cities.

Finally, this book is a history of the invisible because, in addition to real natural tigers, it also deals with supernatural ones. The supernatural tiger, as we will see later on, is not always visible to ordinary mortals.

The American anthropologist Clifford Geertz introduced the term "theatre state" for Bali in the nineteenth century (Geertz 1980). Some scholars have criticized this notion, but we can borrow the image without accepting all the implications. If we visualize the states of the Malay world, the colonial state included, as stages upon which the normal human drama is acted out, this book takes the reader backstage. Yet the tiger is not only the guardian of the area backstage, the forest; he is also to be found on the *kayon*, the marker used by the puppeteer to demarcate the stage of the Javanese shadow play.

Environmental History, Wild Nature, and the Orient

The main theme of the book is the interaction between humans and tigers/leopards, with the natural environment serving as interface. The book explores how changes in the behavior of one party influenced the actions of the other, mediated by environmental change. It is, therefore, also an exercise in environmental (or ecological) history. Briefly put, environmental history deals with the mutual influence of humans and the environment. Human beings exert influence on the environment, and the thus altered environment influences human beings differently than before these changes occurred (Boomgaard 1997a, 2).

We are discovering that landscapes are forever in a state of flux. As this is often the result of very slow, almost imperceptible processes, contemporary observers may very well have missed them (see also Schama 1996). Forests and other "wild" areas have long been seen as timeless, as places where time had stood still. Nowadays, scholars and lay observers alike are very much aware of the changes, often for the worse, in landscapes, but even in less hectic times "wild nature" was not an unchanged and unchangeable entity.

The reader will see how environmental change, often but not always manmade, influences the tiger's habitat directly and indirectly. It is also shown how the tiger's reaction to such disturbances has influenced human behavior in turn.

The "stage" of this book is the area covered by what are now the states of Indonesia, Malaysia, and Singapore.[2] A large part of this area is rather homogeneous culturally. It also shares many natural features, like climate, flora, and fauna. I will refer to this area as the Malay world.

The Malay world is part of what is often called the Orient. I will not attempt to position my book in the ongoing debate on Orientalism, a debate that received its kick-off with the publication of Edward Said's book with the same title (Said 1979). Let me just say that the Orient evoked reactions, images, and sentiments that were often not based on solid information. This complex of im-

4

ages then started to live a life of its own. Such ideas played a role particularly during what is often called the age of modern imperialism (1870–1914), when the Europeans in Asia—that is, the ruling class of the colonies—started to draw firmer dividing lines between themselves and the people they ruled.

This book examines Western perceptions of the Oriental natural world. These ideas no doubt were an important force in the creation of the Western view of the Orient.[3] Many white Westerners came to see the Orient as a whole as a dangerous place. Mortality was, indeed, high, partly because of the many endemic and epidemic diseases, the hot climate, and bad habits, like the excessive consumption of alcohol. Many Europeans died in imperial wars or were killed during uprisings of indigenous people. The tropical forests were thought to be filled with all kinds of dangerous animals, like elephants, rhinoceroses, crocodiles, snakes, poisonous insects, and, of course, tigers. A theme that appears throughout the book is this fear of dangerous animals and the question of how warranted it was.

I also address indigenous perceptions of Oriental nature and how they changed over time, as well as whether a sharp distinction can sensibly be drawn between Western and Eastern perceptions of nature. In fact, given the differences in views of nature between various groups in Europe in almost any period, it would be nothing short of miraculous if uniform views existed across levels of development and across classes in the Malay world.

Killing the Killers: The Role of Individuals and the State

The tiger is, like all big cats, a carnivore and a predator. Tigers kill game and domesticated animals, including pets, a feature that did not endear them to humans. More importantly, tigers were also reputed to kill humans. It was the so-called man-eater who was responsible for such atrocities. Nowadays, man-eating is very rare, and various tiger specialists have recently argued that it was never important, more an "Orientalist" myth than anything else. This book sets the record straight about man-eating.

Various indigenous states seem to have been instrumental in attempts to destroy large numbers of tigers. State-sponsored hunting was one option; organizing ceremonies in which tigers were killed was another. The latter activity, to be found in central Java from 1600 onward, will be analyzed in a separate chapter.

Among Europeans (and also among many indigenous people) the general opinion was that tigers who had killed cattle or people had to be destroyed. In 1820, tigers were perceived to be such a threat in Java that the *Bataviasche Courant,* the official Government gazette, printed an article proposing the establishment of a Society for the Extermination of Tigers in Java.[4] That proposal came to naught, but there was no shortage of attempts, both by the colonial state and by individual Europeans, to rid the areas concerned of these dangerous animals.

The state promised rewards (bounties) to all those who captured or killed a tiger. We are particularly well informed about this topic, and the bounty system and the impressive quantity of reports it generated are an important key to understanding the relationship between humans and tigers. Obviously, hunting and trapping are also phenomena to be dealt with extensively.

The Tiger's Image

To the inhabitants of the Malay world, tigers were certainly not merely animals to be trapped and hunted. Tigers are protagonists in many myths, legends, fairy tales, and fables. They can be found in the *wayang*, the Javanese and Balinese shadow theater, as well as in other popular performances. They are also encountered in paintings, carvings, and sculptures.

Earlier I described the current book as a history of the invisible, and that is true in more sense than one. There is—at least in the literature—a whole range of tigers who are supposedly the embodiments of invisible forces: ghosts, spirits, dead souls (or souls of the dead), or whatever term one prefers. Important motifs in this respect are the ancestral tiger, the tiger familiar, and the weretiger, to be compared to the European werewolf. The information available on this topic is overwhelming, although it is not always easy to find out what the informants may have meant. However, for those who are familiar with the study of popular culture (micro history), such problems are nothing out of the ordinary. These data, no matter how difficult to interpret, are one of the few keys to understanding indigenous attitudes in the past. This book, therefore, is about not only natural tigers but also supernatural ones.

It may disappoint some of my readers, but I do not present an analysis of the many animal fables in which the tiger figures prominently. I refer to some of them only in passing. The analysis of the themes and motifs of these stories is very much the work of a handful of specialists.

Tigers also used to be important in the imagery of the West. This changed after the Second World War, when the Western countries lost their colonies in the Orient, the Malay world included. Tiger stories ended up as bedtime stories, taken seriously only by very young children. For grownups, tiger stories became associated with the rather boring ramblings ("tall stories") of older relatives, a symbol of the Empire's faded splendor.

Since the notion has spread (roughly from 1975 on) that tigers might be on the verge of extinction, tigers have made a remarkable comeback in the West. They are now on television regularly, competing for the viewer's attention with soap operas and science fiction. The quality of these films is often very high, and they have done a tremendous job in making people aware of the plight of the big cats, particularly that of the tiger.

The tiger's recent popularity may, in the end, be instrumental in producing the funds that are needed to save the species, and that is something to be grateful for. However, propaganda on the tiger's behalf, although no doubt well intended, is often as one-sided as was the colonial image. The tiger is now represented as a harmless being that only seldom becomes dangerous, and then not without provocation. This stands in sharp contrast to the colonial image of the tiger as a cruel, gore-covered tyrant of the wilderness, a permanent threat to his human neighbors. Here I present ample data that should enable the reader to take a position between these two extremes.

Do Animals Have a History?

What about the tiger's perception of us? This book is an exercise in human history, but is it also an exercise in tiger history? In other words, do tigers (and leopards and clouded leopards) have a history, as opposed to a past? The theologian and philosopher Martin Buber thought they did not:

> Beasts of prey have no history. A panther can indeed have a biography and a colony of termites even state annals, but they do not have history in the great distinguishing sense of human history as 'world history.' A life of prey yields no history. (Buber 1965, 108–9)

However, it will be shown that such a clear-cut distinction is problematic. I discuss the question as to whether tigers are influenced in their behavior by the proximity of humans and by changes in human behavior. It will also be discussed whether humans adapt (sufficiently) to tigers, whether such adaptations vary between places and periods, and how these mutual adaptations seem to imply learning processes at both sides of the frontier between humans and tigers. Here the narrative touches on recent debates regarding the terms "wild" and "tame," "humankind" and "nature," which no longer seem to represent opposite sides of sharp boundaries.[5]

It is one of the advantages of studying a long time period and a variety of places that differences in time and place emerge, making it possible to evaluate the "historicity" of tiger behavior. So much of our knowledge about tigers is based on data regarding one subspecies, the Bengal tiger, and most of it dates from the years after 1900. It is time to challenge the monopoly of the twentieth-century Bengal tiger.

The Tiger and the Scholar

Historians have not been in the front ranks of those who have studied the tiger over the last 400 years or so. Their interest in animals has always been quite marginal, even regarding domesticated animals. As animals were not supposed to have a history, this lack of enthusiasm does not come as a total surprise. Furthermore, historians describe and analyze things from the past; that is, by definition, what they are supposed to do. Often, therefore, the historian's subject matter is no longer with us. Fortunately, the tiger is still among us, although it is anyone's guess how long his presence will last. But for once, the historian was just in time.

In contrast, biologists have been eager students of the tiger's varying fortunes, and thanks to their unceasing efforts, we can now confront the "tall stories" about the tigers to be found in the older literature with the findings of specialists. However, many biologists, past and present, do not have a sense of history. Often enough I have found that they incorporated data of half a century or more ago in studies purported to refer to the present. The notion that animal behavior might change over time seems to be as alien to naturalists as it is to historians and philosophers.

Of course, biologists are very powerful scholars, as they are the givers of names (although, of course, in the early stages they had to depend upon lay observers). In fact, they define the terms of the debate, and I will show that what we now call tigers is not at all the same as what was thus named in the eighteenth century. It is historians, however, who, with the advantage of hindsight, may attempt to judge how well biologists have exercised their powers.

Anthropologists of the past (including amateur ethnographers, such as colonial civil servants, missionaries, and physicians) had a sharp eye for the invisible. Knowledge of the supernatural tiger largely is based on their writings. Most of them were less interested in the natural tiger. The problem with modern anthropologists is that some of them assume that beliefs and attitudes found among the tribal groups of today reliably reflect the beliefs once held by all people when the world was younger. Again, what seems to be lacking is the notion that it is highly unlikely that present-day beliefs and attitudes can have remained unchanged for many centuries. After all, humans have multiplied and have changed the environment beyond recognition, and tigers are now so rare that an encounter with one is about as likely as that with a UFO. In the Malay world, a whole generation has grown up that knows as little about tigers as Europeans do.

In this book I combine the findings, approaches, and theories of historians, biologists, and anthropologists, in addition to the descriptions given by contemporary lay observers from the Malay world itself and from Europe. Being a historian myself, I may have erred when using the data, methods, and theories of other disciplines, even though I have often consulted their representatives. Nevertheless, I hope to present a multifaceted picture that will allow more than one interpretation.

There are still tigers in the Malay world, but their numbers are dropping, and some subspecies have disappeared or are about to disappear. Although this book was written before they were all gone, the "fall" of the tiger is an important theme.

This book is in so far a product of traditional historical research that it is almost entirely based on research in libraries and archives. Apart from one site visit and conversations with people from the Malay world, it is not based on fieldwork. Most of the records I have used were the products of the colonial states concerned and the white travelers who visited the area or lived there. I did use some indigenous sources, but they constitute a small minority. My information, therefore, is biased. I have tried to compensate for these biases, and I discuss methodological problems when and where appropriate.

2

Meeting the Tiger and the Other Big Cats

The Malayan Peninsula is today the only region of the areas studied in this book where the tiger, the leopard, and the clouded leopard all can be encountered (see Table 2.1), although few people ever have done so. If a meeting with a tiger or a leopard is (and was) rare, very few people, apart from the local population, have ever seen the clouded leopard in the wild. Other areas had only one or two big-cat species in historical times, and it has always been a riddle as to why this was the case. The Malayan Peninsula, Sumatra, Java, Bali, and Borneo were once, during the driest periods of the Pleistocene, all part of one landmass, the Sunda Shelf. Sea levels were then up to 150 m lower than they are today, and one would expect all three animals to inhabit all five areas mentioned in Table 2.1; their differential presence is, therefore, puzzling.[1] Why does Java have the leopard, and why is it absent from the other Indonesian islands? Why was there no tiger on the island of Borneo, and why no clouded leopards in Java and Bali? I will deal briefly with these questions, although I do not pretend to have the answers.

Some fifteen years ago, two Dutch zoologists suggested that leopards might have been introduced to Java during the Middle Ages for ceremonial/ritual reasons. As will be shown later (Chapter 8), there are indeed rituals in which tigers and/or leopards play a role, but leopards evidently were used only if no tigers could be acquired. Why would they have imported leopards when tigers were abundantly available? Moreover, fossils have been reported from Java, and that makes the case for a late introduction rather weak. Besides, it is difficult to imagine that people were able, for example in c. 1500, to ship sufficient numbers of leopards to Java for successful breeding in the wild, since leopards often react very badly when taken captive.[2]

Table 2.1. Distribution of tigers, leopards, and clouded leopards over the Malay world

	Tiger	Leopard	Clouded leopard
Malayan			
Peninsula	x	x	x
Sumatra	x		x
Borneo	—		x
Java	(x)	x	—
Bali	(x)	?	—

x = Present today
(x) = Extinct or almost extinct after 1950
— = Present in prehistoric deposits
? = Recent dubious references

Another riddle is the absence of the tiger from the island of Borneo. Occasionally, reports have suggested that tigers might still be present in remote parts of the island, but the scholarly community has remained skeptical. However, there are some indications that tigers may have been part of Borneo's prehistoric fauna. A single subadult canine tooth of a tiger has been found among the early Stone Age remains (prior to 10,000 BC) from Niah Great Cave. Secondly, real tiger teeth, which the local population claims can be found by digging in the soil, played a role in ceremonies (oath taking) and were worn as adornments by male aristocrats. Finally, the tiger motif is strongly present in many myths, as is demonstrated in detail in the chapter on the weretiger (Chapter 9). As proof of the tiger's former presence in Borneo this may not be sufficient, but the data do suggest that there may have been a Bornean tiger.[3]

Finally, the question can be asked of why there are no clouded leopards in Java and Bali. Prehistoric remains from Java suggest that they used to be part of the fauna but have since disappeared.[4]

Peter Bellwood, dealing with the "disjunct distribution" of many more mammals than the ones mentioned here, seems to support the view that "any major human role in this pattern" is unlikely. He argues that "the reasons appear to be mainly ecological," listing climatic factors among others (Bellwood 1985, 36–37). Based on these assumptions, one could speculate that the leopard, a good tree climber but also a typical savanna hunter, may have left the tropical zone around the equator when climatic change turned it into an ever-wet rainforest zone. This change made it less attractive than the monsoon areas, Java and Bali included, with their more checkered (seasonal) vegetation pattern. The clouded leopard, on the other hand, is generally regarded as a typical dense-forest animal, and it is tempting to hypothesize that this animal was "leaving" Java for Sumatra and Borneo precisely when the leopards were disappearing in the latter islands.

The same climatic change, resulting in a much wetter tropical zone, was unattractive to the tiger living in equatorial regions, because a dense tropical rainforest does not contain much that appeals to tigers. When, therefore, Borneo was turning into an ever-wet forest area, the tiger became extinct, perhaps helped—as some of the Bornean myths suggest—by the few humans to be found there. That tigers did not disappear from Sumatra, by then also much more densely forested than before, should be attributed to higher human population densities there, given the fact that humans create the ecological niches preferred by tigers. But all this is, needless to say, speculation.

The Tiger

Nomenclature, Subspecies, and Numbers

The tiger's scientific name, *Panthera tigris,* is based on a classification of all Felidae, the family of cats, published in 1917 by Reginald Pocock of the Natural History Museum in London. This scientific name was accepted long ago by all specialists, but occasionally we encounter in a newspaper article the older systematic name, *Felis tigris,* dating back to the eighteenth-century designer of the binomial classification system, Linnaeus.

Tigers are, according to "modern" systematic notions, to be found only in Asia, but in earlier times some African and American big cats were also called "tigers" by many Europeans. Leopards, occurring both in Africa and in Asia, were often also called "tigers," namely black tigers, spotted tigers, or even small tigers. In fact, those who wanted to specify that they were referring to what we call a tiger today usually talked about a royal tiger (Dutch: *koningstijger*), a striped tiger, or a big tiger.

The terminology to be found in the languages of the Malay world adds to the confusion. The normal term for tiger in Malaya and Sumatra is *harimau,* with spelling variants including *arimau, rimau,* and *rimo.* In Javanese, Madurese (eastern Java), and Balinese it is *macan* (pronounced "machan"), a term sometimes also used elsewhere in the Malay world, and in Sundanese (western Java) *méong.* In all these cases the user of the term may be referring to the real (royal) tiger, but it is also possible that the term is used more loosely, in the sense of "big cat-like animals." Those who wanted to make clear that they were specifically talking about the royal tiger used terms such as *harimau belang, harimau tunggal,* and *macan besar* in Malay, or *macan gémbong, macan lorèk,* and *macan lorèng* in Javanese.[5]

There are now some 5,000 to 7,500 (real) tigers left, which is not bad compared to an estimate of 4,000 to 4,500 given some 20 years ago by Vratislav Mazák, the then leading tiger expert. However, it is down from over 16,000 about 35 years ago.[6]

Of the tiger species, eight subspecies present in historical times can be distinguished, of which three are extinct or close to extinction. Four subspecies were found in the Malay world (see Table 2.2).[7]

Three of these four are endemic to the islands they are named after. The Indo-Chinese tiger also occurs outside the area mentioned here, Malaya; the figures quoted refer to the Malayan Peninsula only.

The Bali tiger is extinct. Some writers have argued that this may have been the case as early as 1937, the date of the last confirmed kill. I find that rather unlikely, however. H. C. O. Zimmermann, who knew the western Balinese tiger area very well, stated in 1938 that, after 14 tigers had been killed there between 1933 and 1937, there were six tigers in the lowland area and probably many more in the mountains. Based on H. J. V. Sody's data, J. H. Becking dated the demise of the subspecies at c. 1942. It has been extinct almost certainly since about 1955, though rumors that the Bali tiger was still around persisted until the late 1970s.[8]

Until 1997 it was also assumed that the Javan tiger was extinct or about to become extinct, as the latest confirmed sightings, in the Meru Betiri National Park, eastern Java, predated 1980. At that moment, only three to five adult animals were believed to be alive, the last cub having been sighted in 1971. In

Table 2.2. Nomenclature of tiger subspecies found in the Malay world and estimate of present numbers

Location	Subspecies	Taxonomic name	Estimated number
Bali	Bali tiger	*P.t. balica*	extinct
Java	Javan tiger	*P.t. sondaica*	?
Sumatra	Sumatran tiger	*P.t. sumatrae*	400–600
Malaya	Indo-Chinese tiger	*P.t. corbetti*	500–600

The only photograph of a live Javan tiger in the wild, taken in 1938 in the Ujung Kulon National Park, western Java. The Javan tiger was already an endangered subspecies by then. Photo A. Hoogerwerf, collection KITLV

1979, tiger sightings were also reported from the area around Mount Slamet, at the border between western and central Java. In 1987 a team of forestry students found tiger prints, scratchings, and feces in Meru Betiri. Another team, looking for tigers in 1990, again found only prints. In 1994, the presence of a tiger was reported from Banyuwangi, near Meru Betiri, where, according to a newspaper article from the same year, tigers were still supposed to occur. Then, to the complete surprise of everyone, during the forest fires caused by the El Niño-related drought that hit Indonesia in 1997, four adult tigers and two cubs were reported to have come down from Mount Merbabu or Mount Merapi in central Java, far from Meru Betiri. Other alleged sightings of Javan tigers were reported from the Gunung Kidul area in southern central Java in July 1999. However, the presence of tigers in these areas was not confirmed by specialists, who set various "camera traps," a method that had proved its value in Sumatra. So although the Javan tiger might still be counted among the living, the chances seem to be rather slim, and it is unlikely that this will last long.[9]

The number of Sumatran tigers seems impressive compared to the possible handful of Javan tigers, but the subspecies is evidently also endangered. According to a 1996 interview with a World Wildlife Fund (WWF) project coordinator in Sumatra, Ron Lilley, Indonesia exported more than 4,000 kg of tiger bones in the period 1973–1992. At an average bone weight of eight kg per Sumatran tiger, the annual number of tigers killed would have been at least 25, or 500 during the 20-year period covered by the data. As there are now 400–600 tigers left, this implies that the number of tigers was halved during that period. These calculations are consistent with information from 1978, when Sumatra's tiger population was estimated to be about 1,000. Lilley wrote that at that time, 14 tigers were killed every year, though one wonders how he arrived at such a precise figure. The same 1997 El Niño drought that led to forest fires in Java did so in Sumatra, and tigers were spotted outside the national parks, where they are supposed to be safe. The good news is that better counting methods suggest that the upper limit may be 600 instead of the 500 usually found in recent reports.[10]

The most recent estimate on the Indo-Chinese or Corbett's tiger suggests that there are still 800–1,400 animals alive, but the totals are probably higher, as data for Burma, Cambodia, and Laos are not included. Malaysia has between 500 and 600 of these tigers within its borders, according to data from Peter Jackson, which is slightly down from 600–650—a 10-year-old estimate, that, however, is still being quoted in recent publications. Both figures are higher than the 1976 estimate of 300, which, if reliable, would suggest quite some improvement prior to the moderate losses of the last years.[11] I do not regard this estimate as trustworthy.

Physical Characteristics

The island tigers (of Sumatra, Java, and Bali) are somewhat darker and smaller than all mainland subspecies. It is questionable, however, whether nonspecialists would see many differences among the four subspecies from the Malay world. They would certainly see a difference between a Bali tiger, the smallest tiger ever, and the Siberian tiger (*Panthera tigris altaica*), the biggest one alive.[12] The basic coloring of the skin varies from very light among the Siberian tigers to quite dark among the Bali ones.

Of the four subspecies dealt with here, the Indo-Chinese tiger is the largest, although not by a wide margin. It is followed by the Javan tiger, which is marginally larger than the Sumatran tiger, which in turn, is bigger than the Bali tiger. There seems to be some confusion regarding the relative positions of the Javan and Sumatran tigers. Looking at the figures of Sody and Mazák, one has to conclude that the average skull of the (adult male) Javan tiger is larger than that of the Sumatran tiger, although by a small margin. The Javan tiger also weighs more than the Sumatran tiger, namely 140 kg maximum for an adult male of the former and 130–135 kg at the most for the latter. Finally, the body length, including the tail, of most island tigers was probably under 275 cm, and the shoulder height up to 80 cm.[13]

In sources predating the nineteenth century, clearly bent on impressing the folks back home, we find measurements that are obviously unrealistic, like a tiger, mentioned in 1628 near Batavia (present-day Jakarta), measuring 18 feet (c. 6 meters) in length. The following quotation from the Frenchman Sieur Jean de Lacombe of Querçy, who visited Java around 1670, is a rather extreme example of the tall-story genre:

> But the tygers there are so monstrous that it might be thought they endeavoured to attein the greatness of camels: for even a tall man would have sufficient difficulty to raise his hand as high as they carry their backs. I saw once one that had been slain with great ado, for which eighteen men employed no less force than industry to transport it from one place to another. To this prodigious height is added a fury and malignity so great that everything flees before and around them, so as not to be exposed to their butchery.

Almost equally far-fetched, of course, is a tiger as big as a horse, mentioned in a late-eighteenth-century compilation.[14]

The most famous tiger subspecies, the one that is much better documented than any other subspecies, is the Bengal or Indian tiger (*Panthera tigris tigris*), an animal smaller than the Siberian tiger but bigger than the largest "Malay" tiger, the Indo-Chinese one.

The Bali tiger is the darkest of the tigers. The Javan tiger is slightly less dark but darker than the Sumatran tiger. There are, apart from the basic coloring, other differences in coat patterns. For example, the male Sumatran tiger has enormous side-whiskers, almost like a lion's mane. Stripe patterns on the reddish yellow-brown coat also differ among the subspecies. The black stripes of the Javan tiger are smaller and their number is lower than those of the Sumatran and Bali tigers. The stripes of the latter two subspecies are often paired, with small "islands" (lozenges) between the stripes.[15]

In the nineteenth century and earlier we often find the term "black tiger."[16] As many people regarded the leopard as some sort of tiger, and as the modern literature does not recognize black—that is, melanistic—tigers in the Malay world (and very rarely elsewhere), it must be assumed that this term always refers to the black leopard. So-called white, or albino, tigers are less rare, though I know of no recent case of albinism in the Malay world.[17] The *macan putih* (white tiger) found in stories about Java's past may have been a mythical being (see Chapter 8), but it is also possible that these legends refer to real white tigers that existed in times past. The only one in the twentieth century to mention rumors of albino and melanistic tigers in the Archipelago was the hunter J. C. Brasser, but in the absence of any confirmation this can be safely ignored.[18]

Only a handful of specialized naturalists were involved in making these distinctions, and they did not always agree among themselves. In the 1840s, the Dutch naturalist C. J. Temminck suggested that the island tigers were sufficiently different from the Bengal tiger to treat them as a separate (sub)species, but it was not until 1910 that zoologists started to propose distinguishing three subspecies among the island tigers. Such a differentiation seems to have been readily accepted as regards the Sumatran and Javan tigers, but the status of the Bali tiger remained disputed for a long time. In 1912, E. Schwarz argued that the Bali tiger should be accorded subspecies status, a proposal that was backed by Sody in 1933. However, as late as 1958, when the Bali tiger was in all probability already extinct, and again in 1969, when this was certainly the case, authoritative zoological journals published articles denying that the Bali tiger had ever existed. Nowadays, it is generally accepted that the Bali tiger was a separate subspecies.[19]

There may have been a frequent exchange of genes between the Java and Bali subspecies, as tigers, which are good swimmers, were repeatedly reported to have crossed the strait between Java and Bali (the distance is only 2 km). In a recent handbook on the ecology of Java and Bali, the writer admitted that such an exchange was possible but also said that "there is no evidence to support this conjecture." However, I have come across a number of references in the literature, of which one (1849) stated that tigers were known to swim from Java to Bali, while another mentioned people who had witnessed tigers swimming the other way around (1927).[20]

Even the fact that there were tigers in Bali was not generally known. Some older publications stated that the tiger in the Archipelago was limited to the islands of Java and Sumatra. Strangely enough, some authors came up with leopards in Bali even as late as 1984. However, there has never been a confirmed sighting of such an animal. Finally, in many publications it was argued that there were leopards in Sumatra, while, according to contemporary zoologists, there are none. In some cases, this was obviously a confusion of the leopard with the clouded leopard, but sometimes the latter was said to occur in Sumatra in addition to the former. One well-known older handbook on mammals in Indonesia, that of van Balen, mentioned clouded leopards in Java.[21]

Remarkable to the reader of today is the role of hunting in the game of nomenclature. By the early 1930s, when Sody confirmed the existence of three Indonesian subspecies, the Ledeboer brothers had shot so many tigers in

The Bali tiger is the smallest and the darkest of all tiger subspecies. The stripes of the Bali tiger are often paired, with small islands between the stripes. Photo P. J. H. van Bree, in Mazák et al. 1978

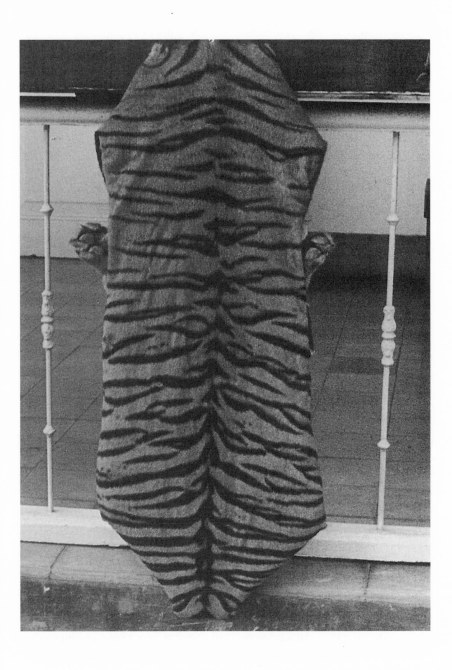

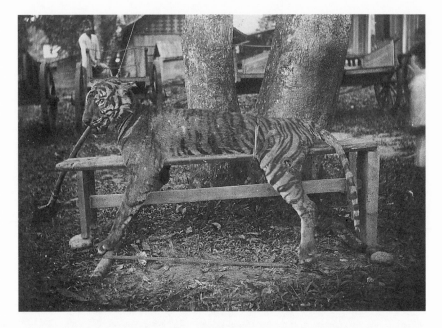

Dead Sumatran tiger, central Sumatra, c. 1915. The measuring rod on the ground indicates that hunters and zoologists were eager to take the measurements of dead big cats. Collection KITLV

Bali, Java, and Sumatra that such a decision could be made with some confidence.[22] The ambiguous role of European hunting, to be dealt with in a later chapter, could not be illustrated better. On the one hand, zoologists very much depended on the activities of hunters and often were both naturalists and hunters. On the other hand, as in the case of the Bali tiger, the time between recognition as a subspecies and extinction could be very short. The same hunters who might enable the identification of the subspecies could be responsible for its extinction.

Finally, the orthodox notion of eight subspecies, of which four exist in the Malay world, is now under attack. Andrew Kitchener has argued recently that this classification was based on very small samples. Instead of eight subspecies with distinctive morphological characteristics, it is more likely, according to Kitchener, that we are dealing with a so-called cline, that is, a continuous and gradual variation over the geographical range due to natural selection. Another possibility is to acknowledge only two or three subspecies. In the two-subspecies model proposed by Kitchener, our four Malay subspecies would be one of the two "new" subspecies (Kitchener 1999).

Procreation

The maximum age attainable by tigers is often given as 20 years, occasionally even 25.[23] According to some authors, however, in the wild they rarely survive beyond the age of 15. They are sexually mature when they are 3 to 5 years old, and it seems that tigresses remain fertile until they are 10 to 12 or even older.

It is often said that tigers are solitary animals, but that applies only to grownup males (and man-eaters). The adult male stays with a tigress only during the rutting season, and incidentally perhaps during the gestation period and briefly thereafter. Then they part company, but the tigress stays with her cubs for about two years (according to some, for a much shorter time), and during this period she does not mate. When, at the end of this period, she leaves the cubs, the tigress will come into estrus almost immediately (tigresses are polyoestrous). She announces this loudly and clearly. As A. Locke, a British hunter in Malaya around 1950, has it: "A tigress is cantankerous if she cannot locate a mate when she wants one and is in an even worse temper after mating because of the rough treatment meted out to her, quite unintentionally, I am sure, by the male" (p. 21). However, with a bit of luck (she is receptive for only a short period), she will find a mate within a few days. In typical tiger areas her vociferous announcements will attract several adult male tigers, who then have to fight it out amongst themselves as to who will get lucky. The mating period is very short, namely three to eight days, during which the tiger and tigress may mate as many as 100 times, making quite some noise in the process. To quote Locke again: "The actual mating produces the most awe-inspiring, prolonged and high-powered caterwauling imaginable." Various authors have argued that during this period tigers are more dangerous to humans than usually.

The gestation period varies between 95 and 115 days. They have litters of two to four cubs, seldom more. If we consider these data in combination, we may expect a tigress with a full life-span to get between 10 and 15 cubs, of whom only half or even one-third survive, implying a survival of between three and eight cubs per tigress. But many tigresses die earlier, and it is therefore more realistic to assume even lower survival rates.[24]

According to a number of recent studies, there is no specific season for tigresses to be in heat. But in actuality, so the argument goes, it occurs more often during certain periods of the year than in others. Most authors seem to regard the rainy season as the period during which most mating takes place, and it is often argued that tigers and tigresses are then most dangerous to humans. A small minority of authors, however, argue the opposite: that tigers are most dangerous to humans during the dry months (because they make so much noise on the dry leaves with which the earth is littered that they can catch no game), when they also have their mating season. Statistical data on the months during which man-eating attacks have taken place, presented in a later chapter, tend to confirm the notion that the tiger was more dangerous during the wet than during the dry months.[25]

As long as each tigress produces, on average, one male and one female cub (the sex ratio at birth seems to be balanced) who live to reproduce, the tiger population will be stable. This means that, generally speaking, each tigress produces a surplus of one or more tigers. It does not imply that, under normal circumstances, tiger populations tend to grow, given that the available tiger habitat is restricted and that the tiger is a territorial animal.

Adult male tigers stake out a territory, which they, being polygamous, usually share with several females. Within those territories the tigers seem to have fixed routes, rendering them vulnerable to hunters and trappers. The tigresses have their own smaller "home ranges" within this area, where they hunt and rear their cubs. Eventually, the adult offspring of the male "owner" of a certain territory will have to move away. Particularly the young adult male must find his own territory. As the number of "openings" is limited, there are often some animals lurking around the fringes of these ranges, waiting for the incumbent to die or biding their time until they are strong enough to pick a fight with him and drive him out. It is likely that these animals at the fringes do not reproduce successfully and may become a threat to humans and livestock, as their access to game has been blocked. Their mortality is probably fairly high.[26] Arguably, they can be regarded as a reserve population that can move in quickly when slots become vacant or when new slots have been "created." This might explain, in some instances, why killing off a few tigers by humans does not seem to make much of a difference, as "reserve" tigers move in almost immediately. It could also explain why environmental changes sometimes seem to be followed by a rapid influx of tigers.

Habitat

Usually, people associate tigers with forests. In 1820, the Briton John Crawfurd quoted the fable of the tiger and the forest, taken from the *Niti Sastra*, a collection of Old Javanese moralistic maxims. In this text, the tiger and the forest are close friends who protect each other. When, on a fated day, the tiger left the forest, it was cut down by men, who then went after the tiger, who could no longer hide in the forest and therefore also lost his life. This is no doubt a felicitous metaphor, and the tiger does, indeed, need the forest as his hideout, but the suggestion should be avoided that he needs nothing but the forest.

Unbroken tracts of virgin forest, like the ones that covered the typical rain-forest zone around the equator not so long ago, are areas unattractive to tigers. To many this will come across as a counterintuitive notion, but in the densely forested tropical areas of yore, tigers were rare.[27] Ground-dwelling herbivorous and omnivorous mammals are scarce in these forests, as there is not much food for them to be found on and under the forest floor, such as roots, bulbs, tubers, nuts, and seeds. There are various mammals, to be sure, but these tend to be arboreal and therefore of not much use to tigers, who are bad climbers.

Where, then, do we look for the tiger? According to Pocock we look for the tiger in areas that meet three criteria: the presence of adequate numbers of prey, abundant supplies of water, and extensive cover where he can establish a lair and avoid the heat of the day.

The tiger will look for forested places where humans cannot easily follow him. Occasionally, tigers made use of natural caves, particularly in limestone areas. This is mentioned several times in sources referring to Java, which, together with Bali, can boast of 1,000 such caves. There is even a Tiger Cave in Java. As caves are also places favored by hermits for contemplation (both in real life and in literature), "holy men" occasionally may have found themselves in trouble. Around 1860, the guardian of the cave hermitage Selamangleng, not far from the town of Kediri, always carried a "fowling piece" (gun).[28]

Almost all writers agree that the prey preferred by the tiger were wild boar and deer. Some sources suggest a preference for boar, on account of its speed being slower than that of deer. Occasionally, tigers also attacked the larger ungulates, like buffalo, seladang, and banteng, but in the Malay area this was probably largely restricted to sick or young individuals, as healthy adults are out of their league—unlike in India, where the tiger is bigger. At a pinch, however, he will eat practically everything, including dogs (in and around the villages), mousedeer, giant turtles, peacock, jungle fowl, and even locusts, spiders, mice, and frogs. The tiger also eats monkeys, despite being a bad climber; the story goes that he mesmerizes them, so that the more nervous ones lose their footing high up in the trees, jumping, so to speak, right into the tiger's jaws. It is a story with an impressive pedigree, dating in India to the 1670s. However, monkeys occasionally forage on the ground, and it seems likely that most monkeys that fall prey to tigers do so on those occasions.[29] Tigers are not strictly carnivorous, and they seem to be particularly fond of the *durian*, a foul-smelling but reportedly delicious fruit.

Areas where deer and boar (and, therefore, tiger) abound are not the densely forested areas but the tall grasses of the *alang-alang* and *glagah* fields, secondary forest vegetation, savanna-like landscapes, and so-called ecotones —that is, transitional zones between biotic communities. Here the term refers particularly to the forest fringes, which are very rich in plant and animal life and also provide cover, as well as to forested areas bordering on cultivated fields, as boar and deer often consume the same crops as humans. It has been argued that the tiger's striped coat, which makes him very difficult to spot in alang-alang-type vegetation, "proves" that this is the habitat he is most adapted to.[30]

In fact, what boar and deer have in common is that they often are found in areas (recently) disturbed by humans. They are clearly culture followers, a term that also can be applied to tigers, who follow the boar and the deer. Human action creates the typical tiger habitats, and areas undisturbed by people are often undisturbed by tigers. Therefore, to some extent, the growth of tiger populations in heavily forested areas depends largely upon the growth of human populations. Tiger populations can grow only if new home ranges are created, and new home ranges can be created only if humans take axe and fire to the forest. Very dense populations will not leave much forest standing, and there is no tiger without forest, even though the forest in itself is not prime tiger habitat. There are few tigers in regions where the forests have gone entirely, but there are also few tigers in regions covered with primary rainforest. Somewhere in between are the ideal circumstances for large tiger populations.

Food Availability and Tiger Density

A tiger can eat 20 to 25 kg per day but needs on average much less. Recent literature suggests that adult tigers need some 3,000 kg per year, and a tigress perhaps as much as 50% more when she has cubs, representing between 40 and 70 kills annually, assuming an average weight per kill of 65 kg. Before World War II, Champion estimated that tigers in India on average killed 50 deer per year.[31] Although the Malayan and island tigers are somewhat smaller, these numbers can be used as an indication of their food requirements.

We have very little data on ungulate biomass in the Malay world, a figure we need in order to estimate the area necessary for the upkeep of one tiger. In fact, I know of only one figure, namely the one published by Seidensticker and Suyono for Ujung Kulon, Java's most westerly nature reserve. In this publication, dated 1980, the ungulate biomass of Ujung Kulon was given as 500 kg per km^2; according to the authors, the reserve therefore could sustain one tiger per 75 to 100 km^2. If the authors assumed, as is generally done, that 10% of the biomass can be taken away annually without negative effects, this would mean an annual consumption of between 3,750 and 5,000 kg. This is more than one adult male needs, but it would be about what could be expected if the authors had included a grownup female and one or two cubs in their calculations.

However, the biomass given for Ujung Kulon is rather low in comparison with a number of areas outside the Malay world. The data for ungulate biomass in six nature reserves in South Asia (Nepal, India, Sri Lanka) varies between 750 and 3,300 kg per km^2, with on average 1,875 kg. In a recent study referring to Nagarahole National Park in southern India, a biomass of over 5,000 kg per km^2 was mentioned, to my knowledge a record. As all of the data, including that for Ujung Kulon, refers to nature reserves, one would be ill advised to use them at face value for estimates of the carrying capacity regarding tigers in an entire country or region.

We have more data on the available surface area per tiger in a large number of Indian nature reserves. In 18 reserves in 1984 it varied between 6 and 55 km^2 per tiger, or, expressed alternatively, between 17 and 2 tigers per 100 km^2. On average, these values were 24 km^2 per tiger and 4 tigers per 100 km^2, respectively. However, in the 1970s the average territory of tigers in India was reported to be 60 to 80 km^2 (or 1.4 tiger per 100 km^2). I assume that the average areas reported were larger because the report referred to all tiger territories, including those outside the nature reserves, where the ungulate biomass doubtless was lower. In Sumatra in the 1980s tiger densities could be as high as 3.7 per 100 km^2 in the lowland forests of Bengkulu, and as low as 1.1 per 100 km^2 in more mountainous habitats, implying, on average, a territory per tiger of 40 km^2.

Data on the prewar Malay world are rare. John Cameron argued in 1865 that there were only 20 "couples" of tigers on the island of Singapore. Although tigers do not really come in couples, let us assume that every couple had two cubs, which would yield a grand total of 80 tigers, or 7 per 100 km^2. I found only two references for Sumatra, dating from the last two decades prior to World War II, one suggesting that a tiger needed some tens of square kilometers and the other discussing a particular tiger with a territory of about 15 km^2.

Fortunately we have an estimate, dating from the years immediately after the war, for Malaya, carefully compiled by the British civil servant and hunter Locke. According to him, the Malayan Peninsula counted c. 3,000 tigers. That implies that on average Malaya had 2 tigers per 100 km^2, taking into consideration the entire surface area within the boundaries of what was then Malaya, and not just the tiger areas.

It seems likely that man-eaters have much larger "territories" than ordinary tigers. Mazák quotes six cases from India and Malaya varying from almost 400 to over 9,000 km^2 per man-eater, or slightly over 3,000 km^2 on average. Here, however, the term "territory" is hardly applicable; these tigers had become nomads without proper home ranges.[32]

The figure quoted for Malaya in 1950—2 tigers per 100 km^2—is probably a fair reflection of tiger densities in the Malay area in the last few centuries. Locally, higher densities must have obtained, probably as high as the one quoted above for a nature reserve in India in 1984 (17 per 100 km²), but it is highly unlikely that such figures ever applied to larger areas. Malaya, at that moment, did not have many areas where tigers were entirely absent. It no longer had the endless stretches of virgin forest that characterized the country in the nineteenth century, nor had it developed large cultivated or urban areas as yet. In that respect, it was not so different from Sumatra at around the same time.

The situation in Malaya and Sumatra was very different, however, from the one in Java and Bali around 1950. But the situation of Malaya in 1950 might reflect tiger densities in Java and Bali prior to 1820, when these islands also had much lower population densities, and not so many almost unbroken wet-rice plains and urban areas as they would have later on.

The Tiger's Meal

The tiger is a "stalk-and-ambush" hunter who, like most cats, relies upon surprise. According to the literature, he seldom runs after his prey; if he fails to get it in one jump, the attack is broken off. However, a 1995 movie on the Ranthambhore National Park in India clearly depicts a tiger running after deer for quite some time, and unless this was a tiger trained to do so, the literature might have to be revised on this point.

Most observers agree that the tiger usually attacks from behind. This applies to both animal and human victims. Prior to the last few decades, this habit contributed a great deal to the tiger's bad reputation. John Cameron, writing about man-eating tigers around Singapore in the 1860s, put it this way: "Though ferocious, they are cowardly to a degree, and while I have inquired into the circumstances attending every death by tigers for a number of years back, I have been unable to find one case where the victim was not come upon unawares, and from behind."

The Dutch naturalist A. Hoogerwerf, for many years the game warden of Ujung Kulon National Park in late-colonial Java, gave the following description: "The method usually followed by tigers in search of prey will doubtlessly consist in moving as silently as possible along regularly used game trails and visiting places where game may be expected, stalking the latter if it has been seen or heard. The tiger's excellent power of sight when it is dark, and its feet, which are perfectly designed for silently stalking, enable this predator to approach its prey very closely." As to the actual methods of killing, Hoogerwerf summed up the possibilities as follows: "Bounding at the throat from below; choking off the victim's breath by grasping or biting its throat from the prey's back, death through strangulation being perhaps most common; wrenching round the head from the back, as a result of which the neck is often broken and the victim may be knocked over by the tiger's jump; in the case of very large prey it was established that a bite on one of the hindlegs just above the hock (hamstringing) seriously severed the tendon, thus rendering these victims largely helpless." The idea that the tiger killed by one crushing blow on the neck, often found in the older literature and already being told in Java around 1630, was abandoned by the well-known tiger specialist and hunter Jim Corbett in the 1940s.

A prey, human or animal, is seldom eaten on the spot where it was killed. Usually the tiger takes the body to a place with shade and near water, because he wants to drink copiously after having eaten his fill. He also seldom eats his kill in one go, unless he is very hungry (or the animal killed was a small one). Normally, the tiger returns once or even more often, over a period of a number of days, to finish his meal. Both habits were taken advantage of by hunters.

One of the more lugubrious but fairly well-documented details regarding the tiger's behavior is that he always tried to find out what happened to a (human) victim that was taken away—and usually buried—by humans. Quoting the hunter Locke once again, "This habit of trying to find out where their kill has been taken is, I think, one of the most ghoulish things about man-eating tigers."

In addition to being accused of cowardly and ghoulish behavior, the tiger was also reputed to be cruel. Various reports mentioned that tigers killed for sport, since they sometimes killed more animals than they could eat. According to Mary Bradley, who came to Sumatra in the 1920s looking for tigers, "The tiger is not a gentlemanly killer like the lion who takes only what he needs; the tiger strikes right and left in his lust for blood. He is as bad in that respect as the cowardly hyena of Africa that will run through a flock of goats hamstringing every one he can reach."

Occasionally, only the blood was sucked from a kill, which was probably perceived as particularly nasty if the victim was a human being. However, most of these instances were probably the by-product of cubs being taught the required skills by their mother. As Locke has it, "Tigers are not as cruel as they are reputed to be; apart from those made sport of by cubs, most animals that they attack are killed instantly." Detailed observation over the last 50 to 60 years has dispelled some of the legends that gave the tiger a bad name.[33]

What did not endear the tiger to his human neighbors either were his cannibalism and his fondness for carrion. One might be inclined to be a bit skeptical about both claims, as those who formulated them seem to have been bent on tarnishing the tiger's reputation as much as possible, but the older reports are largely vindicated on these points by modern research.

Male tigers, usually young adults without a territory of their own, will attempt to chase away or kill the old incumbent of a territory. If this is successful, they will then try to kill the non-adult offspring of the latter. The behavior is also observed among other cats, such as the lion. If the "new" tiger has killed the cubs, their mother immediately comes into season and mates with the new territorial lord. However, it is also possible that she herself will get killed when defending her cubs against the intruder. The older literature sometimes even mentioned that fathers kill their own offspring, but that might be an erroneous observation, although it is not entirely out of the question. Hoogerwerf and Mazák suggest that a parent sometimes kills young cubs if there is not enough food. There are also instances of tigers taking a few bites from a vanquished rival or from another dead tiger.

With regard to carrion eating, the literature gives numerous unsavory examples. The tiger will eat an animal that was not killed by him. The literature cites tigers chasing away other predators from their prey and then finishing the meal themselves. The tiger also takes his time devouring his own kill, returning day after day, even if decomposition is quite advanced, which does not take long in tropical regions.[34]

It was mostly the actual killing and the actions leading up to and following it that earned the tiger his bad reputation. Knowledge of these things, however, also became his undoing, as hunters could and would stalk and ambush the tiger because he is a creature of habit. As we will see in Chapter 3, there are also examples of people who used this knowledge to protect themselves, as did women who were harvesting while under the cover of large baskets, because a tiger walks away when the first attack is a failure!

As a predator, the tiger depends partly on his physical strength. I do not want to try the reader's patience by listing records of tiger feats. Let it suffice to say that he is able to lift or drag much more than his own weight in prey, and that for a long time. He can jump quite far and high, is known to walk enormous distances, and is able to swim across bays, straits, and rivers. Tigers' eyesight and hearing are, according to some authors, much better developed than their sense of smell. They also have such a "pungent body-odor," a "musk-like smell," that local people and trained European hunters were perhaps better at sniffing out a tiger than the other way around. Not all authorities agree, however, that the tiger has a poor sense of smell. He is an indifferent climber, but, if needs be, he will, just like humans, climb a tree.[35]

A Nocturnal Animal?

The tiger is a creature of the night, an attribute that added to the fear so many people felt in tiger areas. It was during the hours from dusk to dawn that most tiger attacks on people could be expected. However, various authors mention exceptions to this rule. It was said that man-eaters often operated during the day. One can also find the opinion that tigers are active at night only in areas where they must adapt to human presence, whereas they are daytime animals in sparsely inhabited regions. In Chapter 3, I present some statistical data on this topic.[36]

If tigers were not often seen during the day, they were, of course, even more invisible at night. Some writers, though, such as the German naturalist Franz Wilhelm Junghuhn, possessing either strong nerves or a vivid imagination, saw the tiger's eyes as "fiery globes in the night."[37]

Many people heard, or thought they heard, a tiger in the night (and sometimes during the day), and did not relish the experience. There might be room for some doubt, though, whether it was really tigers who made themselves heard. "The tigers howl here every night," wrote the American tourist Bickmore, visiting Sumatra in the 1860s. A number of later residents and visitors of Sumatra stated explicitly that they seldom heard tigers roar. The same applies to Java, where, even in the same area, and during periods not that far apart, some travelers hear tigers roaring and/or howling, whereas others say in so many words that tigers are seldom heard. A source from Malaya states that they can be heard growling but do not roar often, while Hoogerwerf, talking about Java, makes a distinction between loud and soft roars, so some of the confusion may be caused by the terminology (growling, roaring, howling). However, some of the growls and roars may have been those of leopards. Another possibility is that some travelers visited tiger areas during the mating season(s), which, as we have seen, were loudly advertised.[38]

Man-Eaters

The fear and loathing that many Europeans felt (indigenous attitudes will be discussed later) toward tigers were largely inspired by the existence of man-eating tigers, often called man-eaters—that is, tigers who specialized in killing and eating people.[39] It was assumed that tigers were naturally inclined to avoid humans and that even the smell of a human being made them turn back. To quote the American hunter Frank Buck, "In most cases the tigers responsible for these deaths are man-eaters, it being an established fact that it is an unusual thing for an ordinary tiger, no matter how ferocious a specimen, to attack a man. In fact, he finds the smell of human flesh repulsive and will lose no time in vacating the spot where this offensive odor reaches his nostrils." And in fact, tigers seldom are seen in the wild or by chance, even by the most experienced naturalist who may have lived for years in tiger areas. However, there are a number of testimonies of people—other than hunters—who happened to come across a tiger.

Those who lived to tell the tale stated that the tiger turned around and walked away. This does not prove much, because the stories of those who disappeared because the tiger did not turn away are, of course, lacking. It is consistent, however, with the notion that the tiger attacks only from behind.

Tigers supposedly rarely attacked people in an upright position, and, if they did so, never from the front. Otto Mohnike has the story, as told by the local population, that the tiger will turn a killed human being with his face to the ground before he starts eating the body, because he cannot look a human in the eyes, not even a dead one. In recent decades, a policy has been based on this notion in the Sundarbans, northeast India and Bangladesh, an area with many human tiger victims; people were given a mask depicting a human face to be worn on the back of the head, thus keeping the tiger from attacking them. It did work for some time, and the number of tiger attacks dropped considerably, but the most recent news is that the tigers are getting wise to these tricks.

Finally, man-eating tigers were reputed to prefer indigenous people to Europeans, a point to which I shall return.[40]

The Leopard

The tiger has always overshadowed the leopard. Smaller than the tiger and less of a threat to humans, the leopard was of much less interest to people. Consequently, we do not have the wealth of information that we do on the tiger. It has also been argued that the leopard is even more elusive than the tiger, so that people seldom get to see him.

If the nomenclature of the tiger used to be a confusing affair, this is probably even more the case with the leopard. In the first place, leopards were often called small tigers, spotted tigers, or black tigers. Secondly, leopards and panthers, once thought to be different species, are now regarded as just different names for one and the same animal. The latter term, *panther*, has been dropped by the specialists in the hope that it will disappear, thereby ending the confusion. In the third place, there are spotted and black leopards. We now know that the black leopard is a melanistic variety of the normal, spotted (yellow skin with large black spots and rosettes) leopard, but for a long time the black variety was regarded as a separate species. Yet authors disagree widely as regards the number of recognized subspecies (7, 15, or over 20). Finally, many authors asserted that there were leopards in Sumatra. Nowadays, zoologists deny any proof of leopards there, and it must be assumed that people were talking about the clouded leopard an entirely different species.

The scientific name of the leopard, is *Panthera pardus*, but in the older literature we find *Felis melas* (or *F. nigra*) for the black variety and *Felis pardus*, the name given by Linnaeus in 1758, for the spotted one, in use until Pocock re-

Leopards were found in Malaya and Java, perhaps in Bali, and not in Sumatra and Borneo. Spotted leopards and black leopards are varieties of one species, not two separate species. Balen 1914

vised the system in 1917. Occasionally we also encounter *Felis leopardus*. By 1850 it had been discovered that black leopards and spotted leopards came from one litter, but even 75 years later some writers still regarded them as separate species.[41] The indigenous names are *harimau bintang* and (*macan*) *tutul* for the spotted leopard and *harimau kumbang* and *macan kombang* for the black leopard.[42]

One gets a fairly accurate picture of leopards if one regards them as small-scale tigers. Their length, height, weight, gestation period, and longevity are all somewhat below that of the tiger. They also go after smaller prey. Information about the procreation process of tigers and their territoriality generally applies to leopards as well. Leopards' hunting methods—"stalk-and-pounce"—are also broadly similar to those of the tiger.

In some respects leopards do better than tigers. As a recent textbook has it: "The leopard has the largest range, west to east, of any species of cat, large or small." He is to be found from southern Africa to China. The same book states: "The leopard is probably the most adaptable of all big cats," and "The species can inhabit dense forest, semi-desert, grasslands and mountainous regions." Some 30 years ago, Hoogerwerf formulated his opinion about the leopard's greater versatility: "The extremely great adaptability of panthers [leopards] and the ease with which they manage to stay concealed—as a result of which they can maintain themselves more easily than tigers in cultivated areas, even in the immediate vicinity of human settlements—are other reasons which may reduce the danger of extermination."

One of the features of a leopard that enables him to do better than the tiger is that he is a very good climber, probably in part because he is smaller. He is therefore better at catching monkeys and birds, and he is known to give terrestrial prey a nasty surprise by simply dropping out of a tree. He also has an excellent sense of smell.

All these things taken together go a long way in explaining why the leopard is so much more successful than the tiger in terms of numbers. The maximum estimate of surviving tigers is 7,500, whereas the lowest figure for leopards is 100,000, but in light of recent estimates for Africa alone it seems highly likely that this is a factor 10 too low. A new method of estimating yielded the unexpected result that there are between 600,000 and 900,000 leopards in Africa south of the Sahara. So the total number of leopards is perhaps not much less than one million.[43]

There are very few reliable "demographic" (life-history) data on individual tigers or leopards, no doubt because one has to observe the animals closely, almost continuously, for a long period of time. I came across such data, collected in the 1980s and 1990s, for one Indian tigress ("Sita") and for one female African leopard ("Umfazi"). Although two cases are far too small a sample for firm conclusions, a comparison of the two "families" yields interesting pointers. The tigress was almost 16 years old at the time that her family was evaluated, and the chances that she will have more offspring are slim, while the leopard was presumed dead at the age of 15, which means that we study her "completed" family.

Sita had six litters with 18 cubs altogether, or three cubs per litter on average. Umfazi had nine litters with (probably) 17 cubs, or two on average. Of Sita's 18 cubs there were 8 who did not make it to independence; of Umfazi's 17, only 5 did not make it. So, although there are differences between numbers of litters and number of cubs per litter, the grand totals are remarkably similar, and the main difference seems to be a higher mortality among tiger cubs. Of the eight dead tiger cubs, six had died within a year, presumably of natural causes. Of the five dead leopard cubs, lions had killed three. The data suggests that, although the tiger has hardly any natural enemies and the leopard does, the survival rate of leopard cubs is higher than that of tiger cubs.

In Asia, the tiger is the leopard's chief natural enemy. It is, therefore, certainly possible that leopards are doing better than before in areas where tigers have disappeared, as occurred in Ujung Kulon National Park (western Java) after 1970.[44]

I am not aware of estimates of leopard numbers in the Malay world, which, in this case, is limited to Malaya and Java, as leopards are not found in Sumatra or Borneo and probably not in Bali. What is certain, however, is that leopards have survived until the present in both Malaya and Java. Also, in the twentieth century there were many more leopards to be found in Java than tigers. The Englishman H. S. Banner, a long-term resident of Java, testified in the 1920s: "Panther [=leopard], both black and spotted, are far more common [than tiger], and their depredations figure almost daily in the Press." Whereas it is unlikely that there were more than 5 to 10 tigers killed annually in Java between 1925 and 1935, one taxidermist alone had prepared 500 leopard skins over the same period. During roughly the same period the Dutch hunter G. J. van der Paardt, a resident of eastern Java, shot 135 leopards in that region alone. Leopards were also more numerous than tigers on the Malay Peninsula. A source dating from the middle of the nineteenth century stated that there were more black leopards in Malaya than tigers. A century later, the hunter Locke called leopards comparatively rare, but he seems to have compared the number of leopards to that in India, not to the number of tigers in Malaya.[45]

Like the tiger, the leopard, particularly the black leopard (usually called black panther), had a bad reputation. In the 1820s, the *bupati* (regent) of Pati, north central Java, showed the Dutch baron Van Aylva Rengers a black leopard.[46] It was a live specimen that had been caught in a trap. According to the baron these animals were rare and only to be found in the forests of the nearby Residency of Rembang. He added, "The family of the black tigers [leopards] is the most vicious of them all, it being impossible to keep them in captivity, but they are rare." Mohnike thought that this—undeserved?—reputation was based on Eugène Sue's novel *Le Juif errant,* in which "la panthère noire de Java" played a bloodcurdling role. Other hunters disliked leopards at least as much as they did tigers. Even today, the black variety has not shed his reputation of viciousness, but it does not seem to be based on factual experience.

The melanistic variety is fairly rare in Africa, somewhat more common in

33

India, and even more numerous in Southeast Asia. Most observers from the Malayan Peninsula state that about half to a majority of the leopards there is black. Although a proportion of 50% or even more is somewhat suspect, given the fact that melanism is a recessive trait in leopards, I am inclined to think that the record goes to Malaya.[47]

Most of the literature suggests that the black form is associated with densely forested regions, because the black leopard would be very difficult to spot in such an environment. However, some writers have pointed out that the spotted variety is very well suited to a forested environment, as the pattern of spots and rosettes mirrors the effects of sunlight in a forest. In fact, various authors have argued that leopards are more often found in any type of forest than is the tiger, even though the latter is strongly associated with the jungle.

It could be argued that black leopards can be expected to favor dense primary forests, whereas spotted ones would be more partial to secondary or planted forests, like the teak forests of Java. This might explain the difference in proportion of melanistic individuals between the Malayan Peninsula and Java, as the former had much more undisturbed forest than the latter, in addition to the fact that in Java disturbed and planted forests were found more frequently than in Malaya. It might also explain the difference between western Java on the one hand, with its high proportion of both primary forests and black leopards, and central and eastern Java on the other hand, with more teak (and comparable *cemara*) forest and a lower proportion of black leopards.

This theory does not, however, explain the observation, dating from the 1820s, that the black variety was extremely rare and found only in Rembang. We will just have to assume that the black leopard was much less often seen than the spotted one in an epoch when forests still covered large parts of Java. The Rembang area, where the exploitation of the teak forests was concentrated, was exceptional only in that there was more chance of a black leopard bumping into a European forest official.[48]

It was assumed that leopards were as afraid of people as were tigers, and that the smell of humans usually would scare them off. Nevertheless, under specific circumstances man-eating did occur among leopards (as it did among tigers). However, whereas India had man-eating leopards as well as tigers, evidence for man-eating leopards in the Malay world is weak. As regards Malaya, the hunter Locke wrote around 1950: "These animals [leopards] are not normally such a menace to human beings and livestock in Malaya as they are in India."

For Java, we occasionally hear stories about leopards attacking people, but according to various authors leopards did not attack humans unless they had been provoked. Hoogerwerf collected 11 stories of leopards attacking people for the years 1929–1939 in which a total of three people were killed. He then says: "The question is whether in all these incidents the panther [leopard] took the initiative or was forced in any way or another to act as he did." In the absence of further details, he argued, "it is therefore not justifiable to regard panthers as a threat to man." For the time being we can conclude that man-eating leopards were hardly an issue in the Malay world. As regards Java, one factor might be that the Javan leopard is smaller than the Indian one, and that attacks on humans are, therefore, less likely. Intriguingly, there is evidence of leopards attacking people from the front.[49]

The Clouded Leopard

Information on the clouded leopard is scarcer than data about the "normal" leopard, perhaps because the former is even more elusive than the latter. Sightings of the clouded leopard are very rare, and the animal has been studied only in zoos. Thomas Stamford Raffles, the British lieutenant governor of Java between 1811 and 1815 and of Bengkulu from 1816 to 1822, was one of the first Europeans to mention and describe the animal. A recent handbook gives the following description of his skin: "The coat pattern is made up of irregular large blotches of black on a brown to yellow background."

The systematic name is *Neofelis nebulosa,* but at the end of the colonial period he was called *Felis nebulosa,* a name that was also in use at the beginning of the nineteenth century. During the intervening period the name found most often was the one given by the Dutch biologist Temminck and then copied by his American colleague Thomas Horsfield: *Felis macrocelis.*

Of the three big cats dealt with in this chapter, the clouded leopard has the most limited distribution, being largely restricted to Southeast Asia. Within the Malay world he is found in Malaya, Sumatra, and Borneo. Nothing can be said about numbers, as even experts do not know whether he is hardly ever observed because he is extremely rare or because he is very good at hiding himself. He is also the smallest of three big cats of the Malay world, with a gestation period and longevity shorter than those of the leopard. [50]

The clouded leopard (Dutch: *nevelpanter*) lives in forests and is an admirable climber who is seldom seen on the ground. This is apparently such a typical characteristic that the various local names are all associated with trees. He is called in the indigenous languages *harimau akar* (root),[51] *harimau dahan* (branch), and *harimau daun* (leaf), although the last name might also reflect the patterns of his skin. Occasionally we find the name tree-tiger used by English-speaking people, and its equivalents in Dutch, *boomtijger* and *boompanter,* in use by Dutch writers.[52]

De Nevelpanter.

Clouded leopards are very elusive and therefore badly documented animals. They were found in Malaya, Sumatra, and Borneo, and not in Java and Bali. Balen 1914

The clouded leopard shares many behavioral features with the leopard and is in many respects a somewhat smaller leopard. In fact, the two are so much alike that many visitors to Sumatra mistook the clouded leopard for the leopard, particularly the melanistic variety.

Opinions differ as to whether the clouded leopard is dangerous to humans. Raffles, as quoted by Horsfield, and the British naturalist R. W. C. Shelford, writing in the 1910s about Borneo, thought not. Another naturalist, the Scandinavian E. Mjöberg, who visited the same region somewhat later, and Mohnike, who worked in Sumatra several times in the middle of the nineteenth century, were less sanguine.

I have never heard of confirmed killings of people by clouded leopards. Their usual fare is dogs (although they seem to be scared of some dogs), pigs, smaller mammals, and birds. This suggests that he is a competitor of the leopard, which, in the areas where their distribution overlaps, could lead to conflicts. In the Malay world, it is only in Malaya that both species can be found, but there is no information on clashes between them.[53]

People and Big Cats

Java was populated by humanoids at an early stage. *Homo erectus* remains were found by the Dutch scholar Eugene Dubois in Trinil in 1891. These humanoids lived there probably not before 1.2 million years ago, but some of the remains are much younger, and *Homo erectus* was probably present in Java until 200,000 years BP (before present). Then the climate changed, and open woodland fauna became a humid forest fauna; *Homo erectus* may have become extinct locally, along with various other mammals. When the climate became drier again, *Homo sapiens,* the modern human, arrived on the scene, probably between 100,000 and 60,000 BP.

Tiger specialists have suggested that the dispersion of tigers over East and Southeast Asia was completed two million years ago and that differentiation, resulting in various subspecies, started more than one million years ago. This could mean that tigers inhabited Java before *Homo erectus* did, and certainly before the arrival of *Homo sapiens.* Based on fossil remains, area specialists now assume that tigers were present in Java from one million years ago. However, the oldest remains are those of extinct subspecies of the tiger (*Panthera tigris trinilensis, P.t. oxygnatha,* and *P.t. soloensis*), and the modern Javan tiger does not appear until 80,000 BP. One could suppose that each subspecies evolved from the one preceding it, and the literature does seem to suggest this, by calling *Panthera tigris* in Java "a holdover." If this is indeed the case, the tiger may have been more tenacious than *Homo erectus,* who is supposed to have become extinct during the more humid period. And, if we accept that *Homo sapiens* came from outside the area, the tiger was already present when modern man arrived in Java.

From more recent ("subrecent") prehistoric times we also have fossil tiger remains, at least from the Mesolithic period, between 10,000 and 5,000 BP. Strangely enough, such remains are absent in finds from the Neolithic period, roughly between 5,000 and 3,000 BP. Nevertheless, the modern Javan tiger was still present in historical times, possibly even until today. As it is unlikely that the tiger became extinct and then was reintroduced in subrecent times, the lack of evidence in Neolithic strata should not be given too much weight.[54]

One might speculate that human activities in Java led to lower tiger densities. This does not contradict the hypothesis I formulated above, namely that in tropical rainforest zones tigers are culture followers. Mesolithic Java was characterized by a more open woodland fauna, and this was no doubt an advantage to the tiger, who, therefore, may have increased in numbers for purely climatological reasons. However, during the Neolithic period human activity increased and may very well have started to limit the number of tigers.

Conclusion

We are used to thinking of the tiger as the king of the "jungle." Forest cover is, indeed, one of the elements the tiger needs for his survival (the other two being prey and water). Nevertheless, large tracts of undisturbed, primary rainforest are not the tiger's preferred habitat, as prey densities in such areas are low. Boar and deer, the tiger's main prey, prefer areas recently disturbed by humans. Tigers, therefore, are found in the same areas. They are culture followers. The highest preference goes to disturbed areas near forests.

Under normal circumstances, tigresses produce more offspring than is necessary for a stable population. Therefore, tiger populations can grow, provided humans create the areas where such expansion can take place. Up to a point, growing human populations led to increasing tiger populations. This point was reached long ago, though perhaps not so long ago as some may have thought.

Tigers had the reputation of being cowardly, ghoulish, and cruel. It was mostly the actual killing and the actions leading up to and following it that earned the tiger this reputation. That they were largely nocturnal, could and occasionally would kill humans, showed cannibalistic features, and were fond of carrion hardly improved their standing. Although nowadays we no longer think in such terms, as it is now deemed unjustified to apply human characteristics to animals, recent research regarding these habits lends credence to many of the older descriptions upon which these opinions were based.

Tigers are now immensely popular, which will make a big difference for attempts to save the tiger. This popularity has made it hard for some people to believe that the older claims regarding "bad" behavior are true. Some details are, indeed, in all likelihood products of overactive imaginations, but much in the older reports has been vindicated by modern research. Many European naturalists admired the tiger for his strength, his beauty, and the graceful way he moves, but all too many people hated and feared the tiger. This was largely based on his actual behavior, but the tiger's "badness" was no doubt exaggerated and was "translated" into "spiritual" terms. To many Europeans and "Malays," the tiger became the personification of evil. This has contributed to his disappearance in many areas, just as his present popularity may save him in the end.

3

The Tiger: Friend or Foe?

Only 50 years ago, the tiger typically was viewed as an enemy to humans. Tigers did, after all, kill people, cattle, and dogs. Although some argued that tigers were content to subsist on a diet of game wherever that was abundant, most people knew hair-raising stories about tigers who had become man-eaters or cattle-killers. These stories circulated in both tiger-populated countries and tigerless regions; oral tradition, lurid newspaper accounts, and children's books that took their cue from Rudyard Kipling's *Jungle Book* (Shere Khan!) had shaped a global image of the tiger that would take a long time disappearing.[1]

Nowadays, with the tiger on the brink of extinction, people find it hard to imagine that tigers or, for that matter, wolves, lions, and other large predators could ever have posed a threat to humans. For example, a recent book on the Indian tiger contains a chapter titled "The Myth of the Man-eater" (Sankhala 1993, 117–25). However, the historical record overwhelmingly favors the view that the tiger was mankind's most implacable enemy. Table 3.1 presents the numbers of people annually killed by tigers in Java between c. 1820 and 1904 and in Sumatra between 1862 and 1904.[2] Particularly the earlier figures are impressive, but even the 50 people killed on average per year in Java between 1882 and 1904 may astonish those who have regarded man-eater stories as fairytales.

Victims of the Javan Tiger

I have collected some 30 stories of individuals killed or attacked by tigers, dating from the years between 1633 and 1687, and another 40 stories of tiger

Table 3.1. Average number of people killed annually by tigers in Java and Sumatra

Period	1820–30	1850s	1862–81	1882–1904
Java	400	200	90	50
Sumatra	—	400	180	60

aggression dating from the nineteenth century, mostly from the years between 1812 and 1869. These are all individual cases, and remarks like "many people are killed annually by tigers" are not included. For the lack of stories from the eighteenth century I have several explanations. In the first place, in the seventeenth century almost all stories were about tiger attacks around Batavia, and as cultivation expanded, their frequency may have dropped. In the second place, such stories may have become "old news," and eighteenth-century writers could have deliberately refrained from telling them. Finally, the *Daghregister,* or daily register, kept by a high official of the Dutch East India Company (VOC) in Batavia—an important source for the seventeenth century—has not yet been published for the eighteenth century. Daily newspapers, publishing many a tiger story from all areas in nineteenth-century Java, only started their appearance after 1800. After c. 1870, tiger attacks on people were less frequent than before.

In the stories from the seventeenth century the number of European casualties was low. Only 3 out of 30 cases are known to have been Europeans, and three other cases may have been. The first named European to be killed by a tiger was the game warden Louis van Brussel, in 1668, for whom such a death was an occupational hazard. The other two certain cases were a Scottish sailor (c. 1650) who survived the encounter and a European soldier who had left his post (1657). The Scot had clasped the attacking tiger in a bear hug until his companions could set the man free; he got off with no more than a few sizeable gashes in his shoulders.[3]

In five cases reported in 1644, Chinese people, probably mostly farmhands, were the victims. The Chinese dominated the production of sugarcane around Batavia, and tigers apparently felt quite at home in the cane fields, probably because these areas were also the regular haunts of wild boar and because the cane afforded protective covering. One of the Chinese was caught from behind during the day, when he was looking for tigers, together with some soldiers, in the cane fields; the soldiers saved him in the nick of time. Two Chinese were killed during the night, one in the cane fields, the other one in his house.[4]

In six other cases non-Chinese and non-Javanese Asians were involved. Twice slaves were the victims, there were three cases of freedmen, and in one case two Amboinese were caught. The death of one of the freedmen was odd enough, or grisly enough, to be reported in detail: "Was found near the fort Rijswijck a Mardijcker [freedman], whom the tiger had caught and killed, the tiger having damaged his body nowhere except at the neck, where he had sucked all the blood from his body and had left him thus" (D 2.10.1657).

One slave was caught by a tiger around midnight on Ancol, a private estate near Batavia, while sitting up over a fire (fires were believed to keep tigers at bay) in an open shed, surrounded by 15 or 16 other slaves who were asleep. While he was being dragged away to the nearby forest, the other slaves fired a number of shots and generally made so much noise that the tiger let go. The two Amboinese were soldiers in the employ of the VOC on campaign in the Krawang area, immediately to the east of Batavia. One of them was standing guard precisely because a tiger alert had been issued, and the other one was asleep inside the camp. Although many of the soldiers fired at the tiger, he escaped unharmed.[5]

There are 11 reports of tiger encounters with Javanese people. In one case, during the war between the sultan of Banten and Batavia in 1650, a tiger carried off a Javanese standing between two Dutchmen. Most Javanese victims mentioned in these reports were woodcutters and soldiers on patrol or standing guard.[6]

Finally, in a few cases it cannot be established to which group the victim, or almost-victim, belonged. Here we encounter one of the best stories, in fact a story that is probably too good to be true, and, moreover, possibly plagiarized. The German adventurer Elias Hesse, who came to the Archipelago in 1680, reported on a soldier sitting at the beach not far from Batavia "filled with melancholic thoughts." All of a sudden he found himself trapped between a tiger lurking in the bushes behind him and a crocodile in the sea in front of him. When the tiger jumped, the soldier ducked; the tiger fell into the water and was caught by the croc and dragged into the sea. Another German, P. Philippus, who published his adventures in 1673, told a similar tale, only it was supposed to have happened in India in the 1630s. In three nineteenth-century tales tiger-crocodile fights are mentioned, but no human in between. In all three cases the victory went to the croc. A similar story was told in Malaya on the eve of the Pacific War, but here the crocodile and the tiger killed each other.[7]

For the nineteenth century some 40 "tiger stories" are available, and there was a much larger body of more general tales about the tiger-human relationship to which I will sometimes refer. Again, the number of Europeans who were attacked was very small: I came across only two cases, of which one is dubious, while in the other it was not the British merchant himself who was the victim but one of the horses drawing his four-wheeled carriage. This happened on the main road between Cirebon and Tegal, on the border between western and central Java, in 1825. Just a year before, a tiger had caught the only Chinese person in this sample. This occurred on the same post road, but this time on the border between Priangan and Krawang, both in western Java, when the Chinese walked home at nightfall, usually regarded as typical tiger time (Nagel 1828, 17–18, 63; Epp 1841, 60). In all other cases it is explicitly stated that the victim was Javanese or it may be readily assumed.

In almost 30 cases at least one of the victims was an adult male. But adult women are explicitly mentioned in 5 reports, and there are 12 examples of children being snatched away by tigers. Women *and* children under attack made, of course, a very good story, and one such tale, appearing first in a newspaper, was repeated by various authors. The scene was a hamlet near the village of Sajira in Banten, regency Lebak, where, on 11 April 1839, a woman lost her three children, including an eight-month-old baby, in one day to a tiger. She herself was so badly wounded when defending her baby that the newspaper article, dated 8 May, did not expect her to live. What made the story even more "Oriental" was that the local population saw the slaughter as punishment for the infringement of a taboo. The nearby Mount Dangka, believed to be the abode of the ancestral spirits, had been desecrated by a European visitor, and the tiger, often regarded as the embodiment of an ancestral spirit, had communicated the wrath of the ancestors by chastising the local population—not the European trespasser. When a tiger was killed a few days later, the population was convinced that this was the Dangka tiger.[8]

Stories about a mother or a father retaliating against the tiger who tried to drag away a child, or a man who defended his wife and child, were popular and often retold. Sometimes both child and tiger were killed.[9] Similar stories can be found about people being rescued or revenged by another family member.[10] As a rule, villagers would seek revenge when one of them, or one of their animals, had been attacked by a tiger. This topic must have appealed to European readers of that period, and one such story was copied several times.[11]

Attacks on children alone also made gruesome, eagerly narrated stories. Listen to the American traveler E. R. Scidmore: "The briefest stay at Tosari equips a visitor with tiger stories fit for tropical regions; and my envy was roused when some Tosari tourists told of having seen a child who had been seized and slightly mangled by a tiger" (Scidmore 1899, 266).

A theme often found is that of the young buffalo-herd being caught by a

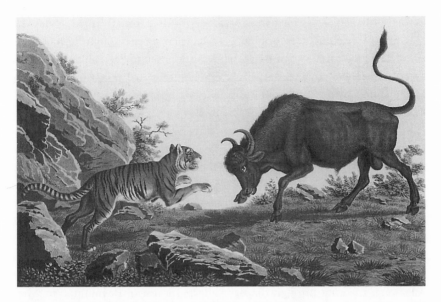

Tiger attacking a water buffalo. In fights between *kerbau* (water buffalo) and tigers, either in the wild or in arranged combat, the water buffalo was usually victorious. It was a favorite theme of many a European author. Pfyffer zu Neueck 1829

tiger. Such boys were obviously more at risk than others from their age group, as they not only took their charges to the "wilder" areas near the village but also left the village at dawn and returned at dusk, precisely those periods of the day when the tiger was most active. Sometimes, the boy survived the encounter. The best-known story, however, is that of the buffalo coming to the rescue and chasing the tiger away. This theme will be familiar to the readers of Multatuli's famous novel *Max Havelaar* (1860), where it was immortalized as part of the moving story of Saidjah and Adinda.[12] Perhaps Multatuli took his cue from one such an event that took place on 26 September 1824 in the regency Sumedang, Priangan Residency, a tale repeated by several authors.[13]

Finally, I twice came across a motif similar to that of the well-known European fairy tale "Hansel and Gretel," in which parents who have nothing left to feed their children in desperation take them to a forest, leaving them to be eaten by wild animals. The two stories I found are dated 1820 and 1844, respectively, years with very high rice prices and even famine.[14]

Most victims were grownup males. Among male occupations, some were particularly dangerous. People with outdoor occupations were obviously more at risk than those who remained indoors or at least in the village. For example,

in the 1840s, a tiger ate the man who carried the mail from the town of Banyumas to Fort Cochius near Gombong in Bagelen, even though he had been
"armed" with a torch. A burning torch was supposed to keep all tigers at a re-
spectful distance, so it was assumed that the rain had put it out. Between
Malang and Lawang, Pasuruan Residency, two postmen had already lost their
lives owing to tiger attacks, according to a report dated 1845. Another mailman, plying the tiger-infested main road between the towns of Besuki and
Banyuwangi, had undergone the same fate. However, some Javanese believed
that tigers would leave them alone as long as they were carrying government
documents. One Javanese, transporting documents for an Assistant-Resident,
on meeting a tiger was said to have squatted, all the while murmuring "*surat
kanjeng Kompeni*" (letter of the high government) until the tiger walked
away.[15]

Being a straggler in a line of coolies was another hazardous position. In
1814 or 1815, Raffles, then lieutenant governor of Java, traveled—by day—to
Ajibarang, trekking through the tiger-infested forest of Dayaluhur (in what
was to be known as the Banyumas Residency). One of his followers "was actually seized by one of these destructive animals, and much torn before he could
be rescued by his companions." Some 15 to 20 years later this also happened to
a coolie of the Dutch traveler J. Olivier, also on the road to Ajibarang. In fact,
the wording of this adventure is so similar to the passage quoted above that the
author may be suspected of having plagiarized Lady Raffles. As it was, not un-
reasonably, generally believed that the tiger would always grab the last person
in a line, an old horse often was positioned to follow the train of people.[16]

Villagers were never entirely safe even within the walls of their own
house.[17] Tigers did not have much trouble jumping through a thatched roof or
walking straight through a door or wall.[18] These activities clearly captured the
imagination of European narrators, given how frequently they can be found in
our rather small sample. The motif reflected the danger embodied by the tiger
and the frailty of indigenous human life much better than any lengthy description of local living conditions could ever have done. Unsurprisingly, the
sparsely populated eastern (Probolinggo, Besuki, Banyuwangi) and western
(Banten, Priangan) Residencies were the setting of most of these stories.[19]

In some of these areas, people could survive only by constructing strong,
high fences or stockades around their cottages, or by building elevated houses
either in trees or on very high poles. In these regions, the post stations along
the post road and the government rest houses also were stockaded. To many
Europeans, an overnight stay in one of these establishments was as near as
they ever would get to experiencing the tiger threat.[20]

Several attacks on people in their houses took place at night, and it was during the hours from dusk to dawn that tiger aggression was expected. Those who lived in tiger areas hurried home when the sun was about to set and did not leave their village until after sun-up. If travel between these moments was unavoidable, people traveled in groups and with torches ablaze. But even then people could be caught, as witness the mailman story.[21]

In many areas, there was no guarantee that tigers would not try to catch people in broad daylight. Of the c. 40 "individual" stories, 20 specify the time of the attack. Eight of these encounters took place at night, eight during the day, and four in between, at sunset. Six of the eight daytime stories are set in the "tiger nest" Residencies of Banten, Priangan, and Besuki. Here, the Javanese traveled only in groups, even during the day, and armed themselves with lances and/or guns. European travelers were surrounded by a large number of followers, also armed. In 1777, when the Swedish naturalist Carl Thunberg visited the Buitenzorg area, not far from Batavia, two of the soldiers accompanying him continuously blew their horns in order to keep the tigers at a distance. In some of these areas Javanese peasants and European planters never went unarmed when at work in the fields.[22]

While tiger attacks seem to have been fairly equally divided between day and night, the frequency distribution over the year was rather skewed, in fact more skewed than the one found for the seventeenth century. The highest frequency was, again, to be found in April, the period of the end of the wet and the onset of the dry monsoon; there were no cases reported for May. Almost all the other cases were found during the wet monsoon, particularly in December, January, and March. Of the 18 cases dating from the nineteenth century for which the month was known, only 3 took place during the dry season, if April is regarded as the last month of the rainy season. For the seventeenth century the distribution was somewhat less pronounced, comprising 7 out of 23 cases.

The observation that the tiger might be at his most dangerous during or at least at the end of the wet season is confirmed by a number of sources. For the Priangan Residency, Junghuhn wrote that the tigers left the low-lying, marshy areas, where they usually could be found during the rainy season, to invade the higher regions, where they were absent during the remainder of the year, following the wild boar and deer that did likewise. In his answer to queries of the Governor-General, dated 1854, the Resident of Yogyakarta, also known as Yogya, reported that the tigers left the inhospitable regions where they used to dwell in March, April, and May. That was the period that the tigers were at their most restless and dangerous. Reporting on the "tiger scare" of 1894–95, the Resident of Jepara stated that it was well known that tigers left the inhabited areas during the dry season, only to return during the wet monsoon. The Resident of Banten, commenting on the "tiger plague" in his area in 1887–89, said that with the onset of the dry monsoon, most problems would be over for the time being, as the villagers would then set fire to the grasslands, depriving the tigers of their cover.[23]

Although these data confirm the findings of my samples, they do not offer much of an explanation, apart from the fact that marshes become too wet for most animals during the monsoon rains. My explanation would be that the crops ripening at the end of the rainy season attract game, and the tigers follow in their wake. In addition, based on data about Sumatra, to be presented presently, it may be assumed that this annual trek was also utilized by the tigers as their (main) mating season. Several writers have emphasized that tigers are at their most aggressive when in heat, and this is probably also what the Resident of Yogyakarta meant when he talked about tigers being "restless."[24]

Fortified and Deserted Villages

If people had to live under the constant threat of a tiger attack, both during the day and at night, they sometimes not only surrounded their houses with a strong and high fence but also turned their entire village into a fortress. Inside the village, fires were kept burning throughout the night by villagers keeping watch. But all those precautions were not sufficient to deter a determined tiger. When Junghuhn visited such a village in the regency of Sukapura, Priangan Residency, in 1847, several families were mourning recent losses. Fortified villages seem to have been rare, however, and I found only three reports to that effect, citing cases in Banten and Priangan.[25]

More often, people living in such areas, feeling beleaguered by tigers, were reported to have yielded to the tiger, leaving their villages altogether. This was observed in Banten, Priangan, Krawang, Probolinggo, Besuki, and Banyuwangi, typical tiger areas, but there are two early reports (of 1803 and 1806) referring to the regency of Batang, Pekalongan Residency.[26] This might suggest that in earlier times, abandoning villages because of the tiger threat may have been far more common. Unfortunately, detailed information on the circumstances that made people leave is usually lacking.[27]

Quite some information is available on the situation in the regency of Caringin, Banten Residency, where a "tiger plague" was raging between 1887 and 1889. The events took place in the district of Cibaliung, where shifting cultivation (the practice of "slash and burn") was still being practiced on a large scale. In 1887 the population of Pasir Salak, where over a few days a number of people had been killed by tigers, and that of Bojongkoneng—both fairly large villages—fled to less dangerous areas. They were in such a hurry that they left their stocks of rice behind. Later on, hunger drove them back to their tiger-infested villages, albeit only temporarily, in order to collect their rice. In his letters to the Resident of Banten, the Assistant Resident of Caringin reported that some villagers from another district, Panimbang, belonging to the same regency, also wanted to leave their homes, equally disturbed by tigers. However, the fate of the people from Pasir Salak and Bojongkoneng kept them from moving. The Assistant Resident asked the Resident for 2,110.50 guilders in order to give them the necessary means to support themselves, thus enabling them to leave their villages. In his supporting letter, the Resident of Banten added that the tiger areas of Caringin were now more or less in a state of anarchy, as the civil servants no longer dared to visit the region. In the end, after a lot of tarrying, no money was given, but the Resident was empowered to issue higher rewards for the killing of tigers, something he had not asked for.[28]

The Caringin tiger plague was a *cause célèbre,* leading to questions in the Dutch Parliament. It was a complicated issue, because it seems that the villagers in question had been strongly urged by the local officials to settle elsewhere—so strongly that they may have moved against their will. One of the reasons the officials wanted to remove these people was that they were slash-and-burn agriculturalists, and discouraging shifting cultivation in Java was official policy. Resettling farmers from tiger-beleaguered villages in wet-rice areas that had become depopulated after the eruption of the Krakatao volcano in 1883 was thought to be a clever move in the battle against this form of agriculture. When the "refugees" were permitted to return home, they did so.[29]

As a result of the last "tiger plague" in Java (at least in the period for which there are good statistics), in 1906–7, reports are available on what were possibly the last "deserted villages" owing to aggressive tigers.[30] They were located on the border of the Ujung Kulon peninsula, now a nature reserve, in the same regency, Caringin, that had seen the tragedies described above. One of these villages, Cibunar, had been first wiped out in 1883 by the tidal wave caused by the Krakatao eruption. It had been repopulated and counted some 500 inhabitants when it had to be left for the last time, on account of the tiger plague.[31]

Livestock and dogs were even more at risk than people. Data on this topic are scarce, and those that are available do not make a distinction between tigers and leopards as causative agents, or between animals killed and wounded. About half the number of animals reported killed or wounded came from the Priangan Residency (see Table 3.2).[32]

In some areas, such as southern Banten and southern Priangan, the risk seems to have been a calculated one, at least for the more well to do. It was more expensive for those who owned large numbers of animals to build stables strong enough to withstand a tiger attack than to lose an occasional buffalo calf from a herd that was left to roam freely.[33] For the majority of Javanese peasants, however, such losses were disastrous; for them, it was their one and only

Table 3.2. Number of livestock killed or wounded by tigers or leopards in Java, 1897–1904

Year	Large livestock	Small livestock
1897	517	671
1903	362	1094
1904	401	1144
Average	427	970

goat or buffalo that was subject to loss. Occasionally, such losses were reported by European authors, but they did not stir much popular response, although there was some concern among the colonial bureaucracy.

Other economic side effects of tiger behavior also received some attention, particularly when state-sponsored activities were at stake. In the Priangan in the early nineteenth century, coffee plantations apparently were spots favored by tigers. This feature found its way into civil-service correspondence, as a single sighting could make the population most reluctant to go back to the coffee, rubber, or tobacco gardens. Even a century later, plantations were still reported to face these problems.[34]

Workers on sugar plantations could be in danger as well, as witness the Jepara tiger scare in 1894–95. In 1894, tigers in the district of Banjaran killed 40 laborers, often in broad daylight. One third of this total, 14 people, had been killed between 10 November and 17 December. During the first five months of 1895, another 23 people became victims of the tiger. Then the killings stopped, partly because a planter named IJ. J. G. van Dijk, attracted by the higher rewards offered by a government decree of 8 April, had shot three tigers. It was an area with many sugarcane fields, located at the foot of Mount Muria, and was well known for its many wild boar, against which the cane fields were protected by sturdy palisades. Nevertheless, during the tiger plague, the coolies often refused to work in the cane fields, and European plantation employees brought along a repeating rifle on their tours of inspection.[35] That cane fields were an attractive habitat for tigers was already demonstrated above, citing data from 1644. In that respect, not much had changed in 250 years.

Work in the forests was another activity frequently interrupted by the appearance of tigers. The first nineteenth-century complaints date from the very beginnings of the colonial Forest Service, in 1808.[36]

The Tiger Threat as a Ruse and a Metaphor

As a rule, reports on tiger threats were taken seriously by officials and by European employers, and their veracity was very rarely doubted. One report, on forest labor in the Semarang Residency, dated 1818, was an exception. It suggested that fear of tigers was being used as an excuse for not showing up for corvee labor in the forest. This may serve as a reminder that some of the tiger sightings may have been fakes, the tiger threat being used as a "weapon of the weak" (Scott 1985). Another possible fake alarm, dated more than a century later, certainly has the ring of truth. In or shortly before April 1922, Lieutenant Karel Baron van Hardenbroek, posted near Bandung in the Priangan, was ordered to take 50 soldiers with him to the nearby regency of Garut, where a tiger plague had been reported. He was told that in a period of two months, some 100 head of livestock had been slain by tigers. No tigers were sighted, however, and there were only a few recent prints. The local population was most uncooperative. Hardenbroek concluded that the tiger plague reports had been a cover-up for a cattle-rustling operation.[37]

Normally, reports on tiger killings focused on the victims, but occasionally there was some information on the perpetrators as well, mostly of a quantitative nature. Travelers and civil servants alike were wont to state that certain areas were made unsafe by large numbers of tigers. In fact, expressions such as "jungle-covered and tiger-infested" appear so frequently that the term "tiger-infested" was often not much more than an *epitheton ornans* for an underpopulated, "wild" area. Occasionally, when high food prices or oppressive policies had led locally to an increase in banditry, some areas were declared "unsafe" on account of the many bandits and tigers.[38] It is possible that bandits indeed sought refuge in areas inaccessible owing to high tiger densities, but it is also possible that the tigers were thrown in for good measure. The same considerations apply when we find reports on areas that are uninhabited owing to the insalubrity of the region (because of malaria), the presence of pirates, and that of tigers.[39] Nevertheless, in the early decades of the nineteenth century, when tigers were still more or less ubiquitous, such phrases were more than just metaphors for many of the less densely populated regions. And even in the later part of the century, when in some areas the tiger was on his way out, the expression "tiger-infested" was far from meaningless, particularly in western and eastern Java.

"Tiger Nests" in Java

Going from west to east over the island, we start with the Residencies of Banten and Priangan, real "tiger nests" throughout the nineteenth century. The German physician H. Breitenstein, posted in Multatuli's Lebak (Banten) around 1880, called it "the Empire of the Tiger" (Breitenstein 1900, II, 59). In these two adjacent Residencies the presence of tigers was the rule, and tigerless regions were the exception. Such a situation was rare, however, and usually tigers were concentrated in certain areas.

One such area was the Weleri Forest, surrounding a stretch of the post road between Pekalongan and Semarang, running more or less parallel to the north coast. Here, the changes in tiger density can be followed from decade to decade, as it was a well-traveled route. J. H. Janssen, who drove through this area in 1828, referred to it as the so-called Tiger Forest, where tigers could be heard roaring left and right. Occasionally the tigers showed themselves on the road. Junghuhn also mentioned tigers when he traveled the same road in 1844. However, when S. A. Buddingh visited the region in the mid-1850s, he reported that there had been a lot of tigers in the Weleri Forest in the past, but that so much teak had been cut that their numbers had dropped. As witness the many tiger-traps, they had not disappeared entirely. In the late 1850s, Professor W. H. de Vriese could speak of the Weleri Forest as formerly infamous on account of its many resident tigers but now not so dangerous, as the tigers went away when the trees were felled, and in many places it no longer merited the name "forest."[40]

A similar story could be told about another stretch of post road that could also boast of a tiger forest: that between Surakarta and Ngawi, in the Residency of Madiun.

The regency of Blitar, Kediri Residency, was another well-known tiger area and, according to Junghuhn, the largest "tiger nest" of Java in the 1840s. In 1830, when it came under direct Dutch rule, it was an uninhabited wilderness. It remained largely uncultivated until around 1860, when European tobacco growing started in the area. The crop was not much of a success, however, and even around 1900 large tracts of land were under forest cover. By then, the Forest Service had taken over the exploitation of the teak forests found there, which afforded the tigers some protection. Blitar was the last place where the once-famous tiger-sticking ceremonies were performed, probably until 1906, and also a focus of weretiger beliefs. (The tiger-sticking ceremonies, pitting tigers and leopards against people with spears, and the weretigers, beings that could shift between human and tiger shapes, will be dealt with in later chapters.) Within the regency, the district and forest of Lodoyo were assumed to have the highest tiger density. In contrast to the road between Surakarta and Ngawi, Blitar was somewhat off the beaten track, so the usual descriptions by "tourists" are largely lacking, but there are government reports and observations by people who worked in the area.[41]

We have now reached the so-called Easthook, comprising the Residencies of Pasuruan, Probolinggo, Besuki, and Banyuwangi. Only the northern plain of this area was cultivated at the beginning of the nineteenth century. The southern parts of the first three Residencies and Banyuwangi in its entirety were very thinly populated and largely covered with forests. Population did increase in these areas during the nineteenth century, but even at the end it was still a fairly wild region. Nowadays, there is a nature reserve, Meru Betiri, and until recently it was believed that this was the land of the last Javan tigers.

One place in this region was mentioned several times as a tiger nest: the area around Klakah, on the road from the town of Probolinggo to the town of Lumajang.[42] Another tiger nest was reached if one continued on the road from Klakah to Lumajang-town, entering the Lumajang plain that stretches away to the south coast.[43]

The place that was probably mentioned most, the area between the towns of Panarukan, in Besuki, and Banyuwangi, formed an exception to the rule that the northern part of the Easthook was well populated and cultivated. This part of Besuki was taken up by a volcano, Mount Baluran, which has been a nature reserve since 1937; it was the backdrop of Java's most northeastern point, Cape Sedano. The cape and the adjacent slopes of the heavily forested Baluran were favorite spots for tigers and hunters alike until the very end of the colonial period.[44] What made the area famous, or rather infamous, was the road at the southwestern foothills of Baluran connecting the Residencies of Besuki and Banyuwangi. Here the tiger-infested forest of Sumberwaru was to be found. It was an area of many deserted villages and stockaded post stations, a place to which no one in his right mind traveled at night or alone.[45]

It is not unlikely that some of these areas, particularly those positioned along well-traveled roads, acquired part of their reputation from being written up by popular authors. As out-of-the-way places were seldom visited, we cannot expect many reports on such areas, and although remote regions are not necessarily full of tigers, some of them certainly were. It could even be argued—as it was argued by some writers of the period—that high tiger densities kept people from settling in certain areas. As there was no need to construct roads leading to "empty" areas, these places would not attract many visitors, and high tiger density could go unreported until a naturalist or a hunter came along. High tiger densities, therefore, sometimes went unreported precisely because they were high.

Mountains were avoided by most nineteenth-century European travelers. They also seem to have been avoided by most Javanese, sometimes because mountains were regarded as forbidden or sacred places. In the pre-Islamic past, many of these mountains had not been avoided entirely, given the fact that the few intrepid botanists and hunters who did climb them often found ruins of Hindu temples and tombs. The presence of these remains partly explains the reluctance of the Javanese to set foot on such mountains, which, in turn, explains their often unspoiled vegetation, making them excellent refuges for tigers (Boomgaard 1995, 55). In addition to Baluran, mentioned in the literature as a typical tiger mountain of the Besuki-Banyuwangi area, various other mountains and mountain complexes in eastern Java and the eastern part of central Java are described as prime tiger habitat. According to Junghuhn, the heavily forested limestone hills of northeastern central Java counted more tigers than people.[46] Finally, Mount Muria in Jepara Residency, source of one of the last tiger plagues, in the 1890s, was known as a tiger retreat long before the area attracted so much bad publicity.[47]

Tiger Families

I return briefly to the personal tiger encounters, which usually feature an individual or a small group of people coming across just one tiger. This was to be expected, as tigers, unlike lions, hyenas, or wild dogs, are not gregarious animals. However, there are a handful of reports about confrontations with more than one tiger.

Andries de Wilde, landowner of Sukabumi (Priangan), wrote in 1830 that tigers sometimes operated in groups of five, six, or even more animals. On Sukabumi, one such group had taken away six people within one week. This, if true, is the record number of tigers acting as a group to be found for Java.[48]

In July 1855, Angayuda, village head of Merayan, Rembang Residency, constructed a tiger-trap provided with poisoned meat because he had seen many tiger prints. Two days later, he found an unconscious tigress in the trap, together with four dead cubs.

In another story, a 50-year-old Javanese, Pak Enting, was attacked and killed at night on the private estate Cimapak in the district of Cibarusa, Buitenzorg Residency, in or just before March 1863, when guarding his fields in a gubuk. When villagers from the surrounding area found his remains, they went looking for the tiger in the nearby forest. They were confronted by four large, snarling tigers, who were unimpressed by the crowd that was out to get them.

Finally, there is the moving story of Bapak Kaira, inhabitant of the village of Cikadokan, private estate Teluk Pucung, in the eastern quarter of the Environs of Batavia. On 28 December 1841, he was chopping wood in a nearby forest when two tigers attacked him. They smashed his head before his son and the other villagers could come to his rescue. When he had been buried, the tigers remained in the neighborhood of the village, according to the inhabitants in search of Pak Kaira's body. The sheriff of Bekasi had tiger-traps constructed, but when this did not produce results, he organized a collective hunt, during which Pak Kaira's son killed one of the animals, a tigress.[49]

It may be assumed that these tiger groups were either females with their cubs or young adolescents, young siblings who stuck together for a short while after their mother's departure, or mature male–female couples during mating season. In de Wilde's story, the numbers mentioned are very high indeed, as a mother with four cubs is about the maximum number to be encountered outside zoos. However, rare cases of two parents with cubs also can be found in the literature (Mazák 1983, 62).

Leopards

In the literature on India, we encounter many a tale about man-eating leopards. However, in Java cases of humans being killed by a leopard were rare. As discussed in Chapter 2, the black leopard, a melanistic variety of the normal, spotted one, had a very bad reputation.[50]

Although in Java leopards hardly ever killed people, they did attack them, but even that was not generally known. Most authors who reported on aggression by leopards stated that only one who had been cornered or who was hungry would attack people. The Javanese evidently were afraid of the leopard, certainly when one "stalked down the village street in broad daylight," but, if under attack, they would not hesitate to kill one with their daggers. In Java, the leopard has survived until this day, but he was already rather rare in most areas prior to 1940. Nevertheless, several reports on people attacked by leopards date from the 1920s.[51]

The most likely explanation for the difference in lethality to humans between the Indian and the Javan leopard is that the Indian leopard was bigger on average than the Javan one. Environmental factors could have played a role as well: Game in India's driest areas was rarer during the rainless period than it was in Java during its dry monsoon. Finally, whereas many Javanese thought that some tigers were inhabited by the souls of human ancestors, such beliefs were not held about leopards. In at least some areas of India this distinction was not made, perhaps precisely because the Indian leopard was bigger and more dangerous. If Indian villagers refused to defend themselves against attacking leopards, this may very well have reinforced the inclination of the latter to see humans as fair game.

Sumatran Killings

There are fewer "individual" stories available regarding tiger killings in Sumatra, only some 30. Only two of these predate the nineteenth century. The period 1900 to 1950 produced some ten stories. In accordance with our findings for Java, the majority of the victims were grownup males, and the attacks were about equally divided between daytime and night.

European victims are not recorded. A fair number of the Asian victims were foreigners, namely Chinese and Javanese, often plantation coolies.[52] It is likely that non-Sumatran Asians are overrepresented in our sample, as stories told by Europeans were often set in surroundings with large concentrations of "foreign" Asians: plantations, railway construction sites, and military outposts, all of them largely dependent on imported labor. Nevertheless, these people may have had more than their fair share of mortality owing to tigers, as they had been transplanted into an alien environment for which they lacked the "coping mechanisms" developed by those who had grown up there. It is even likely that the tiger population of these areas had grown, as European enterprise had been responsible for their partial deforestation, thus creating ecotones attractive to game.[53] This effect was probably restricted in scope and duration, but it must have had a profound influence on the always-precarious balance between tigers and humans.

There are only three stories in which the month of the attack is specified. Although all three cases fall within the rainy season, this is too low a proportion of the already small sample for any conclusion. Fortunately, additional evidence links the period of the wet monsoon with the fruiting season of many trees, which attracted game that had to leave the lower lying areas because of flooding. The game was followed by tigers, who, as one author seems to imply, availed themselves of this period for mating.[54] This tallies with the data on Java.

The balance between tigers and humans was upset by more than only Europeans' activities, as suggested by a number of reports dating from the last decades of the eighteenth and the early ones of the nineteenth century, when the European presence was still fairly restricted. In 1773, the Rawas area, part of the later Palembang Residency (southern Sumatra), "was said to be virtually depopulated because the people were so fearful of attacks by tigers." William Marsden, an official of the British East India Company, whose information came mostly from the Bengkulu area (southern Sumatra), described the situation in the 1780s as follows: "The tigers prove to the inhabitants, both in their journies [sic] and even their domestic occupations, most fatal and destructive enemies. The number of people annually slain by these rapacious tyrants of the woods, is almost incredible. I have known instances of whole villages being depopulated by them." A few years later, around 1810, the comments of the British surgeon and naturalist Benjamin Heyne on Sumatra in general were rather similar. In 1816, the British Resident of Mukomuko, part of the Bengkulu area, had an equally gloomy story to tell: "[At Mukomuko tigers] have become uncommonly fierce and numerous throughout the country, and with the further calamity occasioned by the failure of the paddy crop, it is truly distressing. The gardens are neglected, and desertions take place which I apprehend will prove highly detrimental to the pepper vines."

The first two quotations suggest a certain timelessness, as if tiger aggression were a structural problem. In the latter case, however, the aggression is depicted as something new, and the text could imply a connection between crop failures and the depredations by tigers, as a harvest failure influences the availability of game. The other instances of ravages committed by tigers also might have been of a temporal nature.[55]

Some of these reports might have exaggerated, although in later years we still hear occasionally of deserted villages,[56] as we did for Java. On the other hand, the tiger threat may have been bigger in the years between 1770 and 1820 than it would be later on. We have no exact figures for the number of people annually slain by tigers prior to the 1860s and 1870s, when on average fewer than 200 people were killed annually on the whole island. However, the data we do have suggest much higher death rates in earlier years (see Table 3.3).[57]

Even if the figure for Lampung, which seems to be inflated, were to be halved, we would still find more than 800 people killed per year, and that only for four Residencies, albeit the ones where mortality owing to tiger attacks was higher than elsewhere. This suggests that the average number of people annually killed in the whole island may have been 1,000, or more than double the

Table 3.3. Average number of people killed annually by tigers in various Sumatran Residencies, 1818–1855

Area	Year	Number of people killed by tigers
Bengkulu	1818	100
Lampung	1820	675
Palembang	1854	300
Tapanuli	1855	100

figure to be found for Java in the 1820s (see Table 3.1). On the other hand, the data mentioned here may refer to extraordinary years and therefore might not necessarily be representative. It is difficult to avoid the conclusion that the tiger threat was more formidable than it would be later on, and that people in sparsely settled Sumatra were more at risk than the inhabitants of densely populated Java.

Sumatran Themes and Motifs

There are, inevitably, many similarities between the Javanese and the Sumatran stories. Again we encounter the postal services as an object of the tiger's aggression, only this time it is the mail coach plying the road between Lubuksikaping and Rao, division Rao, in the northern part of the Residency of Sumatra's West Coast. The mail coach was attacked in 1911 while crossing the forest of Panti, an infamous tiger haunt, and the driver of the coach was killed. As was the case in Java, some Sumatrans believed that tigers would not bother those who transported government documents. The then British Lieutenant Governor of Bengkulu, Raffles, recounted such an experience in 1818: "The coolies, in passing through the forest, came upon a tiger, crouched on the path; they immediately stopped and addressed him in terms of supplication, assuring him they were poor people carrying the Tuan Besar [Raffles], great man's luggage, who would be very angry with them if they did not arrive in time, and therefore they implored permission to pass quietly and without molestation. The tiger, being startled at their appearance, got up and walked quietly into the depths of the forest." It is a fascinating notion that the tiger, the "King of the Wilderness," was apparently supposed to have granted diplomatic immunity to representatives of his colleague, the colonial state.[58]

Sumatra also offers the familiar stories about people who refused to leave their houses at night and who, if circumstances or officials forced them to travel between sundown and sunrise, would do so only in groups, carrying arms, and with burning torches. Even inside their homes, people were not always safe from tiger attacks. In the most dangerous areas, villages or individual houses were fortified. Bickmore, visiting the island in 1865–66, gave the following description: "Tanjong Agong is a small village, of only eighteen or twenty small houses, each of which is placed on posts six or eight feet high. A ladder leads up to a landing, which is enclosed by a fence and a gate, to prevent the tigers from entering their houses." But even when such precautionary measures had been taken, people fell victim to the more enterprising tigers. Stockaded forts, established by the military, were not exempt from attacks, either.[59]

Some authors have left particularly graphic descriptions of what it meant to live in areas where the tiger threat was a more or less permanent feature. The following impression comes from Raffles, when he visited Bukit Kabut, an area immediately outside the town of Bengkulu, in 1818: "One of the villagers told me that his father and grandfather were carried off by tigers, and there is scarcely a family that has not lost some of its members by them. In many parts the people would seem to have resigned the empire to these animals, taking but few precautions against them." Raffles, who wanted to establish his country residence precisely in that area, was not to be intimidated: "I am doing all I can to resume the empire of man, and, having made open war against the whole race of wild and ferocious animals, I hope we shall be able to reside on the Hill of Mists [Bukit Kabut] without danger from their attacks."

Oscar von Kessel, who visited the Batak area in 1844, came across people who did take precautions: "People were busy planting rice in the fields near the village, and there I saw, to my amazement, that the women carried out this work under large baskets, made for this purpose from plaited rattan. This was a means to protect themselves against the royal tiger, who was often to be found in this region and who was very dangerous, as it is a well-known fact that the tiger, though usually attacking people unawares and from behind, walks away if the first leap fails." This report is, to my knowledge, the only example of Indonesian women protecting themselves, at least in a defensive way, against tiger attacks while at work outside the village. I found one example of "offensive" protective measures taken by women. This comes from the Gayo area in Aceh Residency, where the German biologist E. Bünning, visiting the area in 1938–39, came across a group of five women and a boy who all carried bush knives. According to Bünning, they were thus armed on account of the many tigers in the area (Bünning 1947, 49–50).

Apart from the general measures taken by men who had to travel (operating in groups, armed and at night, with lighted torches), information is lacking on protective measures taken by males working in areas troubled by tigers. Javanese men at work in such areas were always armed with daggers, and there is no lack of stories of tigers being fended off or even killed by a Javanese with this weapon. However, as this dagger seems to have been part of their normal, every-day attire, this may not have been directed specifically against tigers. Tales about Sumatran males successfully fending off a tiger attack are very rare indeed, and in those cases the weapon is a spear, not a dagger or another kind of knife. It is tempting to assume that the type of weaponry made a difference and that, therefore, Javanese males stood a better chance to survive a tiger encounter than a Sumatran man did.

In 1847, Mohnike visited Tebingtinggi, the western division of the Palembang Residency, where the number of tigers and the losses of human lives owing to attacks of these animals were very large. Of the 47 coolies he employed in the village of Bungamas, no fewer than 17 showed scars resulting from an encounter with a tiger, all acquired recently in and around the village, and that while the survival rate of tiger victims was very low.

Finally, German physician Max Moszkowski, who visited the Siak area in 1907, remarked: "The tiger is a coward. He never attacks from the front, and always only people who are alone. Nevertheless, the tiger plague in Central Sumatra is very large, not a single village that does not pay its annual tribute in human lives to the tiger." This goes to show that, in contrast to the situation in Java, the tiger threat was far from over in Sumatra by the beginning of the twentieth century.[60]

"Tiger Nests" in Sumatra

The number of tigers in Sumatra was much larger than in Java, and they could be found everywhere, apart from the always-submerged swamp areas of the East Coast. Few stories are set in the swampy Residencies of Jambi and Riau. However, the German explorer Wilhelm Volz, who traveled through many regions of northern Sumatra around 1900, included the swampy mangrove belts among the habitats where tigers felt themselves at home. In all probability tigers could live in the swampy areas of eastern Sumatra, as they do nowadays in the Sundarbans, an estuary on the border between West Bengal in northeastern India and Bangladesh; however, they left these regions during the rainy season.[61]

An area that may have had more than its fair share of aggressive tigers was the Panti Forest, in the division of Rao, a northern part of the Residency of Sumatra's West Coast. The area retained its bad reputation at least up to the 1920s. The local population called it "garden of the tigers," while Volz used the term "tiger paradise."[62] The adjacent area, home to the Mandailing Batak, was equally infamous for its many tigers.[63]

In southern Sumatra, Mount Dempo, on the border between the Residencies of Bengkulu and Palembang, had a bad reputation. Local people called it "the region of the tigers" or "the barracks of the tigers." This reputation was shared by the adjacent, most western division of the Palembang Residency, Tebingtinggi.[64]

In comparison with Java, Sumatra seems to have had fewer areas that were well-known "tiger nests," probably because the tiger was practically ubiquitous. Sumatra was also less popular with tourists, who, as I have shown when dealing with Java, were responsible for the reputation of at least some of these regions. It is probably no coincidence that one of the three areas of Sumatra with such a reputation, the Panti Forest, was crossed by the main trunk road connecting the northern and the central parts of the island.

Clouded Leopards

Data on the other big cat in Sumatra, the clouded leopard, are rare. According to most authors, he was neither aggressive nor dangerous to humans. Even the killing of livestock is seldom mentioned, and if it is, it seems to have been restricted to small animals like pigs. However, Mohnike stated that he could be dangerous to humans, although he had to admit that the people of Sumatra and Borneo, the other Indonesian region where the clouded leopard was to be found, did not fear the animal.

Finally, given the paucity of information on this elusive animal, it is perhaps worth stating that according to one author, Tideman, the clouded leopard usually operates in small groups.[65]

The Tiger as a Friend

One has to look hard at the voluminous literature on tigers in order to find indications that tigers were not always and not everywhere looked upon as deadly enemies. On theoretical grounds it could be argued that the literature at our disposal is biased against such information, and that peaceful coexistence between humans and tigers is therefore underreported. After all, this literature was largely written by Europeans, who may have been inclined to overemphasize the tiger threat.

Turning now to concrete examples of good relations between tigers and people, we can discern several themes. In the first place, several observers argued that in some regions of Java and Sumatra indigenous people refused to kill tigers who had done nothing wrong, because they were actually quite useful. They kept the number of wild boar in check, animals that did considerable damage to the crops. In Sumatra, people even had been known to deposit carcasses of wild boar near their arable lands in order to attract tigers specifically for that purpose.[66]

Tigers killed not only wild boar but also a wide range of other game. Although this could have been perceived by the hunting and gathering groups of Malaya and Sumatra as competition, at least one of these groups, the Malayan Semang, were grateful to the tiger for his help in killing game for them. As a tiger almost never eats his kill in one go, tribal groups in the neighborhood could share the spoils. This also has been reported from India. The nomadic Kubu, and the Lubu, shifting cultivators from Sumatra, are also on record as eaters of carrion, so they may have shared the attitude of the Semang toward the tiger in this respect.[67]

Several sources, all dealing with Java, mention the so-called *macan bumi,* or village tiger. Such a tiger, having lived in the neighborhood of a particular village for a long time, was fed meat by the villagers at a set time. He never harmed any of the villagers and kept "foreign" tigers away.[68] In a later chapter, I will deal with this curious phenomenon in more detail.

The motif of the neighborly tiger shades imperceptibly into another theme: the ancestral tiger. The notion that some tigers were inhabited by ancestral spirits was reported by many authors, not only from Java but also from Bali, Sumatra, and Malaya. Ancestral tigers were, in principle, harmless and even beneficial to "their" villagers. The ancestral tiger, however, was a "friend" who, in the eyes of many, was also a strict disciplinarian and was certainly to be feared. Indeed, fear of the tiger, a few quoted exceptions apart, is the all-pervading theme in the tiger-human interaction.

4

Man-Eating Tigers

Tigers often are divided into three categories, namely game-killers, cattle-lifters or cattle-slayers, and man-eaters.[1] Boundaries between the groups are, however, somewhat blurred. "Man-eater" is the term used for a tiger who routinely kills and/or devours humans. It is not applied to those who, because they were disturbed or felt threatened, once or twice have killed a human being. These animals, basically just game-killers or cattle-slayers, occasionally are called man-killers.[2] Mazák, the Czech writer of the most authoritative single-authored textbook on the tiger, distinguished two broadly defined causes of man-eating: inability of a tiger to hunt other prey because of old age or wounds, and a lack of game and cattle (Mazák 1983, 130).

Specialists on the big cats tell us that, as a rule, tigers and leopards leave people alone. Nevertheless, the historical literature on Indonesia abounds with reports on people killed by tigers. That this was not just a quirk of the vivid imagination of Europeans in an alien environment is proved by the statistics published annually between 1862 and 1904 for Java and Sumatra, by Residency (administrative unit), on people killed by tigers.

Man-eating by tigers is almost a thing of the past, restricted to a few cases now and then in Nepal, northern India (Uttar Pradesh, Bengal), Bangladesh, Malaysia, and Sumatra.[3] Around 1900, however, some 1,200 people were killed annually by tigers and leopards in the part of India that was under direct British control. In Sumatra, 60 people were annually registered as having been killed by tigers, and in Java that number was only slightly lower, at 50.

For selected years we have also data for Java and Sumatra on numbers of tigers and (clouded) leopards destroyed or captured. This enables us to com-

Tiger and deer. According to many authors, tigers came in three categories: game-killers, cattle-lifters, and man-eaters. Balen 1914

pare the data on both people killed by tigers and tigers and leopards killed by humans.

The data for Sumatra, where Dutch colonial administration was still expanding at the time, are probably less reliable than those for Java. There is also more background information on Java, which enables me to explain differences between regions, and trends and fluctuations in the figures. The analysis will therefore focus on Java. Similar data available for India will be used for a comparative perspective. Prior to the nineteenth century, quantitative data for Java are rare but not entirely absent. We do have qualitative data for Sumatra, Java, and Bali for the entire period dealt with here.

I must deal briefly with the question as to whether the statistics can be regarded as trustworthy. Bengt Berg, the Swedish tiger-hunter-cum-photographer who trekked through the Indian jungles in the early 1930s, did not think much of the reliability of the Indian statistics. In his opinion, Indian village heads were wont to attribute unusual deaths to the activities of tigers and leopards, reporting them as such to the officials. On the contrary, Jim Corbett, another famous hunter in the 1920s and 1930s, argued that humans killed by man-eaters were underreported. The British Indian government itself seems to have had comparable misgivings, because they discontinued the annual publication of statistics on killings—though not the data gathering—in 1927, owing to the unreliability of the data.[4] Most writers, though, have used the figures without much hesitation as rough indicators of the order of magnitude of the man-eating problem.[5] The figures for Java are fairly reliable, although occasionally one encounters numbers that seem a bit odd. The data on Sumatra are probably somewhat shakier, as Dutch rule was established later, in some cases (such as on Sumatra's East Coast) even during the period under consideration.

Between 1862 and 1904, figures of people killed by tigers in Java and Sumatra were published annually in the *Koloniaal Verslag* (Colonial Report). The gathering and publication of these data was linked to a government decree dated 8 August 1862, No. 7. This decree put the system of bounties for killing tigers, leopards, and crocodiles on the same footing for all Residencies of Java and Sumatra (cf. Chapter 5 for a detailed treatment of bounties). The unified system of bounties was abolished in 1897 because it was deemed expensive and inefficient, but the collection of data continued. In 1905, the Residents were ordered to send in more detailed statistics on people and cattle killed by tigers and leopards (and on tigers and leopards captured or destroyed). At the same time, however, the publication of these data was stopped, for reasons unknown.

Data on captured or destroyed tigers and leopards, by Residency, in Java and Sumatra were collected but, those for 1852 apart, never published. For a restricted number of years they can be found in the archives, namely for 1858–60, 1897, and 1903–4.[6] The same data for Java alone can be reconstructed for 1833 from the amounts to be paid out in bounties, mentioned in the budget for that year. As they reflected expectations based on experiences of former years, these data should be regarded as approximations of average numbers killed in the early 1830s.[7]

Figures for isolated years or series of years on individual Residencies and lower administrative units (regencies, districts), on tigers and leopards captured or killed, and on humans killed by tigers can be found throughout the literature and the archival records. Occasionally, they will be used to fill in gaps and to correct other data. There are also some isolated figures for Bali.

For India, annual data, broken down by administrative unit, are available for people killed by tigers and leopards and for tigers and leopards captured or destroyed from 1875 to 1895. Data on people killed are available for the years 1896 to 1904. As in the Netherlands Indies, the collection of the data was obviously linked to the bounties paid out for captured and destroyed animals. For various reasons, I have left out the data on Burma, Ajmer, and Coorg. As a proportion of the annual totals, the omitted figures are insignificant.

The figures on India and Sumatra refer to the areas under direct British or

Dutch control. In the case of Sumatra, this means that the area for which data are available c. 1870 is not the same as that around 1900.

Data on population and surface area for Java and Sumatra have been taken from or calculated on the basis of Boomgaard and Gooszen (1991). Data for India were taken from the *Statistical Abstracts*.

Finally, I have used material on Java dating from the period between 1605 and the 1850s. They are derived from a huge variety of sources. Many of them are not of a quantitative nature. Their reliability is not easily established, but, taken together, they tell a coherent and consistent story.

Man-Eating in Seventeenth-Century Java

The Dutch arrived in Java just before 1600 and established the headquarters of their East India Company (VOC) on the northwest coast shortly afterward. The location was the city of Batavia, present-day Jakarta, founded on the ruins of an older town in 1619. Apart from the coastal area, the place was surrounded by swamps and forests, which, as time went by, had to give way to houses, walls, arable lands, and orchards. Tigers troubled the people of Batavia from the very beginning, and they are mentioned in the sources as a threat to humans and their animals as early as the 1620s. High VOC officials, such as the Governors-General Pieter de Carpentier, Jacques Specx, and Joan Maetsuijcker, organized tiger-hunting parties, thus probably combining business with pleasure.[8]

At least since 1644, money was given to people who had captured a tiger or a leopard (and also for rhinos, crocodiles, and large snakes) on presentation of the animal to the Governor-General. Initially, the money seems to have been given as a reward, or rather a tip, as one of the earlier sources phrases it. In 1648 this payment was already regarded as customary, a premium that those who captured a ferocious animal could expect to receive. Evidently, the VOC was interested in stimulating the killing of tigers and other dangerous and/or large animals.

Do we have any idea how many tigers were being killed? A source dated c. 1670 suggested that tigers were captured near Batavia every day. This sounds very much like hyperbole, but then the author may have meant that at least 365 tigers (and leopards) were captured around the town. In 1748 some 80 "tigers" were destroyed in the area adjacent to the Environs of Batavia. This area would be more or less covered in the nineteenth century by the Residencies of Buitenzorg and Priangan, where in c. 1830 some 100 tigers and leopards were killed annually.[9]

Is it possible to establish the extent to which tigers posed a real threat to

Java's population in the seventeenth and eighteenth centuries? Most Europeans in Java certainly perceived the tiger as very dangerous. The first known European source to mention the tiger in Java is Edmund Scott's report of his journey to the Indies (1605). In Banten (western Java) he saw a "furious beast, called by them a matchan."[10] These animals killed many people around the city of Banten, and the king often went tiger hunting with his followers.

Governor-General de Carpentier reported in January 1625 to the board of directors of the VOC in the Netherlands that tigers killed more of his people around Batavia than the enemy (that is, the people of Banten, western Java) did, taking in the year 1624 the lives of 60 persons. Given Batavia's small population at that time (some 6,000 people), this was a considerable loss.

The Dutch physician Bontius, who lived in Batavia from 1627 to 1631, was an astute observer of all things natural and not one to repeat fairy tales. In what is probably the earliest Dutch treatise on the Java tiger, he argued that tigers prefer people, with their badly developed sense of smell and low speed, as prey, compared to water buffalo and game. That was the reason that tigers were often to be found in the vicinity of human settlements.

In 1644, the *Daghregister* of Batavia—the official VOC diary—mentioned eight individual cases of people attacked and mostly killed by tigers during the first four months of the year.

In 1659, a group of Malay woodcutters working in Krawang, to the east of Batavia, returned to the city because in two months 14 of their people had been killed by a tiger or tigers. In March of the same year, the *Daghregister* mentions an increase of the number of tigers in the lowlands, as witness the daily reports of people and cattle killed by tigers.[11]

Therefore, it seems that tigers posed, indeed, a threat to the local population. If we calculate the share of these killings in all causes of death, assuming that the figure given for 1624 is reliable and representative, the proportion must have been quite significant.[12]

All these data suggest that man-eating was a serious problem in western Java in the seventeenth century, not only in heavily forested areas like Priangan and Krawang but also, and perhaps even more, around the two relatively large population centers of Banten and Batavia. This runs counter to current opinion, as expressed by the view that "historically, a low incidence of man-eating has been correlated with localities where there was an adequate supply of natural prey and extensive habitat, into which human encroachment was only gradual" (McDougal 1987, 445). With the exception of the port cities of Banten, Batavia, and Cirebon, and a number of smaller coastal towns, western Java at that time was largely covered with forests, with only a sprinkling of small towns and villages in the upland areas. The population density of the area around 1600 could have been 20 to 25 persons per km², but it is not inconceivable that the real density was even lower.[13]

If we accept such a situation as "gradual human encroachment" and the large expanse of uninhabited waste as "extensive habitat," there is still a theoretical possibility that the supply of natural prey was not adequate. After all, the tropical rainforest in its more pristine state, although extremely rich in animal species in general, is not known for its abundance of relatively large, forest-floor-dwelling mammals like wild boar and deer, the tiger's preferred prey animals. However, the forests in western Java at that time were often broken by patches of secondary growth and arable lands, not to mention the areas where forest cover was absent because the land was too wet, too dry, or too high. As this situation made for a fair number of ecotones, the favorite spots for wild boar and deer, we may expect to find an abundance of game, as, indeed, we do find in the sources.[14] So although McDougal's conditions have been met, we are confronted with a situation in which the incidence of man-eating was high. The abundance of game notwithstanding, every year many people were killed by tigers, even to such an extent that Bontius could suggest that tigers preferred humans to animals.

So why this unexpectedly high incidence of man-eating? In the Introduction, I cited the commonly held opinion of modern writers that, as a rule, tigers avoid human beings. In their view, man-eating is exceptional, if only because in real tiger-country game is abundantly available, and only a few tigers per thousand are man-eaters.[15] According to various authors, one of the reasons for this state of affairs is that tigers—as long as they are not man-eaters—have a natural, ingrained respect, fear, mistrust, or aversion of human beings. Another almost universally accepted (and related) notion is that the tiger is a nocturnal animal, beginning his activities shortly before dusk and starting to look for cover at dawn. Recent studies, however, have shown that tigers operate during the day as well, particularly in those areas where human settlements are few and far between. Corbett and Fend argue that man-eaters invariably became active during the daytime because they adapted themselves to humans as diurnal animals.[16]

In the seventeenth century, tigers killed people and cattle both during the day and during the night. These tigers were truly opportunistic animals, killing where and when they met with easy prey. They were not afraid to come to the edge of the city, venturing right up to the walls and occasionally even entering the town.[17] Neither do they seem to have feared human beings in general, although they may have learned at an early stage to leave Europeans alone, as the latter almost invariably carried firearms outside the city walls. The 60 people killed in 1624, for instance, all were Asians, as were most of the victims mentioned in the *Daghregister*. Evidence for this supposition can also be found in the often-repeated story that Europeans did not have much to fear from tigers, and that, given a choice, the tiger always picked an Asian out of a mixed group of Europeans and Asians. This story appeared as early as 1662 and was still being told in the early twentieth century.[18] Another story, for which I have only found examples dating from a later period, may also be read as proof of the tiger's opportunism rather than evidence for his fear of humans: It is the conviction that tigers will predominantly attack stooping people, mostly indigenous women and children who are harvesting, cutting grass, defecating, or gathering wood. People in an upright position, the typical posture of humankind, would be much less at risk, according to this story.[19] I fail to see why this should point to a basic fear of people rather than to the tiger's ability to learn that indigenous women and children were easier prey than indigenous men, who were often armed with a dagger, just as tigers seem to have been able to distinguish between Europeans with firearms and indigenous people without them. Those who fear that the story of the tiger preferring "natives" to Europeans might have racial or supremacist overtones may rest assured that there is another story to redress the balance. In some areas the crocodile was believed to leave the indigenous population alone and devour Europeans only (e.g., Aylva Rengers 1844, 383–84). But that is a story much harder to credit than the alleged, rather "rational" preferences of the tiger.

It seems certain, therefore, that tigers did not avoid humans, particularly in situations where some humans were an easier prey than a formidable adversary, such as the wild boar. What may have been an additional factor around Batavia in the early seventeenth century was the lack of experience with tigers of many of the recently arrived inhabitants of this booming town. At every moment in time, the majority of the inhabitants, both European and Asian, consisted of immigrants, often from tigerless regions. Of the Asians who were killed by tigers and of whom we know the nationality, only a small minority was Javanese.

There may be alternative explanations for the many tiger killings recorded in the sources. Small numbers of man-eaters may have been responsible for a large majority of the killings, or there could have been sudden peaks in man-killing owing to extraordinary circumstances.

In India, man-eating tigers and leopards have been known to kill hundreds of people each year. The record of registered kills attributed to one animal seems to be the 700 victims of a tigress operating in the central provinces at the beginning of the twentieth century. A good second are the 436 victims of the Champawat tigress, who in the end was hunted down by Corbett around 1910.[20]

I am not aware of Indonesian tigers that killed on this scale. Although this lack of data may be partly caused by a different method of registration—numbers of kills per tiger were not systematically registered—I am inclined to believe that the enormous numbers cited for India cannot be applied to Indonesia. The record for Indonesia seems to be 69 kills, followed by 39 and 22 kills by one tiger, all reported from Sumatra in the 1920s and 30s.[21] Nothing comparable even to this more modest scale of kills per tiger can be found for Java. When in 1894–95 63 people were killed in the district of Banjaran, Residency of Jepara, it was estimated that this had been caused by 15 tigers "only."[22] In the literature, a sudden increase in killings is never specifically attributed to the appearance of a man-eater but almost invariably is said to reflect the growing number of tigers in general. In Java, tigers were sometimes regarded as reincarnated ancestors, and many would not kill them without good reasons (cf. Chapter 8). But if a tiger was guilty of cattle lifting, or if he had turned man-eater, the local population who wanted revenge would relentlessly pursue him. If the animal could not be destroyed, the population would call in the help of the local colonial government. In contrast, in India man-eaters were often not pursued by the local population because they regarded them as evil spirits or weretigers and feared their vengeance.[23] Given this difference in attitudes toward man-eaters, it is doubtful that the large numbers of victims in early-seventeenth-century western Java should be attributed to a few man-eaters only.

The second alternative explanation is that the large numbers of killings could have been peaks caused by special circumstances, which therefore cannot be regarded as representative for normal years. Such a sudden outburst (sometimes called a "tiger plague") could be stimulated by a sharp increase in human or animal corpses (from epidemics, epizootics, famines, and wars) or a lack of game and cattle (from epizootics or droughts).[24]

The year 1624, when 60 people were killed by tigers in the surroundings of Batavia, was a year of high rice prices throughout Java. In and around Batavia, however, the situation was not alarming. The VOC subsidized the retail price of rice, and in the surrounding countryside rice and sugar were doing well.[25] Under these circumstances a tiger plague is not likely to have occurred. On the other hand, the above-mentioned description of tiger behavior by Bontius, who lived through two sieges of Batavia by the armies of Mataram (central Java), in 1628 and 1629, may have been influenced by the circumstances produced by these wars. In both cases, the retreating Mataram armies left large numbers of corpses, which may have made man-eaters of a fair number of tigers.[26]

In 1644, another year with many registered tiger kills, there were no wars, agriculture around Batavia was thriving, and rice prices in the city were low, due to an abundant supply from Mataram and places outside Java. The only setback was an outbreak of smallpox, but as the victims of this epidemic were no doubt immediately buried, this cannot have influenced tiger behavior.[27]

Finally, in 1659, the 14 Malay woodcutters killed in Krawang may have been the indirect victims of local dearth (and famine?) owing to a rice-harvest failure. Batavia itself, however, had plenty of rice, and agriculture in the environs was doing well and expanding.[28] Therefore, the daily reports of people and cattle being killed by tigers around the city cannot be explained by unfavorable circumstances turning tigers into man-eaters. It is more in keeping with the facts to assume that the gradual expansion of rice and, particularly, of sugarcane cultivation attracted increasing numbers of wild boar, which in turn led to a growing tiger population.

We have witnessed two processes, both conducive to an increasing incidence of man-eating, namely a structural and a periodical process. The gradual expansion of Batavia's population, its cattle, and its arable lands—and therefore of a game-rich ecotone—may have led to a growing tiger density around the city. There were opportunistic tigers, moreover, who had no reasons to fear humans in general. This is what I would call a structural process, as opposed to the periodical disasters that could turn opportunistic tigers into full-fledged, specialized man-eaters.

In the end, the expansion of agriculture into areas at quite some distance from Batavia gradually removed the threat of man-eating tigers from the city. In the eighteenth century, man-eating became the headache of the adjacent regions.

Data available on central and eastern Java before 1800 are very meager, as the Dutch were thin on the ground before the closing decades of the eighteenth century. There is, however, one fascinating piece of information, dated 1620, to be found in a letter to Batavia from a Dutchman held captive in Mataram. He wrote that the ruler of Mataram, Sultan Agung (r. 1613–1645), had sent out his people to capture 200 tigers, which had taken them three months. Agung had pitted these tigers against his men, "sitting in the Javanese way, with pikes" (Colenbrander/Coolhaas 1919–53, vol. 7 no. 1, 608). As I argue in Chapter 7, this may perhaps be read as an attempt to rid the countryside of marauding tigers, in areas where they had become so numerous that individual villages could no longer be expected to cope with them. However that may be, there was a constant demand for live tigers (and leopards) from the central Javanese courts, where they were used for ritual tiger-stickings and tiger-buffalo fights. This demand increased during the closing decades of the eighteenth century, when the indigenous rulers of the areas that had been taken over by the VOC around 1750 started to imitate these court rituals. Although it is rather unlikely that the destruction of man-eaters was the main purpose of these rituals, the ultimate effect may have been a lower tiger density.

Java from 1800 to the 1850s

Taken as a whole, eastern Java was the most sparsely populated part of Java during this period. It had an astonishing abundance of game, and no European hunting to speak of. Western Java had a somewhat higher population density, and northern central Java had the highest number of people per unit of land. These data suggest strongly that man-eating was inversely related to population densities.

Quantitative data on people killed by tigers for almost all of the Residencies of Java are not available prior to 1862. However, we do have isolated data on Banten (for 1820) and Priangan (for 1828–29 and 1855–60), the areas that were responsible in the 1860s and 1870s for 4.3 and 35.7%, respectively, of all killings. If these percentages can be applied to the 1820s and 1850s as well, the estimated average annual number of people killed by tigers in Java as a whole would be about 500 in the 1820s and about 200 in the 1850s. Given the annual averages for c. 1870 (90) and c. 1890 (51), these estimates suggest a sharp downward trend throughout the nineteenth century, which becomes even sharper if we calculate per-capita deaths caused by tigers (see Table 4.1).

It is possible, of course, that the relative contributions of Banten and Priangan calculated for c. 1870 cannot be applied to the 1820s. Even then, the Java total must have been much higher then than after 1862, since the number of deaths in Banten and Priangan alone was over 200 in the 1820s.[29]

There are two years for which data are available, by Residency, on tigers and leopards captured or destroyed for the whole of Java prior to 1858: 1833 (or rather the early 1830s) and 1852. The total numbers of animals killed for these years are c. 1,100 and c. 900, respectively, but the figure for 1852 is almost certainly too low. As in the years after 1858, these data were the by-products of government decrees, allowing individual Residents to offer bounties for tigers and leopards captured or destroyed.

An increasing number of official reports and travelogues on the hitherto "dark" regions of Java become available after 1800 and particularly after 1815. As the territory under direct Dutch rule expanded after the Java War (1825–1830), it is sensible to distinguish two phases within this period, namely 1800/15–1830 and 1830–1860.

During the first period, information on the so-called Principalities (southern central Java) is very scarce, owing to a limited Dutch presence. Of the remaining areas, western and eastern Javanese Residencies are most frequently

Table 4.1. People killed by tigers, and tigers and leopards destroyed in Java, 1820s–1850s, totals and figures per unit of land and population (annual averages)

Period	Total	Per unit of land*	Per 1 million population
1820–1830			
animals killed	1,100	8.1	155
people killed	500	37.0	70
	(400)	(29.6)	(56)
ratio	2.2		
	(2.8)		
1850s			
animals killed	900	6.7	82
	(1,000)	(7.4)	(91)
people killed	200	14.8	18
ratio	4.5		
	(5.0)		

Note: Data in parentheses are estimates and calculations based on assumptions mentioned in the text.
*Animals killed per 1,000 km²; people killed per 10,000 km².

mentioned as tiger regions. Apart from one dubious reference, the island of Madura, in the east, is not mentioned as a big-cat area, and it may never have had any tigers. The Residency of Batavia (the city and its Environs) is seldom mentioned, no doubt because by then tigers had almost disappeared.[30] Therefore, Batavia and Madura apart, the sparsely settled western and eastern Javanese Residencies were typical tiger areas.

Of the six northern central Javanese Residencies only Semarang is frequently mentioned as a tiger area, but it is clearly not in the same league with the typical tiger regions of western and eastern Java. Data on the other five Residencies and on the Principalities of south central Java are scarce. One of the few reports from the latter area, namely on the region adjacent to Semarang in the (later) Residency of Surakarta, confirms the data on southern Semarang as a tiger area. It was said that in the district of Getas, tigers attacked men, women, and children even in the marketplaces. In the same area Carolus Hamar de la Brethonière, leaseholder of the district, had killed 71 tigers in eight years (Nahuijs 1852, 198; on this hunter see also Chapter 7). Regarding the other Residencies, absence of reports does not always mean absence of tigers. Nevertheless, at least in the coastal lowlands of north-central Java, the tiger was not much of a threat.

Regarding western Java, on the contrary, stories abound of tigers who had no fear of large human settlements, who roamed around in broad daylight, even on highways (once attacking a carriage drawn by two horses), and who dragged people from their cottages. Coffee gardens, often laid out in upland areas at the fringe of "virgin" forests, were favorite tiger haunts. The Dutch, though, who lamented the loss of production caused by the refusal of the indigenous coffee planters to venture into tiger-infested gardens, suspected the locals of using tigers as a pretext. Neglected or abandoned arable lands also were favorite spots.[31]

Eastern Java had similar and possibly even worse conditions. Tigers were everywhere, from the seashores to the rims of the volcano craters; in the forests, the alang-alang wilderness, and the grassy highlands; and along the roads. We read of encounters with and attacks by tigers in broad daylight, but fear of the tiger was strongest at night, and people traveled only during the day and in groups. Perhaps it was the tiger's constant and terrible roaring and "howling" at night, not mentioned in the western part of the island during these years, that made people even more afraid of nocturnal travel.[32]

The ubiquity of the tiger and the fear he inspired, particularly at night, was one of the reasons that the penal settlement for indigenous people, Sukaraja, had been established in the "green desert" of Banyuwangi. People did not run away from this place, not even at night, and of the very few who attempted to do so, their skeletons often were found in the forests after some time. Many villages were surrounded by a stockade. Other villages, even those along important roads, were deserted because of tigers. According to one source such abandoned villages could be found in other regions of Java as well, but not so frequently as in Probolinggo, Besuki, and Banyuwangi.[33]

A broadly similar picture, pertaining now to southern central Java as well, characterized the period 1830–1860. Western Java was still an important tiger area, with a concentration in the Residencies of Banten, Priangan, and Krawang. Tigers were found—often during the day—in "virgin" forests, where they killed palmwine-tappers, woodcutters, and gatherers of forest produce; they also appeared in bamboo forests, swamps, deserted *ladang*, alang-alang and glagah wastes, indigo fields, on the beach, and in the mountains.[34] Tigers killed people in front of their houses, or even inside the house after having torn open the thatched roof. Therefore, people built elevated houses and stockaded villages, which did not keep the tiger from jumping over high bamboo fences, however.

Finally, such attacks led to deserted villages. In one forested region, communication between riverine villages was only by water because of the tigers.[35]

For eastern Java we find similar stories. It might be significant that during this period travelers and officials in this region begin to emphasize the nocturnal character of the tiger's activities. It seems likely that a growing European and Asian population, with a concomitant increase in land reclamation and hunting, had a direct and indirect (through the changed behavior of game) influence on the tiger's behavioral patterns.

Information on the northern part of central Java during this period does not differ much from the earlier data. Man-eating is seldom reported in our sources. However, this does not mean that man-eating and tigers were entirely absent. The big surprise in southern central Java, until then largely unknown to Europeans, is Kediri and to a somewhat lesser extent Madiun, both sparsely settled Residencies. For the other six Residencies tigers were seldom mentioned. The large number of tigers in Kediri is not so strange after all, as the Residency borders on eastern Java, tiger country *par excellence*. In fact, in the early nineteenth century, Kediri, Malang (southern Pasuruan), Lumajang (southern Probolinggo), Bondowoso (southern Besuki), and Banyuwangi can be regarded as an almost unbroken chain of wildernesses, forming an ideal tiger habitat.[36]

People Killed by Animals, 1860–1900

Richard Perry stated that "With the exception of Singapore, there are no historic records of any country suffering a mortality from man-eaters comparable to that experienced for so long and so widely in India." Mazák's opinion is very similar: regarding numbers of people killed by tigers, India holds the record. In mainland Southeast Asia, according to him, man-eating is far more rare, and this applies even more aptly to Indonesia. McDougal thinks that man-eating was rare in Sumatra from c. 1880 on, and that in Java tiger habitat had almost disappeared around 1850, with man-eaters being dispatched swiftly.[37] Mazák's statement is phrased in the present tense, but its context suggests that it might equally apply to an earlier epoch. If that is true, all three authors seem to suggest that, compared with India, Indonesians in the nineteenth and early twentieth century had nothing to complain about. In fact, this seems to be borne out by the figures at our disposal (see Table 4.2).

In India, the number of people killed by big cat carnivores was ten times as high as that of the two Indonesian islands taken together. However, a rather different picture emerges if we relate the number of people killed to the total population or to the surface area of the various regions (see Table 4.3).

Table 4.2. Numbers of people killed by tigers and leopards in India and Indonesia, 1882–1904 (annual averages)

| | | Killed by | |
Region	Tigers	Leopards	Total
India	889	317	1,206
Sumatra	58		58
Java	51		51

As regards the number of people killed per unit of land, India still holds first place, at least in around 1890, but the differences are much less pronounced than they seemed before. If we look at the probability of being killed by a big cat, as expressed per unit of population, India loses its leading position to Sumatra, and by a broad margin at that. The relationship between population

Table 4.3. People killed by tigers and leopards in India and Indonesia, 1862–1904, totals and figures per unit of land and population (annual averages), and population densities (c. 1900)

Region (pop density)	Total		Per 10,000 km²		Per 1 million population	
	c. 1875	c. 1890	c. 1875	c. 1890	c.1875	c. 1890
India (105)						
by tigers	810	889	4.0	4.4	4.4	4.2
by leopards	229	317	1.1	1.6	1.3	1.5
both	1,039	1,206	5.1	6.0	5.7	5.7
Sumatra (10)	120	58	4.4	1.6	54.5	17.6
	(180)					
Java (180)	90	51	6.7	3.9	6.1	2.2

Notes: The actual years used for the columns headed "c. 1875" are 1862–81 for Indonesia and 1875–81 for India; the years for the columns "c. 1890" are 1882–1904. Figure in parentheses for Sumatra is an estimate of the total average annual kill by tigers if one includes the area not yet under direct Dutch rule c. 1875, which is included in the data for 1882–1904.

density and number of people killed per unit of population seems to be *linear, though inverse:* the lower the population density, the higher the per capita probability of being killed by a tiger and/or leopard, and the other way around.

The same relationship applies, as a rule, within regions. In India the per capita chances of being killed were highest in thinly populated Assam and the Central Provinces. In Sumatra, the relatively well-populated Residency of Sumatra's West Coast showed the lowest per capita incidence of killings by tigers. This relationship existed in Java as well for the period 1800–1860.

Up to now we have been mainly comparing different regions, but what happens when we compare the areas in different periods? Regarding the Indonesian regions, a clear trend is visible in Table 4.3. All indicators from c. 1875 are much higher than the ones from c. 1890. Although population densities around 1870 were appreciably lower than around 1890, the total number of people killed by tigers, and therefore the numbers killed per unit of land and people, were two or three times higher during the earlier period. Given a linear and inverse relationship between population density and per capita deaths from big cats, this was to be expected.

The figures for India do not share in the downward trend for Indonesia. Here we see a slight increase in both the numbers of people killed and the population itself, which makes for a stable per capita number of deaths by big cats and a slowly growing number of killings per unit of land.

Animals Killed by People

The average number of people killed by tigers annually seems to have diminished much more rapidly in Sumatra than it did in Java. Several reasons might account for this discrepancy. Theoretically, it could have been the result of a higher rate of disappearance of typical tiger habitat. Another possibility is that in Sumatra larger numbers of tigers were being killed by humans than in Java. Finally, it is also possible that tigers and people came to live further apart as the clearing of land continued.

The first possibility mentioned is rather unlikely. In both Sumatra and Java, population growth and the expansion of Western agricultural enterprise were responsible for a high rate of land reclamation, possibly to the detriment of tiger areas. However, there is no evidence that this pressure was higher in Sumatra than in Java. Furthermore, as was discussed in Chapter 2, under certain circumstances the clearing of land also led to the creation of new tiger habitats. This was more the case in Sumatra than in Java. At any rate, there was much more tiger habitat left in Sumatra than in Java, both in absolute and in relative terms.

Turning to the second possibility, the killing of tigers (and leopards) by hu-

Table 4.4. Tigers and (clouded) leopards captured or destroyed, people killed by tigers and leopards, the ratio between these figures, and tigers as a proportion of the three big cats in India and Indonesia, 1858–1904 (annual averages)

Region	Period		Tiger proportion
	1860–75	1890–1900	1890–1900
India			
tigers and leopards killed	4,708	5,428	26%
people killed	1,039	1,206	
ratio	4.5	4.5	
ratio (tigers only)	(1.8)		1.6
Sumatra			
tigers and clouded			
leopards killed	489	349	80%
people killed	120	58	
ratio	4.1	6.0	
ratio (tigers only)	(3.3)		4.8
Java			
tigers and leopards killed	1,431	496	13%
people killed	90	51	
ratio	15.9	9.7	
ratio (tigers only)	(5.3)		1.3

Notes: Data on tigers and leopards captured and destroyed in Sumatra and Java are available for 1858, 1859, and 1860, and for 1903 and 1904. Some discrepancy exists, therefore, with the years for which average numbers of people killed have been calculated, namely 1862–81 and 1882–1904. For India, there are figures on the destruction of tigers and leopards for the period 1875–95, while data on people killed are available for 1875–1904. Figures in parentheses are calculated or estimated ratios between tigers killed and people killed by tigers.

mans, the available data suggest that the higher rate with which the number of people killed by tigers diminished in Sumatra than in Java cannot have been caused by a more relentless hunting down of these animals in Sumatra (see Table 4.4). Not only was the total number of animals killed in Java higher; the ratio of animals killed to people killed, which in Sumatra was comparable to that of India, was higher in Java as well.

However, the total numbers of animals killed mask varying tiger–leopard ratios. Although precise figures for Java c. 1860 are lacking, probably no more than one-third of the animals killed were tigers. At the turn of the century, the proportion of tigers to leopards is not more than one-seventh, or about 65 on average (and a ratio of animals to people killed of 1.3). At the same time, the proportion of tigers to leopards killed in Sumatra was four-fifths, or 280 on average per year (ratio 4.8). Clearly, the number of tigers killed in around 1900 and the ratio of tigers destroyed to people killed were higher in Sumatra than in Java. However, if the 1900 proportion of tigers to leopards obtained in Sumatra in c. 1860 as well, pressure from hunting may have been higher in Java at that time, both in absolute terms and relative to the number of people killed (5.3 versus 3.3). Therefore, in Sumatra around 1900 the number of tigers being killed was much higher than in Java (where tigers had become rather rare), which was a reversal of the situation around 1860. This is part of the explanation of the higher rate with which the number of people killed by tigers diminished in Sumatra than in Java.

Concerning the third possibility mentioned above, data from Bali (see Chapter 10) suggest that tigers kill few people if the areas inhabited by humans and typical tiger country are neatly separated. It could be argued that in Sumatra during the nineteenth century, people and tigers were increasingly being kept apart by the pattern of land clearing and the growth of towns. This process created concentrations of people on the one hand and, at some distance from the centers of civilization, concentrations of tigers on the other. This may very well have had a downward influence on the number of humans killed by tigers.

Related to total surface area, hunting pressure was highest in Java and lowest in sparsely populated Sumatra (see Table 4.5). If, however, we relate the

Table 4.5. Number of tigers and (clouded) leopards captured and destroyed in India and Indonesia, per unit of land and population, 1858–1904 (annual averages)

Region	Per 1,000 km²		Per 1 million population	
	1860–75	1890–1900	1860–75	1890–1900
India	2.3	2.7	25.8	25.5
Sumatra	1.8	0.8	222.3	83.1
Java	10.6	3.8	114.3	17.5

number of tigers and (clouded) leopards captured and killed to the population of the various regions, the pressure was highest in Sumatra. This might be linked to the fact that Sumatra also registered the highest per capita number of people killed by tigers, which, however, perhaps partly due to this high hunting pressure, was declining rapidly (see Table 4.3).

Stable Response, Flexible Response, or Massive Retaliation

In India the relationship between the predators and people seems to be fairly stable: low population growth rates—the lowest of the three areas—seem to be matched by a gradual increase of the number of people killed and the number of animals captured or destroyed. All rates are moderate compared to other areas and not subject to big changes in the period under consideration. In terms of strategy—if we see tigers and people as two parties involved in a long-term conflict—I would like to call this a "stable response."

On the contrary, Sumatra, sparsely populated but with a more rapidly growing population, is characterized by outsized rates and rapid changes. In the 1870s, the number of per capita deaths caused by big cats was ten times as high as that of India, but owing to a per capita hunting pressure that was also ten times higher, both indicators were decreasing at a high rate. Nevertheless, at the turn of the century, these deaths were still three times as high as those in India. The ratio between tigers killed and people killed, which in India decreased gradually, had not only been higher in Sumatra at the beginning of the period but had even increased considerably at the end. The battle between humans and tigers was far from over. Here, obviously, the response was far from stable. This strategy of tit for tat, of giving as good as one gets, could be called one of "flexible response."

In Java, with a population density around 1870 comparable to that of the British part of India in 1890 and with a much higher rate of population growth, there was a notable shift in the relationship between humans and big cats. Its position c. 1870 in all respects surpassed that of India by an appreciable, although sometimes moderate margin. Java had a higher number of deaths by tigers per unit of land and population, higher ratios between tigers killed and people killed and between tigers and leopards killed and people killed, and higher hunting pressure per unit of land and population. At the end of the century it had moved to a situation in which it scored lower than India on all indicators save two, namely the number of animals killed per unit of land and the ratio between tigers and leopards killed and people killed. These indicators reflect predominantly the high incidence of leopard hunting, because the number of tigers available to be killed had become very low. This state of affairs, in turn, was the result of very high hunting pressure during the earlier years of the period. Although the number of people killed by big cats per unit of land and population in Java in the 1870s was not much higher than that in India, the Javanese response had been one of "massive retaliation." Around 1900, therefore, the war between people and tigers in Java was almost over.

As such numerical data are not available for Bali, a similar analysis cannot be carried out for this island. However, as we will see in Chapter 10, we have sufficient qualitative evidence to hazard a fairly shrewd guess as to the changing relationship between the Bali tiger and humans. While in around 1850 people and tigers hardly bothered each other, hunting pressure increased rapidly after the turn of the century. This was very similar to the situation in Java, only worse; the strategy might be considered one of "total" instead of "massive" retaliation.

The Effect of Population Density

Low numbers of people were killed per unit of land in sparsely populated areas (Sumatra), high numbers characterize the middle-range areas (Java in the 1820s), and low rates again obtain for densely inhabited regions (India and Java in the 1850s and 1900; see Figure 4.1).

There is some logic to these curvilinear statistical relationships. In low-population-density areas, the low probability of being killed by a tiger, expressed per unit of land, was partly the case because there were fewer people and partly because there were, consequently, fewer tiger habitats, which depended largely on human activities. In high-density areas the low probability of being

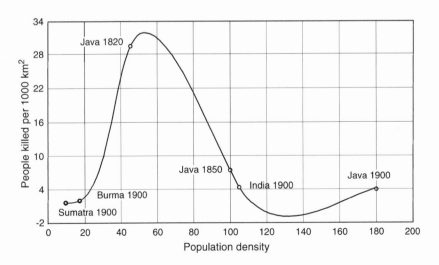

Fig. 4.1. Population density of selected areas related to the number of people killed by tigers.

killed was due to a supposedly lower tiger density caused by hunting and loss of habitat. The middle-range areas seem to have had the "ideal" mix of population density and tiger/leopard density regarding the chances, per unit of land, of being caught by a tiger or leopard.

The figures for per capita number of people killed, including those for Java before 1860, confirm the hypothesis of an inverse linear relationship. Early nineteenth-century Java, with its lower population density, presents much higher numbers than the figures for the latter part of the century, when the population had grown considerably; these numbers are similar to those of sparsely populated Sumatra. This relationship—decreasing per capita killings while the population increases—is reflected in the data on per capita tiger and leopard hunting. In the lower density areas, with high per capita numbers of people killed, the figures for big cats destroyed per unit of population are equally high. In the high-density regions per capita hunting pressure is low. Therefore, the relationship between per capita numbers of killed animals and population densities is also inverse and linear. The most likely explanation for both phenomena is that human populations grew much faster than tiger populations, which, during the period studied here, were declining, stagnant, or at best increasing very slowly.

Regional Differences in Java after 1860

Numerical data per Residency for 1858–1860 on "tigers" captured and destroyed confirm the inverse relationship between population density and tiger troubles, so long as the per capita number of tigers and leopards being shot is a good indicator for tiger problems. The correlation coefficient (Pearson's rho) calculated for 20 Residencies, $r = -0.69$, does indicate a fairly strong link.

If we plotted these data in a graph, Tegal would be the only Residency entirely out of line, with a clearly above-average population density and a much higher than average per capita number of destroyed tigers and leopards. As the figures are consistently high three years in a row, and as the data used by the central bureaucracy are of the same order of magnitude as the ones reported by the Resident for the early 1860s, a simple clerical error can be ruled out. When the series of data on people killed by tigers starts in the early 1860s, there are very low figures, in keeping with the high population density of Tegal. So the killing of tigers and leopards in Tegal was unrelated to the number of human victims. This is also suggested by a newspaper article reporting the death of 27 tigers in three months, caused by the use of *walikambing,* a natural poison that the local population spread on the remains of the horses, buffaloes, and goats that had been slain by "tigers," to which the latter almost invariably returned after some time. It is certainly possible that the heavily forested, mountainous, and "empty" hinterland of the thickly populated coastal area of Tegal still housed many tigers and leopards. It is likely that their natural prey was disappearing rapidly, given the c. 10,000 wild boar killed annually in the early 1860s, turning the tigers and leopards into cattle-slayers.[38]

In the period 1862–1881, most Residencies with an above-average per capita incidence of people killed by tigers were characterized by low population densities: Banten, Priangan, Krawang, Kediri, Probolinggo and Besuki/ Banyuwangi. Also, very low per capita figures of people killed by tigers are invariably found in Residencies with high population densities: Cirebon, Tegal, Banyumas, Bagelen, and Kedu. There are of course a number of cases that do not live up to expectations, but the correlation coefficient, calculated for 21 Residencies, of −0.55 indicates a reasonably strong link, albeit somewhat weaker than the link between population density and per capita tigers/leopards destroyed.

As a rule, figures for tigers and leopards killed cannot be separated for this period, let alone cattle-slaying and man-eating tigers. Neither do we have data on cattle taken by big cats. A more roundabout way of finding out what went on is to single out the Residencies with a very high ratio between "tigers" killed and people killed. Given an average ratio of 18.7 to 1, I regard 60 and over to 1 as very high.[39] The Residencies with very high ratios are Tegal (853), Bagelen (120), Madiun (88), Cirebon (86), Banyumas (73), and Rembang (61). What these Residencies had in common is that, with the exception of Cirebon, they were all mentioned as suffering from depredation by wild boar in the 1850s and 1860s, which were therefore pursued relentlessly and killed in large numbers. Aside from the 10,000 wild boar killed annually in Tegal in the early 1860s, in Rembang 8,546 wild boar were killed in 1857. For the other Residencies figures are lacking, so we have to make do with qualitative statements. For Cirebon, I could only find a source dating from the 1820s that reported extraordinary numbers of wild boar.[40]

It is certainly possible that an overkill of wild boar gave rise to larger numbers of cattle being killed by tigers and leopards, which, in turn, led to intensified attempts to get rid of the big cats. Specific circumstances in some Residencies may have contributed to the high ratios, like the presence of the Forest Service in Rembang, with its avidly hunting employees, and the garrison of Gombong in Bagelen, with its equally enthusiastic military huntsmen.

Finally, in three Residencies the ratio between tigers killed and people killed was less than half the ratio for the whole island, namely in Batavia/Buitenzorg (3.3), Priangan (8.1), and Probolinggo (6.8). The explanation for Batavia/ Buitenzorg is not hard to find. It was no longer a tiger area itself, and people were killed by "visiting" tigers from the adjacent Residencies Banten, Priangan, and Krawang. The indigenous and European population of the Residency was no longer accustomed to hunting these tigers down, and the animals withdrew to the neighboring areas after their forays. The explanation for Priangan and Probolinggo, with the highest and second highest per capita number of people killed, respectively, is probably simply a lack of European hunters in combination with the vast, largely uncharted and impenetrable wildernesses where the tigers could hide themselves.

The ratios between tigers/leopards killed and people killed in these areas, low for Java, would have been normal in India (see Table 4.4). As the very high ratios in Java were found in Residencies where large numbers of wild boar were killed annually, thereby depriving tigers and leopards of their natural prey and turning them into cattle-slayers and man-eaters, this overkill of wild boar might go a long way in explaining some of the differences between Java and India. However, overkill of wild boar was a reaction to wild boar nuisance, which, in turn, may have been caused by excessive destruction of tigers and leopards. Initially it may have been a rather modest difference, to be explained by different attitudes toward "revenge" on marauding big cats of the indigenous people of India and Java and the demand for these animals for rituals in Java. This difference would then, through a positive-feedback mechanism, lead to more wild boar nuisance, wild boar overkill, an increased incidence of cattle-slaying (and sometimes man-eating), and, finally, even higher numbers of tigers and leopards being killed. It is, however, a self-limiting mechanism; if one kills enough tigers and leopards, the cattle-slaying and man-eating will eventually stop.

During the entire nineteenth century, the total number of people killed by tigers shows a downward trend. Between 1830 and 1860, total numbers of tigers and leopards destroyed were rising. Therefore, the ratio between "tigers" killed and people killed, originally comparable to that of India, was rising even more steeply, whereas that of India remained at the same level. Given these divergent ratios, and the contrast between India's stable level of man-eating and Java's decreasing numbers, I am inclined to regard hunting pressure as the main cause of the decline in Java between 1830 and 1870, rather than loss of habitat. Land reclamation was a slow process before the 1870s, gradually pushing the edges of the tiger-inhabited wildernesses inwards without posing a real threat to his way of life. There were exceptions, to be sure, like the increasing isolation of Mount Muria in Jepara. Another case in point seems to be Kediri between the late 1850s and early 1870s, when large-scale teak production and the rapid expansion of smallholder tobacco may have temporarily upset the always precarious balance between people and tigers.[41]

After 1870, the year in which the Agrarian Law permitted 75-year leases of wasteland to Europeans, the number of European agricultural enterprises in Java's inland areas would increase considerably, as did the number of European hunters—often the same leaseholders or their representatives. Loss of habitat was now increasing rapidly, as these enterprises were almost invariably established in typical tiger country, particularly in Banten, Priangan, Kediri, Probolinggo, and Besuki. Unfortunately, there are no numerical data on hunting for the years between 1860 and 1897, and although the figures around 1900 are much lower than those dating from the late 1850s, it is not known when these figures started to drop. However that may be, around 1900 the tiger and, to a lesser degree, leopard populations had been reduced to such an extent that annual figures of tigers and leopards killed could only drop even further.

"Tiger Plagues" in Java after 1850

In 1886 and 1887, the total numbers of tigers killed were 126 and 116, respectively, which is as high as or even higher than the annual average number killed in the 1860s (117). Between 1875 and 1886–87, the trend of tigers destroyed had been upward. Variation around the mean was more pronounced after 1875 than before. The explanation of this phenomenon is that "tiger plagues" (sometimes called "tiger epidemics") came to dominate the annual fluctuations more than they had earlier, at least during the period for which annual data per Residency are available.[42]

There were tiger plagues before the late 1870s, to be sure. The killing of 147 people in Priangan in 1855, twice the annual average for that period, looks like such a plague, probably related to the drought in that year. We have no all-Java total for that year, but it seems safe to assume that the Priangan figure for 1855 was responsible for half the total number. Such a high proportion was again reached between 1877 and 1880, when Priangan was responsible for about 45% of all deaths by tigers in Java, perhaps partly owing to a series of harvest failures.

However, apart from Priangan Residency, where the number of people killed by tigers was always high anyway, no single Residency had ever been responsible for more than 15% of the total number of people killed by tigers before 1875. In 1875, in general a rather bad rice year owing to drought, Probolinggo was responsible for 26% of the Java total. In 1882, 1884, and 1885, Banten was good for 28%, 27%, and 25%, respectively. This must have been related to rinderpest and a severe malaria epidemic followed by famine, as well as the eruption of Krakatao in 1883, which generated a tidal wave that left behind an enormous number of unburied human corpses.[43]

Jepara—Mount Muria—and Probolinggo had tiger plagues in 1879 and Kediri in 1880. Adding these numbers to those of the Priangan tiger plagues of 1877–1880, about 58% of all people killed by tigers had been the victims of tiger plagues during these four years. Never before had such a high average proportion been reached in any period of four consecutive years. This may have been related to the series of bad harvests that hit Java during these years.

Between 1882 and 1884 a similar situation obtained when, in addition to Banten, other western Javanese Residencies—Batavia-Buitenzorg, Priangan, Krawang—were struck by tiger plagues as well, probably also related to rinderpest and malaria. Another tiger plague hit Rembang in 1883. Taken together, the tiger plagues in the period 1882–1885 were responsible for 51% of all human killings by tigers.

However, worse was to come in 1886 and 1887, when Banten was solely responsible for 51% and 53% of all deaths caused by tigers, respectively, thereby surpassing even Priangan. If we add to these figures those of the tiger plagues in Cirebon and Besuki/Banyuwangi during these years, the average percentage taken care of by tiger plagues becomes 68%, another record for two years in a row. Apart from that, the absolute figures for Banten alone—64 and 61 people killed by tigers, respectively—were higher than any other figure for a single Residency since 1862, Priangan included. Finally, the series of tiger plagues in Besuki/Banyuwangi would continue in 1888 and 1889.

The last big bangs, at least in the period for which we have annual statistics, came in 1894, with a tiger plague in Jepara (Muria) that accounted for 65% of all deaths caused by tigers—another record—and one in Semarang in 1901, good for 45% of the Java total, probably owing to a severe flood. What must have been the last tiger plague in Java ever occurred in 1946, when in southern Banyuwangi 64 people fell victim to tigers in 10 months. Alas, we know nothing about the circumstances, but it may be assumed that it had something to do with war and revolution (*Verslag* 1940–46, 143).

Reviewing the evidence just presented, it can be said that after 1875 man-eating, up to then a phenomenon to be found in all Residencies, if not annually at least once in two or three years, became largely concentrated in a much smaller number of regions: the Residencies of Banten, Priangan, Krawang, Cirebon, Jepara, Kediri, Pasuruan, Probolinggo, and Besuki/Banyuwangi. From a *basso continuo* to life at the fringes of "wild" areas, man-eating became increasingly restricted to specific areas and even there under specific circumstances only.

Perhaps 1875 can also be seen as the year of birth of the "real"—that is, specialized—man-eater. If we take Priangan as an example, it is impossible to argue that prior to 1875 man-eaters were only those tigers incapable of acquiring other prey, either because of personal characteristics or owing to a general scarcity of game. The phenomenon was much too general and widespread for such an explanation. People were living in relatively small valleys between large tracts of mountainous wildernesses, and there were few regions where tigers did not sooner or later wander into the village area. The "birth" of man-eaters can perhaps be demonstrated most convincingly in the case of Banten. Up to 1881, man-eating occurred regularly, but in small numbers, probably due to the fact that "culture" and "nature" were rather neatly separated, with the tigers in the southern wastelands and the people in the northern districts. Then, however, European entrepreneurs started to acquire long leases for large tracts of "jungle" in the southern area, with all the land reclamation and hunting such an acquisition entailed. All of a sudden Banten was hit by a series of tiger plagues, starting in 1882 and lasting until 1888, with annual numbers of people killed by tigers that were much higher than those of the 1860s and 1870s. The series of plagues was triggered by a number of disasters that may have been responsible for an increase in the number of tigers. After the supply of corpses had dried up, the tigers could no longer find sufficient food in their by now largely ruined habitat, once an inexhaustible source of prey. This episode proved to be the tigers' last stand in Banten, and between 1889 and 1904, people killed by tigers were registered in only seven years, and in low to very low numbers at that.

Conclusion

There was an *inverse linear* relationship between population densities and *per capita* numbers of people killed by tigers. In other words, in areas with low population densities, the number (per head of the population) of people killed by tigers was relatively high.

The numbers of people killed by tigers *per unit of land* had a *curvilinear* relationship to population densities. Thus, in low- *and* high-population-density areas, the probability of being killed by a tiger, expressed per unit of land, was low. In the former case, that was true because there were few people per unit of land; in the latter, because there were few tigers. Only in the middle-range areas (population densities neither low nor high) was the chance, per unit of land, to be caught by a tiger high.

That man-eating in the past was only important in India cannot be maintained in view of the evidence presented here. Whether the incidence of man-eating is expressed as per unit of land or per unit of people, Sumatra and Java scored higher than India at various points in time. Only regarding the number of people killed by a single man-eater was India easily at the top of the list.

Man-eating as a specialized activity of decrepit individuals or of those who have no alternative prey available is probably a modern phenomenon, in Java perhaps not older than the 1870s, where it came into being when the tigers were about to disappear. Earlier sources suggest that the tiger used to be an opportunistic predator who made a "rational" choice between easy and difficult, unarmed and armed, weak and strong.

Modern observers, who formulated the now orthodox view, never knew the tiger before he learned to avoid humans, and conceived of the tiger—or, for that matter, any animal—as an ahistorical being. Tigers, however, can and do learn. They adapt their behavior to changing circumstances, and the tigresses transmit what they have learned to their offspring, which is what history is all about.

5

Ancestors for Sale: Bounties for the Big Cats

In tropical areas under European overlordship, holding out rewards for capturing or killing fierce animals was a widespread phenomenon. For example, the Dutch offered rewards for jaguars (then also called tigers) in their Caribbean colony Suriname, for lions and leopards (equally called tigers) in the Cape colony in South Africa, and for crocodiles in Sri Lanka. The British offered rewards for tigers, leopards, and various other animals in India and Burma. The story of the tiger bounties in the Malay world is, therefore, part of the much larger story of how Western trading companies and governments attempted to rid the tropical areas where they held sway of dangerous animals, or at least of animals that were perceived to be dangerous.

Java under the VOC

Tigers troubled the people of Batavia from the very beginning of the Dutch presence. In response, high VOC officials organized tiger-hunting parties, and at least one Governor-General, Pieter de Carpentier, had a tiger-trap constructed. However, the officials themselves rarely were active in attempts to rid the countryside around the town of tigers. Fairly soon their role seems to have evolved to giving money to people who presented them with captured or killed tigers. This is mentioned for the first time in a source dated 1644: "Today, a large tiger, a female, was captured near the village of Jan Cleijn, Javanese, and brought in. The Governor-General rewarded aforesaid Cleijn and his people with 30 Reals of eight."

Initially, the money seems to have been given as a reward, or rather a tip, as one of the earlier sources phrases it, to people who had captured a tiger or a leopard (and also for rhinos, crocodiles, and large snakes), on presentation of the animal to the Governor-General. In 1648 this sort of payment was already regarded as customary.[1]

We do not know when and why the local population started to present the Governor-General with captured or killed ferocious animals, but it is possible that the Javanese just continued to carry out a customary exchange, the Governor-General now taking the place of an indigenous ruler. For instance, the population of Banten (western Java) captured tigers who were then presented to the Sultan, "who keeps always some of 'em in his palace, and looks upon that as a piece of great state" (Fayle 1929, 76–77). The Sultans may have kept live tigers at their court in order to show that they, the Sultans, the lords of the land and therefore of civilization, were superior to the lords of the forest and therefore of the wilderness, of chaos—namely, the tigers. The tigers were seen as captive rivals who should be treated well, as they were the equals of the Sultan in rank, as is suggested by the following quotation: "And when one of them brings forth a young one, it is so much taken notice of, that all the canon round the castle are discharged, and great rejoycing [sic] and pastimes are made upon the occasion" (Fayle 1929, 77). So the birth of a tiger cub was greeted with the same pomp and circumstance as the birth of a royal baby! The rulers of Mataram also kept tigers at their courts.

One wonders whether the Governors-General fully understood the symbolic implications of their being regaled with large, dangerous animals, and what they did with the live ones. What we do know is that the Governor-General often received wild animals as presents from other rulers, and that he, in turn, presented rare, strange, or otherwise valuable animals to them. Although the Governor-General, who was, after all, a merchant, often got rid of these animals as soon as possible by presenting them almost immediately to some other ruler, some space must have been reserved for the shelter of these presents, in other words, a kind of zoo. That is, indeed, what the well-known Dutch clergyman and writer François Valentijn encountered when he visited the "stables" for strange animals in the Castle of Batavia in 1694. He saw, among other animals, a black bear and a very large tiger. One day, however, the tiger's cage had not been locked properly and the tiger escaped, only to be shot by Captain Winkeler with a flintlock. The Governor-General's "zoo" would be mentioned several times in the eighteenth century.[2]

The rewards given for wild animals killed or captured varied from 50 guilders in the 1640s to almost 25 guilders (or 10 Rixdollars) later on.[3] Occasionally, if a tiger encounter had been particularly horrid and the person who had killed the tiger extraordinarily brave, the Governor-General could show his appreciation by bestowing a much larger reward. Such was the case in the

A "tiger" shot in the "Castle" of Batavia. From the early seventeenth century onward, people who presented a captured tiger—dead or alive—to the Governor-General in Batavia (now Jakarta) received a reward or bounty. A tiger held captive in the Castle—the headquarters of the VOC (Dutch East India Company)—once escaped and was shot dead. The artist who tried to illustrate this episode in the drawing reproduced here, c. 1720, depicted a leopard instead of a tiger, a normal mistake prior to 1850. Valentijn 1724–26, vol. 4, no. 1

1670s or 1680s with a freedman who had been employed by the Governor-General. Together with another freedman he had been hunting pigeons and wild boar, and while they were resting a tiger had attacked them. His colleague, with only a burning fuse to defend himself—apparently he was hunting with a matchlock—had been killed immediately. The person who lived to tell the story had fired his "fowling piece," which only wounded and enraged the tiger, who then bit off three of his assailant's fingers. Nevertheless, he succeeded in reloading his gun and killing the tiger with his second shot. After having spent the night in a tree with the corpse of his colleague, he returned to Batavia, where he was rewarded with 12 guilders "and a set table for his life, besides his former pay, and withal a corporal's place" (Fayle 1929, 33–34).

Johann Wolffgang Heijdt, a German who lived in the Archipelago from 1735 to 1740, mentioned that a bounty of 10 Rixdollars (Rxs) was paid out to those who had killed or captured a tiger, leopard, panther, or rhinoceros.[4] This must have become the standard payment, because in 1747 the bounty was fixed by official publication at 10 Rxs for "tigers"—of all sizes—and rhinoceroses.[5]

Under normal circumstances, 10 Rxs would get a Javanese twice his rice requirement for an entire year.[6] Given this impressive amount of money offered for a dead tiger or rhino, it is not surprising that the response was rather satisfactory: between the middle of October 1746 and the end of August 1747, 60 rhinos and 26 "tigers" had been killed in the areas adjacent to the Environs of Batavia. Between September 1747 and the end of 1748, another 526 rhinos and 80 tigers were destroyed there. This was becoming too expensive, and the bounties for rhinos, which were now declared not to be dangerous after all, were abolished. In 1762 the bounties for tigers in these areas also were rescinded, because, as the official publication had it, the need for these expenses was no longer as strong as it used to be, but in reality probably because paying out these bounties had become too costly.[7]

Between 1762 and 1817, when the first decrees reinstating the bounties were issued, the only references to premiums are to be found in response to a circular letter from Governor-General Daendels dated 5 May 1808.[8] The wording of two of the answers suggests that at that moment premiums were being offered in Tegal but not in the Buitenzorg-Priangan area, where they had been abolished in 1762. The British Lieutenant Governor of Java, Raffles, issuing instructions to the Residents by Proclamation of 15 September 1812, wrote: "They [the Residents] will also take measures in the proper season to destroy destructive wild beasts."[9] The measures taken by the Residents may have included the promise of bounties, as the case of Tegal suggests, but there was no published proclamation of the central authorities to that effect.

Bounties under the Dutch Colonial State

In March 1817 the Resident of Cirebon, western Java, requested the permission of the Governor-General to offer the same reward for catching or killing tigers that had been paid before, in view of the fact that the number of tigers near the capital of the Residency had been increasing continuously. By decree of 29 March 1817, the Resident was authorized to pay f.12 for a tiger. By the same decree it was decided "to request from all other Residents a report regarding the regulations, now in existence or formerly in force, stimulating the destruction of tigers and other beasts of prey."[10] This decree, however brief, is interesting for several reasons. First, the Resident clearly refers to the payment of bounties in former times. It is unlikely that this was a reference to the rewards paid prior to 1763, as almost 55 years had lapsed since then. Therefore, bounties must have been paid in a more recent period, but they had been abolished. Second, the amount of money authorized by the Governor-General is less than the 10 Rxs the VOC had paid between 1747 and 1763. At the conversion rate of 1811, the Rixdollar had a value of f.1.6, so that "the same reward . . . that had been paid before" would have been f.16, not f.12.[11] The decree offers no explanation for this deviation from the Resident's request. Third, the Resident based his request on the increasing number of tigers near his capital. This may have been just a ploy to get more money, but the possibility exists that the tiger population was in fact growing. Finally, the Governor-General's request for information from the other Residents might indicate that he was contemplating a more centralized approach to the threat posed by tigers. I have not been able to locate answers from the Residents, which implies that the General Secretariat forgot to implement this decision, or the Residents could not be bothered to answer the request, or the answers never led to a decision by the Governor-General.

From 1817 to 1825, several Residents did request to be allowed to offer bounties for captured and killed tigers, and occasionally also for rhinos.[12] Most requests mention increasing numbers of tigers, particularly in 1817 and 1821. These increases, or rather these increasing numbers of attacks or of tigers showing themselves near inhabited places, may have been partly related to abnormal weather conditions. The agricultural years 1816–17, 1817–18, and 1818–19 were unusually dry.[13] Also, there were harvest failures in 1817 in Cirebon, the first Residency to request permission for bounties, owing to the drought.[14] During droughts, wild animals do not find sufficient food in forests and other uncultivated areas, and they show up near human settlements, places they normally avoid, and they attempt to get hold of cattle, pets, and people. The year 1819–20 was rather dry, but 1820–21 was very wet. Very wet years are also problematic for humans and animals alike. That 1820 was a bad year is confirmed by various reports from the Residents, who mentioned high rice prices, harvest failures, or even famine in 11 Residencies; one report specified the causes of the harvest failures as mortality among water buffaloes and inundation. This was followed by another bad year. Apparently, most Residencies were confronted in 1821 with droughts, at least in one case in addition to floods. Again, 11 Residencies reported very high rice prices and harvest failures. This situation continued in 1822. The problems in 1821 and 1822 were compounded by the arrival of cholera in 1821.[15] In fact, such a prolonged period of weather anomalies, harvest failures, and epidemics as occurred between 1816–17 and 1821–22 would not be repeated until the period 1843–44 to 1851–52, probably also years of increased tiger activity.

Bad weather may not have been the only reason that more tigers came out of the woodwork, as witness the following remarks made by the Resident of Pekalongan. In 1823 he reported "that he had been compelled by the increased clearing of waste lands, both for the cultivation of coffee and for other crops, to be alive to the destruction of wild animals, who, as it were dislodged from their hiding places by aforesaid clearings, in the preceding month had taken away several people and animals." An increase in land clearing may, indeed, have dislodged the tigers from their hiding places. However, there could have been an actual increase in the number of tigers. Land clearings in densely forested regions create food-rich ecotones that attract wild boar and deer. These animals, in turn, attract large carnivorous predators. In the 1820s, Java still had many heavily forested areas, and it is certainly possible that clearings not only "dislodged" some tigers but caused a real increase of their numbers as well.

Given that the average annual income of an agricultural family around this time was f.45 (Boomgaard 1989, 119), receiving a bounty could mean a lot. The Resident of Semarang suggested paying a bounty of f.22, according to him the amount that had been paid in former times. This is probably not true, but the mistake is easily explained.[16] The mistake—if it was one—started a life of its own, and the Governor-General allowed bounties of f.22 in Tegal, Surabaya, and the Priangan as well. In Priangan, the Resident himself had proposed this amount, which would become the standard reward in 1854. In all other cases the amounts were lower, either because the Residents proposed lower amounts or because it had been left to the discretion of the Governor-General. It was probably not a coincidence that the maximum amount stipulated for most Residencies was f.16, or the equivalent, based on the exchange rate of 1811, of 10 Rxs, the bounty that had been fixed by decree in the eighteenth century. In other Residencies the amount for a real tiger was f.12 or less, and bounties for "small" or "young" tigers (i.e., leopards) were in many cases also lower. In Banyuwangi the rewards were very low, but here the Resident employed indigenous tiger hunters, officially appointed in 1817. Their numbers were reduced in 1830, and the entire institution was abolished in 1838.[17] A similar situation obtained in Priangan starting in 1821, but it was discontinued, perhaps as early as 1825.

After 1825, there is a gap of almost ten years in the series of tiger-bounty decrees. This was no doubt partly caused by the Java War (1825–30), which relegated even tiger attacks to the category of minor problems. More importantly, most (if not all) Residents had by then received a ruling that enabled them to offer bounties, so even if there had been no war, the number of decrees that could have been issued was very limited.

In the Netherlands Indies budgets for 1823–25 and 1833 no bounties were recorded as having been paid for the island of Madura, probably because there were no tigers. In Batavia and Krawang the tiger bounties were not listed separately but came under the heading "bounties for catching criminals and for the destruction of wild animals."[18] Evidently, tiger bounties had been tagged on to an older regulation, and therefore a separate decree had not been deemed necessary.

After the Java War, five Residencies were added to the territories under direct Dutch rule, and money for tiger bounties was budgeted for these Residencies at least since 1833. Bounties had been restricted to Java, but as the Dutch started to establish their rule over parts of Sumatra, the Dutch Governors and Residents in these areas also wanted to reward those brave enough to capture or kill a tiger. The first request for permission to offer bounties for captured or killed tigers came in 1838, from the Governor of Sumatra's West Coast.

Unification

On 2 February 1853, the General Secretary sent a circular letter to all Residents in Java.[19] They were asked to report on whether there were tigers to be found in their Residencies, what the results had been of the measures taken to get rid of them, and what measures should be taken to exterminate the tiger. The letter contains no indication of why the Government all of a sudden would be interested in these data. The action came at the end of a long period of droughts, floods, high rice prices, harvest failures, epidemics, and famine in the years 1843–44 to 1851–52. It is likely, therefore, that the initiative had been prompted by increased attacks of tigers on humans and cattle.[20]

The sometimes detailed reactions of the Residents have been preserved, and they are used throughout the book.[21] Here it may suffice to mention that most Residents doubted whether the tiger could be exterminated but believed it would be helpful if higher rewards could be offered. At their present level, most rewards were barely sufficient to compensate those who caught a tiger for their expenses (the construction of a trap, the sacrifice of a goat or other animal as bait). Moreover, tiger catchers were often forced by indigenous officials to share the bounty with them. A minority of the Residents argued that bounties hardly played a role in the number of tigers being killed, as the people did not kill tigers who had done no damage. A number of Residents proposed to appoint official indigenous tiger hunters. The latter idea was turned down by the Council of the Indies, because it had not worked in the past (in Banyuwangi and Priangan). The Council agreed with higher bounties and suggested offering f.22 for each tiger, regardless of age or species, because all tigers were, according to the Council, equally dangerous. The maximum amount that could be paid for a real tiger was f.22, and until 1854 only three Residencies were authorized to pay that maximum. The Council's advice was remarkable: Of all the Residents, only two had argued along the same lines, whereas all other Residents had wanted to maintain a differentiation between tigers and leopards. As the Governor-General concurred with the advice of the Council, the decree was formulated accordingly. From this date onward, the Residents in the Principalities—Yogyakarta and Surakarta—were also authorized to offer rewards.

In August 1861, another circular letter regarding tiger bounties issued by the General Secretary reached the Residents. They were now asked whether Government should continue to pay bounties for spotted and black "tigers" (in other words, leopards), or whether it could be assumed that the indigenous people themselves would take care of their property (i.e., livestock). The majority of the Residents felt that, although leopards were less dangerous than tigers and seldom if ever attacked humans, it would be a mistake to abolish the rewards entirely, as leopards did kill cattle. If rewards would no longer be offered, the number of leopards would surely increase. In some Residencies, the existence of professional tiger hunters was reported. It was felt that abolishing the bounties for leopards would discourage these people. However, many Residents also thought that the rewards for leopards could be lowered somewhat, provided that the bounties offered for tigers would remain at the same level or would even be increased. Leopards were easier to catch or kill than tigers, and the present system of one bounty for all species therefore stimulated people to concentrate on leopards. Only a small minority of the Residents argued that all bounties could be abolished, because the indigenous population killed tigers and leopards out of revenge, not because of the bounties, and because a "blameless" tiger or leopard would not be killed no matter how high the reward offered.

The Council of the Indies partly followed the majority opinion, advising the Governor-General to offer higher rewards for the killing of tigers and lower ones for leopards, or even to abolish the rewards for leopards altogether. According to the Council, it was important that the Residents take a strong stance in these matters: "Only the orders of a higher authority can overcome the superstitions of the indigenous people that keep them from killing tigers. If he acts under orders, according to his notions he is no longer responsible for his actions. In this case, Government surely ought not to respect such superstitions." In the decree of 8 August 1862, No. 7, based upon these reports and considerations, the bounty for killing a striped or royal tiger was established throughout the Indies at f.30, and that for a spotted or black "tiger" at f.10.[22] By now, average income for an agricultural family was higher than it had been around 1820, partly owing to inflation, but this does not seem to have played a role in the considerations. A bounty of 30 guilders now represented between one-quarter and one-third of a peasant family's income.

Two minor regulations derived from the considerations upon which the decree of 8 August 1862 had been based were published at the same time. One allowed the Residents to encourage those who wanted to become professional tiger hunters by advancing them firearms, powder, and lead. The second contained a model for the registration of "accidents," that is, people who had been killed by tigers, crocodiles, snakes, and other animals; the Residents were to send in this information at the end of each year. The Colonial Report for 1862 contained the first overview of these data, immediately attracting the attention of the Dutch Parliament (N. 1866, 492).

In September 1895, the Residents again received a circular letter from the General Secretary on the topic of tiger bounties. This letter had been inspired by two rather contradictory recent developments. On the one hand, an Inspector of Finance had written to the General Secretary that in his opinion the bounties for tigers in Palembang (southern Sumatra) could be abolished, because they did not motivate the population to catch more tigers than they already did. The Resident of Palembang agreed that this was, indeed, true. On the other hand, the Residents of Banten and Jepara recently had asked to be allowed to offer higher rewards, as parts of their Residencies were being terrorized by tigers. This had been the case in the division Caringin in Banten between 1887 and 1889 and in the district of Banjaran in Jepara, where additional funding had been requested just a few months earlier (February 1895). The Governor-General had approved of higher bounties under these exceptional circumstances, the record being f.200 in Caringin in 1888 and 1889. This particular case even attracted the attention of the Dutch Parliament.[23]

Residents were now asked to evaluate the effects of the bounties. Almost all Residents from Java wanted the bounties to continue for both tigers and leopards. However, the Sumatra Residents thought that tigers—there are no leopards in Sumatra—were not killed because of the rewards and that, therefore, there was no need to continue the bounty system.

Having read the Residents' reports, the Director of the Department of the Interior argued that in Residencies for which data were available (Banten and Priangan), lower bounties for leopards after 1862 had hardly led to fewer leopards being killed, although the total numbers of these animals surely must have been reduced due to hunting and the clearing of land. He did not share the opinion of the majority of Java's Residents and sided with those of Banten and Priangan, who both suggested that the bounties for leopards could be rescinded. The Resident of Priangan even argued that leopards were not only relatively harmless but also useful, as they kept the wild boars in check.

The General Secretary summarized the arguments of the Residents and the

Director of the Department of the Interior: bounties for leopards (Java) to be abolished, those for real tigers in Java to be maintained, and those in Sumatra to be discontinued. His summary noted, too, that it might be a good idea to re-voke the regulation allowing Residents to encourage Indonesians who wanted to become professional tiger hunters by advancing them firearms. An increase in the number of firearms among the indigenous population was undesirable, and if someone wanted to shoot tigers he could always borrow a gun from a European.

These arguments were sent on to the Council of the Indies for their consid-eration and advice. The Council, in turn, deplored the absence of good statistics upon which such advice should have been based. They argued that the avail-able evidence did not justify any decision for or against the continuation of premiums, but that it could not be true that bounties for tigers were effective in Java whereas they were not in Sumatra. Indigenous beliefs regarding tigers were surely the same in Java as they were in Sumatra, and if the Java Resi-dents wanted to continue the bounties, they were just more concerned about proper compensation for indigenous tiger catchers than were their colleagues in Sumatra. The Council therefore suggested abolishing all premiums in Java and Sumatra as an experiment and collecting good data in the meantime. These measures had the added advantage of cutting back considerably on ex-penditures. If occasionally tigers would locally turn into a major threat to hu-mans and cattle, bounties, even higher than those allowed by the decree of 1862, could be offered on a temporary basis.[24]

The Governor-General reached a decision on 3 April 1897. By decree of that date, No. 29, all bounties were abolished and the regulation regarding firearms was revoked.[25] A circular letter of the same date was published, telling the Residents that they could temporarily offer (higher) rewards if tigers became an extraordinary nuisance. They were also asked to send in monthly statistics on tigers and leopards captured or killed and on cattle and humans killed by tigers and leopards.

Comparing the three major nineteenth-century decrees (1854, 1862, 1897) that regulated the tiger-bounty system, it becomes clear that the Council of the Indies and the Governor-General had two out of three times ignored the sug-gestions of the majority of Residents, at least partly. In 1854 the Governor-General and the Council pegged the bounty for all species of "tigers" at one and the same level, instead of allowing higher bounties for real tigers and lower ones for leopards. In 1897 they abolished all bounties, including the rewards for tigers and leopards in Java, against the advice of an overwhelming majority of the Residents. It could be argued that in 1854 the Council had thereby handed down a death sentence for many more leopards than the situation, as perceived by the Residents, warranted. They made up for that decision in 1897, giving more tigers and leopards a new lease on life than the Residents had intended. It is a rather chilling thought that such a small group of people could decide, on rather whimsical or at least badly motivated grounds, the fate of so many animals, be it for better or for worse.

The system had its share of unintended victims. In 1862 the Resident of Madiun wrote, in response to queries from the Government, that people attempted to collect bounties for "wild cats," pretending they were spotted leopards. In 1867 the Resident of Cirebon reported discovering that a large number of *macan congkok,* a kind of tiger cat, had been killed for bounties in the Kuningan Division over the last few years. In 1866 bounties had been paid for 164 of these animals.[26] In 1895 the Resident of Banten wrote, in response to the September circular letter of the General Secretary, that skins of "tiger cats" often had been presented for bounties and that it was hardly possible to distinguish between the skin of a mature tiger cat and a young leopard. In response to the circular letter, the Resident of Bagelen answered that tigers were too clever to be caught in traps, but that they did catch "tiger cats," who were as dangerous to livestock as were tigers. There was a lot of confusion in the literature about the smaller cats, but these authors probably were referring to what is now called the leopard cat (*Felis bengalensis*) or, possibly, the fishing cat (*Felis viverrina*).[27]

In 1906, the Resident of Banten was still paying out "substantial bounties." They were probably too substantial in the eyes of the Governor-General, because in 1907 a limit was set to the amounts that could be paid out in areas where tigers still posed a threat: f.25 for a tiger and f.10 for a leopard. This was a far cry from the f.200 allowed during the tiger "crisis" in Banten in the late 1880s. Finally, in 1922 the General Secretary wrote to the Residents that they were no longer required to send in statistics on tigers captured and killed.[28] Apparently, in the eyes of Government, this kind of information served no purpose anymore. Nevertheless, the bounty system was never abolished entirely, and, at least in Sumatra, the tiger threat was far from over.

Bali

The decree of 8 August 1862 did not apply to this island until it became a Residency in its own right, in 1882. People killed by tigers, though, were registered much earlier, at least since 1862, when four victims were reported. These data likely had been gathered by a Dutch civil servant detached by the Assistant Resident of Banyuwangi, who was supposed to supervise the affairs of Bali. However, in most years for which data on tiger victims are available the number was zero, which implies either that tigers did not pose much of a threat or that the registration was incomplete. The former possibility is confirmed by the Resident's answer to the circular letter of 12 September 1895. The Resident wrote that the tigers had retreated to the few forested areas that remained, and the villagers, living far from the forests, were seldom molested by them. Bounties, therefore, were not required for his Residency. In 1897, three real tigers (there were probably no other "tigers" in Bali) had been killed, there were no human victims, and only three head of livestock had been attacked. However, a few years later, in 1903, tigers killed 53 cattle, although only six tigers were taken to task for this. Apparently, the tiger had not entirely lost his bite.

Sumatra

We do not know whether the indigenous population presented their own rulers with live tigers, as the Javanese did in the seventeenth century. There is a very late suggestion, dated 1926, that this was the case "in former times" in the tiny Sultanate of Asahan (East Coast): "When in former times a tiger had been captured, it was customary to bring the animal before the ruler, who then, while *gong* and cymbals were struck, had his *panglimas* engage it in mock-battle (*menecaki*). The tiger is, after all, the ruler of the forest! After the performance the hunter could take his tiger home" (Hamerster 1926, 88). Here the tiger was not held captive at the court of the ruler, but, as in Java, the tiger was regarded as a highly esteemed adversary of the king.

Information on rewards offered by Europeans for killing tigers in Sumatra prior to 1800 is scarce. Around Bengkulu (southern Sumatra) tigers were quite a problem, "the heads being frequently brought in to receive the reward given by the [British] East India Company for killing them" (Marsden 1811, 118). It is not clear when the British, who had been there since the seventeenth century, had started to hand out rewards, or how effective this measure had been. Benjamin Heyne, who visited the area in 1812, was not impressed as regards the latter point: "Pecuniary rewards for destroying them [the tigers] are here held out by this Government as in other parts of India, but it is very seldom indeed that any is claimed; the Bencoolese being too superstitious and too indolent for such enterprises" (Heyne 1814, 427).

Likewise, little is known concerning Dutch attempts before 1800 to reduce the tiger population near their "factories" by means of rewards. The Dutch reestablished themselves in parts of southern and central Sumatra in the 1820s and 1830s, and the oldest decree seems to date from 1838. In that year, the Governor of Sumatra's West Coast asked permission to offer bounties for each tiger that would be presented, dead or alive, in his Northern Division, "and this in order to check the ravages, committed there by these animals among people and livestock."[29] The Governor was allowed to do so. In 1846 this permission was extended to Bengkulu, Lampung, and Palembang—that is, to all the southern administrative units where tigers were found; there were no tigers on the islands of Bangka and Belitung. The amount to be offered was fixed at f.10.[30]

Although the year 1854 brought unification of the bounty system in Java, the same system was not immediately applied in Sumatra as well. The Governor-General might have preferred to wait until Sumatran civil servants themselves would ask for the same treatment before extending such an expensive system to Sumatra. Some of the heads of local administration were apparently paying close attention to the Government Gazette, because the Resident of Palembang and the Governor of Sumatra's West Coast in 1854 requested permission to implement the recent tiger-bounty decree in their regions. Their requests were based on the large numbers of people who were killed annually by tigers: 300 in Palembang and 100 in the Mandailing Division of Sumatra's West Coast alone. Permission to do so was granted without further ado.[31] By 1858, all Sumatran Residents were paying the bounties established for Java.

The year 1862 brought the same differentiation of bounties to Sumatra as was described for Java, the only difference being that there are no real leopards in Sumatra but only clouded leopards. At that time, such a distinction was made only by a handful of scholars and not by civil servants.

During the years that followed, the area under Dutch authority expanded, and so did the working of the tiger-bounty decree. In 1895, when the next major revision of the bounty system was about to take place, rewards were being paid out in three more administrative units, namely Sumatra's East Coast, Riau and Dependencies, and Aceh and Dependencies. These Residencies were only the nuclei of what they would become later on. Therefore, the bounty decree of 1862 was in force in relatively small areas, of which the plantation region around Medan was by far the largest. Taken together, all the areas under effective Dutch authority at that time did not cover much more than about half the island.

Bounties to be paid out on a routine basis were abolished in 1897, partly based on the almost unanimous opinion of the Sumatra Residents that the rewards were not effective. According to them, no tiger was killed because of the rewards that were offered, nor had the promise of bounties led to the creation of a group of professional native tiger hunters. The latter observation had been made earlier in the printed report of the central Sumatra expedition that took place between 1877 and 1879. Most civil servants attributed this lack of enthusiasm to indigenous superstition, but one Resident (Bengkulu) argued that the bounties were just not high enough: professional rhino and elephant hunters made more money per animal killed, because of the high prices they obtained for elephant tusks and rhinoceros horns. Even so, bounties did attract some professional hunters. Westenenk mentioned one man, a *haji*, who, as a devout Muslim, did not believe in the special relationship between tigers and humans and therefore had no qualms about killing a great many tigers for a reward. The bounties also attracted adventurous and/or poor (Indo-) Europeans. In 1909, one Indo-European, who called himself Jonkheer—the title of a Dutch nobleman—van Alphen, claimed to have shot so many tigers (67) that the Resident refused to pay him any more rewards, because he was believed to have shown the same tiger skin more than once.[32]

In contrast to the Sumatran officials, almost all Java Residents had wanted to retain the bounty, at least for real tigers. This remarkable difference of opinion may have been based on actual differences in attitude toward tigers between the Javanese and the people of Sumatra. In the nineteenth century, Sumatrans seemed much more hesitant to go after tigers than were the Javanese (see the discussion of the "ancestral tiger" in Chapter 8). Therefore, the Council of the Indies was mistaken when they argued that indigenous beliefs regarding tigers in Java and Sumatra were identical.

Although after 1897 bounties could still be obtained when the tiger situation was extraordinarily threatening, some officials, apparently convinced that tigers should be killed under ordinary circumstances as well, started experiments with penalties instead of bounties. In the Upper Kampar Division, Sumatra's East Coast, every village was ordered to build a tiger cage with a trap-door, to be constantly provided with live bait (goat or dog) and to be controlled regularly. Failure to do so would be punished with a fine of f.20. The system was quite successful: Between 1905 and 1911, 100 tigers were trapped, and only five times a fine had to be imposed.

However, this system did not always work, and in the 1910s or 1920s a man-eater in the same Division managed to avoid all the traps set for him. After the tiger had killed 17 people, the Collector offered a bounty of f.100 and published an appeal to tiger hunters in some of the Java journals. This prompted a reaction from the famous tiger hunters the Dutch Ledeboer brothers (cf. Chapter 6), who in the end declined to come over, as the whole enterprise would be too problematic and time-consuming. Finally, when the tiger had killed 22 people, the local population constructed another kind of trap, consisting of two heavy beams, suspended over a pit with a howling dog, that were supposed to be released when the tiger would touch a trigger mechanism. The next morning the tiger was found crushed by the beams.

Until 1932, bounties were being paid out in Rokan, a Division near that of Upper Kampar. When the system was abolished, the number of tigers became quite abundant.[33]

It is not quite clear how the Collector of Upper Kampar could have offered a reward of f.100, given the limit of f.25 set in 1907. It may have been authorized by the central authorities by means of an unpublished decree. It may also have come out of his own pocket, as was sometimes done under exceptional circumstances. Between the 1910s and the 1940s, bounties were sometimes offered by institutions other than the central authorities in Batavia. Several areas in Sumatra were semiautonomous, which implied that they had their own budget. Such was the case in the Divisions of Asahan and Langkat, Sumatra's East Coast. In the early 1920s Asahan offered, on a routine basis, f.25 for each tiger killed, and Langkat had an annual budget in the early 1930s of f.3,000 for the destruction of noxious animals, tigers included. The latter case is a warning against reading too much into such figures without further evidence, because the Assistant Resident discovered that much of this money was not spent on bounties but had disappeared in the pockets of an indigenous official. Another possibility was that private enterprise offered rewards, as happened in the late 1910s, when the large tobacco and rubber estates in Deli, Sumatra's East Coast, promised f.50 per tiger killed. This attracted European hunters, who, if need be, could survive on f.100 per month. Rumors that such bounties were being offered even caused a "tiger rush" in the area.[34]

In 1904, 344 real tigers were registered as killed in Sumatra, and 71 clouded leopards. In the same year, some 60 people had been registered as killed, no doubt by real tigers. In addition c. 2,250 cattle, buffaloes, and horses had been killed or wounded, and c. 2,900 smaller livestock. In comparison, between 1860 and 1880 approximately 120 people had been killed on average per year in a much smaller area, which implies that the tiger threat had certainly decreased during the later decades of the nineteenth century. However, it had not yet disappeared when in 1897 bounties as a routine measure were abolished.

The earliest nineteenth-century decrees on bounties, all issued for specific Residencies in Java, had made a distinction between large and small tigers. We now call the "large tiger" royal tiger or just tiger, and the "small tiger" is called leopard. Later on (c. 1860), a distinction was made between striped or royal tigers and spotted and black ones. The spotted or black tiger is now recognized as one species, the leopard. From 1838 onward, this terminology was also applied to Sumatra. Here, however, the real leopard is and was absent, and the only big cat apart from the tiger is the clouded leopard. Therefore, terms like small tiger or spotted and black tiger, if applied to Sumatra, refer to clouded leopards. Under the terms of the tiger-bounty decrees, these animals were also captured and killed, and those who handed in a clouded leopard skin were given the appropriate award.

Borneo

The only other area in the Indonesian Archipelago where clouded leopards are and were found is Borneo (Kalimantan). One might have expected that tiger-bounty decrees would have been declared valid for Borneo as soon as Dutch authority expanded there, in the later decades of the nineteenth century. This, however, never happened. The circular letter of 1895 had, strangely enough, been sent to all heads of local administrative units in the Netherlands Indies, including the two Residents of Dutch Borneo. They answered that there were no tigers in the regions under their authority and that the questions posed in the circular letter therefore were irrelevant. Strictly speaking they were, of course, right: there are, and were at that date, no real tigers in Borneo. But apparently they did not know that the clouded leopard fell under the terms of the tiger-bounty system and, therefore, in legal terms, had to be regarded as a tiger. The Residents of Borneo probably never petitioned the Governor-General to extend the working of the tiger-bounty decrees to Borneo, perhaps because they were unaware of the existence of clouded leopards in their Residency (which is unlikely) or because the clouded leopard is rather harmless, at least to humans. Another possibility, that the clouded leopard was never called "tiger" by the local population, does not seem to be the case.

The Malayan Peninsula

Although the Dutch had been in possession of Malacca since 1641, there is no evidence of tiger bounties prior to 1800. Chinese and European sources do mention the presence of tigers and leopards around and sometimes even in the city in the fifteenth and sixteenth centuries, when Malacca was a thriving and expanding settlement, first under its own rulers and later under the Portuguese.[35] Under Dutch rule, however, there was no expansion into the surrounding countryside, as there was around Batavia. The need for tiger bounties arose in Batavia because of this expansion, as tigers increasingly became a nuisance to the people in the recently cleared areas. As Malacca's population did not spill over into the environs of the city, there was perhaps no need for rewards.

The earliest evidence for tiger bounties dates to 1825, the last year of Dutch rule over Malacca.[36] In 1825, the British took over Malacca, thereby strengthening their presence on the Peninsula, consisting at that time of Penang, Province Wellesley, and Singapore.

When Raffles founded the British settlement of Singapore in 1819, the island was one large jungle and virtually uninhabited. During the first two decades under British rule there were no tigers, or they did not show themselves. Problems seem to have started around 1835, when Chinese migrants had begun to clear the jungle for gambier and pepper plantations. Tigers are supposed to have come swimming—which would have been quite possible—from the mainland (Johore) and started bothering the settlers. Around 1850, it was rumored that tigers took a toll of one Chinese per day on average, which led to questions in the House of Commons. Colonel Butterworth, the Governor of the Straits Settlements (in office 1843–1855), answered that to his knowledge not 365 but only 200 people were killed annually by tigers. Even if the latter estimate was more near the mark, as a proportion of a population of some 50,000 people this was still considerable.[37]

Small wonder, then, that rewards were being offered since c. 1840, and high rewards at that: $100 for each tiger, dead or alive. Results were minimal, however, and the reward was lowered to $50, only to be increased again around 1860. Then an additional $50 was put up by the merchants' fund, bringing the bounty back to its original level. Still, during the four years from 1860 up to and including 1863, the reward was claimed only 10 times, which caused at least one observer to think that the total number of tigers responsible for all these killings was low, perhaps not more than 20 "couples." In the early 1860s the official death rate of tiger victims was down to 125 a year, but it was suspected that many cases were concealed, as the Chinese planters wanted to avoid the bother of an official investigation and feared that coolies would refuse to work at their plantations if they acquired a bad reputation. By the 1870s the death rate was said to be a dozen or so a year, probably largely due to the ongoing disappearance of the jungle. This was low by former standards, but still high enough for an occasional "scare." Another scare must have been finding a tiger under the billiard table in the Raffles Hotel shortly before 1900. After the turn of the century an occasional tiger still visited the suburbs of Singapore, but tigers were no longer a real problem.[38]

From the 1870s onward, British authority spread to the Malayan sultanates, and so, apparently, did the tiger bounties. In the late 1870s a reward of $25 for a tiger was mentioned for Selangor. In Perak in the 1870s $50 was being paid for a tiger, but the bounty was seldom claimed. In Malacca in 1879 lower rewards were being paid—$15 for a tiger. Maxwell, writing around 1900, mentioned at least one professional indigenous tiger and crocodile catcher who made a living from the rewards he received. Judging by his name—Abdulmanap bin Muhammad Arsad—he was a Muslim who apparently no longer shared the beliefs regarding tigers and crocodiles that kept so many of his countrymen from going after these animals.[39]

Between 1900 and 1913 bounty amounts paid out for the "destruction of wild beasts" in Malacca are comparatively high, fluctuating between $200 and $675 (in 1905) per year. Between 1914 and 1924, the amounts generally fluctuated between $75 and $175, but after 1924 the upper limit was $78.10 and the lower limit $4.90. So the trend was clearly downward, and if the reward for a tiger was still $15, evidently in some years no tigers had been captured at all. At the turn of the century, most Malayan states were probably paying $25 for an adult tiger and $10 for a young one (cub?). Around 1950 rewards of varying amounts were still being paid for cattle-killing and man-eating tigers in some of the Malayan states, Trengganu being one of them.[40]

Around 1925 the Sultan of Johore, a great tiger hunter himself, offered bounties of $100 for every tiger captured alive, not so much in order to rid his sultanate of these animals but rather to stock his private zoo (Buck and Anthony 1930, 140–41). Would he have been aware of the fact that he was doing what the Sultan of Banten did three centuries before?

Conclusion

Rewards had been offered in Java during at least some 200 years, in Malaya for at least 125 years, in Sumatra during more than 100 years, and in Bali for not more than 15 years. Given the fact that Bali was the first area where tigers became extinct, the length of the period during which rewards where being offered was clearly not the most important causal factor in this respect. The fact, however, that Java came a good second suggests that the duration may not have been entirely unimportant.

Can we establish whether the system of offering bounties fulfilled the purpose for which it had been designed? Bounties were designed first and foremost for the destruction of real tigers. It was, after all, the tiger who could turn man-eater or cattle-killer. Leopards, at least the Indonesian ones, very seldom became man-eaters. They did kill livestock, but they rarely killed mature cattle or buffaloes, restricting themselves largely to goats, dogs, and poultry. Prior to the second half of the nineteenth century, the Dutch, and, for that matter, the British, used the term "tiger" almost always in a generic sense that included the leopard of Africa and Asia and the jaguar of America. Tiger, therefore, meant "big cat," rather than royal tiger. Scientists like Bontius were aware of the existence of more than one species of big cats, but the VOC officials perhaps not. Before 1860, when the Dutch more systematically started to make a distinction between striped (real) tigers on the one hand and spotted or black ones on the other, they usually differentiated between big and small (or even young) tigers. This does not suggest a strong awareness of the existence of different species, with clearly distinguishable characteristics. Bounties for "small" tigers were sometimes, but by no means always, lower than rewards for "big" tigers. Originally, this was probably just because the trophy of a big animal was more highly esteemed than that of a smaller one.

It is tempting to suggest that leopards and clouded leopards—and even leopard cats—were the victims of the real tiger's behavior. This notion is supported by the fact that there were no rewards for clouded leopards in tigerless Borneo, whereas in tiger-rich Sumatra killing the same animal was rewarded with a bounty. In the real tiger areas, anything called "tiger," by virtue of the mere fact that people had bestowed that name upon it, fell under the terms of the bounty decrees.

Particularly between 1854 and 1862, a great many leopards were killed because the reward paid out for a leopard was the same as that for a tiger, whereas it was much less dangerous and easier by far to catch or kill a leopard. By then, however, most European Residents had begun to understand that they were dealing with several species, and in 1862 the system of one bounty for all "tigers" was abolished.

Having established that the rewards probably caused the deaths of many unintended victims, the question remains whether they also caused the destruction of more real tigers than would have been killed without them. The rewards certainly attracted Europeans and Indo-Europeans as professional tiger hunters. Some Europeans, particularly soldiers, went after tigers as a sideline in order to supplement their meager paycheck. In 1861 and 1895, several Residents objected against lower bounties or argued for higher bounties because they expected that European hunters would be very sensitive to changes in the amount offered. One Resident, however, argued that those Europeans who hunted as a hobby would show up as soon as it was known that tigers were making a nuisance of themselves, bounties or not.

The question becomes more complicated if we turn to the indigenous population. It has often been argued that in most areas where tigers could be found, killing them just for the heck of it was anathema, at least to the common man. There was a strong awareness, so the argument goes, that tigers and people were somehow related. Tigers, therefore, were killed only if they had "sinned," that is, had killed a human being or a domesticated animal. Then, revenge was permitted, at least in Java. In Sumatra, the fear of tigers and their supernatural powers was even stronger (see Chapter 8).

Not all people from the Malay world seem to have fitted this model, and not all "tigers" were equally feared. Most Dayak tribes in Borneo, for example, had no qualms about killing clouded leopards (Bock 1882, 153). Also, the Javanese were much less hesitant to kill a leopard than a tiger. Killing or catching a leopard was probably easier than going after real tigers, but the possibility exists that the leopard was also less dangerous in a spiritual sense.[41]

Some indigenous groups in Java and Sumatra may not have shared the misgivings of the majority as regards tigers. This may have applied to the Batak in northern Sumatra and to the people of Banyuwangi, at the eastern rim of Java.

Occasionally, indigenous individuals, particularly orthodox Muslims, became professional tiger hunters who made a good living from the bounties they received. In these cases, the bounty system had the desired results. However, specialized tiger catchers were not "created" by the bounty system. Indigenous society had always known so-called tiger-charmers, who, by virtue of their special, supernatural knowledge, were supposed to be able to lure "guilty" tigers into a trap (see Chapter 9). Theoretically, the new breed of tiger catchers differed from the old tiger-charmers in that they had turned full-time professionals who also killed blameless tigers; however, the evidence to date is only suggestive.

The influence of bounties was not restricted to just a handful of Indonesian hunters. Many Residents reported that Indonesians seldom killed tigers because of the reward offered, but many of them also admitted that without the bounties even fewer tigers would have been killed. According to the Residents, the bounties were used to defray the expenses that catching or killing a tiger entailed. If bounties were to be abolished, going after tigers would be regarded as a waste of time, energy, and capital goods (goats, beams for a trap). If these observations are to be trusted—and I have no reason to think that they are not—the bounties must have made a difference, although perhaps not as much of a difference as the Dutch officials would have liked.

Bounties, therefore, almost certainly caused the death of many tigers. The amounts offered were certainly impressive enough. Still, where "blameless" tigers were concerned, many people may have had to make a choice between a sizeable increase in income—or, in a bad year, any income at all—and a clear conscience. In 1895, the Resident of Bengkulu wrote that he was familiar with one case where an old chief refused to collect the bounty for a tiger he had captured, because he did not want to sell his ancestor. This was most exceptional, however. "Guilty" ancestors should be killed, and if one got some money for defraying expenses, so much the better.

6

Hunting and Trapping

Hunting as a historical phenomenon is associated mostly with kings and no-blemen on the one hand and primitive hunter-gatherers on the other. The lat-ter hunted for food, the former for status, and both hunted in order to free the countryside from dangerous predators and pests. The hunting and trapping of tigers—and occasionally leopards—involved a range of motives. Hunting or trapping tigers as food seems to be fairly rare, but killing a tiger in self-defense or in revenge is not. Also, tigers were killed in order to rid the environment of these dangerous animals. Examples of the commodification of the tiger include the killing of tigers in order to use their bones in Chinese medicine and in or-der to display the tiger skin as a status marker. Finally, tiger hunting could be a pastime.

Sometimes, people did *not* attempt to kill the tigers surrounding them, even when the animals did quite some damage. And if they did hunt them, they used a variety of means.

Kings and Noblemen

Hunting by Javanese royals is a theme encountered in early Javanese and Portuguese sources. The fourteenth-century Javanese epic *Negarakertagama* gives a detailed description of a "royal chase" of the ruler of Majapahit (eastern Java). About a century and a half later, the Portuguese traveler Tomé Pires, who visited Java c. 1515, gave the following account of the king of Sunda (western Java): "The king is a great sportsman and hunter. His country con-tains stags without number, pigs, bullocks. They do this most of the time." A similar testimony was given about "the Javanese heathen lords" of the central

and eastern parts of the island. Another Portuguese writer from the same period, Duarte Barbosa, was equally impressed with the Javanese ruling class.

However, neither indigenous nor Portuguese sources mention tiger hunts.
The large mammals that served as objects of these royal hunts are wild boar,
wild cattle, and deer.[1] In the long list of hunted animals enumerated in the *Negarakertagama*, the tiger is conspicuously absent.

Around 1600, the princes of Banten, Jakarta, Cirebon, Gabang (western
Java), Mataram, and Tuban (central Java) are described as hunters. The only
ruler who was explicitly named as a tiger hunter was the Sultan of Banten. It
was reported that many people around the town were killed by tigers, and the
ruler, accompanied by all his people, hunted them down, both during the day
and at night.[2] That last piece of information is a bit strange, as a "beat hunt"
during the night is virtually impossible.

In the seventeenth century, the rulers of Mataram had deer parks and other
game reserves laid out for hunting purposes. Such reserves could also be found
in the seventeenth and eighteenth centuries in western Java (Priangan,
Krawang, and Cirebon).[3] Some of these hunting grounds were fenced in. In
some cases, such as those reported from Mataram dated c. 1650 and c. 1695,
the tigers had been removed from the enclosed hunting grounds before the
ruler would take his pleasure there. The VOC ambassador Rycklof van Goens
visited Plered, the court of Amangkurat I, Susuhunan of Mataram (r. 1645–
77), several times. According to van Goens, the ruler had at his disposal, to the
south of the court, "an incredibly large game-park, where he keeps, for his
pleasure and for the hunt, several thousand deer, rhinoceroses, wild cows and
excellent large bulls . . . , as well as wild horses and other animals; each species
separately enclosed between the mountains with heavy oak [teak] fences; between which one can hunt freely without any hindrance from tigers, snakes,
or other vermin" (Graaf 1956, 215–16). An indigenous Javanese source refers
to Susuhunan Amangkurat II (r. 1677–1703) and his court at Kartasura in the
years around 1695: "The ruler then ordered wild animals from Mataram to be
driven to Kartasura, where they were given a place within an enclosure to the
west of the pond. The animals were chased along a road that had been fenced
off with wattle-work made of branches and bamboo. Deer, roe, mouse deer,
wild bulls and cows, etcetera, thus arrived within the enclosure of the pond.
Only the tigers and the wild boar were killed" (Olthof 1941, 256).

It seems that the Sultans of Banten hunted tiger, whereas the rulers of
Mataram did not. This is a remarkable and rather unexpected difference.
Around 1600, the Banten sultanate was sparsely populated, and the area
cleared for agriculture probably did not go far beyond the immediate environs
of the city of Banten. As western Java belongs ecologically to the tropical rain-

forest zone, the forested areas, covering almost the entire sultanate, did not contain large numbers of big terrestrial game and therefore did not have many tigers. Mataram, on the other hand, located in a monsoon forest zone, had many more densely populated areas where land clearing had created ecotones attractive to game (cf. Chapter 2). This must have led to much higher tiger densities there than in Banten. Therefore, the Bantenese rulers should have been only marginally interested in hunting tigers, whereas the princes of Mataram should have been more like their contemporaneous Indian colleagues: "The [Indian] kings take great pleasure in hunting tigers, both for the purpose of ridding the country of them and saving the poor people, and also because therin [sic] are the valour and bravery of their noblesse shown forth and proved" (Gray/Bell 1887, vol. 2 no. 1, 347).

Two factors are to be taken into account in interpreting these deviations from behavior predicted on the basis of assumed tiger densities. In the first place, the fact that ecotones attractive to tigers in Banten were limited to the area surrounding the capital might have been the cause of high tiger densities around the city, even though the average density in the sultanate was low.

In the second place, the Mataram ruling elite did have a mechanism that had the dual function, observed in India, of getting rid of tigers and of enabling the aristocracy to show its prowess. Tiger rituals at the courts of central Java (discussed in greater detail in Chapter 7) seem to have developed from tiger hunts supervised by the ruler. The first description of such a hunt comes from Valentijn, who lived in Java around 1700. On the occasion of a general meeting of the royal princes and the nobility, a number of solid structures were built for the ruler, the princes, and their women, on an open field. Then, about 10,000 pikemen went to an area where a tiger had been spotted, in order to surround it and drive it to the place where the spectators were waiting. When the tiger had been surrounded, it tried to escape and was caught on the pikes (Valentijn 1724–26, vol. 4 no. 1, 203–4). In the eighteenth century such hunts developed into court rituals, and although the central Javanese rulers did not themselves hunt tiger, they employed professional tiger catchers in order to provide them with tigers for their rituals. These were the so-called Tuwa buru people, governed by their own noblemen.[4] In 1744, when they were mentioned in the European sources for the first time, they numbered 1,200 *cacah*. The cacah (pronounced "chachah") is a unit of taxation, and it is also a rough indicator for numbers of families, one cacah supposedly representing one family. In all likelihood the Tuwa buru people paid their taxes in kind, namely in live tigers and deer. In the nineteenth century they were still being employed by central Javanese rulers to the same end, although the number of people thus engaged had been reduced drastically. In 1853, the Sultan of Yogyakarta employed only ten Tuwa buru people.[5] The tiger rituals would be an important element in the gradual disappearance of tigers in central Java.

Royal hunts also took place in seventeenth- and eighteenth-century Sumatra by the princes of Aceh, Pedir (in northern Sumatra), Palembang (in southeast Sumatra), and Banten (in the Lampung area of southern Sumatra). They went after elephant, deer, and wild buffalo. Only in one case, that of Sultan Iskandar Muda of Aceh (r. 1607–36), is it known that a royal hunted tigers. Whether all these princes really took an active part in the pursuit of dangerous game is not certain. Malay Sultans were supposed to love hunting, and therefore indigenous sources often depict them as great hunters.[6] However, there seems to be no evidence of hunting grounds exclusively for the royals in Sumatra.

It is perhaps slightly disappointing that we do not hear more about tiger-hunting royals in Sumatra. Java's lack of elephants—animals that were most useful for hunting—may have been an element in the reluctance of Javanese rulers to hunt tigers. This situation did not apply to Sumatra, and the Sumatrans knew how to tame elephants for hunting. What may have been lacking, however, are large grassy plains. In India, these plains were the favorite hunting grounds for royals who wished to hunt tiger from the back of an elephant. Such fields could be "beaten" for tigers by large numbers of followers with dogs, the king having made himself comfortable in a howdah on the elephant's back. Thus, the risks to the king were relatively minor, whereas the chances of encountering a tiger—grassy fields were their preferred habitats—were fair. This is not to say that one cannot hunt tiger in a dense forest, but rulers and nobility did not undertake this kind of hunting.

Even around 1900, when quite some forests had been cleared and when more climax vegetation than before had been turned into secondary forest, the hunter Whitney could write that in Malaya, Sumatra, Lower Burma, and southern Siam "the jungle is too dense and continuous" to hunt tigers from the back of an elephant. He added, "In fact, as compared with India, almost no tiger hunting is done in these countries, and that little consists of sitting up over a kill, or, in the dry season, over a water hole" (Whitney 1905, 117, 290).

The situation on the Malayan Peninsula was broadly similar to that in Sumatra. From the fifteenth century onward rulers were mentioned as hunting deer and buffalo and trapping—or "noosing"—elephants. Indigenous sources depict Sultan Iskandar Syah of Perak (r. 1752–65) as a genuine Malay ruler: he "engages in kingly pursuits, like elephant trapping, tuba fishing, and buffalo hunting." The Sultan would go to the upland area where the elephant trapping was taking place in order to have a look at the activities, but he himself did not take an active part in them.[7] Tiger hunts, however, are not on record prior to 1900, no doubt for reasons similar to those pertaining to Sumatra. Although there are trained elephants, the scarcely inhabited rainforests of Malaya were not attractive to tigers, and the large, open grassy plains of India, needed for royal tiger hunts with elephants, were lacking.

Not until the early twentieth century is there evidence of tiger-hunting Malayan royals. Around 1925, the Sultan of Johore was referred to as a "real hunter . . . , the greatest of them all." He was, moreover, a great tiger hunter. Between 1898 and 1927 His Highness had shot 35 tigers, all on display in his palace. The Sultan also owned a "deer park," where his collection of "strange" animals was housed, among which were some tigers. He paid $100 for every live tiger presented to him.[8]

Around that time, the Malay Peninsula had become more densely populated, and large tracts of forest had been cleared. Thus, many ecotones attractive to deer and wild boar had been created, which, in turn, had attracted more tigers. By then there were also more grassy plains conducive to royal hunts. In addition, reliable and accurate firearms had become available, lowering the risks to the hunter of a tiger encounter.

Tiger-hunting rulers in Sumatra after 1800 do not appear in the record. As regards hunting nobles, the heads of lineages, clans, and districts, the latter often Dutch "creations," may or may not have been noblemen, depending upon local custom. Information that could establish whether such a chief was a member of the nobility is often not available. Also, when chiefs were tiger hunters, they often were involved in punitive expeditions, organized ex officio, against tigers who had killed cattle or people. Although some of these chiefs took an active part in the actual hunting, the brunt of it was usually borne by the peasantry.

Sumatran chiefs led such hunts: the first one I know of took place shortly after 1800, led by the Demang Osman (Palembang); one some time before 1880, involving the Kejuruan of Lhoong (Aceh); and the last one in the 1910s, with the Tuangku Bagindo-Maro of Rao (Padang Highlands). The hunt in Palembang is the only example of a post-1800 tiger hunt from the back of an elephant in Sumatra. The Kejuruan of Lhoong, probably a real aristocrat, claimed to have played an active role in the actual killing of the tiger. In the last two cases the hunt was undertaken because a tiger had killed someone.[9]

After 1800 tigers were hunted by the Javanese aristocracy and members of the royal families. The Dutch writer and traveler Johannes Olivier mentioned tiger hunts by the Priangan aristocracy in Cianjur around 1820. Around 1840, a hunting club existed in Surakarta, of which the members were Europeans and indigenous princes. They hunted wild boar and deer and occasionally killed a tiger. One of the members was a 16-year-old prince who killed a suddenly appearing tiger with one shot from his double-barreled shotgun at seven

Hunting from the back of an elephant. Although fairly general among kings, aristocrats, and high-ranking civil servants in British India, this manner of hunting was very rare in the Malay world. The drawing represents a tiger hunt in Palembang, southern Sumatra, around 1800. Olivier 1836–38, vol. 2

yards distance. In the same area the Mangkunegara had a pleasure ground where the aristocracy went hunting, perhaps tiger hunting, as the Mangkune-garan lands even around 1850 had still a fairly dense tiger population. In 1895, the Mangkunegara had a private zoo, where he kept tigers, bears and orang-utans.[10]

Punitive expeditions organized by district heads, like those mentioned above for Sumatra, were common in Java and probably undertaken more frequently there than in Sumatra. The destruction of noxious animals had been written into the instructions formulated by the Dutch for the regents, but the actual task of getting rid of tigers was normally organized by a lower dignitary, such as the head of a district.[11] Tiger hunting, then, was official business, although the Resident of Pasuruan in 1895 warned against tiger hunts undertaken by district heads and lower Dutch officials as a pastime for visiting friends. In nineteenth- and twentieth-century Java, under Dutch rule, most of these Javanese officials would have been regarded as members of the aristocracy.[12]

"Primitive" Hunters

There existed, and often still exist, a number of distinct "tribal" entities in the Malayan Peninsula and Sumatra. Some of these were mainly hunter-gatherers (foragers), whereas others could be qualified as semi-sedentary peasants (as opposed to sedentary peasants, who formed the majority in these areas in the nineteenth and twentieth centuries). The foragers of note here are the Semang of the Malay Peninsula and the Sumatran Kubu. The semi-sedentary peasants studied here are the Senoi and the Aboriginal Malay in Malaya and the Lubu, Sakai, and Mamak of Sumatra. Elsewhere (Boomgaard, in press) I have dealt with these "tribes" and their attitudes toward killing tigers in more detail. Here I summarize my findings.[13]

It is not easy to generalize the data on these seven groups. A tentative conclusion is that the more sedentary tribes—Aboriginal Malay, Lubu—were less hesitant to kill and eat tigers than were the more nomadic ones. This may have been related to a higher incidence of atrocities committed by tigers in the areas of these semi-sedentary groups, where gaps had been created in the climax forest vegetation, thus attracting more game and, therefore, more tigers. Even though a large share of their food requirement came from agriculture, these hunting communities may have captured so much game that tigers were forced to kill an occasional human, dog, or goat, thus inviting retaliation.

It could be questioned whether the presence or absence of specific weapons may have influenced attitudes toward tigers. The two groups with the fewest inhibitions against hunting tigers, the Aboriginal Malay and the Lubu, possessed both the spear and the blowpipe. The only other group with this combination was the Senoi, about whom not enough is known to place them firmly in one category or another. The spear and the blowpipe (with poisoned tip) both could be used to kill tigers, but it is conceivable that people armed with both—as opposed to just one of them—felt more confident that they were a match for the tiger. One is tempted to speculate that the same conditions that made for an increase in the quantity of game and, therefore, of tigers, namely the creation of ecotones, had also prompted the use of this combination of weapons.[14] Another factor could have been that the nomadic groups ate carrion and may have seen the tiger as a provider of food. Most of the semi-sedentary groups are not on record as carrion eaters. As non-Muslims, the latter may have seen the tigers as competitors for wild boar, being therefore more inclined to go after them.

Most groups may have relied more on traps than on face-to-face contacts for catching tigers. This probably does not apply to the Semang, but the other tribes had either spring-spear traps or pitfalls with stakes with sharp points, or both. Tigers could and did walk into these all-purpose traps and were thus killed or at least seriously injured. The typical "Malay" tiger-trap, specifically designed for catching tigers, was not found among these groups. Several explanations suggest themselves, of which the least likely is that they were not

Kubus with spear and hunting knives (above) and Sakai-Semang with blowpipe (opposite). Nomadic and semi-sedentary groups in the Malay world were able to kill tigers with these weapons. Adams 1928 (Kubus); Skeat and Blagden 1906, vol. 1

familiar with these traps or not able to make them. More plausible is the possibility that they were unwilling to spend the not inconsiderable amount of time required to make them, or that they had insufficient dogs or goats (or were unwilling to part with them) to bait these traps. They may also have had "ideological" objections. The trapping of a tiger in a spring-spear trap or a pitfall could be regarded as "fate," whereas catching a tiger in a tiger-trap could not, and the groups may have feared that the use of such a trap would provoke the wrath of the spiritual entity embodied in the tiger. Finally, it is also possible that the tribal groups lacked the spiritual specialists who, according to most Sumatran peasants, were needed to make these traps work.

Information is lacking concerning the supernatural beliefs of the Lubu and the Sumatran Sakai, but all other tribes believed that tigers were inhabited by spirits, often those of shamans, dead or alive. It was considered ill advised to kill these tigers, as they protected the camp, kept "real" tigers away, and even provided their people with game. Moreover, revenge would await those who killed such a tiger. However, evil spirits could also inhabit tigers: among the Semang, such a spirit could be the "soul" of a living, evil shaman. Apparently, people did not dare to attack these tigers.

The notion prevailed that if a person was killed by a tiger, that person surely must have done something wrong, and the tiger killing him was a representative or embodiment of higher forces. In such cases, revenge was not called for. Among the Aboriginal Malay, however, either there were ways around the prohibition to kill supernaturally endowed tigers or the people were able to establish whether a specific tiger was a real or a supernatural one before killing him. The fact that they did not have the specific tiger-traps suggests that even the Aboriginal Malay stopped short of killing tigers at random.

Finally, many people in these communities feared the tiger, although some (Aboriginal Malay, Lubu) seem to have had a more relaxed attitude than others (Semang, Mamak). One is tempted to speculate that the gap between semi-sedentary peoples and tigers seems to have widened, the forest and its animals became more alien, and the tiger began to be seen more as an adversary than as a close—though certainly greatly feared—relative, as was still the case among the nomadic tribes.

Sedentary Peasants

In Java, Bali, Sumatra, and Malaya there is no sharp dividing line between sedentary and semi-sedentary peasants. Sedentary peasants are those cultivators who have been living in one village for a long time, were often born there, and may very well die there. In many but certainly not all cases, their ancestors had also lived there. Sedentary peasants are often the proud owners of a permanently cultivated piece of land, but they can also practice shifting cultivation. Their houses are often more solid than the abodes of the semi-sedentary cultivators.

Until recently, peasants have always hunted, partly in order to protect themselves, their animals, and their crops, and partly for food, often a welcome addition to their meager fare. In some areas farmers also hunted (and still hunt) for recreation. Nowadays, however, peasants are not necessarily hunters, as game is now rare and protected in many areas.

Java

In the nineteenth century, shifting cultivators could still be found in the southern districts of western and eastern Java, but the large majority of the population lived in permanent villages and were in the possession of permanently cultivated fields (with or without fallow).

Information on tiger hunting and trapping by Java's peasantry in the period prior to 1700 is rare and lacking in detail. Most of this information refers to the area around Batavia. Often mentioned are "traps," and in some cases it is clear that these were typical tiger-traps, solid wooden constructions with a trapdoor and provided with (live?) bait. The earliest reference, dated 1627–31, deals with a tiger-trap constructed by the Governor-General Pieter de Carpentier, but he must have followed a Javanese example. This may have also applied to a trap set by Chinese, mentioned in a source dated 1644. A few times it is specified that tigers were caught alive in these traps.[15]

Only two references may be found to pits (pitfalls) with bait, in one case live and in one case with stakes. The reference to the stakes, dated 1632–46, is somewhat suspect or at least remarkable, as it specifies that these were iron stakes, whereas all later sources refer to bamboo stakes. One source, dated 1682–86, describes a real tiger hunt carried out by the peasants of Banten. The German Christoff Frick reports that thousands of Bantenese armed with pikes went to the area where tigers had been observed. There they surrounded a tiger and drove him to a place where a trap with a trapdoor had been positioned, into which the tiger, all escape routes having been cut off, was then forced to enter.[16] No references have been found to nooses or poison before 1700, both mentioned in nineteenth-century sources.

A compilation of older sources, published c. 1730, presents a neat although brief summary of the means employed by the Javanese to capture or kill tigers. According to this text, the Javanese hunted tigers by surrounding a place where a tiger was expected with large numbers of armed people (with lances) who made a lot of noise. They also used traps, pits, and nooses.[17] The only element lacking here was poison. Most later sources note that trapping was the normal way to get rid of tigers. Almost all information dates from the nineteenth century, as real tigers had become scarce after 1900.

The technique reported most often is the use of the specific tiger-trap (*bekungkung*).[18] There was some variation between traps, but it was basically a wooden cage, made of young trees, driven firmly into the ground. It had one or two open sides, and it contained dead or—more often—live bait, usually a bleating young goat. In many cases there was a partition within the traps with one opening, so that the goat would not be killed when a tiger entered the trap. When a tiger or a leopard entered the trap, he triggered a mechanism that released a trapdoor, closing off his only exit. In such a trap, tigers or leopards were caught alive, which was imperative if the animal was to be used in tiger ceremonies (see Chapter 7). The fact that the victim was alive may also have assuaged any possible feelings of guilt among those who had captured him.[19]

Tiger-traps were doubtless an indigenous invention. However, their use may have increased during the nineteenth century because of Dutch influence. In individual Residencies, the Resident ordered the indigenous regents to have them erected in all the relevant areas. This not only led to a numerical increase but also placed the responsibility, and therefore the "guilt," for tigers being captured in such a trap on the shoulders of a higher authority.[20] A system of bounties for every tiger or leopard captured or killed also contributed to the population's willingness to go through the trouble of constructing these traps.

The effectiveness of these traps has been judged differently. According to the Hungarian hunter Count Andrasy, who traveled over Java in 1849–50, some 400 tigers annually were captured in these traps. In the Residency of Banyumas, the regent employed a certain Surakendaga, a specialist in the construction of tiger-traps who in three years had thus captured 6 tigers and 27 leopards. However, tiger-traps did not always work, either because individual tigers were too smart to be caught in one or because the local population did not "service" the traps frequently enough. In 1889, an anonymous author stated that the results of these traps were meager, among other things because tigers had learned to avoid them. It should be mentioned, too, that at that time tigers were no longer all that thick on the ground.[21]

Somewhat less frequently mentioned are pits or pitfalls. The indigenous term used for these pits is *borangan*, named after the sharp pointed bamboo stakes, *borang* (also *ranju*), found at the bottom of the pit, which was covered with branches and dirt. Occasionally the stakes were also placed on those locations of a tiger path (according to many authors tigers had fixed routes) where the tiger had to jump. In order to enhance the attractiveness of a pitfall, bait was sometimes suspended from a tree just above the covered pit. In 1853 some Residents reported their objections to using these pitfalls, as they were a threat to cattle and innocent passersby. That may be the reason that they were hardly found in similar later reports by the Residents on the same topic.[22]

Nooses are much less often recorded, and details are lacking. One source, dated 1883, names a "spring-noose," again without details. However, the term suggests a contraption that was described for Malaya: "The top of a long springy sapling is bent over and secured to the ground." "The wire [or rope], fastened securely to the top of the sapling, ends in a running noose left lying open flat upon the ground." Leaves and twigs conceal the noose. If the tiger sets one foot in the noose, he goes up in the air."[23]

In the nineteenth century the use of poison was frequently reported. The first writer who wrote about using poison to kill tigers was Raffles. His source was the American naturalist Thomas Horsfield, who stated that "in some districts their [the tigers'] number has been sensibly diminished by this poison." Raffles also stated that the same poison was used to kill wild boar. In the reports of the Residents from the early 1850s, the term most often encountered for tiger poison is *walikambing*. Walikambing (*Sarcolobus spanoghei*) was the best known of all vegetable poisons, although the effects on tigers varied. Often they were killed outright, but sometimes they just became dizzy, and some authors stated that drinking water would revive them entirely. The poison was normally applied to a recent tiger kill, as the tiger, who rarely devoured a kill in one go, could be depended upon to return to it. As the effects of the drug were uncertain, it was imperative to check upon the tiger after his meal and finish the job of the poison if he was only dizzy. According to most sources many tigers were killed with walikambing. Poisoned meat was sometimes used in combination with tiger-traps.[24]

Walikambing was also used to kill wild boar. Apparently, the poison quickly lost its power, because the Chinese sold this meat for human consumption. One source even mentioned that tiger poisoned with walikambing could be—and sometimes was—eaten. In a much later publication, A. Hoogerwerf, who had been in charge of the nature reserve Ujung Kulon (Banten) between 1937 and 1950, gave his opinion that most tigers had become the victims of eating poisoned wild boar. This is rather unlikely if the first two statements are true, unless the boar had been poisoned with something stronger than walikambing. This could have been the case, as arsenic was sometimes mixed with walikambing, and plants containing strychnine were also said to be used occasionally for tigers. As late as 1936–37 four of the few remaining tigers were killed in Priangan (Cianjur) and Banten (Caringin) with poisoned carcasses.[25]

Traps, pits, and nooses were all Indonesian inventions, and walikambing likely was as well. The spring-gun (also gun-trap), or *weleng*, may or may not have been an indigenous invention, but the guns were probably imported. A gun—sometimes two—was connected to a trip wire, with or without bait. These contraptions were reported in 1837 (Krawang), in 1853 (Banyumas), and in 1862 (Probolinggo). In 1889 an anonymous author, probably a civil servant, recommended it, having seen its excellent performance in Priangan. The Residents of Banten and Priangan mentioned it in their 1895 reports to the Governor-General. In Banten, the spring-gun had proven itself quite effective, having wounded or killed 80 tigers during the 1887–89 tiger "epidemic" in Caringin. In Priangan, most tigers were killed by this means, according to the Resident. In 1938 spring-guns and poison used in the district Cibaliung, regency Pandeglang (Banten), had rendered tigers and leopards so rare that they no longer bothered the population.[26]

The indigenous term for the spring-guns is in Sundanese, the language of western Java, the region to which all sources on spring-guns except one (from Probolinggo) refer. According to the dictionary (Heringa), the trap could also contain a weapon other than a gun. It is tempting to speculate that this must have been a spear and that the spring-spear trap, so often to be found among the "tribal" groups, had been adapted for a gun. However, only one source, dated 1883, records spring-spear traps as one of many traps, snares, and the like employed by the Javanese. Another source, dated 1895, uses a term that possibly referred to a spring-spear trap. In any case, the fact that the spring-gun was largely restricted to western Java seems to point to Batavia as the source for this invention. Given the paucity of references to the spring-gun, it may never have become very popular, perhaps because the Dutch discouraged the possession of firearms among the indigenous population.

One could well ask, if all these means to capture and kill tigers were so successful, whether there were any tigers left to be hunted. The answer is a qualified yes. Prior to c. 1855, tigers (and leopards) could be found in every Residency of Java. Between 1855 and 1905, the tiger disappeared almost entirely from the central Javanese Residencies, but in a number of places there were still leopards. In western and eastern Java the tiger had survived to around 1900, but not in large numbers. The leopard had done somewhat better.

So, up to 1900, hunting of tigers was indeed possible, and there is sufficient evidence that the Javanese did hunt them. Alas, there are very few sources on this topic predating the nineteenth century, and the ones available are not much help. The early-eighteenth-century compilation referred to above states only that the Javanese took great pleasure in hunting tigers, driving them to a place where a noose had been placed. According to a manuscript dated c. 1780 the number of tigers had increased considerably in the areas of Java's Northeast Coast since that region had been ceded to the Dutch (between 1743 and 1746). Before then, every regency had been obliged to deliver annually a (fixed?) number of tigers for the court rituals of the central Javanese kingdom of Mataram, an obligation that had now ceased to exist. Apparently, the Javanese of this region did not keep up the same level of capturing these animals of their own free will. [27] In the early eighteenth century Valentijn had described a tiger hunt under the supervision of the ruler. The first European to describe a tiger hunt without royal involvement was Frick, followed by Salmon, but the best description is one given by Raffles:

> On receiving information of the retreat of a tiger the male inhabitants are sometimes called out in a body, by the orders of a chief, each man being obliged to be provided with a spear, the common weapon of the country. The place where the animal is concealed is surrounded: a double or triple range being formed, according to the number of hunters, and he is roused by shouts, by the beating of gongs, or by fire. The place where he is expected to attempt his escape is carefully guarded, and he is generally speared on the spot. In many districts, where the population is not deficient, the appearance of a single tiger rouses the neighbourhood, and he is infallibly destroyed by the method described.

Tiger hunts were organized by local, indigenous chiefs, like regents, but usually by the lower ranking district heads, heads of subdistricts, or village heads. The phrasing "rouses the neighbourhood" might suggest that villagers also might have done so at their own initiative. Raffles' description is almost certainly based on a report dated 1808 from the Resident of Surabaya, Frederik Jacob Rothenbühler, to Governor-General Daendels. Here it was said that tigers were rare and that, when the indigenous people spotted one, the animal would be pursued by hundreds of villagers.

Later sources seldom specify whether the tiger hunts were organized by indigenous officials or by the villagers themselves. Most participants were armed with lances, but the "chiefs" often possessed (old) guns. Some writers mention tiger hunts organized by local European officials, such as the Resident, Assistant-Resident, or Collector.[28] Since the period of Raffles, the Residents had been charged with taking measures to destroy tigers. However, the notion of a collective tiger hunt clearly predates their presence.

The 1853 reports of the Residents confirm the importance of indigenous tiger hunts. Of the 19 reports containing information on means to capture tigers, 15 mention traps and other "means at a distance," whereas tiger hunts held by villagers can be found in 10 reports. In five of these reports it was specified that tigers would be hunted only if they had killed human beings or livestock. In only six Residencies both traps and hunts were encountered. The Residents of Priangan and Pasuruan said that general hunts were impossible in the more forested areas. Motives are lacking for the other non-hunting Residencies, but at least in two cases (Buitenzorg and Kedu) tigers had become so scarce that going after them was no longer necessary. Many Residents argued that tigers were not hunted systematically owing to indigenous superstitions. A tiger who had done no wrong could very well be an ancestor who, far from being dangerous, protected his village (see Chapter 8). Only one Resident stated that the population was afraid that killing too many tigers would lead to an increase of the number of wild boar, an animal that did considerable damage to their crops. Finally, in the Yogyakarta Residency, one of the so-called Principalities still governed by native rulers, the population could call in the help of a court official specifically appointed for this purpose, if they were unable to catch a marauding tiger.

After 1860 not much is heard anymore about these collective tiger hunts. The 1861–62 reports of the Residents do mention what seems to be (but may not have been) a new phenomenon: Javanese who made a living catching tigers and leopards. They are recorded in Priangan, Madiun, and Besuki. In the 1895–97 report we meet the Aris of Pamotan (Malang), who was said to have killed 40 tigers.[29] The "professional" Javanese tiger hunter was seldom mentioned prior to 1860, although of course the Yogyakarta tiger mantri and the Banyumas tiger-trap specialist could arguably be seen as their predecessors. In the eyes of the Javanese, there may have been no difference whatsoever. They were just two examples of what the Dutch called tiger-charmers, dealt with in

Chapter 8, the biggest difference being that this new breed of tiger-charmers was armed with guns or rifles. It is tempting to speculate that the increase in bounties decreed in 1854 had enabled a number of Javanese to buy guns and thus become professional hunters of tigers and leopards.

Finally, the population of some areas was less hesitant to kill all tigers on sight. In 1853 the Resident of Banten reported that the people of the northern, more densely populated areas of his Residency hunted down all tigers, irrespective of their behavior regarding humans and cattle. This was in contrast to the southern, densely forested regions of the Residency, where "blameless" tigers were left in peace. In 1895 the Resident of Besuki reported that the people of the Banyuwangi regency were avid hunters who, certainly stimulated by the bounties offered by the Government, liked to go after tigers, unlike the majority of the people in his Residency.[30]

By way of explanation it should be pointed out that southern Banten was an area where shifting cultivators were still predominant. Northern Banten had been populated by sedentary peasants for ages, and the Sultans of Banten had been going after tigers at least since c. 1600. These differences in environmental circumstances and economic and cultural development seem to explain the observed variations in hunting patterns.

In ecological terms, Banyuwangi was more similar to southern than to northern Banten, but its population consisted of some local people and immigrants from many areas of the Indonesian Archipelago, including places where tigers were unknown. It is possible that this mixture of cultures made for an attitude regarding tigers that was notably different from tendencies among the Javanese. Madurese hunters in Banyuwangi, for example, had a reputation of bravery, which may have been reinforced by their lack of knowledge of tiger behavior (and therefore lack of fear), given that there were almost certainly no tigers on the island of Madura. However, there may have been a more utilitarian reason for the peculiar attitude of the Banyuwangi people: In contrast to most Indonesians, they were allowed firearms (Stohr 1874, 2; Groneman 1902, 19).

Bali

Information on indigenous tiger hunting—or indeed on any tiger hunting—in Bali is very scarce, but it appears that at the turn of the twentieth century the local population would attempt to kill a tiger only if it had attacked humans or livestock. In that case they would set up a spring-gun near the remains of the tiger's kill. Given that there was not much "tiger trouble," the level of indigenous tiger hunting was probably low.[31]

Sumatra

Around 1685, the German adventurer J.W. Vogel mentioned a spring-gun (or rather three guns at the same time). However, he states explicitly that this method was introduced and employed by the Dutch, and it is not clear whether the Sumatrans were also using it.

In the late eighteenth century, Marsden asserted that the Sumatrans did not like to hunt tigers: "from a superstitious prejudice, it is with difficulty they are prevailed upon, by a large reward which the India Company offers, to use methods of destroying them [tigers], till they have sustained some particular injury in their own family or kindred, and their ideas of fatalism contribute to render them insensible to the risk." This notion was to be repeated throughout the nineteenth and early twentieth centuries by almost all sources. Amazingly enough, he also mentions "the heads [of tigers] being frequently brought in to receive the reward given by the [British] East India Company for killing them." So either the British had succeeded in convincing Sumatrans that "blameless" tigers should also be killed, or the number of "guilty" tigers was very high. The latter possibility seems more likely. Some of the tigers brought in came doubtlessly from traps, as Marsden notes: "Their traps, of which they can make variety, are very ingeniously contrived. Sometimes they are in the nature of strong cages, with falling doors, into which the beast is enticed by a goat or dog enclosed as a bait; sometimes they manage that a large timber shall fall, in a groove, across his back; he is noosed about the loins with strong rattans, or he is led to ascend a plank, nearly balanced, which, turning when he is past the centre, lets him fall upon sharp stakes prepared below." Evidently, Sumatrans used the same tiger-traps, sharp stakes (sometimes in pits), and nooses found in Java. (For Java, however, only one reference records the "balanced plank" mentioned here.)[32]

Tiger-traps with goats (and, in the Batak area, dogs) are frequently recorded. The terms used are *penjara* and *kandang (harimau)*. Gustav Schneider, traveling through parts of Sumatra from 1897 to 1899, even stated, no doubt exaggerating slightly, that there was a tiger-trap near every village. Unlike the Javanese, many Sumatrans believed that a tiger would walk into a trap only if it was set by a specialist (*tukang macan, pawang rimueng*) who had put a curse on the tiger. This, of course, is none other than the "tiger-charmer."[33]

Only one source notes the spring-spear trap (*belantek*) so often encountered among the tribal groups. It seems that a belantek was redundant if a real tiger-trap was available. The spring-gun is recorded more often. The terms used here for this contraption are *poting*, a Batak word, and, interestingly enough, *be-*

Various types of Sumatran tiger-traps. These traps could be found among the sedentary peasants of the Malay world. *above,* Model of a specific tiger-trap in central Sumatra, c. 1880. Hasselt 1882. *below,* In the Padang Highlands, Sumatra's West Coast, c. 1900. Collection KITLV *lantek malam,* suggesting that a gun had indeed taken the place of the spear, as noted earlier with regard to Javanese spring-gun terminology. Before the 1880s spring-guns are mentioned only once, in the 1680s, and as a contraption of the Dutch. This is a much earlier reference than the ones to Java, Bali, and Malaya, which date from the 1830s or later, and it demonstrates the European origin of this particular kind of trap. What the Sumatrans apparently did not use was poison. Only two sources state that they did (1850s, 1920s), one source explicitly denies it (1895–97), and the other sources do not name poison at all. Two Sumatran Residents argued that tigers did not touch poisoned meat, so the available poison must have been different from that of the Javanese. Around 1880, the Collector De Jager promised some Acehnese chiefs poison from Java, which implies that they had no effective poison themselves.[34]

Generally speaking, the settled Sumatran peasantry chased tigers far less than did the Javanese. The Sumatra Residents, advising the Governor-General in 1895, were unanimous in their judgment that bounties did not lead to an increase of the number of tigers killed (while their Java colleagues were in favor of continuing the bounty system). Not only did Sumatran peasants normally refuse to go after tigers who were "blameless," but even tigers who had "sinned" were often left alone, certainly if the victims were only pets or livestock. There are both natural and supernatural explanations for their reluctance.

The natural one is that Sumatra had a much larger proportion of its surface area under forest cover than Java, while most Sumatran forests were also more impenetrable than many Javanese ones. The kind of collective hunts in Java were here hardly possible, although they were not entirely absent. For example, in or shortly before 1935 hunting parties led by a civil servant killed 70 tigers in Bengkulu, where the killing of wild boar with poison had led to a "tiger epidemic."

The supernatural explanation (see also Chapter 8) is that the Sumatran peasantry, as much convinced as the Javanese that tigers could be harmless and even helpful ancestors, put more emphasis on the ancestral tiger as a "moral force" than did the Javanese. If a tiger had killed someone, that individual surely had done something wrong and had now been punished by his ancestor.[35] The tiger as a moral force was not unknown in Java, but it was less pronounced, and it did not keep the Javanese from hunting them down if they killed humans or livestock.

In Sumatra, the death of a tiger was also more often surrounded with ceremonies to beg forgiveness from the animal than was true in Java, testifying again to the greater unease felt by the Sumatrans when confronted with a marauding tiger.

Fear of invasions of wild boar may well have been one of the reasons that the Sumatran peasantry was reluctant to chase tigers. Such was the case in the Upper Kampar region, where around 1930 the population refused its cooperation for the killing of tigers. Another reason is that the Government often confiscated the firearms in their possession.[36]

Finally, not all Sumatrans were afraid to kill tigers, even the ones that had not killed a human being. Examples are the Acehnese, the Batak, and the Rawas people from Palembang. The Batak in particular seem to have had a rather cavalier attitude toward tigers, decorating their dwellings with skulls and hides of tigers and even eating tiger meat.[37] The Batak area was much less forested than most Sumatran regions, and their beliefs differed in various respects from those of the other Sumatrans, so a different attitude regarding tigers is not entirely unexpected. Also, the Acehnese and the Batak had more and better guns and revolvers than other Sumatrans, particularly since the start of the Aceh War in 1873.[38]

The twentieth century offers evidence of a professional Sumatran tiger hunter. He was an orthodox Muslim and therefore supposedly not bothered by the supernatural aspects of the tiger. Here, again, is a link with the tiger-charmers, often also orthodox Muslims.[39]

Malaya

The Malayan sedentary peasantry employed the panoply of traps and snares encountered on the islands. John Newbold, writing in the 1830s, stated that nooses and pitfalls were used to catch tigers, elephants, and rhinos. He added: "The tiger is sometimes destroyed by placing part of a buffalo near his haunt and poisoning the spring to which he retires for the purpose of slaking his thirst; by shooting him as he devours the bait, or by spring guns." This listing is not complete, but it is remarkable for what it mentions and what it does not. Newbold does mention the spring-gun, perhaps a recent introduction, around the same time that the first one was recorded for Java (1837). In a later source it is called *belantek pesawat*, thus linking it to the spring-spear trap. Newbold does not list the specific tiger-trap, recorded for Java and Sumatra in the eighteenth century. However, it was observed in the hinterland of Singapore in 1848, and it is hard to imagine that it would have been entirely absent on the continent, even though it does not appear in the literature prior to c. 1900. The term used was the same as the Sumatran one, penjara. Newbold does not record the use of the spring-spear trap (belantek) either, a contraption to be found in the literature of a later date. There were several belantek varieties, of which Richard Winstedt described one that "has been aptly called the 'slapping spring-spear' [belantek parap or parak] and consists of a powerful elastic arm (of sapling) bound horizontally to two trees or posts with a fire-hardened spike or spear fastened at right-angles to the slapping end which latter is held back by a strong noose." The mechanism is activated when an animal comes into contact with the trip-wire stretched across its path. It was frequently in evidence amongst the tribal peoples of the Peninsula, but it is possible that the sedentary Malays had not much use for it, preferring the specific tiger-trap and the spring-gun, as did the sedentary peasants of Java and Sumatra. By the 1940s the belantek had become obsolete.[40]

Newbold does not mention the probably less popular *penurun,* a wooden spear suspended over a game-track, and another trap based on a similar principle—a heavy mass of logs falling on a tiger and crushing him. Newbold lists poison, but he is the only author to do so, and details are lacking. Looking at all the available evidence, it seems that the sedentary Malayan peasantry used the specific tiger-trap and the pitfall most frequently.[41]

Malayan peasants are not on record as avid tiger hunters. The collective chase, so often to be found in Java and somewhat less frequently in Sumatra, seems to be absent. As Newbold has it: "The Malays of the Peninsula, as well as their brethren of Sumatra . . . have a superstitious aversion to slaying tigers, which are considered in many instances to be receptacles for the souls of departed human beings, nor can they be prevailed upon to make any attempt to do so until the tiger has committed the first aggression, by carrying off a man or some of their cattle." Emily Innes, living in Selangor in 1876–77, even argued that "natives, we knew, never went out to shoot tigers" and that "the Malays have all sorts of superstitions about tigers, and consider it very unlucky to kill one." This was no doubt somewhat exaggerated, as Newbold had listed among the means employed by the Malays to kill a tiger "shooting him as he devours the bait." Nevertheless, such an action was rare indeed. Even the less direct confrontation with the tiger by means of the construction of a tiger-trap was accompanied by the Muslim trap specialist's explanation that it was not he but Mohammed who had set the trap. And if a tiger had been killed, the dead animal was given a public reception in the village like that of a war chief or champion, with dancing and fencing demonstrations.

Hunting tigers with shotguns by Malays increased, together with the number of shotguns, during the late nineteenth and twentieth centuries. Just after 1900 it was said that most tigers killed by Malays, who came to collect the bounty issued by the Government, had been killed with guns and no longer in pitfalls. When the indigenous population was forbidden to use guns, as was the case during the Japanese occupation and during the time of the "Emergency" just after the war, the number of tigers increased notably.[42]

Here, again, is the probability of a link between increased tiger hunting by the indigenous population and the existence of bounties that could be used to buy—gradually improving—guns. Also apparent is the advent of the professional indigenous tiger hunter, making a living out of the bounties offered by the Government for the extermination of these animals. Around 1900, Maxwell met such a person, nicknamed Manap Rimau (Tiger Manap) owing to his extraordinary skill in shooting tigers. His real name was Abdulmanap bin Muhammad Arsad, no doubt a good Muslim and therefore in theory less impressed by supernatural properties of tigers. Once again, I would suggest that the professional indigenous tiger hunter is a modernized version of the tiger *pawang* ("tiger-charmer"), who set the tiger-traps, often to be found in the sources.[43]

Meat, Skins, and Bones

I want to consider briefly the eating of tiger meat and the possible commercial value of other tiger "parts." In other words, I turn here to the question of whether the "commodification" of the tiger and the other big cats was an important motive for killing them.

Eating tiger meat clearly was rare. It was eaten in seventeenth-century Batavia, where it was believed to be a cure for asthmatic afflictions. In the 1850s to 1880s, tiger meat was said to have invigorating and antirheumatic properties and to be a cure for many complaints. It was valued highly by the aristocracy of the Javanese Principalities, and the Chinese paid good money for it. Even meat from a tiger killed by poison was eaten. However, neither the consumption of tiger meat nor the sale of it to the Chinese is ever mentioned as a motive for killing a tiger. Among the indigenous peasantry, only the Batak are on record as (habitual?) consumers of tiger meat, apart from rather late and isolated references to individuals from other areas. There is the story of a man from Lampung (southern Sumatra) who wanted to kill a tiger in the 1930s because the meat was supposed to cure skin diseases. A group of Javanese who almost starved to death during the revolution against the Dutch, between 1945 and 1949, killed a tiger in the Krawang area (western Java) and ate it. They found that it cured them of their skin diseases.[44]

A Chinese source dated 1436 claimed that the island of Belitung, off Sumatra's southeast coast, exported skins of (clouded) leopards, in addition to those of bears and deer. In the seventeenth century exports are mentioned of tiger skins from the Coromandel Coast (India), Siam, Cambodia, and Korea, but not from the Malay world.[45]

The Batak apart, indigenous people seldom if ever decorated their houses with tiger skins. The tiger skin as a trophy may have been a European "invention," although occasionally local aristocrats displayed the visible results of their prowess. It is not clear whether this was done only by "Westernized" rulers and nobles. Statements on the value of tiger skins are rare and somewhat ambiguous, but the impression is that Javanese and Sumatrans seldom shot tigers in order to sell the hides. In the 1820s, Roorda van Eysinga proposed that tiger skins should be exported from Sumatra, which would generate a trade in a valuable commodity, thus inducing the Sumatrans to kill tigers. This clearly suggests that there was no such trade at the time. Around 1860, the Resident of Madiun (central Java) reported that leopard skins had a higher monetary value than tiger skins. The former were sometimes bought at a price as high as or even higher than the bounty to be paid out by the Government for a leopard captured or killed. In his view, therefore, bounties for leopards could be abolished, but those for tigers could not. Around 1880 tiger skins, particularly from Sumatra, were sometimes exported to Europe, but as a rule they did not leave the Archipelago, and even there they did not constitute a regular article of commerce. What may have happened is that people tried to sell a hide when they had been obliged to kill a (man-eating) tiger, as witness the experience of the French traveler Xavier Brau de Saint-Pol-Lias in Aceh around that time. The German physician and explorer Max Moszkowski stated explicitly that to the Sumatran villagers who captured a tiger, the skin had no value. Indeed, tiger skins often were spoiled because local people had stabbed them repeatedly with their knives and spears in order to vent their anger and/or increase the strength of their weapons—an effect attributed to the immersion of the latter in tiger blood.[46]

In contrast, the hides of the clouded leopard of Borneo often could be found in the markets of central Kalimantan, and they were exported to places like Sulawesi and Sumbawa. Strangely enough, the monetary value of these hides was probably much lower than that of tigers and leopards, at least around 1880. The skin of a clouded leopard could be had for f. 5 or so, whereas a real leopard skin could easily bring f. 25 in Java. Of course, even f. 5 could mean a lot in a barely monetarized society such as that of the Dayak, but the monetary value may not have been the deciding factor regarding the killing of clouded leopards. The attitude of the Bornean Dayak toward the clouded leopard was rather callous, and killing one was not a big deal, particularly as their hides were much sought after for Dayak war costumes.[47]

Today, the quest for tiger bones to be exported to mainland China and Taiwan is the main reason that so many tigers are still being killed. Although the use of tiger bones as "medicine" could be a long-standing tradition, the enormous sums of money that these bones command seem to be a fairly recent phenomenon. In fact, prior to the Second World War, the sale of tiger bones was hardly ever mentioned, let alone as a motive for killing these animals.

Only two references point in this direction. The first one is about a tiger skull given to some Chinese in Malaya in 1876, which they would use to produce a medicinal powder. The second one is the observation of the German traveler H. Morin, visiting Java in 1907, that Chinese apothecaries in (western) Java often sold "parts" of tigers. The first person to mention the high value of tiger bones was the British tiger hunter Locke, living in Malaya around 1950: "To the Malayan hunter of to-day the bones of the tiger he shoots are of the greatest saleable value." One is left to speculate that the very fact that at that moment tigers were becoming scarce in some areas may have been the cause of the rising prices of tiger bones, which, in turn, hastened their demise.[48]

The only parts of the tiger the indigenous people were interested in were the teeth and the claws, which were worn as talismans, and the whiskers, which, when ground up, were supposed to be a potent poison or, if burned, a cure for impotence. Teeth and claws of the clouded leopard were used in the same way.[49] No evidence points to a trade in these items.

Finally, there was a market for entire tigers, dead or alive.

Hunting by Peasants

Summing up the findings from the preceding sections, we can say that among the sedentary peasantry, trapping tigers and leopards was more important than hunting them. The specific tiger-trap was one of the main instruments in this respect, separating the "peasants" from the "tribes." The use of poison may have been largely restricted to Java. As trapping is a more or less "invisible" activity, not much in evidence in official reports and the writings of naturalists and other travelers, the prominence of trapping over hunting may have led to the impression that fewer tigers were killed than was actually the case.

Java is also the area where collective hunts took care of the remainder of the tigers who had made the villagers uneasy. In Sumatra these hunts seem to have been rare, and they were not recorded for Malaya, in both cases perhaps because the natural environment was less conducive to such endeavors. In Sumatra supernatural reasons played at least an additional role in this respect.

The feeling that "blameless" tigers should not be killed, as they could very well be ancestors who meant the villagers no harm, seems to have been fairly widespread among the populations of Malaya, Sumatra, Java (and Bali). This aspect is dealt with more extensively in Chapter 8. But some groups apparently were immune to such feelings, as witness the cavalier attitude toward tigers of the Acehnese, the Batak, and the Rawas people in Sumatra and the populations of northern Banten and Banyuwangi in Java. In three out of these five cases the presence of firearms seems to have played a role.

More mundane reasons for a certain reluctance to kill all tigers, like the fear that this would lead to an invasion of wild boar, were occasionally given in the sources. It may very well be that such notions were underrepresented in the colonial sources, as "superstition" was a much more appealing, generally accepted explanation among colonial civil servants. This is not to say that local "beliefs" had nothing to do with indigenous attitudes toward tigers, but it may have been just one factor among many.

Whatever the weight of these factors, it could be argued that during the later part of the nineteenth century certain individuals, perhaps mostly orthodox Muslims, were slowly but surely weaned from such "animistic" beliefs. Spurred on by a generous bounty system and by the increasing availability of more dependable firearms, which they could, moreover, afford to buy with the reward money, they embarked upon a career of professional tiger hunting. It is tempting to see these people as a modernized version of the "tiger-charmer," the expert in tiger-lore and in constructing tiger-traps, to be found in many sources dating from an earlier epoch.

It could be argued that the presence of the colonial state with its bounties and of European technology, as embodied in guns and rifles, stimulated the killing of tigers by the indigenous peasantry. But the basic mechanisms of hunting and trapping were already in place before the European presence made itself felt. At least in the case of Java, the tiger was on his way out before bounties and improved firearms could make much of a difference.

Fear

The tiger was greatly feared among some of the Malayan and Sumatran tribes dealt with above. However, the Aboriginal Malay and the Lubu, two semi-sedentary groups rather close to becoming full-time agriculturists, may have feared tigers less than did the real nomads. This notion, that the fear for tigers diminished as agriculture became more important, may lead some readers to expect that sedentary peasants would no longer fear tigers all that much, or even that they would lose their fear entirely. That, however, is certainly not the case, at least as regards the majority of the peasantry of the Malay world. There is no shortage of stories about villagers who lived in constant fear of tiger attacks or eventually left their villages because of them. Even killed or captured tigers, particularly in Malaya and Sumatra, were shown deference.

Occasionally, and perhaps mainly when a tiger had been killed by a European or by an indigenous ruler, which would take the villagers off the hook in a spiritual sense, fear would express itself not as deference but as hatred or pent-up rage. When Mohnike shot a tiger who had just killed a 16-year-old girl in Palembang in 1847, the inhabitants vented their fury on the animal by sticking their weapons into its dead body. The American animal trapper Charles Mayer, who hunted in Malaya and Sumatra during a period of 18 years between 1900 and 1920, recounted two such instances. When he had killed a tiger in the Palembang Residency, "the men began to heap insults on the dead creature. They spat on him and called him names." When he shot a cattle-killer in Malaya, an animal that was regarded as a ghost by the population because it had never been sighted, "the natives were overjoyed that the evil spirit was dead. They cursed it in all varieties of the Malay language and spat upon it."

Moszkowski, visiting Siak (Sumatra), graphically describes a similar experience in 1907. A tiger had been caught in a tiger-trap, and the entire village presented itself in front of the cage, "gave him a firm talking-to, called him names and insulted him, goaded and wounded him with their lances and knives, until he was finally shot with an old gun. Even the corpse was maltreated."

Deep hatred was also said to be felt by the Javanese who lived in areas troubled by tigers. That was the reason that they enjoyed the tiger-sticking ceremonies (see Chapter 7) so much; the more tigers killed during these occasions, the better.

Consider these words from the American animal catcher Frank Buck, who hunted in India and Malaya during the 1910s and 1920s and who thus formulated the reactions of the indigenous people from Johore (Malaya) on the killing of a plantation coolie by a man-eater: "One has to have a good comprehension of the wild world-old superstitions of these natives to appreciate fully what happens inside them when a man-eating tiger appears. All the fanaticism that goes with their belief in strange devils and ogres finds release when a tiger, their enemy of enemies, kills a member of their ranks. They act like a people who consider themselves doomed. Going into a delirium of fear that leaves them weak and spiritless, they become as helpless as little children."[50] The modern reader becomes a bit suspicious when a Westerner from the colonial period writes about the native population of the Malay world as "little children" swept up in "fanaticism." Such terms provided a welcome background against which the big and brave Western hunter could portray himself as their savior. It reminds us of the dangers of using colonial sources when attempting to write a "history of mentalities" of colonized peoples. However, sources do vary considerably regarding the attitude of Malay people toward tigers. Most sources were quite specific as to time and place and did not indulge in facile generalizations.

A striking feature of this ensemble is the real threat that tigers posed in many of the societies under discussion here, details of which are given in several chapters. In a period that witnesses the rapid disappearance of many subspecies of the tiger, the notion of the tiger as a threat to humans is neither easy to grasp nor popular, but man-eating was not a myth.

In addition, tigers were said to be both greatly feared in many of these groups and venerated as the embodiment of ancestors. This has led some writers to argue that the attitude of the indigenous population toward tigers was ambiguous: the tiger as friend *and* foe.[51] My reading of this paradox is different. The fact that many people regarded tigers as ancestors who could have a benign influence does not imply that tigers were seen as "friends." Such a tiger would not hesitate to punish his offspring if they committed an offence against the rules laid down by the ancestors. The ancestor-tiger was a strict disciplinarian who, like a ruler or a deity, could be benign if he so desired but who was mostly greatly feared in his wrath.[52] The tiger is the King or Lord of the Forest, and, as a real king, he is basically unpredictable, thus keeping people in awe of him.

It is too Romantic a notion that, because some tigers were regarded as ancestors, and because many Malays avoided killing tigers, tigers were not feared or hated. Calling the tiger "grandfather" may have fooled the tiger, but it should not fool us.

The Availability of Firearms

The use of firearms by Malay individuals and groups increased during the second half of the nineteenth and the first half of the twentieth century, at least insofar as the Europeans did not (try to) stop this. Guns were the only weapons that European tiger hunters had in common with their Malay counterparts, and it is therefore fitting that a short section on firearms should link the indigenous and the European parts of this chapter.

When the Portuguese gave their first descriptions of Malaya, Sumatra, and Java, there were already arquebusses (hook-guns) and muskets in evidence, presumably partly provided with matchlocks. Those weapons were probably largely imported from Pegu (Burma), Siam, China, Japan, and perhaps Europe, but by the sixteenth century, Indonesians had also started to produce matchlocks themselves.[53]

In the seventeenth century, the Dutch introduced snaphaunces and (other) flintlock guns, blunderbusses, carbines, fowling pieces, and pistols.[54] Ignition of most of these firearms was based on the flintlock principle, which must have been quite some improvement over the matchlock type if one wanted to hunt tiger.

In the nineteenth century, technological change went into higher gear. It started with the introduction of the percussion lock ("detonating lock"), along with the percussion cap containing fulminate. Hunting guns with a detonator lock became available in Europe in the 1820s. In 1841, all flintlock firearms of the army in the Netherlands were converted to percussion weapons, and they likely reached the Archipelago not much later. They are mentioned for the first time in 1854. Rifles, or guns with rifled barrels (with spiral grooves), had already been used by hunters in Europe for quite some time, certainly since the eighteenth century, before they were adopted by European armies. The Dutch army introduced them between 1850 and 1860, but in Indonesia hunting rifles were mentioned as early as the 1820s. Self-contained and self-primed cartridges, replacing separate balls, gunpowder, and primer, became readily available in the 1850s and could almost immediately be found in Indonesia. They were a necessary precondition for the successful introduction of breechloaders (as opposed to the older muzzleloaders), which conquered the Dutch army from 1867 onward. Double-barreled shotguns—very important when, as in the case of tigers, a quickly fired second bullet could mean the difference between a hunter's life and death—were in the Archipelago in 1838 (and possibly earlier). But the real repeaters, namely the revolver and the repeating rifle, were not introduced, or even invented, until much later. The Dutch army obtained revolvers after 1873, and repeating rifles became available in 1888. In Indonesia, revolvers were mentioned in 1881 and repeating rifles in 1890. Often-named brands of the latter were Mauser and Mannlicher.[55]

Compared to the slow spread of the flintlock gun and the long period that it reigned supreme, the changes between for example 1850 and 1890 were both more rapid and more far-reaching. Within half a century, firearms had become more dependable and accurate, loading had become easier, and the number of bullets that could be fired in succession had increased, as had their muzzle velocity and stopping power.

The indigenous population did not keep up with these rapid changes, although at first they seemed to have followed European developments closely enough. They did adopt matchlocks and start to produce them at a very early stage. Around 1700, many flintlocks had found their way into the Javanese armories, and the Javanese had also begun producing flintlocks themselves. At the end of the eighteenth century at the latest, flintlocks were also being produced in Sumatra. However, the first signs of technological stagnation regarding firearms were already visible around 1800, when a number of areas (Bali, Minangkabau) were still producing matchlocks. Muskets without any lock at all were still being used in some areas in the nineteenth and twentieth centuries, as were matchlocks and flintlocks. In the early twentieth century, Indonesia was a veritable museum of old muzzleloaders that were still seeing action, more often than not homemade or at least products of local industry.[56]

Until the 1950s, Indonesians and Malayans did not produce a more advanced weapon than the flintlock, and even the rate of adoption of more modern imported weapons was very low. The problem with modern firearms was not only that they were more expensive but also that indigenous people could no longer make their own shot or bullets and had to buy cartridges, which made the use of these weapons even more expensive.[57] It is questionable, therefore, whether nineteenth-century European hunting equipment influenced indigenous hunting practices all that much. Of course, it did influence European hunting in Indonesia.

Another factor influencing the availability of firearms, both old and modern, among the "Malay" population was that the colonial rulers often tried to restrict their possession to a carefully selected elite. In 1822 the Dutch made the import of firearms in Indonesia a Government monopoly of which only guns for hunting and "luxury" firearms were excluded, although even then a permit was necessary. The possession of firearms was allowed to Europeans and their offspring and to indigenous civil servants. All other Indonesians (and "foreign Orientals") needed a permit. According to additional regulations, dated 1828, these permits had to be renewed annually. But these rules were not strictly enforced, and, particularly in times of war, smugglers supplied firearms to those Indonesians who could afford them.[58]

During times of war or unrest, the Dutch often rounded up the guns of the indigenous population. This happened several times in Sumatra during the nineteenth and twentieth centuries, and reports sometimes stated that the number of tigers or elephants had increased because of these measures. So even the flintlocks may have made some impact.[59]

Hunting by Europeans

The Dutch colonial state was, unlike the British Raj, not a hunting state. Neither was the Dutch East India Company (VOC) that preceded it. To be sure, in the seventeenth century the Governors-General and other officials in Batavia, the VOC's headquarters, did employ professional hunters for their table. Occasionally, they themselves left Batavia for a short hunting trip in the—then still pretty wild—neighborhood. Deer and wild boar were the usual victims, but from time to time the gentlemen went after a marauding tiger. The Governors-General Pieter de Carpentier (r. 1623–27), Jacques Specx (1629–32), and Joan Maetsuijcker (1653–78) all participated in tiger hunts. When, however, the Environs of Batavia were turned into arable lands, somewhere during the second half of the seventeenth century, both the game wardens and the shooting parties disappeared.[60]

This situation did not change much when, after 1800, the Dutch colonial state took over from the VOC, at least not for the first three-quarters of the century. "We did not hear of any Dutch gentlemen who are sportsmen [hunters]; but had Java continued in the English possession, I have no doubt it would ere this have been celebrated for its field sports," as the Englishman Joseph Jukes, visiting Java in 1844, commented. Or, shorter but equally dismissive: "The Dutch do not hunt," affirmed Charles Whitney, who hunted in Sumatra some 60 years later. Rupprecht, crown prince of Bavaria, visiting Java in 1903, was more specific, stating that the Dutch hunted small game only.[61]

From today's perspective this would seem to be admirable behavior on the part of the Dutch, yet the statements just quoted somewhat exaggerated Dutch abstinence from hunting, particularly around 1900. Certainly, compared with British India, Dutch colonial hunting was a much less important feature of colonial rule. It did exist, but on a much smaller scale, not unlike the difference in scale between the Raj and the Netherlands Indies. Dozens of books were published on tiger hunting in India alone, whereas books on tiger hunting in Indonesia are virtually absent, and even books on hunting in general seem rare. No more than eight books on hunting in Indonesia written by Dutchmen may be found; of these authors, at least two were Indo-Europeans, one of whom wrote his book in Javanese and had it printed in Javanese characters![62]

Indonesian tiger hunts themselves were also by far less showy and grand. In the Indonesian Archipelago there was nothing to be compared with the tiger hunts sometimes lasting for months on end, with hundreds of elephants, organized by Indian maharajahs in the honor of visiting British royals.[63] Neither was there any European in Indonesia who came even near to the 1,000 tigers supposed to have been shot between 1832 and 1862 in India by one hunter alone.[64]

Nevertheless, shooting game by Europeans in Indonesia was not negligible, and it may have increased slightly between 1800 and 1870, probably to the same degree as the number of Europeans and the influence of the Dutch colonial state expanded. The higher echelons of the colonial bureaucracy—Governor-General, Governor, and Resident—are not on record as great hunters.[65] Lower officials—such as a Collector—did hunt from time to time, probably mostly in the line of duty, as when they were called upon to stop the activities of man-eating or cattle-killing tigers.[66]

Most hunters seem to have been planters or military men. That the military hunted is more or less self-explanatory: these were men conversant in the use of firearms. That owners or administrators of estates or plantations were often avid hunters is not hard to understand. As their lands were frequently established in "wild" areas, they often started their hunting careers when they attempted to rid their grounds of "pests." Some planters had links to the local indigenous aristocracy and were sometimes related to them and copied their hunting behavior. In other areas they had indigenous concubines and started local Indo-European dynasties in which the hunting traditions were transmitted from father to son.

European hunter with indigenous assistant. Drawing, c. 1880, from one of the few books on hunting in Java written in the colonial period. When the Dutch started hunting tigers as a sport, c. 1870, the tiger density was already low. Rhemrev 1884

Such an Indo-European planter-cum-hunter was J. Dezentjé (d. 1840), leaseholder of Ngampel, in the Principalities, who was married to a Javanese princess. Another one was Carolus Hamar de la Brethonière (1798–1868), leaseholder of Getas and Ngasinan, who killed between 120 and 190 Javan tigers. This discrepancy in count is rather large and may have been caused by the unreliability of the one source upon which all estimates in the literature are based, namely de la Brethonière himself.[67] Nevertheless, it seems to be beyond dispute that he held the record for nineteenth-century Java. If the latter estimate is correct, it is almost certainly the all-Indonesian record for the nineteenth and twentieth centuries. Of two other European hunters it is known only that they shot over a hundred tigers each (had it been much over a hundred, that figure would have been recorded, no doubt). Of one of them, all that is known is his name, Hofman, and the fact that he shot Sumatran tigers. He did his shooting probably before 1910. More is known about the other big-game hunter, A. J. M. Ledeboer. He shot his tigers in Sumatra, Java, and Bali between 1900 and 1940. He held the lease of a large estate named Kalisat, in the Residency Bondowoso (eastern Java), where he attempted successfully to restore the depleted deer population. He was a prominent member of the

Netherlands Indies Association for the Protection of Nature, which counted many well-known hunters among its members. Very few people at that time could see anything wrong or even strange in the combination of big-game hunting and concern for the preservation of nature, and certainly not if the game being hunted consisted of tigers. Tigers, after all, were large-scale game-killers.[68]

Before 1870 European hunting was not restricted to Java, but it seems to have been rather rare in the Outer Islands.[69] After 1870 hunting, big-game hunting included, became much more fashionable among the Europeans in Indonesia. This was partly, and perhaps largely, a question of numbers. The Dutch empire expanded considerably and not always peacefully between 1870 and 1910, and the enlarged military presence made for more hunting. With the Agrarian Law of 1870 it had become much easier for Europeans to obtain long land-leases, and many Dutchmen availed themselves of this opportunity. Ledeboer was a representative of this group. At the same time there was an increasing interest in obtaining land concessions for tobacco planting in Sumatra (Deli). The new estates in Java and Sumatra often had to be cleared in or near heavily forested and other uncultivated areas. This attracted a lot of game, often harmful as regards crops, domesticated animals, and pets, or dangerous for humans. Planters who wanted to protect themselves and their properties thus turned hunters. These new estates, particularly those in Java, also attracted quite a few members of the Dutch aristocracy, who already had a hunting background before they came to the Archipelago.[70]

There was also a general increase in the number of Dutch people who came to the Indonesian Archipelago, and this increase (this time including women) spurred the development of a new "white" imperial morality. It was directed against the slack morals of the old European colonists (drinking, concubinage, whoring, and laziness), and espoused sobriety, self-control, and physical exercise, or, in other words, "clean living." Hunting, a "manly sport" par excellence, became a recognized means to stay fit and healthy, which, moreover, kept men out of mischief. The "Sunday hunter" was born.[71]

Another precondition for the birth of the Sunday hunter was the increasing availability of better guns and rifles. It goes without saying that soldiers and planters profited from this development as well. A number of people, no doubt encouraged by these more reliable firearms, started to specialize as tiger hunters, either as a pastime or as a living. In addition to Hofman and Ledeboer, others who should be named include van Alphen, Buma, van Dijk, Jahn, Patrick, and Synja. The only professional hunter of this groups was van Alphen, an Indo-European who styled himself "Jonkheer," a Dutch noble title.

Tiger shoot, Sumatra. Even in the 1930s there were still so many tigers in Sumatra that it was possible to shoot three in one day. Denninghoff Stelling 1966

In 1909 he told a visitor that he had killed 67 tigers, presumably mostly in Sumatra, in order to collect the Government bounties for these animals. Indo-Europeans, permitted to own firearms, seem to have regarded hunting as an essential feature of Indo-culture. Particularly during economic recessions, when many of them became unemployed, they often turned to hunting (although of course not necessarily tiger hunting) as a means of earning a living.[72]

Increasing numbers of Europeans also came to the Archipelago in the nineteenth century as collectors of specimens of what was then called natural history. This was not an entirely new phenomenon. Rich private persons had formed "curiosity cabinets" in the seventeenth and eighteenth centuries, and in the eighteenth century learned societies started to collect all sorts of preserved animals, a task that was taken over by museums in the nineteenth century. What was new in the 1800s was the number of people involved and the numbers of specimens collected. To a scholar like C. L. Blume, who around 1820 asked the people of Priangan (Java) to collect animals, including tigers, for him, this was a sideline. But after c. 1850 naturalists like Bernstein, Horna-day, and Wallace came to the Indies as full-time collectors, financing their undertaking with the proceeds of their sales to museums.[73]

Demand for live tigers must have increased considerably during the second half of the nineteenth century as circuses and zoos became more popular. Traveling animal shows (menageries) had preceded both and were sometimes turned into circuses or zoos, but they did not disappear entirely. Zoos came into being in Europe in the first half of the nineteenth century (London, 1829; Amsterdam, 1838; Antwerp, 1840; Berlin, 1844), but their proliferation dates from the second half. In the United States, zoological gardens did not appear before 1890. Around 1900, zoos were also being established in Latin America, Africa, and Asia. The menagerie of the Dutch van Aken brothers was, to many Dutchmen who came to the Indonesian Archipelago before 1850, their only point of reference regarding tigers and leopards. The van Aken brothers, who showed their animals all over Europe, are an interesting example of the transition of traveling animal shows to zoological gardens. Cornelis van Aken sold his entire menagerie to the founders of the Amsterdam Zoo, including the four tigers he owned, and Cornelis's brother Willem sold his collection to the newly founded Antwerp Zoo.[74]

The circus, another nineteenth-century phenomenon, flourished during the second half of the century both in Europe (Carré, Corty Althoff, Hagenbeck, Krone, Renz, Sarrasani, and Strassburger), and in the United States (Barnum & Bailey, Ringling). Circuses sometimes featured wild-animal acts, but their popularity seems to have come fairly late in the century, when the German Carl Hagenbeck, animal dealer and circus owner from Hamburg, introduced his training method. Hagenbeck had been active as an animal dealer since the 1860s, selling to zoos and circuses. Originally he sent his animal catchers to Africa, partly because Charles Jamrach from London more or less monopolized India. However, when his African supply was blocked by war, he turned to Asia. In 1885 his half-brother John Hagenbeck established himself as an animal catcher in Sri Lanka, from where he sent expeditions to India, the Malayan Peninsula, and the Indonesian Archipelago. At that time there were already several central markets for the trade in wild animals, established to cater to zoos and circuses; most notable were those in Calcutta and Singapore, where among other animals tigers and leopards could be bought. Charles Mayer mentioned that there was always a market for live tigers, and Frank Buck stated that there was a regular trade in tigers and leopards. That market, however, got in trouble during the Depression of the 1930s. In 1931–32 very few tigers were caught in Siak (Sumatra) because there was no longer a demand for them in Singapore.[75]

People like Buck, Hagenbeck, and Mayer were a new breed of specialists, often remaining in the area for one or two decades. Apart from buying on the specialized local markets, they organized hunting expeditions themselves and created local networks of indigenous people who would catch animals for them. They were interested in live animals, to which hunting methods had to be adapted, but the local environmental impact was the same: the animals left the area.

There are no exact quantitative data on how many tigers, leopards, and clouded leopards were caught by animal trappers in the "Malay" world during these years. Given the growing number of zoos and circuses and the high death rate of these animals in Europe, we may assume that demand was high and probably constantly rising, although recessions did slow the trade. It is likely that hundreds of big cats from these areas were shipped to the United States and Europe.[76]

Summing up, it can be said that although hunting tigers and leopards by Europeans did not reach the levels of British India, it was not absent, and it increased considerably after 1870. This applies to Sumatra and, to a lesser extent, Java. The professional animal catchers never went to Java, because big game had become scarce or at least very difficult to capture, but people like Buma, Ledeboer, and Patrick may have made up for this. Leopards in Java were less scarce and were still avidly hunted in the 1930s.

Bali, where Dutch influence had been limited prior to 1900, became a popular tiger hunting ground for Europeans after the turn of the century. Around 1935 tigers there were hunted so intensively that some experts predicted that they would become extinct within a few years. The professional animal catchers did go to Malaya, but it is possible that they did not get all that many tigers. At least one author stated, in 1905, that "of tiger-hunting there is but little," and another one, writing about the 1930s, said, "There are greater difficulties in Malaya than elsewhere in bagging a tiger." So it is at least questionable that European tiger hunting in Malaya increased all that much.[77]

By the First World War the period of growth in European hunting was over. Three elements may have been responsible for this process. First, military intervention in the Indonesian Archipelago was much less important after c. 1910, and it may be assumed that hunting by the military decreased. Second, the creation of European-run estates also slowed down. In Java, the creation of forest reserves and the growth of indigenous agriculture had claimed most areas where new estates could have been staked out. In the Outer Islands similar processes operated, and many estates had gone bankrupt because operating them on an economically sound basis had proved more difficult than had been anticipated.

Third, authorities began to limit hunting by law: the first ordinance for the protection of wild animals was published in 1909. Although the ordinance was hardly effective outside Java, it recognized that the state had a role to play in the protection of endangered species. Another step in this direction was the establishment of the first nature reserves in 1919. More rigorous game laws were published in 1924 (introducing hunting permits) and 1931 (forbidding the export of a large number of wild animals or their products).

Finally, in 1932 an ordinance for the creation of wildlife reserves was put on the Statute Book. Similar developments took place in Malaya. Although tigers and leopards were never regarded as protected game, they profited, of course, from the creation of wildlife reserves. The game protection laws probably slowed down the activities of professional animal catchers, as it was—supposedly—much less worth their while to go after tigers and leopards alone (Foenander 1952; Boomgaard 1993a, 1999). European tiger hunting had certainly not stopped at the eve of the Second World War, but life had been made more difficult for serious hunters.

Iron and Steel

Two additional factors were closely linked to the European presence and may have had a marginal influence on tiger and leopard mortality: the introduction of the iron (or steel) tiger-trap (sometimes called gin-trap) and the introduction of the motorcar.

The iron tiger-trap, constructed like a giant mousetrap, which closed shut when a tiger set one foot in it, was mentioned for the first time in 1896. The traps were produced by a factory in Haynau, Germany, and could be bought in Batavia for f. 30 or f. 40. They were used by the plantation owners in Sumatra (Aceh, Asahan, Deli, and Padang) and somewhat later also in Java (Priangan, Besuki). Originally, the Government stimulated their introduction, but later on their use seems to have been forbidden as being too dangerous. Various late examples of the use of these things suggest that this prohibition was not always effective. Due to their high cost, iron and steel traps were probably mainly used by (Indo-) Europeans. There is only one known example of villagers buying such a trap, in south Sumatra probably in the 1940s or 1950s. Somewhat comparable, because it also was made of steel, was the steel wire-noose snare introduced and publicized by the British Military Administration in Malaya in 1945–46.[78]

From about 1915 onward, tigers were sighted in the beams of car headlights, thus presenting an easy target for someone with a firearm. Also, tigers were being killed because they collided with a car (at night). Tigers were

The arrival of the motorcar. From 1915 onward tigers were reported as colliding with cars or being shot from them. Cars also made for easier transport of the trophies. This photograph was taken in Sumatra in the 1930s. Denninghoff Stelling 1966

sighted from cars during the day as well, but perhaps not as easily shot. Similar information comes from French Indo-China.[79]

The White Hunter's Impact

European tiger hunting, particularly between 1870 and 1915, seems to have made a difference, at least in Sumatra, Java, and Bali, and perhaps less so in Malaya. In most areas, although not in Bali, the increase in European private hunting was over with the First World War. Tiger and (clouded) leopard hunting probably remained more or less at the same level until the Depression of the 1930s, when a (slight?) drop must have occurred.

In Java, European private hunters probably came too late to have much of an impact, although the bounties and the guns and rifles almost certainly did. The fairly rapid disappearance of the tiger noticeable since the 1850s had been set in motion before Europeans had become active participants, and they do not seem to have done much more than rounding up the last stragglers.

It certainly could be argued that the Dutch in the Indonesian Archipelago were less fascinated by and given to tiger hunting than were the British in India. But they did hunt tigers, and other Europeans and Americans made up for the lack of enthusiasm displayed by the Dutch. To the tigers it may not have mattered that much whether they were killed or captured by Dutch or by other Western private hunters.

7

Tiger and Leopard Rituals at the Javanese Courts, 1605–1906

The rulers of central Java did not often go on tiger hunts and never personally killed tigers or leopards. Instead, they had tiger-killing rituals. This chapter traces the history of two such rituals, involving tigers and leopards, enacted at the royal courts and in some regional centers of Java.

Rituals are about the social order and the cosmic order, reproduction and the ancestors, life and death. Rituals reflect, often in a convoluted way, natural and supernatural constellations, but also try to influence them. As most of these realities and beliefs are subject to change, rituals cannot be expected to remain unaffected. It is even worth contemplating the question as to whether rituals are, indeed, agents of change themselves. Finally, rituals can mean different things to different groups, and the social order of the ruler is not necessarily the social order of the peasantry. Given all these premises, it seems reasonable to expect a complicated interplay of changing realities, beliefs, and rituals.

Evidence related to the rituals can be found as early as 1605 and as late as 1906, providing a basis for reconstructing the development of the rituals themselves and of the relationship between them, with special attention to local variation. Moreover, I link these developments to changes in Javanese society at large. Finally, I present some speculations regarding the changing and sometimes group-specific symbolic meaning and value of these rituals. Often it is not possible to know what various performances meant to the people concerned, and, unlike modern anthropologists, scholars dealing with the past are not in a position to ask them. However, some older interpretations, sometimes based on just a handful of references and suffering from a lack of attention to detail, can be discarded by a simple chronological presentation of the data.

The Animals, the Rituals, and the States

The two rituals to be analyzed in this chapter are the fight between a tiger/ leopard and a buffalo, and what could be called tiger/leopard sticking. In both ceremonies the tiger is often a real tiger, but it could also be a leopard; sources often did not make the distinction between these animals.[1] During the later part of the nineteenth century, observers increasingly used the terms "panther" and "leopard" for the black leopard and the spotted leopard, respectively. In this chapter I will use the term "tiger" in a generic sense, except where it is necessary to specify that the discussion refers to a real tiger.

The buffalo in the tiger-buffalo ritual is really a water buffalo (*Bubalus bubalis*), which was perhaps introduced in Java in its domesticated form a long time ago (but it may have been indigenous) and had become feral in some areas. European sources almost invariably use the term "buffalo"; they sometimes specify that a "wild" (feral) buffalo was used.[2] Occasionally, a "wild bull" was pitted against a tiger; this was the *banteng* (*Bos javanicus*).

The first ritual to be described briefly is the tiger-buffalo (*sima-maésa*) fight. The buffalo is led to a large cage or an enclosed place near the palace. Then a tiger in a small cage is placed near the opening of the enclosure, after which his cage is opened. Usually, the tiger has to be forced to leave his cage, and both animals have to be "stimulated" to start fighting. As a rule, after a few skirmishes, the buffalo wins by taking the tiger on its horns and crushing or goring him.

The second ritual is the *rampogan sima* or *rampog macan*, to be rendered in English as tiger sticking. In this event, a number of small cages with tigers are placed on a large square near the palace, surrounded by three or four rows of spearmen. One cage is opened, and the tiger is forced to leave it. The tiger tries to find an opening in the ranks of spearmen; failing that, he attempts to jump over their heads. Usually, he is caught on the points of the spears and thrown back; this is repeated until the tiger is dead or totally exhausted. The same procedure is followed with the other tigers. Occasionally tigers have managed to escape.

Around 1630 there were only three important political entities left, all of them of a recent origin. Mataram, which by then covered central Java and parts of western and eastern Java, was the largest state. Its rulers were styled "Sultan" or "Susuhunan." The capital of the state frequently moved to another spot. The remainder of the island comprised the sultanate of Banten in the west and the city of Batavia, between Banten and Mataram, founded by the Dutch East India Company (VOC).

Between 1677 and 1705 Mataram lost its influence in western Java (Priangan, Cirebon) and the island of Madura, to the northeast of Java, to the VOC. The sultanate of Banten lost much of its independence. During and after a civil war ending in 1755, Mataram had to cede the entire north coast and most of its eastern districts to the VOC. The remainder, the southern part of central Java, was divided between the Susuhunan of Surakarta (Solo) and the Sultan of Yogyakarta (Yogya). The area of these so-called princely states, or Principalities, was seriously reduced in 1812 and again after the Java War, which lasted from 1825 to 1830.

Early Testimonies

No mention is made of either ceremony in the numerous and detailed Javanese sources predating the seventeenth century, nor in the Chinese and Portuguese sources that deal more or less extensively with Java. The first reference to a tiger in a ceremonial context dates from 1605. Edmund Scott, head of the British establishment in the town of Banten (western Java), was present during the prolonged festivities surrounding the circumcision of the young Sultan of Banten. When the prince of Jakatra arrived to pay his respects, a procession was staged of many "strange animals" in cages, placed on buffalo-drawn carts, "among which was one furious beast, called by them a *matchan*." Scott's further description makes it clear that this was a real tiger.

The next reference, dating from 1620, is more detailed and contains some basic elements of the tiger-sticking ritual as it would develop later on. Two Dutchmen, imprisoned in the tollgate of Taji, near the capital of the central Javanese kingdom of Mataram, wrote to the Governor-General of the VOC in Batavia that the ruler of Mataram, Sultan Agung, had sent out his people to capture 200 tigers, in order to have his men fight them.[3]

We cannot be sure that the prisoners in the tollgate, even though they were not imprisoned all the time, actually witnessed these fights. Fortunately, the next reference comes from someone who undoubtedly was an eyewitness. Rycklof van Goens visited the court of Mataram five times between 1648 and 1654 as a VOC ambassador. He tells us that the ruler—Sunan Amangkurat I (r. 1646–1677)—sometimes organized fights at the "Tournament Square" between *banteng* and tiger or between banteng among themselves. Van Goens was favorably impressed: these were both hard and cruel fights, and well worth seeing.

The "Tournament Square" must have been the *alun-alun* (called the *medan* in the Malay-speaking areas and India), which was an unpaved outer courtyard found outside the gate of every royal palace and residency of a regent.[4] Jousting tournaments, a tradition dating back at least to the early fifteenth century (but perhaps not much earlier, as they are not mentioned in the fourteenth-century *Negarakertagama*), were held regularly at the central Javanese courts at least until the beginning of the nineteenth century, sometimes on the same day as the *rampogan sima*. It seems that the lance tournaments, at least at the princely courts, did not survive the Java War.[5]

Van Goens's testimony is the earliest evidence for the *sima-maésa* ritual, albeit with a banteng instead of a buffalo. This is the only mention of banteng-banteng fights at a central Javanese court.

The palace of Sunan Amangkurat I at Plered is the first one for which we have evidence for the existence of a permanent tiger cage. For the later capitals—Kartasura, Surakarta, and Yogyakarta—sufficient contemporary evidence indicates permanent tiger cages in the compound from 1686 onward. They were always located in a corner of the northern outer courtyard, at least since the nineteenth century always in the southeast corner.

The tiger cages were fairly large and could contain a considerable number of animals. Around 1850, the tiger cage of the Surakarta palace usually held seven, eight, or nine tigers, which made for high mortality. The cages must have been quite large by the early eighteenth century, because in 1703 Sunan Amangkurat III (r. 1703–1705/8) locked his uncle Pangeran Puger and the latter's family members in the tiger cage of the Kartasura court.

In the early years of the twentieth century, when tiger rituals were no longer performed at the central Javanese courts, the Yogyakarta palace had various, probably smaller permanent cages, which by then (1900, 1907) almost always contained only leopards, as the real tiger had become rare. In 1915, the tiger cages of the Surakarta palace had disappeared; it was reported that the last captive tigers recently had been taken to the City Park.[6]

One is tempted to assume that the presence of permanent tiger cages at the central Javanese courts, at least from 1686 onward but possibly even earlier, points to the regular occurrence of tiger rituals. However, it is also possible, as will be shown presently, that the tigers were kept prisoner in order to demonstrate the king's power over his rival, the King of the Forest, and, by extension, over "wild" nature.

Nicolaus de Graaff, the first contemporary European to describe the permanent tiger cage in 1686, is also our sole authority for the occurrence of tiger-tiger fights at the Kartasura court. If we combine this reference with the one—also unique—given above on banteng-banteng fights at the Plered court c. 1650, we may perhaps conclude that this was a time of experiments with animal fights. No fixed ritual had taken root as yet. This should caution us against far-reaching symbolic interpretations of these rituals, based on the tiger-buffalo combination of the ritual as it "solidified" later on.

Finally, the Sultan of Banten also kept tigers in his palace (1682; cf. Chapter

5). There is no evidence, however, that he used them for animal fights or for rampog rituals. It is perhaps not a coincidence that, at least in 1605, the Sultan, unlike his Mataram colleague, did participate in tiger hunts (cf. Chapter 6).[7]

Rituals in the Eighteenth Century

The record includes some fascinating though perhaps not entirely trustworthy particulars regarding Amangkurat III, the ruler who locked his uncle in a tiger cage. In 1703, according to Valentijn, the Sunan built a little house made of stone or brick on his alun-alun, where he could safely watch the fight between a thousand naked women and a number of tigers. Certainly, Valentijn cannot have been an eyewitness to these events, as he was not even in the Archipelago at the time. Moreover, Amangkurat III was anti-VOC and therefore unpopular among contemporary Dutch authors. This story might reveal more about Valentijn's vivid imagination than about Amangkurat's inclinations, yet it would be unwise to discount the story entirely. It is probably an exaggerated account of a punishment meted out by Amangkurat to Raden Ayu Lembah. There is a drawing of three of her (naked female) servants in a cage with three tigers, an event that should have taken place in the same year, 1703.

Valentijn had more to say about the role of tigers at the court of Mataram. As he visited Java several times and remained there, particularly in 1706, for a number of months, he may have witnessed some of the things he described. He is the first observer to mention what could be called a "trial by tiger," a cross between an ordeal and a punishment. If a royal scion or a member of the high nobility had done wrong, he was sometimes permitted to fight a tiger with a ceremonial dagger. If he worsted the tiger, he was allowed to live. Valentijn is also the first to notice the "execution by tiger," in which criminals were thrown to tigers (or elephants). After Valentijn's reference, which must be dated 1706 or earlier, buffaloes, crocodiles, elephants, or snakes are no longer mentioned as executioners, a role that earlier sources had attributed to them. This role fell now exclusively to the tiger. Perhaps the seventeenth century was also in this respect an age of animal experiments.[8]

Trial by tiger and execution by tiger are mentioned in various sources of a later date, sometimes by Dutch or Javanese eyewitnesses. In two instances, a Javanese sentenced to fight a tiger was pardoned after intercession by a Dutch official. In both cases, a tiger-buffalo fight was staged instead of the execution. Raffles mentions a case of a criminal who had fought so valiantly, first against a real tiger and then with a leopard, that the ruler made him a *mantri*.[9]

Finally, another example of trial or ordeal by tiger can be found in Mataram's banishment policy. If the ruler wanted to be rid of a member of the

Tigers and naked women. "Sunan Mas [Amangkurat III] gloating over the punishments and cruelties being inflicted on his orders, 1703." Copy of an undated Javanese painting. The story behind this scene is no doubt the source of Valentijn's exaggerated account of tigers being pitted against one thousand women. Collection KITLV

nobility, he banished him to the "wild" areas of Lodoyo or Aya, in the expectation that tigers would eat him.[10]

References to post-1800 trials or executions by tiger are based on erroneous interpretations of older sources. This form of execution had become virtually obsolete when, in 1812, the British abolished it by treaties with central Javanese rulers.

The earliest evidence regarding a tiger ritual from an indigenous source, the *Babad Tanah Jawi* (*Chronicle of the Land of Java*), must be dated around 1700. When Sunan Amangkurat II (r. 1677–1703) suffered from a serious paralysis of the legs, he took a vow to organize a large tiger-sticking ceremony.

Although references to a rampogan sima ritual, or something from which it may have developed, date from 1620 and 1700, we owe the first description of the event to Valentijn. He calls it a tiger fight and notes that it also called tiger catching. On the occasion of a general meeting of the royal princes and the nobility, a number of solid structures were built for the ruler, the princes, and their women, on an open field. Then, about 10,000 pikemen went to an area where a tiger had been spotted in order to surround it and drive the tiger to the place where the Sunan was waiting. When the tiger had been encircled entirely, he tried to escape and was caught on the pikes. Usually, one or two Javanese lost their lives in these encounters.

If this is an accurate description of what happened, then at this time the tiger-sticking ritual differed notably from the nineteenth-century "model" sketched above. The location of the action was apparently not the alun-alun, but it must have been somewhere outside the capital. It was, indeed, a tiger hunt—Valentijn's "tiger-catching"—more than anything else. It is important to note that the ruler did not participate in the hunt, even in the final stage.

It is not until the 1780s that sources record another description of a rampogan sima, this time from Surakarta. The ritual seems to have evolved in the direction of the nineteenth-century "model." The place of the action seems to be the alun-alun, where the ruler appeared regularly (every Saturday?) for a spectacle that usually began with a lance tournament "and ended with a rampogan sima, in which the Sunan's men, armed with pikes, formed a square around a tiger, advanced on it together, and killed it." Although the ceremony is now "localized" and confined to the palace grounds, it still contains elements of the hunt, albeit of a tiger apparently captured beforehand and no doubt stored in the permanent tiger cage.[11]

After Van Goens's testimony, dated c. 1650, Valentijn is the first one to mention the sima-maésa fights, which he may have witnessed in 1706. He observes that the ruler occasionally pitted tigers against buffaloes, wild oxen (that is, banteng), and other animals. The next reference in time dates from 1739, when Sunan Pakubuwana II (r. 1726–1749) visited the tombs of his ancestors in Kota Gede and Imogiri. The Sunan, who had received a lioness as a gift from the Governor-General, staged a fight between this animal and a buffalo or banteng. The lioness lost.[12]

These early-eighteenth-century descriptions are the last ones to mention banteng in the context of the tiger-buffalo fight. With one exception, dated 1843, all later references are to buffaloes.

There is a dubious description, dated c. 1775, by J. S. Stavorinus, who seems to have mixed a tiger-buffalo fight with a tiger-sticking ritual. It is also possible that he did indeed witness a rare attempt to combine both rituals. His testimony is important, because he is the first one to mention the "formal" row of pikemen, four deep, who surrounded the field of action. His description is supposed to refer to a tiger-buffalo fight, but the row of pikemen is an element that, at least in later descriptions, belongs to the tiger-sticking ceremony (the tiger-buffalo fights took place in a large cage). This also applies to his description—again, the first such one—of the persons who had to open the tiger cages and then had to make the formal greeting to the ruler. They were permitted to walk slowly back to the circle of pikemen only when the ruler had given a sign to that effect.

Our next witness is the Swedish naturalist Carl Thunberg, who visited Java in 1777–78. According to Thunberg, the Javanese princes, on the occasion of public festivities—possibly the three annual court festivals—staged various shows ("spectacles") for the people, including fights between wild animals. He himself witnessed a fight between a tiger and a buffalo, where the latter, hesitating to attack his adversary, was goaded into action by being whipped with a type of leaves that caused blisters.

Thunberg's description is important because it links the tiger-buffalo fight with public festivities. For 1783, we find an explicit link between one of the three big annual court festivals and a tiger-buffalo fight at the Yogya court, the Dutch Resident being present.[13] Visits to the courts by high VOC representatives were another reason to stage a tiger-buffalo fight.[14]

A 1792 source records, probably for the first time, a tiger-buffalo fight in Yogya followed by a rampog macan.[15] The tiger who lost but survived the tiger-buffalo fight subsequently was used, along with two other tigers, for a rampog. A few thousand men, armed with pikes, had formed a square, in the center of which three tiger cages had been placed. The tiger who had survived the buffalo was so exhausted that he did not care to participate in the ceremony; he was finished off by ten men. Although it is not explicitly mentioned, this might be the first example of the rampog as it would be described so often in the nineteenth century. If the men had advanced on the tigers—as they had in the 1780–90 description—instead of waiting for them to jump into the pikes, it would not have been necessary to mention the finishing off of the exhausted tiger. Raffles, who was the first one to give a vivid and extensive description of the nineteenth-century "model," also mentions the finishing off of tigers tired from a sima-maésa fight.[16]

In the nineteenth century the tiger-buffalo fight followed by tiger sticking, now divested of its last hunting features, would become the classical combination at the central Javanese courts. Apparently, the link between the lance tournament and the rampog macan had been broken, although the tournaments would continue up to the eve of the Java War. The last example of such a tournament being followed by a rampog macan dates from 1788, when Greeve visited Yogya.

Finally, just before the century closes (1798), evidence indicates that the regents of the areas ceded to the VOC in 1743–45, namely the north coast and the eastern districts, had started to imitate their former sovereigns. They were now also staging tournaments, animal fights (including tiger-buffalo fights), and rampog rituals for their European visitors. Before 1745, these ceremonies had been royal prerogatives, and for regents it was forbidden even to own tigers, along with other regalia, such as elephants, wild buffaloes, dwarfs and otherwise deformed people, and cannon above a certain caliber. If such regalia came into the hands of a regent, he had to present them to the ruler.[17] Throughout the nineteenth century and until the early decades of the twentieth, elephants, dwarfs, and other anomalous people would be part of the royal pomp in Solo and Yogya, when the Sultan and the Susuhunan came out for the major annual court festivities. They seem to have survived the tigers and their cages by a few years.[18]

The first description of tiger rituals being enacted by regents comes from the journey of Sebastiaen Cornelis Nederburgh, who, as Commissioner-General, visited a large number of Regencies along the northeast coast in 1798. Apart from more peaceful artistic demonstrations, he was also treated to dancing/boxing/fencing shows, horse races, lance tournaments, rampog macan, and a wide variety of animal fights, only some of which were of the "royal" tiger-buffalo kind. Tiger cats are mentioned a number of times, perhaps as a kind of poor man's tiger. The rampog macan described in this source is the one of the "model," where the tiger jumps into the pikes. Nothing is recorded of a tiger-buffalo fight followed by a tiger-sticking party, nor the tournament-rampog combination. Evidently, the regents copied the behavior of their former overlords, but the rituals were far from perfect copies of the court ceremonies. Staging a successful tiger-buffalo fight or rampog macan required experience, skill, and money. One of the skills required was catching a tiger alive. To this end, the rulers of Mataram and their successors from Solo and Yogya could, at least since 1744, engage the Tuwa buru people, professional catchers of deer and tiger (cf. Chapter 6). It could well be that the regents were insufficiently equipped for the tiger rituals and therefore had to make do with tiger cats and other substitutes.[19]

The appearance of tiger rituals in Regencies outside the Principalities might also be linked to the fact that after 1745–55 these regents were no longer under the obligation to provide the central Javanese rulers with tigers. As an unchecked proliferation of tigers may have posed problems to the peasantry, it is not unthinkable that the regents decided to go on catching them, but now for their own tiger rituals. However that may be, one gets the impression that both European and Javanese officials did all they could to entertain the Commissioner-General. Although it would be unwise to draw a sharp line between ritual and entertainment, the latter element seems, in this case, to have been more important than the former.

Changing Rituals

With the tiger rituals on the verge of their nineteenth-century "solidifica-tion," the turn of the century seems to be a good vantage point for some re-flection, before continuing the chronological narrative.

It is unlikely that either ritual predated the seventeenth century. They are, therefore, not of "a very ancient origin," as was suggested by Vincent Houben (1994, 82), who based his opinion on the mistaken assumption that a cere-mony must be very old if a part of the ceremony is formulated in Old Javanese.

The story of the tiger rituals clearly demonstrates that rituals are in flux, shedding some of their features, and merging with other, possibly older ele-ments. As there does not seem to have existed an indigenous Javanese tradi-tion of ceremonies in which tigers played a major role, the question arises, Where did these later rituals come from? I can think of two possible answers, one related to the quest for safety from marauding and man-eating tigers and the other one to reasons of state—answers that are not mutually exclusive and can be easily combined.

Tigers were already a threat to humans in early-seventeenth-century Java. There is no hard evidence that central and eastern Java were equally terrorized by tigers during this period, but they must have been numerous, given that Sultan Agung's people captured 200 specimens in three months in 1620. Un-like the late-sixteenth- and early-seventeenth-century Moghul emperors, the central Javanese rulers were no tiger hunters. They did hunt extensively, sometimes for months on end, but they did not go after tigers (cf. Chapter 6). If the king was not a tiger hunter and if it was, nevertheless, desirable to rid the country of tigers, ritual killings presided over by the king seemed to be a perfect solution. The more so as Mataram, in the early seventeenth century, was a young and aggressive state, bent on expansion, where rank at court was inti-mately linked with one's place in the military, and where prowess in danger-ous encounters was at a premium.

This would explain the 200 tigers killed in 1620. It would also explain the seventeenth- and eighteenth-century rampogan sima, before it lost its hunting characteristics. Its move from the countryside to the alun-alun somewhere during the eighteenth century might have to do with increased population densities around the capitals. Under such circumstances, tigers would move away from the royal palace, and it would be necessary to stage the ceremony henceforth with captured animals. The alun-alun was, of course, a perfect set-ting for this restyled ritual, given the fact that it could be enacted here in com-bination with a lance tournament, emphasizing its "prowess" aspect. It was also the stage of the tiger-buffalo fights.

The origins of these fights date to the early seventeenth century, when the young state of Mataram, with a shaky royal lineage and a country-bumpkin reputation in comparison with the richer and older states of the north coast, was badly in need of spectacular court ceremonies. It would be logical for the rulers to look to other more famous courts for examples to follow. The sultanate of Aceh could have served their purpose, or, even better, the court of Moghul India at Agra or Delhi. In both cases there were animal fights around 1600, often with elephants but also involving lions, buffaloes, bulls, and tigers.[20] Aceh may have imitated the Moghul court, so Mataram could have followed the Moghuls' example, either directly or indirectly. These were Muslim courts and therefore appropriate as models for Muslim Mataram. Mataram may have been an "agrarian" and "inland" kingdom, but Sultan Agung had sufficient diplomatic contacts to be aware of the activities of his more illustrious colleagues. Another possibility is that the Mataram rulers copied the "trial by animal" and "execution by animal" from the Moghuls or from Aceh's Sultans.[21]

As there was a shortage of elephants in Java, they were too expensive to be used in animal fights; given a total absence of lions, experiments with tigers, buffaloes, and banteng, in all possible combinations, were a logical choice. It would be unwise, therefore, to make too much of the symbolical significance of the tiger-buffalo pair for the Javanese before the "crystallization" of these rituals into the classical tiger-buffalo fights, probably somewhere around the middle of the eighteenth century. As noted, the banteng dropped out of the game after 1739 and before 1775. This is exactly the period when Mataram lost much of its territory to the VOC. It is likely that there was a sharp drop in the supply of available banteng, not only because so many areas had been lost but also because by then the remainder of Mataram was more densely populated than it had been in the seventeenth century.

The loss of the outlying regencies and the increased population density of the core areas may also have prompted the rulers to combine the two tiger rituals. When tigers are becoming scarcer, it makes sense to stage a tiger-sticking ceremony after a tiger-buffalo fight, because a tiger that survives the first ritual can be used in the second one.

Changes in the natural environment and in the political fortunes of Mataram, therefore, go a long way in explaining the "classical" form of the rituals under discussion. In the 1790s, the two rituals more or less merged, which was a logical step at this stage of their development. At the same time, they spread to the Regencies under the sway of the VOC, with a probable shift in emphasis away from prowess and pomp of state to entertainment. This, in turn, may have influenced the status of the rituals as they were staged at the courts, from the point of view of both the Dutch and the Javanese.

Rituals in the Nineteenth Century

For the early decades of the nineteenth century, we have the detailed and beautifully worded testimonies of two high British officials, Thomas Stamford Raffles and John Crawfurd, in Java during the British Interregnum (1811–1816). Raffles called the rampog at the courts an "amusement," as did Crawfurd, who used the term "diversion" for the tiger-buffalo fight. Raffles is the first, and possibly the only, author to state that, generally speaking, "the smaller species of the tiger" (that is, the leopard) was selected for the rampog macan.[22] One is tempted to assume that real tigers had become somewhat rare in the princely states and that their use in rituals had to be restricted to the tiger-buffalo fight, or else Raffles was mistaken. Raffles also mentioned that if a tiger survived the encounter with a buffalo, he was to be destroyed in a rampog. This seems to have become the new orthodoxy, at least at the courts of Yogya and Solo. The combination is mentioned on the occasion of the visits of several Governors-General to the courts.[23] Other Europeans also witnessed the combination of a tiger-buffalo fight and a rampog party at the central Javanese courts, for example, W. R. van Hoëvell (1840), Junghuhn, and J. Rigg (both 1844). In all these cases, the Residents of Solo or Yogya also were present.[24]

It is possible that tiger-buffalo fights and the rampog macan did not resume immediately after the end of British rule in 1816, when the territories of the central Javanese rulers had been reduced considerably. Just prior to his departure, Raffles had witnessed both ceremonies in Yogya in January 1816. The Dutch writer J. Olivier, who came to Java in 1817, also mentioned them, but he seems to have copied Raffles's *History*. When the Dutch traveler J. B. J. van Doren visited Solo in 1822, he was present during a conversation between the Susuhunan and the Resident. When the latter mentioned the rampog macan, which had not been performed for a number of years, the Susuhunan promised to stage one.[25]

Tiger rituals continued to spread to Regency capitals outside the princely states. As in 1798, however, they constituted only one item in a range of possible "amusements" and very seldom were part of the by-now classic combination of a tiger-buffalo fight followed by a rampog macan. Apart from the Regencies of the north coast and eastern Java, where these rituals were recorded in 1798, they now were also mentioned in many other Regencies, including those that had come under direct Dutch rule after the Java War.[26]

I have found only one example of a tiger-buffalo fight followed by tiger sticking outside the Principalities, namely that in Cilacap (Banyumas) in 1858, at the arrival of the new Resident of Banyumas. It is not clear whether this ceremony was organized by the regent or by the European officials.

Rampog macan. **Tiger-sticking ceremonies developed from tiger hunts in the central Javanese kingdom of Mataram. They could still be observed in the nineteenth century and even during the first few years of the twentieth century. The scene in this chromolithograph is probably a Regency capital, and the period is the 1850s or 1860s. Collection KITLV**

In 1862 a tiger ritual (tiger-buffalo fight) is mentioned to have occurred outside Java, in Palembang, on the island of Sumatra, where these rituals were probably not indigenous. In this case it is clear that it had been organized by the Resident. This also applies to Banyuwangi, Java, where the Assistant Resident staged tiger-buffalo fights c. 1870.[27]

Instead of being court rituals in which the indigenous rulers could display their warriors' prowess and the splendor of their courts, the tiger rituals had degenerated into entertainment for European visitors, staged in practically all Regency capitals, and sometimes even organized by the Dutch and exported outside Java. It is likely, though, that the rituals as they were enacted at the central Javanese courts remained somewhat more solemn than the performances in the Regency capitals (Hoëvell 1840, 299). In the latter places the tiger-buffalo fight was often a failure, and the regents or European officials sometimes added other animals for extra fun.

The proliferation of tiger rituals between 1830 and 1870 must have seriously depleted the stock of real tigers and leopards. And in fact, the Java tiger

Tiger-buffalo fight (left) and tiger sticking (right) in Cilacap, Banyumas, in 1858. The high bamboo cage on the left contains the water buffalo. The much smaller cage with the tiger is barely visible behind the spectators. The strange, inverted bathtub-like structure to the right contains the people who, should the tiger refuse to leave his cage, must force it out, either by prodding the animal or by setting fire to the cage. Jagor 1866

population decreased considerably during the second half of the nineteenth century, partly owing to the tiger rituals.

The period 1830 to 1870 is legendary as the time when the Cultivation System was instituted. Under this initiative, the colonial government geared a significant proportion of Java's agricultural sector toward export production. It does not seem too far-fetched to suppose that the Dutch took over not only the Javanese economy but also the rituals of Java's rulers in order to boost the authority of the regents, who were pivotal for a smooth functioning of the system of compulsory cultivation and corvee obligations. In the process, the Dutch introduced these rituals in places where they were unknown before, possibly adding new features as well, thus "inventing" age-old traditions.[28]

Precisely when and why the tiger rituals at the courts disappeared remains something of a mystery. One of the last reliable eyewitness accounts dates from 1862. The very last witness account is dated 1882 and refers to the classic combination of a tiger-buffalo fight followed by a rampog macan in Yogya. Thereafter, visitors and writers of compilations still mentioned court rituals, but these reports seem to have been hearsay. What may have confused these writers is the fact that the tiger cages and the tigers—mostly leopards by then—were still there, up to the early years of the twentieth century. The last accounts of tiger-buffalo fights outside the courts are dated c. 1870. [29]

It certainly seems that the tiger rituals had become rare after 1880, in keeping with the evidence that tigers had disappeared from the Principalities by then (cf. Chapter 10). For example, an 1881 source deals in great detail with all ceremonies enacted at the central Javanese courts, but it does not describe the tiger rituals.[30] Another source, dated 1883, states that the demand for living tigers had diminished greatly, owing to the fact that tiger rituals had become rare.

In only one area, the Residency of Kediri, is there reliable evidence that at least one ritual, the rampog macan, was still taking place after 1870. It is even possible that these rituals did not reach Kediri until the 1880s. In 1884, a rampog macan was staged on the occasion of the arrival of the railway to the town of Blitar, capital of the regency of the same name.[31] The rampog macan was also staged in the town of Kediri, capital of the regency and Residency of that name. Several witnesses described the rituals fairly extensively, and there are even some photographs of these latter-day rampog macan. In both centers, a festival commemorating the end of the period of fasting seems to have been the usual occasion for a rampog ritual. The last year with a tiger-sticking ceremony in the Kediri area for which there is a trustworthy witness is 1906.[32]

It is not difficult to explain, at one level of reality, why the tiger rituals disappeared almost everywhere in the 1870s, why they did continue in Kediri, why they came so late to this area, and why they stopped being staged in the early years of the twentieth century. The answer to most of these questions is, of course, that the supply of real tigers and leopards was crucial for the survival of the rituals. By 1880, real tigers had become very rare in the Principalities and in most other areas of central Java, Kediri being an exception. The rituals came late to Kediri because before 1870 it was an underdeveloped area, with very few Dutchmen with an interest in staging such ceremonies. In all probability, the rampog macan came to Kediri—at least to Blitar—with the railway. But even in Kediri real tigers (and possibly leopards) had become something of a rarity after 1900, which spelled the end of the rampog macan. The eruption of Mount Kelud, near Blitar, in 1901, may have hastened the disappearance of the big cats. Banteng, wild boar, leopards, and tigers were killed or left the volcano area just before or during the eruption (Koning 1919, 193; Wormser 1941, 180).

There are some difficulties with this explanation, if only because there were other areas around 1880 where tigers were still to be found in reasonable numbers, such as Banten and Priangan in western Java and Besuki and Ban-

Rampog macan in Kediri, c. 1900. *above,* Five tigers or leopards have already been killed, one tiger is "on stage," and three animals wait to make their entrance. *below,* After the party. Of the eight animals killed, only one is a tiger, by 1900 already rare in Java. Collection KITLV yuwangi in the east. In most of these cases, however, the areas concerned always had been underpopulated, and a tradition of staging such rituals was lacking. They were also largely outside the cultural sphere of influence of Mataram, which may have rendered the rituals less meaningful.

This explanation—the disappearance of the tiger—can be easily combined with causal links between the disappearance of the rituals and changes in the Javanese economy and society around 1870. The Agrarian Law of this year meant the beginning of the end of the Cultivation System. Henceforth, the colonial government was no longer directly responsible for the production of export crops, and it was no longer necessary to boost the prestige of the regents as props of a state-sponsored plantation system. In the Principalities, the Dutch tried to modernize the rule of the Sultan and the Susuhunan as well.

The courts had been losing territories and power during the eighteenth and early nineteenth centuries (1743–55, 1812, 1830), and it may well be that they adapted their need for ceremonial performances that emphasized prowess and the splendor of the royal lineage. The rulers had given up the trial and execution by animal around 1800; the lance tournaments had disappeared after 1830, the tiger rituals around 1880; the tigers-kept-prisoner would vanish shortly after 1900, the tiger-pens somewhat later; and finally, the elephants and the dwarfs disappeared. As the rulers were confronted with increasing financial difficulties, this list of abolished rituals and regalia can also be read as a series of cutbacks.

The Symbolic Value of Tiger Rituals

Raffles was probably the first European observer who discovered that there was more to the tiger-buffalo fights than met the eye. He wrote: "In these entertainments the Javans are accustomed to compare the buffalo to the Javan and the tiger to the European, and it may be readily imagined with what eagerness they look to the success of the former." The tiger is fierce and dangerous, but in the long run he is worn out by the buffalo, with its formidable staying power, although under normal circumstances a plodding, slow animal. Several European witnesses were aware that the Javanese reacted disappointedly when the tiger won.[33] The symbolic value of these encounters may have formed part of the process in which a number of possibilities—tiger-tiger, banteng-banteng, tiger-buffalo/banteng—was narrowed down to just one, namely the tiger-buffalo fight. Symbolism may have been important as early as 1709, when a tiger almost killed a buffalo in the presence of the Susuhunan and the VOC Commissioner. The Susuhunan had the fight stopped. Another sign that the Javanese—at least at the central Javanese courts—saw the buffalo as a symbol of themselves can be found in the fact that in at least two instances, buffaloes took the place of pardoned Javanese who were destined to fight tigers (1783, 1789).

One source suggests that the Dutch forbade the tiger-buffalo fights in the early twentieth century for political reasons, because the tiger always lost. This seems unlikely, since the tiger-buffalo fights seem to have disappeared before Indonesian nationalism became significant, but it is nevertheless interesting that such an explanation could be given, based on the testimony of a Javanese informant.[34]

If this was the view of the courts, perhaps to some extent shared by ordinary Javanese, one can also imagine that the ceremony had yet another meaning for the peasantry. They may have seen it as an encounter between agriculture (the buffalo, plow animal to many Javanese) and "wild" nature (the tiger), a conflict that in this ceremony was almost always resolved in their favor.

So in the eyes of the court the tiger was the outsider, the European (Dutchman), the rival power to Mataram. He was also a rival king in another sense: the lord of the forests, the wilderness, or even of "wildness" (a view also ascribed to the peasantry) and chaos and, by extension, the embodiment of evil. The ruler of Mataram, on the other hand, is the representative of civilization, order, and, by extension, of good.

One might expect the king of Mataram, as the representative of order, to challenge the lord of chaos, for which hunting seems the most appropriate form. This is indeed what the Moghul emperors did around 1600: They kept tigers (and lions) prisoner at their court, as they would have done with other rival lords. The same applies to the Sultans of Banten.

The kings of Mataram, however, did not hunt tigers. This unexpected behavior is related to the Javanese concept of power. The ruler had to exude power, which in Java had—and perhaps still has—the connotations of "refined," "aloof," "cool." It therefore would be improper for a Javanese king to show prowess in battle. By extension, he could not himself attack his major rival, the tiger, but should be seen supervising the hunt. His subjects were not always eager to attack tigers, given the supernatural properties of the latter, so a tiger hunt, developing into a localized rampog macan staged and supervised by a ruler sufficiently aloof so as to counter possible supernatural ill effects, was the perfect solution.[35]

The alun-alun, apart from being a practical location, was also an ideologically appropriate place for this ritual, at least if one agrees with Denys Lombard's interpretation of its symbolical meaning. He suggested that the alun-alun, with two fenced-in *waringin* trees (*Ficus benjaminica*) in its center, symbolized domesticated nature.[36] It is perhaps not a coincidence that the tigers surrounded by a square of pikemen seem to be a mirror image of the waringin with its fence.

If the Javanese ruler was regarded as refined, the Dutch were often seen as rude and coarse—attributes linking them with the tiger. Abdullah bin Abdul Kadir, writing about Malacca around 1810, remarked: "At that time there were still not many Englishmen in Malacca and people looked upon them as tigers because of their misbehaviour and aggressiveness" (Abdullah 1970, 72). It is unlikely that the opinion of the Javanese regarding the Dutch was much different.

The tiger not only represents evil; he also can *be* an evil person who has turned himself into a tiger—in other words, a weretiger. Belief in weretigers in Java is documented from the early nineteenth century onward but could be much older. In the nineteenth-century sources the weretiger is associated particularly with the forests of Lodoyo near Blitar and the village of Gadhungan, both in the Residency of Kediri (see Chapter 9).

Lodoyo has been associated with tigers at least since the seventeenth century. As noted, it was one of the areas to which the rulers of Mataram banished members of the nobility in the expectation that they would be eaten by tigers. As the tiger often leaves humans alone, the association in this particular area with "bad" or weretigers is not inexplicable.

Therefore, Kediri, apart from being a real tiger and leopard area c. 1900, was also regarded as a well-known weretiger region, perhaps owing to its past as an area of banishment. One is tempted to associate the popularity of the tiger stickings in Kediri up to the early years of the twentieth century with these weretiger beliefs, whereas these beliefs, in turn, may have been reinforced by the rampog macan.

Finally, the tiger should not be thought of as a purely negative force. When the rulers had people "judged" by tigers, both at the courts and in the areas of banishment, the tiger seems to represent a moral force, perhaps even the king himself. A guilty person would be killed, but the innocent would live. In the lives of the peasants, the ancestral tiger played a similar role. He protected "his" village, and no harm would be done to those who were virtuous and who followed the rules laid down by the ancestors. However, the ancestral tiger would punish trespassers of these rules (cf. Chapter 8).

Conclusion

We have witnessed the rise, diffusion, temporary "merger," and fall of two rituals, the tiger-buffalo fight and the tiger sticking (rampog macan) ceremony.

Neither can be traced in sources prior to the seventeenth century nor found in reliable eyewitness accounts later than 1906. The two ceremonies had been combined at the central Javanese courts between the late eighteenth century and the 1880s, and most descriptions, among which are the most detailed and evocative ones, have come down to us from this period. This abundance of latter-day eyewitnesses has obscured the relatively recent origin of the ritual in its "solidified" form and the separate origins of the constituent parts. It has also led to an overemphasis of the supernatural character of the rituals and to gratuitous references to symbolic meanings surviving from an age-old past.[37]

The tiger-sticking ritual seems to have developed from a tiger hunt supervised by the ruler, who did not take part in the actual hunt and who may have combined attempts to rid the countryside of marauding and man-eating tigers with an occasion for Mataram's warriors to show their prowess. When the tigers in the immediate surroundings of the capitals became rare, the rampog macan moved to the court, where it could be combined with another show of martial valor, the lance tournament. Meanwhile another ritual had been introduced to the royal court: fights between big and dangerous animals, particularly tiger, buffalo, and banteng, in all possible combinations, also performed at the alun-alun. The court of the young kingdom seems to have copied these ceremonies from older and grander courts, like those of the Moghuls and Aceh. In the second half of the eighteenth century the number of possibilities had narrowed down to the tiger-buffalo fight, always enacted in the presence of high-ranking Dutchmen.

In the late eighteenth century four developments, taking place roughly at the same time, shaped the "solidified" phase of the rituals. The rampog macan lost its last hunting features; it became disengaged from the lance tournaments; at the courts it became the sequel to the tiger-buffalo fight; and both ceremonies spread, though hardly ever in combination, to the capitals of the regents. During the nineteenth century, particularly between 1830 and 1870, a further geographical proliferation of the rituals took place, in a number of cases clearly on the initiative of Dutch officials. This was the period of the Cultivation System, during which the Dutch went out of their way to strengthen those features of indigenous society that were conducive to an uninterrupted flow of cash crops for the European market. One of these features was the authority of the regents. Without too much exaggeration, it can be said that the "age-old" rituals in the Regency capitals were by and large a Dutch creation.

Around 1880, the ceremonies disappeared all of a sudden, and only the rampog macan "survived"—having been introduced there recently—in one area, Kediri, where the last documented ritual was enacted in 1906. Apart from the fact that this was an area where tigers were still much in evidence, it was also weretiger country.

The disappearance of the rituals after 1880 was doubtless caused partly by their very success between 1830 and 1870: real tigers and, to a lesser degree, leopards were vanishing rapidly from the more accessible areas. At the same time, the courts may have adapted their public role to their reduced power and purse, while the Dutch colonial state was in the process of turning rulers and regents into civil servants. Private capital replaced the state as manager of the economy, and high population growth rates replaced the regents as suppliers of cheap labor. The need to enhance the regents' authority with pomp and splendor was gone.[38]

Tiger-buffalo fights originally were just one of many possibilities among the fights between large animals, but the increasing scarcity of banteng, combined with ritual attempts to defeat the Dutch, particularly after the VOC had reduced the power of Mataram in the real world (1677–1709), may have narrowed down these possibilities to the tiger-buffalo combination. The presence of the Dutch, therefore, may have been instrumental in shaping the "classical" form of this ritual.

The tiger representing the Dutch may be interpreted as a variation on an older and more universal theme in which the tiger stands for the forces of death and destruction and therefore chaos and evil, which threaten the social order (village, state) from outside. One assumes that this aspect appealed more to the peasants, who, during the rituals, repeatedly witnessed the defeat of the forces of death by the life-giving powers represented by the buffalo, the central Javanese plow animal. Less abstractly, king and subjects may have seen this ritual as a representation of the superiority of "culture" (agriculture) over "nature" (the wilderness).

With the standardization of the animal fights into the tiger-buffalo fight sometime in the eighteenth century and the increasing need for a more economical use of tigers, a "merger" with a previously unrelated tiger ritual, the rampog macan, seemed to become desirable. It was supervised by the ruler, who thereby could be seen to make the world safe for his subjects and to triumph, as the representative of order, over chaos. In a supernatural or moral sense it could be seen as an attempt to maintain the cosmic balance between good and evil. To spectators, the connotation of evil may have been linked particularly with weretiger beliefs. In its "localized" form, therefore, the rampog macan was a logical sequel to the tiger-buffalo fight.

It is the irony of history that during the nineteenth century, the Dutch, by then the real rulers of Java, used these rituals—in which they were killed in effigy—as a prop for the colonial state, and perhaps also as a means to get rid of the tiger. The rituals started to disappear when, in the most tangible sense, civilization had triumphed over wild nature and therefore tigers had become even more rare. On a higher level of abstraction the tiger had triumphed over the buffalo, in the sense that the Dutch were there to stay—at least for the time being. Neither the Dutch nor the courts were interested in a continuation of the rituals.

8

The Ancestral Tiger: From Protection to Punishment

In the Malay world, the majority of the population did not kill tigers unless the tigers had killed people or livestock first. Many people conceived of tigers as animals inhabited by human spirits, or, to be more specific, by ancestors, and we will now have a closer look at this belief.

Village Tigers

"I have been told that there are villages, visited daily by the tiger, where he will get a certain portion of meat, because that will keep him from causing people harm and from robbing them." Thus the Swedish surgeon J. A. Stützer, visiting the Cirebon-Priangan region (western Java) in 1786–87, wrote in his diary, presenting the first European testimony of the *macan bumi,* or village tiger (literally, "tiger of the land").[1] Stützer, who also reported even stranger tales, did not record his opinion of this curious piece of information. Given the overwhelming number of stories of atrocities committed by tigers in Java, it seems hardly credible that his informants could have come up with such a "tame" tiger tale. Did Stützer get his story wrong, or were the Javanese pulling his leg?

This and similar stories are encountered so often in later sources that one must conclude that Stützer accurately reported what his informants had told him. Around 1820, the Dutch writer J. Olivier Jz., visiting Java, came across a village in the Environs of Batavia (western Java), between the private estates of Tanjung-East and Tanjung-West, that according to the inhabitants was visited regularly by a macan bumi. The tiger daily entered the village in order to get his piece of meat, which was always left in a particular spot, without harming anyone. The Dutch scholar P. P. Roorda van Eysinga, writing about Besuki (eastern Java) in 1841, reported that the Javanese had told him of the existence of "good" tigers, dwelling in the neighborhood for a long time, who had never robbed the people of their cattle.[2]

In 1854, all the Residents of Java had to report to the Governor-General on the policy in their Residencies regarding tigers. The Resident of Yogyakarta (southern central Java) wrote, "The so-called *macan bumi*, a tiger said to have been born in the area around a particular village or [at least] belonging there, is honored by the villagers, who do not want him to be killed or chased, because he does no harm to people and cattle from the village, clears it from noxious game and even keeps alien tigers from invading the area." The Resident of Kediri (southeastern central Java) reported that in many villages tigers were being fed and that the inhabitants even prepared offerings for them.[3]

The phenomenon of the macan bumi was not restricted to Java, although the term probably was. Sophia Raffles, second wife of Thomas Stamford Raffles, accompanied him when he was Lieutenant Governor of Bengkulu, Sumatra. Writing about Sumatra, she commented, "When a tiger enters a village, the foolish people frequently prepare rice and fruits, and placing them at the entrance as an offering to the animal, conceive that, by giving him this hospitable reception, he will be pleased with their attention, and pass on without doing them harm." Apparently, Lady Raffles was not convinced that the tiger would be fooled by such a reception. Judging by the material from Java, she may have been wrong. However, perhaps one should make a distinction between feeding a tiger (with meat) and making offerings (of rice, etc.). One is tempted to assume that the first policy made for more satisfied, eventually perhaps even almost tame, tigers.

A reference from Malaya dated c. 1950 suggests that something akin to the macan bumi may have occurred there, too. Beyond the Malay world, Herman Wiele, a big-game hunter in India before 1925, stated that tribal groups in Mysore disliked European tiger hunters because they killed their "best friend." To these people, the tiger was a major provider of meat; they appropriated the game he had killed. Therefore, the village tiger, in the Malay world a protector of the village with whom the inhabitants were on terms of peaceful coexistence, was to these tribal people a prey-sharing partner.[4]

Another category of tigers was not as benevolent as the macan bumi, although still harmless to humans. Charles Whitney, a professional hunter and animal trapper active in India, Malaya, and Sumatra around 1900, observed, "The cattle killer is, in fact, by way of being sociable, prone to take up his abode in the jungle nearby a settlement where, on terms of easy friendliness with the village people, he lives and levies tribute of a cow or a bullock from every three to five days, according to the size and condition of the victim." John Hagenbeck, a German professional trapper working in India between 1885 and 1914, comes up with much the same story. Villagers regarded a cattle-killing tiger mostly as an inevitable nuisance, just as they did the tax-collecting state. One might add that the similarity between the king of the jungle and the king (Maharajah) of the people was not lost on the villagers. Not only did both rulers levy taxes, they also kept out other "kings." Coexistence was still peaceful, but it came at a rather high price.[5]

The tax-levying tiger who is left alone by the population is not encountered in the extensive literature on Java. Typically, the Javanese would never hunt a macan bumi or any other game-killer that had not harmed them or their cattle, but a cattle-slaying tiger would be relentlessly hunted down or at least trapped. Even in Sumatra there was a limit to the level of tolerance or lethargy-cum-fatalism (as the Dutch often called it) afforded a cattle-killer. A Dutch civil engineer, big-game hunter in his spare time, who spent most of his career in Sumatra between 1900 and 1930 mentions a village near the Semangka Bay that for many months had passively suffered the activities of a tiger killing cattle and dogs. However, when the tiger became more daring, walking around in broad daylight and even venturing into the village, the village head called in the help of the narrator (Schilling 1952, 79). Apparently, the price to be paid for coexistence was no longer acceptable.

There is one other dangerous animal in the Malay world with which the indigenous population coexisted peacefully, according to their own stories: the crocodile. This "village crocodile," who is fed and given offerings by the local population and who does them no harm, was mentioned for Java by many authors.[6] The village crocodile was also reported to exist in Sumatra. The testimony of Mohnike is particularly valuable because he was an eyewitness. In 1862, while visiting Bangka, he saw children playing around and even mounting two crocodiles on the bank of a river without being harmed by the animals. The local population told him that these crocodiles had been visiting the same location daily for many years, harming no one. In all these years no other crocodile had taken the life of a human or a pet, either. Having seen this with his own eyes, Mohnike wrote, "There can be no doubt that these animals, in particular cases, have a special knowledge of both specific local circumstances and certain persons, thus being harmless to the latter." This belief, and, for those who have been persuaded by Mohnike's eyewitness account, this phenomenon, was probably as widely distributed as was the crocodile. W. W. Skeat (c. 1900) reported it for Malaya: "The Malays fed it regularly, and said it was not vicious, and would not do any harm."[7]

What do we make of these stories? Cynics might argue that these stories were based almost entirely on hearsay, or that they reflect what Europeans found interesting or, at best, indigenous beliefs. However, Mohnike's first-hand account is quite impressive, and such stories on peaceful coexistence are perhaps less farfetched than one might be inclined to think. As long as they were being fed, tigers may not have been all that interested in cattle (often guarded), pets, and armed humans. Tigers even provided a useful service to villagers by killing wild boar and deer, known to damage the crops. Tigers have territories that they will defend against other tigers, which explains reports of them keeping out "alien" tigers.

This reasoning, to be sure, cannot be generalized for all situations where tigers (or crocodiles) were found in proximity to humans. Obviously, under certain circumstances a tiger will turn cattle-slayer or even man-eater. There-fore, village tigers and crocodiles were probably fairly rare phenomena. This is not inconsistent with the stories just told, which are often specific as to time and place.

Ancestral Tigers

The Indonesians themselves often were not satisfied with a rational expla-nation of the existence of the village tiger or the village croc. In many instances they told the European traveler, missionary, physician, planter, or civil servant that the village tiger was inhabited by the soul of an ancestor who in that guise protected his offspring. For Java, Olivier was the only observer to report this specific connection between ancestors and macan bumi (although many oth-ers made the link between ancestors and tigers in general). He was told that these tigers were ancestors who during their life on earth had prayed continu-ously to be turned into tigers after their death, for a period of 100 years or more, in order to protect their descendants from the attacks of other wild ani-mals.[8]

The ancestor-village tiger link is better documented for Sumatra. Heyne, visiting Bengkulu in 1812, wrote: "The heathenish part of them look upon those ferocious animals with reverential awe, perhaps with a kind of pride, as being animated by the souls of their forefathers and relations, which they feed and worship (to be sure at a distance)." Lady Raffles reported in the same vein.[9]

J. L. van der Toorn, a Dutch civil servant with Sumatran experience, wrote around 1880 that the Minangkabau (central Sumatra) believed that bad peo-ple became tigers or other animals after their death. In order to atone for their sins in their former life, they would be very helpful to members of their family. They would live near their old village, where they would be fed, although peo-ple would attempt to get rid of them. Such a tiger was called a *harimau jadi-ja-dian*. L. C. Westenenk, a high-ranking Dutch civil servant who held several po-

sitions in Sumatra, published similar stories in the early 1930s on ancestral village tigers, collected during a 25-year stay. Locally, the belief in the ancestral
tiger who helps and protects the villagers has survived until today.[10]

On the nineteenth-century Malayan Peninsula such a tiger was, according
to Sir George Maxwell (c. 1900), regarded as *keramat,* a being credited with supernatural powers, and in many cases it was imagined to be a reincarnation of
a deceased celebrity. Such animals would "treat the human inhabitants of the
district honoured by their presence with a benign consideration bordering on
condescension, and a child might drive away a *kramat* tiger that strayed too
near the cattle-folds." The following story, reminiscent of the report of tribal
foragers from Mysore mentioned above, was told about the Semang of Malaya,
also hunters-gatherers (cf. Chapter 6). There, according to the German anthropologist Paul Schebesta, the medicine men who were also ancestors could
turn into tigers after their death. "But such a tiger is not in the least dangerous
for members of the tribe, rather does he help them, e. g. by killing game for
them." Anthropologist Ivor Evans confirmed the existence of such a belief.[11]

Many European sources suggest that the people of the Malay world believed that tigers (and not only the macan bumi) might be inhabited by the
souls of ancestors. Therefore, they would not kill a tiger unless the animal had
"sinned." For Java, many authors who visited the island between the 1830s
and the 1940s described this phenomenon, sometimes called *sima leluhur.*[12]
After the first decade of the twentieth century such reports become rare, and
they almost invariably refer to isolated, quasitribal groups such as the Baduy in
western Java. Since by then the tiger had disappeared from most areas in Java,
this is not entirely unexpected. Nevertheless, even nowadays these beliefs
have not disappeared from Java altogether (e.g., Wessing 1986, 15–44).

The tiger as a reincarnated ancestor was also mentioned in late-nineteenth-
century Bali, where some Balinese were said never to kill a tiger, fearing that
they might kill an ancestor. For Sumatra, reports on the "generalized" ancestral tiger (*harimau roh*) started earlier and continued later than in Java, including into the twentieth century.[13]

Beliefs regarding "human" tigers in Malaya either were more varied and
complicated or else the European reports regarding these beliefs were more
confused than for Java, Bali, and Sumatra. It is certainly possible that these beliefs were, indeed, more varied, given the existence of various tribal groups in
addition to the settled Malays. Most tribal groups seem to see a link between
their shamans (medicine men/sorcerers) and tigers. The shaman is supposed
to have a "familiar" (familiar spirit) who is both a tiger-spirit and an ancestor-
shaman. The shaman is also credited by some with the ability to turn himself
into a tiger, both during his lifetime (as a weretiger) and after his death.[14]

Apart from this shaman-ancestor-tiger-spirit complex, several reports from Malaya argued that tigers were inhabited by the souls of human beings. At the beginning of the nineteenth century, John Newbold put it thus: "The Malays of the Peninsula have a superstitious aversion to slaying tigers, which are considered in many instances to be receptacles for the souls of departed human beings, nor can they be prevailed upon to make any attempt to do so until the tiger has committed the first aggression, by carrying off a man or some of their cattle. " Later in the century, Isabella Bird, who may have taken her cue from Newbold, came up with a broadly similar story. W. E. Maxwell, writing in 1881, asserted, "The Malay addresses the tiger as *Datoh* (grand-father), and believes that many tigers are inhabited by human souls."

What these reports have in common is that they are of an earlier date than the literature on "shamanic tigers." It is likely that the earlier observers reported on the beliefs of the coastal Malays. Later on, as the British penetrated into the tribal inland areas, reports came in on shamanic tiger beliefs. Later researchers stressed that Malay beliefs concerning tigers were incredibly confused and complicated. Evans, driven to distraction by all these stories, at one point exclaimed: "For all I know all tigers may be thought to be human beings who have assumed an animal shape."[15]

There is no evidence of the ancestor-tiger link in stories from mainland Southeast Asia (outside Malaya) and India, at least not in such a general fashion as in Java, Bali, Sumatra and—though somewhat modified—in Malaya, so this connection might be a typical Malay phenomenon. What one does find in tales about India and other places is the well-known Hindu belief in reincarnation, a topic to be addressed presently.

According to many authors, Indonesians would never use the normal word for tiger if one was supposed to be in the neighborhood. Instead, they would almost always refer to the tiger or the tigress as "grandfather" or "grandmother." Less often he was addressed with other kinship terms, such as "father," "uncle," and "older brother." Finally, they also used honorifics like "great lord," "Your Reverence," or "chief (or prince)" when talking about a tiger nearby.[16] The people of the Malayan Peninsula and other countries of mainland Southeast Asia had similar taboos. Various tribal groups in Malaya and Indochina did not use any name at all but stretched out their right hand in the shape of a claw: the sign of the tiger.[17]

Many European observers evidently regarded the use of kinship terms as proof that the tiger was seen as an ancestor or at least a member of the family. However, Indonesians often employ kinship terms, particularly names for older relations, as honorifics. The term "grandfather," therefore, can be used for a real grandfather but also for an older gentleman, and the fact that the tiger is addressed as "grandfather" should not be read as evidence that he was regarded as an ancestor. Nevertheless, the ancestor-tiger link in folk beliefs can be clearly established in many cases, though it was perhaps not as universal as some European writers believed.

Javanese versus Sumatran Beliefs

In 1854 the Resident of Madiun (southern central Java), asked to report to the Governor-General on the tiger situation in his Residency, wrote that only in Java, and not in the Outer Islands, was a tiger killed when he had assaulted people or livestock.[18] Since further information is not available for Bali regarding this point, the following discussion is necessarily limited to Sumatra, the only other Outer Island with tigers, and Java.

Late-eighteenth- and early-nineteenth-century writers on Sumatra emphasized that Sumatran people would capture a tiger only when he had injured or killed one of their family, and even then not always. As Marsden put it, "It is with difficulty they are prevailed upon to use methods of destroying them [tigers], till they have sustained some particular injury in their own family or kindred." E. Presgrave, traveling through Sumatra in 1817, when Raffles was Lieutenant Governor of Bengkulu, was even more cynical about the willingness of the local population to go after tigers: "Even when its jaws are polluted with human gore, a man cannot be prevailed on to kill it in order to prevent it from repeating its bloody feast. If a near relation have fallen its victim, he will perhaps be roused to revenge his death; yet sometimes, even in this, his superstitious prejudices and fears get the better of his ardent thirst for revenge."

Heyne, visiting Sumatra a few years earlier, was somewhat more positive in this respect. In his opinion the people were awed by tigers "as being animated by the souls of their forefathers until they happen to make away with one of the family—then certainly all connection is cut, and the spirit of revenge shows itself more powerfully than that of religion." The German E. von Martens, who traveled through the Palembang-Bengkulu area in 1862, wrote that some indigenous people believed that the spirits of their ancestors dwelled in the tigers and that, therefore, if a child was killed by a tiger, they said that the child had been called by his grandfather. According to Martens, they did not mind this and they would not seek revenge. Some 30 years later the Resident of Bengkulu reported that the population attempted to capture a tiger only if he had killed a human being, and that even then the people begged the tiger's pardon and tried to propitiate him with offerings. He also wrote that an old clan chief refused to accept the bounty for a dead tiger because he did not want to sell his ancestor. Finally, among the "tribal" Mamak around 1900, even when a tiger had killed a human being the people did not go after him but restricted themselves to offerings to the tiger's spirit.[19]

These Sumatran stories have one thing in common: They do not mention the slaying of livestock as a reason for going after tigers. Mohnike, writing in 1874, was the first author to report that the population of Sumatra (in this case Palembang) also caught tigers who killed livestock.[20] Only two other sources describe revenge on a cattle-killing tiger, and these examples may be atypical because they refer to Batak villages. The Batak certainly assumed that there were connections between (some) tigers and the world of the spirits. Nevertheless, they seem to have been less afraid of the tiger's (or the spirit's) revenge, as witness the fact that they decorated their village council houses with bones, skulls, and skins of tigers.[21] Such a daring attitude has not been described for other Sumatran groups, and at least for one Javanese region—Probolinggo (eastern Java)—the literature includes an explicit denial that people would keep tiger skins in their houses, because that would attract the tiger. Nor were the Batak afraid to travel through lonely, tiger-infested regions or to sleep on the soil in forests. One eyewitness even mentioned that they ate tiger meat.[22]

Most sources suggest that the people of Sumatra would turn to a tiger specialist (*dukun, pawang*) if a tiger was killing their cattle, and even sometimes when he had killed human beings. These people were skilled trap-builders, but even more importantly they were in the possession of formulas that would make a tiger walk into a trap or, if he would refuse to do so, would make him die from hunger and thirst.[23]

Finally, in an example mentioned above, dating from the period 1900 to 1930, a village plagued by a cattle-killer called in the help of a European official-cum-hunter (Schilling 1952, 79). The villagers did not go after the tiger themselves.

It seems, therefore, that the Resident of Madiun was at least partly right. Many Sumatran groups would not go after a tiger who had assaulted livestock (or dogs), and even the death of a human being would not always be avenged. In contrast, the Javanese normally would retaliate immediately if tigers had assaulted people or livestock, as mentioned with regard to the tax-levying macan bumi, who apparently was not tolerated in Java.

These impressions are borne out by the figures available for the period 1860–75 on tigers captured and destroyed by people and humans killed by tigers. If one accepts that the ratios between tigers killed and people killed reflect the willingness of the indigenous population to retaliate when humans and/or cattle have been attacked by tigers, in the sense that a higher ratio implies a higher willingness, then the difference between the Java ratio (5.3 tigers killed for 1 human) and that of Sumatra (3.3 to 1) confirms the greater reluctance of the Sumatrans to go after tigers who had "sinned." [24]

Why would Sumatrans have been more hesitant to kill a tiger, even one that has "sinned," than Javanese? There are a number of possible answers. In the first place, there were people in Sumatra who believed that some tigers were keramat, to be translated here as invulnerable. Such a belief may have been reinforced when tigers who had killed cattle or human beings refused to walk into traps. As these tigers must have had some experience with the ways of humankind, they may very well have been rather skilled in avoiding traps. [25] No references to invulnerable tigers have been found in Java.

Second, the expectation that the tiger's relations would avenge him if he had been killed may have been a motive to refrain from doing so. This belief is mentioned for Java, but rarely and only in early-nineteenth-century sources. Perhaps it became weaker when the tiger became more rare and people had less to fear from revenge undertaken by the relatives of a deceased tiger. For Sumatra, more references exist to this fear of the tiger's revenge, all of them in sources of a later date. [26]

Third, many references can be found to totemistic beliefs in Sumatra, or at least vestiges of these beliefs, but none regarding Java. Several Sumatran clans trace their ancestry back to a tiger and are therefore not allowed to eat tiger meat. [27] Such a taboo presupposes the existence of a taboo on killing tigers.

However, it may not be necessary to look only for supernatural explanations, as there is also a natural one. Given the fact that Sumatra was largely covered with impenetrable tropical rainforests, going after tigers was much more difficult there than it was in Java, where more deforestation had taken place and where many of the remaining (monsoon) forests had a less dense undergrowth.

Finally, the presence of a powerful inland state (Mataram) in Java and, more marginally, the VOC in Batavia, both interested in destroying tigers, may have had some influence. It is generally assumed that during the period under consideration, the inland states of Sumatra (Batak, Minangkabau) were rather weak.

The Ancestral Tiger as a Moral Force

Tigers who caused the local population no harm or limited harm were usually left alone. Many believed them to be ancestors who protected their offspring by chasing away foreign tigers and keeping out noxious game. Ancestors, however, are not always benevolent guardians. They are also guardians of the local customary law, which they themselves had laid down in the past. And just as a father punishes infringements of the rules of the house by his children, an ancestor comes down on any villager who breaches the village rules. In other words, the ancestral tiger is seen as a moral force. The corollary of this notion is that a person who is killed by a tiger surely must have done something wrong.

A number of sources cite the tiger as a moral force for Java who punishes several infringements of custom, such as undertaking an illicit love affair, entering sacred areas in order to cut wood or collect fruit, enacting taboo performances, and reciting a taboo poem. Moreover, villagers obviously used the punishing tiger as a mechanism of social control by threatening certain people, putting them to a test of some kind, or attempting to establish the truth regarding certain rumors. These stories were reported as early as 1832 and are still being told.[28]

Similar stories, dating from the same period, come from Sumatra.[29] There are also data on Malaya regarding the tiger as a moral force. The German Rudolf Martin, citing Logan (1847), argued that someone who had been killed by a tiger evidently had angered a *pawang* (shaman), who now, in the shape of a tiger, had meted out retribution.[30]

If the benevolent ancestor in the shape of a tiger is also believed to punish those who have sinned, two interpretive problems emerge. In the first place, if someone was killed by a tiger, was that a "foreign," a "bad," or a "mad" tiger,[31] or was it an ancestor with an axe to grind? In the second place, if the ancestral tiger has killed a villager, should this villager be avenged, or should his death be accepted as a just punishment for his wrongdoings?

Apparently, among the Javanese the idea of revenge predominated.[32] In Sumatra, the Batak went to great length to explain to the (dead, or at least trapped) tiger, or to local guardian spirits, why the tiger had to be killed. This was also mentioned regarding the population of Palembang. As noted earlier, the people of Bengkulu not only asked forgiveness for having killed a man-eating tiger, they also brought him offerings. J. C. Hazewinkel, working in Sumatra between 1925 and 1950, wrote that the population would kill the tiger, but his death would be surrounded by various rituals, and the people would explain to the dead tiger—who was still being addressed as "grandfather"—that killing him had been unavoidable. Finally, in Malaya ceremonies were performed for a tiger who had been killed in a trap, but he was also ridiculed.[33]

Most sources are rather ambivalent on these dilemmas, as the informants may have been. Obviously, there was no clear-cut solution for such situations, and it may be assumed that this ambiguity gave village leaders much leeway when they had to decide whether to prosecute a tiger who had killed a human being.

Reincarnation

The Hindu belief in reincarnation was mentioned by early European travelers in India. The central idea is that someone who has led a morally reprehensible life will be punished in the next life, as his or her soul will dwell in a tiger or another ferocious animal. This idea of punishment is alien to the Malay/Indonesian conception of the ancestral tiger.

The seventeenth-century traveler Edward Terry, who was in India between 1616 and 1619, wrote that certain groups thought that "the soules of the furious, cruell, and revengefull [go] into lyons, tygers, and wolves." John Fryer, visiting southern India between 1672 and 1681, reported that Brahmins believed that the soul of a tyrant would enter a tiger.

The Dutch government Commissioner H. A. van den Broek, touring Hindu Bali in 1817–18, wrote that, according to the local population, people could turn, after their death, into tigers (or other animals) as a punishment. As mentioned earlier, one reference exists to the ancestral tiger in Bali. More than half a century separates these two quotes, but it is nevertheless possible that these beliefs were not mutually exclusive. However, it is also possible that these reports signify local variations. Bali was as typical a tiger area as Java, Sumatra, and the Malayan Peninsula up to the second half of the twentieth century, but it deviated from other Malay tiger beliefs as well.[34]

Hindu beliefs could also be found in those parts of the Malay world that were no longer Hindu in religion. F. C. Wilsen wrote that the people in the Sunda area (western Java) were convinced that every evil-minded or bad person after his or her death was doomed to wander around in the shape of a tiger. He added that this belief also existed elsewhere in Java, but it was particularly strong in the west. The harimau jadi-jadian of the Minangkabau (central Sumatra), mentioned above, was supposed to be a bad person who became a tiger after his death and who in that shape wanted to atone for his sins. This seems to have been a Hindu belief in Muslim guise. The German Max Moszkowski reported a similar belief of bad people turning into tigers after their death from the adjacent Tapung/Siak area. According to him, some people believed that such a tiger would protect his human relatives, while others thought that the tiger went after them.[35]

The Batak, in northern Sumatra, were also reported to believe that after their death, bad people would turn into tigers. It is not clear, however, that this reflects Hindu influences. W. D. Helderman explained that people who had died had to cross a narrow bridge over an abyss in order to reach the land of the spirits. In this endeavor, one needed the help of other spirits, who would come to one's assistance only if one's offspring had made sufficient offerings. If this

Ancestral tiger as moral force? This tiger, shot in 1935 near Alahan Panjang, Sumatra's West Coast, was believed to have been inhabited by the soul of the *bilal,* the recently deceased village "priest" of Gerabag Datar. Members of his family, from whom he had been estranged during his life (and who had to pay his debts), feared his revenge. Collection KITLV

had been neglected, the wandering soul would fall into the abyss, where it became an "evil spirit," turning into a ferocious animal, like a tiger.[36] This sounds very much like an animistic explanation, not a Hindu one.

Spirit Tigers (Guardians, Familiars)

If turning into a tiger after one's death was seen in some areas as a punishment for "sinners," strangely enough it was conceived of by others as a prerogative of "saints." The Dutch expert on Islam, C. Snouck Hurgronje, and the Dutch physician J. Jacobs mentioned this belief as being held by some people in Aceh, in northern Sumatra. The Batak of Simalungun believed that old men who had led an exemplary life would suddenly disappear, turning into tigers, elephants, and snakes.[37] Other Batak, on the contrary, particularly those from the east, believed that bad people would turn into tigers after their death. Perhaps the Batak from the north, who were neighbors of the Acehnese, had been influenced by Islamic Acehnese concepts.

A related but much more widely held notion was that of tigers as guardians of sacred places, notably graves or shrines of holy or otherwise distinguished people or the abodes of important spirits. Such places are called *angker, buyut,* or *keramat.*

A famous location in western Java was Arca Domas, near Pondok Gede, on the Gede Mountain, in the region of what was then Buitenzorg, now Bogor. "Arca Domas" means 800 statues, which were supposed to be Prabu Siliwangi, the last "heathen" king of Pajajaran, and his 800 faithful followers (and/or children and grandchildren), who were turned into stone because they refused to be converted to Islam (c. 1580). Javanese and Chinese inhabitants of the region made offerings to these statues. In the late eighteenth century, when the Swedish naturalist Carl Thunberg visited the place (1777–78), it was still typical tiger country, but in the 1820s tigers came to the area only occasionally. This situation had given rise to the story that all tigers—even those from eastern Java—regularly made a pilgrimage to Arca Domas. By the twentieth century all real tigers had disappeared from the region, but there were still "ghost tigers," namely Prabu Siliwangi and his followers.[38]

There are many other places called Arca Domas in western Java, often believed to be ancestral tombs or at least abodes of ancestral spirits, which are linked to spirit tigers as guardians. There are also many other stories regarding Siliwangi and his men, and other Pajajaran royalty, who had turned into ghost tigers. In the oldest story related to this theme from a Dutch source, dated 1687, large numbers of tigers were said to be guarding the ruins of Pajajaran.[39]

In one of these stories, Siliwangi's offspring were turned into white tigers (cf. Chapter 2 on "real" white tigers), who became the guardians of the Cirebon court. Tombs of Hindu royalty were not the only graves in western Java with white tigers as guardians. A white tiger also frequently visited the shrine of Syekh Abdulmuhyi, a Muslim saint, located in the Priangan, particularly during the month of Mulud. The tiger was harmless to the visitors of the shrine.

Another interpretation of the white ghost tiger in western Java was given by the Dutch missionary S. Coolsma, who was told that an evil spirit in the shape of a white tiger dwelled in every graveyard. This could, of course, be a more orthodox Muslim version of the white tiger as the spirit of a Hindu king.[40]

The white tiger was also associated with two other vanished Hindu kingdoms, Daha/Kediri (southeast central Java) and Blambangan, in Banyuwangi (eastern Java). In the latter area the ruins of the *macan putih* (white tiger) town and temple—possibly dating from the sixteenth century—were visible until far into the nineteenth century.[41]

Kediri, and particularly the forest of Lodoyo (Lodhaya), was known as a weretiger area, and it may be assumed that there is a link between the white ghost-tiger beliefs and the weretiger stories in Kediri (see Chapter 9). Another footnote, related to Lodoyo, is also in order. I mentioned the story dating from about 1820 that tigers from eastern Java would occasionally visit Arca Domas near Pondok Gede. When the real tigers had disappeared from there entirely, probably in the 1860s, the story lived on, but in a slightly adapted form. Haji Moestapa, a former high Muslim dignitary of the Priangan, rendered the story in 1910 as follows. The people of the Priangan said that one should not make too many trips to the mountains during the month of Mulud, because that was the time that the tigers who stand guard in Ujung Kulon, the extreme south-west of Java, changed places with the tigers guarding Lodoyo (Moestapa 1946, 170). The idea of special tiger centers had been preserved, but Ujung Kulon, in 1910 still typical tiger country, had taken the place of Arca Domas.

Sacred places being guarded by (spirit) tigers were also found in Sumatra, as witness many references dating between the 1860s and the 1950s. Belief in these tigers was particularly rampant in Aceh, where almost all graves of "holy" men had their tiger guardians. Some people believed these tigers to be the spirits of the deceased, but others thought that they had been sent by Allah to stand guard. They would harm no one unless someone had aroused the holy man's ire. There is an example of guardian tigers who were obviously thought of as a "moral force" but could be bought off with a fine.[42]

Among the Batak the sacred places were the abodes of ancestral spirits and particularly of the highest-ranking spirits among them. Ferocious animals under their command supposedly surrounded these places. Some tigers were inhabited by these spirits, and tigers in general were regarded as executors of the ancestors' wishes. The Batak often referred to tigers as (evil) spirits or raw-meat-eating spirits. It was assumed that those who had been killed by a tiger had committed some grave offense against customary law. Even if a tiger had been killed, people showed him their rice measures as proof that they did not cheat. These examples demonstrate that the borderline between the ancestral tiger and the spirit tiger guardian may be rather vague, and that the two phenomena are related.[43]

Finally, the ghost tiger also was a guardian of sacred places in Malaya. Such a keramat place could be the dwelling of a spirit (*jin*), or the grave of a "holy" or otherwise important person. A *rimau keramat* (ghost tiger) could be the spirit of the deceased or a tiger with whom the person who was buried there had had a special relationship. Some of the ghost tigers were white. Also, it was thought that one could distinguish the prints of a ghost tiger from those of a normal one.

The belief that souls of deceased kings, chiefs, noblemen, and priests entered into tigers was not necessarily linked to graves with tiger guardians. In a number of references throughout the Malay world, such high-status figures turned into tigers after their death, and graves were not mentioned.[44]

A relationship between sacred places and tigers is indeed plausible. Places called angker, buyut, or keramat were normally avoided by the population, unless they came as supplicants in order to put forward some specific wish (for health, riches, a spouse, children, and high office) to the residing spirit or enshrined king or saint. It was believed that people who desecrated these sacred places, by cutting wood, gathering fruits, or even walking there when they had no business there, would be punished by the attendant spirit tiger, the more so when their thoughts were impure. Moreover, these graves, tombs, shrines, and spirit dwellings usually were located in inaccessible places, such as forests and mountains. Therefore, these "holy" locations, often found in relatively unspoiled, out-of-the-way places, would be largely left alone. These were ideal circumstances for game, and several testimonies assert that sacred spots were veritable wildlife sanctuaries. Such a situation, of course, attracted tigers. Occasionally, tigers killed pilgrims and other visitors to these sanctuaries, thereby reinforcing the notions of sanctity of the place and the existing beliefs about guardian tigers.[45]

It does not seem unreasonable to suppose that this feedback mechanism kept people from felling the (mountain) forests and clearing the "wastelands" where these sanctuaries could be found. Particularly in Java, this state of affairs may have been the cause of a much higher tiger density—and longer survival—than the high population density would have led one to expect. So the story from the *Niti Sastra,* about the tiger and the forest protecting each other, quoted in Chapter 2, was indeed true.

From ghost tigers who may be the spirits of the holy men or chiefs of whose graves they are the guardians to tigers who are at the beck and call of a live saint or king is but one step. In Dutch reports such an animal is called *volgtijger,* literally a following or attendant tiger; in English the best equivalent would be "familiar." Sources differ as to the question of whether this is a real or a ghost tiger. There is a very strong bond between saint or chief and tiger familiar, which often continues even after the death of the person involved. Chief and familiar usually died at the same moment.

In the many sources on tigers in Java there are few references to possible tiger familiars. Snouck Hurgronje mentioned the famous Bantenese saint Haji

Mansur of Cikadueun, who had freed a tiger from a giant shellfish and who therefore could always count on the assistance of tigers. The white ghost tiger guarding the grave of Syekh Abdulmuhyi in the Priangan had been the pet of his grandchild.

In Sumatra, the familiar seems to have been a much more frequent phenomenon. Examples of familiars were reported from Aceh, the Batak area, Palembang, and Bengkulu, but according to some authors this belief was islandwide.[46]

In Malaya, various keramat graves were guarded by tigers who were said to have been the pets of the august persons whose graves they were guarding, one of them being a princess of Malacca named Tuan Putri Gunong Ledang. Presumably, these were ghost tigers who used to be familiars. In the confusing literature on Malayan medicine men/magicians, one often encounters the link between shamans and tigers. Tigers who appear during a shamanistic seance seem to represent the familiar spirits of the shamans. Informants were divided on the question of whether the tiger who appeared during a seance was a real one or not.[47]

Tiger-Charmers

The category of the tiger familiar shades imperceptibly into that of the real tiger who is under the spell of a tiger-charmer. Everyone has heard of the snake-charmers of India, but it is perhaps less well known that there are also people who are supposed to be able to charm tigers or crocodiles.

Stützer, the first European to mention the macan bumi, was also the first person to report on tiger-charmers in Java (1786–87). He called them magicians, and they all were priests, a term that he must have used to indicate a dukun or an Islamic functionary. He also noted that Gerlach, a German overseer for the VOC in Gabang (Cirebon, western Java), never left his house if not accompanied by the local Javanese tiger-charmer. Gerlach described to Stützer three encounters with a tiger in which the magician had made the tiger go away.

At a much later date, in 1854, the regent of Bandung (Priangan, western Java) proposed appointing specialized tiger-catchers. If they were successful, the local population would assume, in his opinion, that these people possessed the required esoteric knowledge, as did such specialists outside Java. This remark suggests that tiger-charmers were unusual in that part of the island. Nevertheless, in 1858, W. F. Hoogeveen mentioned a person in the southern Priangan whom the local population thought capable of charming tigers. A few years later, Barrington d'Almeida, traveling through the Indonesian Archipelago between 1862 and 1864, wrote the following when he visited central Java:

"Men who have the reputation of being expert in tiger-trapping, are supposed by the natives to possess some particular charms, inherited from their parents, or given to them for a special purpose in this world." After 1864, only one reference has been found to tiger-charmers in the extensive literature on tigers in Java, and that was from someone who wrote down his reminiscences in 1910.[48]

As regards Sumatra, the oldest information is derived from a report by the Scottish country-trader Alexander Hamilton, who made many journeys in Asia between 1688 and 1723, on the Minangkabau people (who came from Sumatra) living around Malacca. He wrote, "Their religion is a complex of Mahometism and Paganism, and they have the character of great sorcerers, who by their spells can tame wild tigers, and make them carry them whither they order them, on their backs." There are more data on the nineteenth century. J. L. van der Toorn reported a case of tiger-trappers who used charms to get a tiger to walk into a trap, and A. L. van Hasselt mentioned tiger-charmers who were called in to stop a "tiger plague" (cf. Chapter 6). Xavier Brau de Saint-Pol, visiting northern Sumatra around 1880, mentioned expert makers of tiger-traps and nooses. Gustav Schneider, in Sumatra in the years 1897–99, stated that among the Batak a tiger-trap would work only if a sorcerer had been brought in to cast a spell on the tiger. He also reported extensively on the activities of a tiger-charmer among the semi-sedentary Mamak people.

For the twentieth century there are several references. Hazewinkel used the term *dukun* or *pawang rimueng* for the tiger-charmers. They were middle-aged men, known to be orthodox Muslims, who led an ascetic life. They had acquired this power over tigers by learning esoteric knowledge from older teachers who were also ascetics (and vegetarians). The local population assumed that after the death of a tiger-charmer his soul would enter a tiger. Often, the son would follow in his father's footsteps. *Pawang rimba,* or "woodsmen," were supposed to have a similar relationship with tigers. The tigers carried them on their backs, protected them against other animals, and helped them acquire game and forest products. Such stories can also be found in earlier and later writings on twentieth-century Sumatra.[49]

Data on the Malayan Peninsula are somewhat less abundant; the few references emphasize the pawang's ability to catch tigers. There were also people who befriend tigers by feeding them; henceforth they would be under the tiger's protection. This example suggests that the difference between a macan bumi and a tiger under the influence of a tiger-charmer may not be all that big.[50]

The core element of these stories seems to be that there are people—wizards, magicians, medicine men, priests—who have extraordinary spiritual

Professional woodsmen and tiger hunters. A *pawang rimba* **or** *pawang utan* **was supposed to have a "tiger familiar" and to be a tiger-charmer. The people in the photograph are Acehnese** *pawang utan.* **Zentgraaff 1938**

powers that they can use in order to make a tiger do their bidding. However, these powers can also be used to catch and eventually kill the animal concerned. In other words, these spiritually gifted people have the power to counterbalance the spiritual dangers involved in killing a tiger. A link between spiritual power and tiger catching is also suggested by a number of texts that do not refer specifically to tiger-charmers: orthodox Muslims, who are not supposed to believe in the ancestor-tiger link, and other specialists in spiritual matters were expert tiger-catchers.[51]

Therefore, it is probably not a coincidence that the tiger-charmer/tiger-catcher seems to have been more a Sumatran than a Javanese phenomenon, at least in the late nineteenth and early twentieth centuries. The Javanese were less hesitant to kill a tiger who had attacked their cattle, which implies that they were less in need of a spiritual specialist when a tiger had to be punished. After 1864, tiger-charmers were hardly mentioned in Java, perhaps because their services became increasingly superfluous, as the tiger was by then rare or even absent in many regions.

In the eighteenth century, Java had known a group of professional tiger-catchers, the so-called Tuwa buru people. These people caught tigers for the central Javanese courts, where they were used for the tiger-buffalo fights and the tiger-sticking ceremonies described in Chapter 7. We know next to nothing about these people, but it is certainly possible that they were supposed to possess certain charms for luring tigers into their traps. Tiger-charmers therefore may have played a more considerable role in Java in more remote times.

Conclusion

The tigers dealt with in this chapter were supposed to be either real tigers under the influence of spiritually powerful people, real tigers inhabited by the souls of deceased human beings, or spirits (i.e., souls of the dead) in the shape of a tiger (ghost tiger, tiger spirit). The village tiger, who in some regions was also a tax-levying bully, was sometimes held to be an ancestor, as were other tigers, perhaps even all tigers. He was an ancestor who protected his offspring but who also punished those of his descendants who had sinned against customary law.

Tigers could also be reincarnated good or bad people, or at least animals into which the souls of these people had migrated. After their death, very good people and very powerful people could have (ghost) tigers, often white ones, as guardians of their tombs, perhaps the very tigers that had been their familiars during their lives.

Finally, familiars were but one step removed from tigers who were being held in thrall by tiger-charmers, people credited with the possession of sufficient spiritual power to kill or catch tigers with impunity. These charmed tigers, in turn, were perhaps not all that different from village tigers.

Many of these features can also be found among other cultures, although the details and the combinations in which they occur are specific. Particularly strong is the resemblance between the Malayan shaman-ancestor-tiger-spirit complex and that of Central and South America, with the jaguar substituted for the tiger. In that region, the jaguar served as a guardian of sacred places. In Africa the leopard was a guardian animal for humans, including the element of their simultaneous death. In many areas of Africa leopards and lions were supposed to be inhabited by the souls of humans, particularly those of chieftains, and these animals could therefore be killed only in self-defense. One even encounters the view that an attack by such an animal should be regarded as a kind of tax assessment. The seeking of vengeance was, therefore, not permitted.[52]

9

Devouring the Hearts of the People: The Weretiger

Not so long ago, most people believed in the possibility of metamorphosis, or shape shifting. In Europe this was represented by a belief in werewolves, people who were supposedly literally transformed into wolves, albeit temporarily. This belief in werewolves has given its name to the term "lycanthropy" (from the Greek *lykanthropos,* wolfman), used to describe a number of phenomena, past and present, that have in common a notion of people physically turning into fierce animals. In tropical areas around the world a feline animal, such as the jaguar and the puma in Latin America, the leopard and the lion in Africa, and the tiger in Asia, often takes the place of the wolf.[1] Although other shape-shifters are mentioned in the extensive literature on magic and ghosts in the Malay world, the weretiger is the most recognizable counterpart of the European werewolf.

The Malayan Peninsula

The first reference that may allude to weretigers in the Malay world comes from an early-fifteenth-century Chinese source. Chinese visitors to Malacca told the following story: "In the town there are tigers which turn into men; they enter the markets, and walk about mixing with people; after they have been recognized, they are captured and killed" (Mills 1970, 113). Although this clearly refers to shape-shifters, the direction of the change seems to be wrong: the orthodoxy in were-animal lore presupposes people turning into animals. However that may be, in 1560 the Portuguese ecclesiastic authorities of Malacca, conquered by the Portuguese in 1511, solemnly excommunicated a number of weretigers. At that moment both Europeans and Southeast Asians

apparently shared a lycanthropic outlook. Two features of this story are note-
worthy: The weretigers are encountered in an urban and commercial (market)
setting, and they are killed.

At the beginning of the nineteenth century, many people in Malaya still believed in weretigers, for whom the term (*harimau*) *jadi-jadian* was used.[2] Nevertheless, much had changed during the intervening two and a half centuries,
as witness the following quotation from Abdullah bin Abdul Kadir, who was
born in Malacca in 1797: "Once I believed such things myself, being afraid of
them, because from my youth up I had heard of these matters and people tried
to frighten me. But they are all old wives tales. Since I have gained knowledge
and a little wisdom and have studied books, and especially since I have had occasion to associate myself with intelligent people like the white men, I have
known for certain that all these beliefs are groundless and nothing more than
sheer deceit." A devout Muslim, he added that such beliefs were also un-
Islamic. However, according to the Englishman John Newbold, writing in the
1830s, being Muslim did not keep the Malay from believing in weretigers:
"They will point out men that have the faculty of transforming themselves at
pleasure into tigers, or are doomed nightly to become tigers, returning to their
natural forms by day; this process is termed 'Jadi Jadian.' The belief in Jadi
Jadian is still strong, although powerfully contended against by their Mo-
hammedan priests."

About 60 years later stories still circulated on weretigers, but they had been
given a peculiar twist, or else the earlier reports had left out an important detail, namely the fact that the weretigers were foreigners. Sir Frank Swettenham, a British civil servant in Malaya at the turn of the century, reported as follows:

Another article of almost universal belief [among the peninsular Ma-
lays] is that the people of a small state in Sumatra called Korinchi have
the power of assuming at will the form of a tiger, and in that disguise
they wreak vengeance on those they wish to injure. . . . It is only fair to
say that the Korinchi people strenuously deny the tendencies and the
power ascribed to them, but aver that they properly belong to the inhabitants of a district called Chenâku in the interior of the Korinchi
country. Even there, however, it is only those who are practised in the
elemu sehir, the occult arts who are thus capable of transforming themselves into tigers.

Later, when dealing with Sumatra, we will hear more about Kerinci—today's
spelling of Korinchi—and the *orang cindaku*. Sir Hugh Clifford, another British
civil servant working on the Malayan Peninsula at that time, confirmed the

Weretigers in Sumatra and Malaya. In the Malay world people without a groove in their upper lip were supposed to be weretigers. In Malaya many medicine men claimed the ability to change themselves into tigers. They also had tiger familiars and became tigers when they died, it was said. *above,* **Sumatran weretiger in human shape. Hazewinkel 1964.** *opposite,* **Malayan weretiger (person on the right). Skeat and Blagden 1906, vol. 2**

Sumatran origin of weretigers active in Malaya. He told the story of Haji Abdallah, a trader of the little state of Kerinci, who was caught naked in a tiger-trap, and of other textile-trading hajis (that is, those who had made the Islamic pilgrimage to Mecca) from that area who turned out to be weretigers. It is remarkable, to say the least, that hajis, supposedly orthodox Muslims, were suspected of being weretigers. However, people with extraordinary spiritual pow-

ers, regardless of their specific religion, were often thought to be particularly capable of such transformations. It should also be noted that these hajis were traders, a theme that will be discussed presently.[3]

Shortly after 1900 interest among ethnographers dealing with Malaya shifted away from the Kerinci weretigers and attached itself to the shaman and his tiger familiar, discussed in Chapter 8. As noted, most tribal groups saw a link between their shamans and tigers. The shaman could conjure up a "familiar" who was both a tiger-spirit and an ancestor-shaman. Some people also credited the shaman with the ability to turn himself into a tiger, both during his lifetime and after his death.[4] The shaman, therefore, was, among other things, a weretiger.

The Cambridge Expedition in 1899–1900 met and photographed such a shaman-weretiger—in his human shape—in the little Malayan hamlet of Ulu Aring, deep in the interior of the Peninsula. One of the participants of the expedition gave a rather detailed report of their conversation: "From what he told me it appeared that he had (or believed that he had) the power of turning himself into a tiger at will, in which guise he would feast upon bodies of his victims (whether dead or alive), always, however, excepting and burying the heads." When the shaman wanted to become a tiger, he would say, "I am going to walk," whereafter he went to the hills, burned incense, "collecting smoke in his fist, blowing through it." The narrator continued:

> He next squats on his haunches and leans forward on his hands, turning his head quickly to left and right. "Presently" (I tell the tale in his own words) "his skin changes, fur grows, and a tail appears. Thus he remains from seven to twelve days, during which time he raids the neighbouring cattle-pens till his craving is fully appeased, when he returns to the spot that he started from, squats down as before, and turns himself back by means of saying simply, "I am going home." . . . "On regaining his human form, he is usually extremely sick and vomits up the still undigested bones that he had swallowed in his tiger-shape." It is, I was told, impossible to shoot him, as would otherwise be done, in this stage, as he invariably disappears before there is time to fire a shot.

Kirk Michael Endicott, who studied these beliefs thoroughly, assumed that the weretiger and the tiger-spirit were—originally?—quite distinct notions in Malay thought. In his opinion, the confusion that seemed to occur among Malay tribal groups between the two notions was a product of Negrito (Semang, non-Malay) influence. Negritos did believe that shamans were weretigers. Generally speaking, the Malay tribes believed that a tiger-spirit would enter a shaman who had been brought into trance, sometimes by inhaling incense. The shaman would then start acting like a tiger (as opposed to becoming a tiger). Such beliefs were and are almost universally held among societies in which shamans play a role.[5]

In all probability there was a third notion related to shape shifting among the Malays of the Peninsula. According to Walter William Skeat, the people of Selangor told the following story: "Far away in the jungle the tiger-folk have a town of their own, where they live in houses, and act in every respect as human beings." The houses were largely constructed of human hair, bones, and hides. Periodically, they had "attacks of fierceness" whereupon they went into the forest looking for a victim. The most important tiger village of the Peninsula was on Mount Ledang.[6] Yet another twist is given to this story by Charles Mayer, a big-game hunter, who cited Timar, first wife of the Sultan of Trengganu, as his source. She told him "about a kampong where the houses were made out of human bones and thatched with the long hair of women who had been eaten. The town was built and occupied by tigers, and the headman was a tiger at night but in the day he was a man." Around 1950, Locke sums up various places where such tiger villages were supposedly to be found.

These stories, different variations upon one theme, all describe tigers living together in certain areas, like human beings in villages and houses. "Imagined communities" no doubt, even though this was not what Ben Anderson had in mind when he coined that phrase! These tigers act like humans and sometimes even become humans. However, from time to time they are "mischievous" or have "attacks of fierceness," and then they attack, in their tiger guise, humans or animals. These stories therefore seem to refer to tigers who occasionally turn into human beings, and not the other way around, recalling the fifteenth-century Chinese source mentioned earlier.[7]

Sumatra

If the Malays from Malaya believed the people from Kerinci to be weretigers, what was it that the Sumatrans themselves believed? Marsden, writing at the end of the eighteenth century, obtained most of his information from the Rejang. They lived in an area, later to be included in the Residency of Bengkulu, just to the south of the Kerinci Valley. According to Marsden, "Popular stories prevail amongst them, of such a particular man being changed into a tiger, or other beast." He then goes on to say: "They talk of a place in the country where the tigers have a court, and maintain a regular form of government, in towns, the houses of which are thatched with women's hair." This, of course, sounds remarkably like the "imagined communities" from the Malayan Peninsula. Not much later (1817), Presgrave, who served under Raffles in Bengkulu, visited the region of Besemah (Pasumah), to the south of the Rejang area. When he and his companions visited the "sacred mountain" Dempo, they "passed through what is called by the natives the region of tigers; the superstitious inhabitants of the surrounding country imagine that there is a stream in these parts, which when passed over by a human being, possesses the virtue of transforming him to that ferocious animal, and on his return of restoring him to his original shape."

Mohnike, who visited the area 30 years later (1840s), told the story somewhat differently. According to him, the people believed that there was a large village on the Dempo volcano, entirely inhabited by tigers who could change themselves into humans. In their human shape they visited nearby markets and mixed with other people. Some had married women from adjacent villages, and in one case the bride had discovered the identity of her spouse on their wedding night. This story and other similar ones could be heard in the Rejang and Besemah areas.

As in Malaya, the stories of Marsden and Mohnike seem to be about tigers living in villages who are able to turn into humans. Only Presgrave talks about humans changing into tigers when they cross a stream, perhaps a garbled version of local beliefs, if we accept A. L. van Hasselt's much more coherent, "classical" rendering of the story.[8]

Finally, another 30 years later (in the 1870s), the link mentioned in Malaya between the Kerinci area and "tigers" appears in the report of the central Sumatra expedition. Expedition members were told that there was a district near Kerinci called Banye balingka, consisting of two villages inhabited by the Cindaku people. The "people" of one village could alternate between the tiger and the human shape, those of the other one between the shape of a human and that of a pig:

> At certain times of the year the Cindaku leave their district and prowl the forests in the shape of tigers in order to visit the areas inhabited by humans, looking for prey. When they reach a river too large to be crossed swimming, they change themselves into humans carrying trading packs, which makes them look like itinerant merchants, and ask to be ferried across. Having reached the other side, they resume their tiger shape. Upon reaching a village, they again show themselves as normal people, of whom they can be distinguished only by the absence of the vertical groove in the upper lip between nose and mouth. They will go to a house and ask for a place for the night, and when everyone is fast asleep they will, in their tiger shape, attack the sleepers and devour the hearts of the people. They also fancy livestock.

A number of twentieth-century authors repeated this story almost verbatim—often without reference to Van Hasselt—but also with some "new" details that will be mentioned presently.

These stories all refer to the same phenomenon, and they all come from roughly the same area, namely Kerinci-Rejang-Besemah, with Mount Dempo as its focal point. For several reasons this is an extraordinary area. In the early nineteenth century, most people there were not yet converted to Islam, and those who were had retained much of their "pagan" worldview. The area is largely located within the Bukit Barisan, the spinal mountain range of Sumatra, even then with fairly high concentrations of people in its upland valleys. Some of these valleys had been settled very early, and wet rice has been grown there for centuries if not for millennia. Pollen analysis of a core from Lake Padang in the Kerinci Valley suggests land clearance before 1000 BC and perhaps even as early as 2000 BC. One of the main concentrations of prehistoric stone (megalithic) monuments in Indonesia is in the Besemah area, probably dating from the first millennium AD.[9]

One megalith that has attracted quite some attention is that of two copulating tigers. A. N. J. Thomassen à Thuessink van der Hoop described it as follows:

The Besemah megalith of copulating tigers. The area where weretiger beliefs were rather strong in Sumatra also featured prehistoric tiger megaliths. The photographs show a statue of copulating tigers, with a human head between the paws of the tigress. Thomassen à Thuessink van der Hoop 1932

"The heads of the animals, especially, are very finely finished; the canine teeth and tongue are very clearly indicated. The tigress is grasping with both front paws the head of a small human figure which with both hands is trying to extricate itself from the claws." Although we do not know the meaning of this statue, more than one author has linked it with local beliefs in supernatural tigers.[10] Such links between feline megaliths and beliefs in supernatural big cats are also found elsewhere.[11]

The people of Kerinci were itinerant traders, at least from the seventeenth century onward. Watson noted, "From the earliest mention of Kerinci in the records, it seems that the principal source of wealth was trade, with Kerinci men going back and forth to the West Coast and Jambi taking a variety of forest products and also gold." Gold is dug or panned in the Minangkabau area to the north of Kerinci, and in some of the later Cindaku stories the people always paid in gold or gold dust. The possession of gold suggests wealth, but it is highly unlikely that all temporary migrants from Kerinci were rich, given the following quotation, dated 1818: "As it is well known the Korinchi men frequently leave their country in search of employ in other parts of the Island." Van Hasselt described the Cindaku as looking like itinerant merchants in their human shape, and in the stories from Malaya the weretigers from Kerinci were clearly depicted as hajis-cum-itinerant cloth peddlers. In the late nineteenth century, poor hajis from Kerinci could often be found in the Acehnese countryside, where they could fall back on Muslim charity, paid out of the tithe. A later source suggests that people could prevent the depredations of the Cindaku in their tiger (or pig) shape by giving in to the demands they made while in their human shape.[12]

In other words, many Kerinci people, who roamed all over Sumatra and the Malayan Peninsula, were beggars or at least petty traders who had fallen upon hard times, and they threatened the credulous populace that they would return as animals if their demands were not met. Originally those who left the area temporarily may have been rather wealthy merchants, but as time went on and as the population increased, poor migrants would have taken their place, although they were still rumored to be in the possession of gold dust. In fact, gold in the hands of badly dressed Kerinci people, who moreover had a reputation of being thrifty or even miserly, suggested wealth acquired by supernatural means.[13]

Given the presence of the megalithic tiger images in the area, it is likely that the local population had made the connection between tigers and supernatural powers long before the Kerinci people became temporary or permanent migrants. Vagrants from the Kerinci area, or claiming to be from there, could play upon these fears in order to make a living. That some of these vagrants had criminal sidelines was to be expected. Hazewinkel, who met a strangely dressed tiger-Cindaku with an unkempt head of hair in 1926, reported that the man was given money and food by the population and that, according to the police, he was also an opium-smuggler (Hazewinkel 1964, 52). A connection between weretigers and drugs will be explored later.

It is puzzling that almost nothing is written about Sumatran weretigers being caught and punished. The people of fifteenth-century Malacca captured and killed the weretigers if they could; regarding Sumatra, however, there seem to be only two references, and late ones at that. Hazewinkel mentioned punishment, and he stated that because of it people no longer dared to suggest that they were weretigers. Nevertheless, belief in Kerinci and Besemah weretigers persists to this day.[14]

Among the other groups of Sumatra, belief in weretigers does not seem to have been strong. Jacobs mentioned a belief among the Acehnese (northern Sumatra) that people with distorted feet belonged to a tribe that could assume the human or tiger shape at will. He also stated that the Batak and the Lampung people strongly believed in the possibility of metamorphosis. Lampung, to the south of the Besemah area, could certainly have been influenced by the Cindaku stories, but no corroborating evidence is available on the Batak. Evidence on the Minangkabau is contradictory.[15]

Java

Evidently, no European sources prior to 1800 deal with weretigers in Java. However, these beings are mentioned in indigenous sources. The two Javanese sources I am referring to, the *Serat Cabolang* and the *Serat Centhini,* have been handed down as manuscripts dating from c. 1800, but large sections of these texts may well be older. Both texts are constructed as frame stories, in which groups of people are traveling all over seventeenth-century Java. During their journeys they have long conversations with knowledgeable local "informants," thus presenting an encyclopedia of Javanese culture. In the *Serat Cabolang,* canto 21, the travelers arrive in Lodhaya—on modern maps, Lodoyo—where they receive information on the *macan gadhungan,* or weretiger. In the *Serat Centhini,* cantos 385–86, the travel companions visit the Salakakas Forest, where they meet with 50 people, men and women, who turned out to be weretigers from the large forest. This transpires when they all go to sleep at night, assuming their tiger shape.[16] So, as in Malaya and Sumatra, such beings are primarily tigers. But perhaps it is better to think of them as beings that can assume either human or tiger shape.

The first report written by an (Indo-)European with information on the macan gadhungan dates from 1824. Its author is the translator J. W. Winter, appointed at the court of Surakarta: "The Javanese believe that a human being can change itself into a tiger. This belief is based on the fact that in Surakarta, in the forests of Lodoyo and the surrounding area, there are always many man-eating tigers, particularly during the period called *prasé* or mating-season. It is said that some poor people, who find it difficult to make a living, at this occasion turn into tigers. Such a tiger is called macan gadhungan" (Winter 1902, 85). Someone who wished to do this left the house, hid in the bushes, undressed, prayed, jumped and rolled over as long as it took until the transformation took place. He returned, satiated, before daybreak to the same spot in order to become human again. If someone had stolen his clothes in the meantime, he would have to remain a tiger. Again, here is the region of Lodoyo, Residency Kediri, an area already encountered in the last chapter as a center of supernatural tigers. The "poor people" recall, of course, the Kerinci beggars.

Winter's account, written in 1824, was not published until 1902, and during most of the nineteenth century few data on weretigers came to the attention of the Europeans. The first time that the macan gadhungan appeared in print was in 1870, when the physician J. A. van Dissel published an article on superstitions and customs of the Javanese. He stated that the macan gadhungan was a human being that had changed itself into a tiger by means of sorcery, and that esoteric knowledge was needed for such a transformation.

A few years later (1881) a somewhat more detailed account was published based on stories from eastern Java. Someone without a vertical groove in the upper lip was supposed to be a macan gadhungan, which brings to mind the Cindaku people from the Kerinci area. The transformation always took place at night, when the weretiger was asleep in his human form. The sleeping human body remained where it was while the weretiger performed his ugly deeds. The pugmarks of a weretiger can be recognized because of its extra nail. There was reported to be a village on Mount Lamongan (Probolinggo) inhabited entirely by macan gadhungan. No outsider would ever wish to spend the night there, and the inhabitants would refuse to have people stay overnight anyway, because they did not know when the—unconscious—transformation would take place. In this example there was no physical transformation, but the soul left the body and manifested itself as a tiger—which sounds remarkably like a shamanic experience. G. A. Wilken, who summarized what had been published about the macan gadhungan in 1884, distinguished between a conscious variant, in which people used esoteric knowledge, and an unconscious, hereditary one.[17]

In 1899 came the breakthrough in European knowledge regarding the macan gadhungan. In 1898 the Sinologist J. J. M. de Groot had published a lengthy article on weretiger beliefs in China. This encouraged G. A. J. Hazeu,

J. Knebel, and G. P. Rouffaer to publish their data on Javanese weretiger beliefs a year later.[18] Following are the relevant elements of these stories:

- There are no stories of tigers turning into people.
- Weretigers are always royal tigers (and not leopards).
- Weretiger beliefs are to be found in the Residencies of Banyumas, Bagelen, Kedu, Tegal, Semarang, Jepara, Madiun, Kediri, and Pasuruan. In Banyumas and Pasuruan the beliefs had been imported by migrants. Probolinggo, mentioned in 1881, is, strangely enough, not listed here. This means that weretiger beliefs were to be found in almost all central Javanese Residencies. Data regarding belief in weretigers were apparently absent then in western Java and in the eastern Java Residencies of Besuki and Madura.
- Those who are able to turn themselves into weretigers are in the possession of specific esoteric knowledge that is often transmitted from parent to child.
- If such a person wants to assume the shape of a tiger, he will turn his clothes inside out, recite the appropriate incantations, and turn somersaults thrice, keeping his breath. It is suggested that fasting should precede all this. It seems that the transformation usually takes place at night, but sometimes also during daytime.
- If one steals the clothes a weretiger left behind before his transformation, he will remain a tiger forever. If the weretiger is wounded when a tiger, he will have a wound at the same spot when he has resumed his human shape.
- In their human shape, these people can be recognized by the absence of the vertical groove in the upper lip, by the absence of heels, and by the fact that they will not look at people when spoken to, keeping their head down.
- During the daytime weretigers are wage-laborers, sellers of merchandise in the market, or beggars. Particularly those from Lodoyo annually leave their homes seeking to earn a living, going to Bagelen, Banyumas, and other Residencies (perhaps an echo of the story of the tigers of Lodoyo visiting Arca Domas/Ujung Kulon, discussed in Chapter 8). On these journeys they always carry a stick and a knife. They go from house to house in worn-out clothes, and those who give nothing will be visited later in the tiger shape. This is such a familiar phenomenon that people accosted by beggars always check whether they are dealing with a weretiger. As tigers, they also scare people away from their fields, which enables them to steal maize and sweet potatoes in order to feed their wives and children. So,

some people turn themselves into tigers because they are hungry, in order to grab a chicken or a dog, but others do it because they want to attack someone they bear a grudge. Beggars sometimes wear a tiger-skin in order to make people believe they are weretigers.

• Weretigers sometimes marry human beings.

• Women and men both can be weretigers. In most texts, however, weretigers are male.

• People who have this ability often live together in villages. One of these villages is Gadhungan, in the district of Lodoyo, Regency of Blitar (Kediri); another one is Prata in the Kudus Regency (Jepara).

• If need be, people take the law into their own hands when confronted with a weretiger; he is hunted down by a large crowd and, if possible, killed. Often, however, the weretiger means no harm, and he can be rendered harmless by calling his name or by saying that one is a good friend of his in his human shape.

• Some people say that a weretiger has the ability to become a tiger after his death, a link with the ancestral tiger.

Most of what was printed after 1900 about weretigers in Java repeated these data, or rather part of the data, often without reference to Hazeu and Knebel, the most important sources of knowledge regarding Javanese weretigers. Therefore, the errors found in these sources also were repeated.

Knebel or his informants committed such an error when naming the village Gadhungan in the district Lodoyo as a "tiger village."[19] What makes this statement problematic is that there was and is no village of Gadhungan in Lodoyo. On the maps the only village called Gad(h)ungan is to be found to the northwest of Mount Kelud, just to the southeast of the district capital, Paré. This is not only another district but also even another Regency, and the distance between this village and Lodoyo is c. 50 km. Knebel, who probably never looked at a map, must have assumed that the village of Gadhungan, associated with supernatural tigers (but until 1900, at least in writing, not with weretigers), was a place in the Lodoyo area, typical weretiger country.

The Javanese weretiger was associated with the forest of Lodoyo at least since 1800 and in all probability much earlier. Prior to 1830 this was a wild, almost uninhabited area, entirely covered with forests and swarming with tigers. Even in the early twentieth century Lodoyo was typical tiger country, which enabled the people of Blitar to stage regular tiger-sticking ceremonies even after 1900 (see Chapter 7). It had been an area of banishment for Mataram, the central Javanese kingdom, at least since the seventeenth century. Noblemen who for some reason had angered the ruler were sent there on the assumption that they would be eaten by tigers, or, as Rouffaer suggested, by weretigers. Lodoyo plays a role in Javanese mythology, and at least in one case, in 1888, its fame was used by a group of insurgents in order to attract followers.[20]

Both Gadhungan and Lodoyo were located in the Kediri Residency, an area sparsely populated when it was ceded to the Dutch in 1830. However, in earlier times it had been an important and populous region, as the myths surrounding it suggested. The Hindu-Buddhist State of Daha or Kadhiri had been located here from the eleventh century, until Muslim forces from the north coast destroyed it (c. 1580). In the nineteenth century, its former importance was still visible in the many antiquities found in the area. It is probably not a coincidence that many of these remains were located in and around Gadhungan and Lodoyo.[21] There is an interesting parallel with the megaliths in the Besemah area in Sumatra. Another comparison that suggests itself is that with the so-called *Arca Domas*, the stones and statues found in the area of the former kingdom of Pajajaran in western Java, which were also associated with supernatural tigers, albeit with ancestral tigers (see Chapter 8). In fact, Bogor—near the old Pajajaran *kraton*—and Lodoyo were regarded as the two main (supernatural) tiger centers of Java.

According to legend, the first man who had learned the art of turning himself into a tiger—during the reign of king Jayabaya of Kadhiri, in the twelfth century—and his offspring were still living in the forest of Lodoyo, albeit invisibly.

Prior to 1899 the village of Gadhungan had been associated with certain supernatural tigers (macan putih, familiars).[22] However, it had never been linked, in writing, with weretigers. The term gadhungan derives from *gadhung*, a tuber (the Asiatic bitter yam, *Dioscorea hispida*) with intoxicating properties. A verb based on this word means to intoxicate someone with such a tuber, hence to cheat or deceive someone. The latter connotation also pertains to the word gadhungan, meaning disguise or deceit. So a macan gadhungan is a mock tiger. The term, therefore, has nothing to do with the village Gadhungan, but it is not unreasonable to suppose that people who were not familiar with this etymology just assumed that a macan gadhungan was a tiger from Gadhungan.

However, the village of Gadhungan may have had features conducive to its being associated with weretigers. By a stroke of extraordinary good luck, the written record includes a rather detailed description of the village of Gadhungan, dated 1868. It had at that time 1,040 inhabitants, a fairly large village by the standards of that period, and it was a most remarkable village. It had virtually no wet rice fields and very few other arable lands. Nevertheless, the people were well to do. Their income derived mainly from livestock rearing, the preparation of "wine" and sugar from the *arèn* palm (*Arenga pinnata sv saccharifera),* and the sale of fruits of the *langsep* tree (*Lansium domesticum).* As the villagers had almost no arable lands, the water buffaloes they kept were rented out. The population was very much addicted to the use of opium.[23] It seems likely that people associated this village of wealthy and opium-smoking wanderers, who did not have the usual visible means of support (wet rice fields), with the macan gadhungan, even if the term gadhungan had nothing to do with the village.

According to Hazewinkel, the weretigers of Lamongan had disappeared by the 1950s because their marriages remained childless (Hazewinkel 1964, 45). He does not mention Lodoyo or Gadhungan. But by the 1930s "natural" tigers had become rare in that area, and even the village of Gadhungan seems to have vanished. There is no longer a village Gadhungan in the Kediri region to be found on the relevant map of the *Atlas van Tropisch Nederland*, published in 1938. As it is rather unlikely that the village had disappeared entirely, it could have become a ward of a larger village, or the inhabitants could have changed its name, as Javanese often did if a name turned out to be "unlucky." Given the association with weretigers, the last possibility does not seem unlikely.

Finally, before leaving Java entirely, we should turn our attention briefly to western Java. In the three weretiger texts published in 1899, western Java was not mentioned. Only two references to weretigers are available from that area. The missionary and Sunda expert Sierk Coolsma, writing around 1880, mentioned the term *adén-adén*. This referred to an old woman carrying a large pack containing the clothes she dons when she is alone and in which she is transformed into a tiger (Coolsma 1881, 78–79). More than 20 years later, Christiaan Snouck Hurgronje used the term *maung kajajadén*, or weretiger, adding only that in their human form they always carried a spotted knife (Snouck Hurgronje 1904, 396).

Bali and Lombok

Information on Balinese weretigers is far from abundant. The first European visitor who mentioned this topic was the Dutch physician Jacobs. He stated that in Bali belief in weretigers (*macan dadèn-dadèn*) was general, among the well educated as much as among the common people. According to this belief, every person lacking the vertical groove in the upper lip at certain times could turn himself into a tiger. Many Balinese also believed that tigers lived in a secret district where they had towns and magnificent houses. This sounds like the stories from Malaya, Sumatra, and Java, where many people believed weretigers to be living in towns and villages of their own. Jacobs is one of the very few authors to mention the Balinese macan dadèn-dadèn, clearly in terminology and description a local variety of the Indonesian weretiger.[24]

Various other writers have reported on a phenomenon that has some features of the weretiger but is nevertheless clearly something else: the so-called *léyak* (often spelled *leak*). The first European who mentioned the léyak was Rudolf Friederich, who visited Bali c. 1850. According to his description it was a human being that, by means of certain incantations, could change his shape or make himself invisible, betraying his presence only by a bright sheen, comparable to that of the big Balinese fireflies. The léyaks feed themselves with corpses from graveyards or those awaiting the funeral pyre, but they also eat the entrails of the living, thereby causing their death. They have meetings, like witch covens, on Mount Agung, the abode of their mistress, Rangda. People accused of being a léyak have often been condemned. Friederich, who does not specify into what a léyak can change himself, obviously compared these beings to witches, known to his European audience from their own past and from popular fairy tales.

An interesting addition to this information came at a much later date. In 1912, W. J. M. Plate wrote an article on lycanthropy, using that specific term, on the island of Lombok, the immediate eastern neighbor of Bali. He described a phenomenon called *selak.* Although Plate does not mention the léyak, it is clear that not only are the terms etymologically related, but the phenomena themselves are quite similar. According to Plate, there are three grades of selak. Those of the lowest grade can change themselves into small animals, such as dogs, pigs, and goats. The selak of the highest order (*selak sakti*) can transform themselves into large animals, such as water buffaloes and tigers. The most fascinating feature of the selak sakti is that the people of Lombok thought that those who could assume the tiger shape came mostly from Bali. As there were no tigers on Lombok, whereas they did occur on Bali, it is difficult to find fault with this belief. What makes this information even more interesting is that prior to the Dutch conquest of Lombok in 1894, part of the island had been governed by a Balinese ruler. When in 1891 the people of eastern Lombok rebelled against their Balinese overlord, troops came over from Bali in support of the ruler. It was rumored that these troops included many Balinese who could change themselves into tigers, in order to spread destruction and despondency among the people of Lombok.

Plate also mentioned witchlike covens (with free sex for all participants) and the ability of the selak to fly, another witch feature. He did not report that the selak ate corpses (cf. Friederich), but he emphasized that they sucked blood from living humans, causing their unexpected death. So although the element of shape shifting is present—according to Plate, in order to scare people; the blood sucking was done in the "invisible" (light-emitting ghost or shadowlike) shape—the phenomenon is one of witches or vampires rather than "pure" were-animals, and certainly not the "classical" weretigers known from other areas of the Archipelago. Finally, Plate stated that people often attempted to kill or maim those believed to be selak. The Dutch tried, of course, to stop this. On Bali, léyak were murdered as late as 1920.[25]

The léyak and the selak belong to a category of beings to be found all over eastern Indonesia. Its best-known representative, at least to European ethnographers, is the *suangi*, mentioned as early as in a text dated 1621. The suangi was reported to exist in the Moluccas and on some of the Lesser Sunda Islands. Similar beings, indicated with other terms, are found throughout the area. All these beings have shape-shifting characteristics, usually in addition to an invisible or rather "shining" shadow or ghost shape, and they make people ill by eating some vital organ or drinking their blood, causing lingering or sudden, but in any case unexpected, death. In their human shape, the suangi were often old or disfigured people. The enraged villagers often killed an alleged suangi, with or without benefit of trial.[26]

Most European missionaries, ethnographers, physicians, and other researchers had a hard time deciding what to call these beings. They had clearly lycanthropic features, but they also had much in common with beings that Europeans called witches, sorcerers, and vampires. The Dutch missionary and ethnographer Albert Christiaan Kruyt called them—in Dutch—*weerwolven en heksen* (werewolves and witches), a category as good as any other. Unfortunately, he also included the weretigers of western Indonesia in this category, a judgment that is neither helpful nor warranted by a careful reading of the ethnographic material.

When Alfred Russel Wallace summed up his experiences in the Indonesian Archipelago in the 1850s and 1860s, he suggested that there was a line to the east of Borneo and Bali separating the Indo-Malayan from the Austro-Malayan flora and fauna (Wallace 1869, 21). To the west of this line, now generally called Wallace's Line, there are tigers and leopards, but there are none to the east. It now appears that Wallace's Line is perhaps also a "spiritual" border. To the west is the weretiger as described above, and to the east there is the more undifferentiated were-animal-cum-witch of the suangi type.

Bali and Lombok might be, or might have been, a place where the two spheres overlap, at least partly. Lombok was the only area to the east of the spiritual Wallace Line where a suangi (selak) could assume the form of a tiger, provided it was a Balinese suangi. Bali was the only place to the west of the same line where a local variant of the suangi was to be found.

Borneo

In historical times, tigers do not seem to have inhabited the island of Borneo. The only big cat to be found there is the clouded leopard. Nevertheless, the tiger played a fairly important role in the beliefs and the folklore of the Dayak, the indigenous population of the island, of which the majority lived—and still lives—some distance away from the coast. Skins, skulls, teeth, and images of tigers were regarded as potent charms, more potent than those of the clouded leopard; in stratified societies they could be owned or even touched only by the aristocracy. Male aristocrats were identified with tigers in oral tradition. Some Dayak groups (Kenya, Bahau) regarded tigers as the most powerful spirits they could think of. Another Dayak tribe, the Ot Danum, regarded the man-eating tiger as a mighty deity.[27]

Tigers and weretigers were mentioned in local myths of origin, but they were slain by culture heroes a long time in the past. In another local story, however, a tiger was still supposed to be living on a mountaintop. As mountain peaks were almost invariably held to be the abodes of ancestral spirits, it does not seem too wild to assume that these people were referring to an ancestral tiger.[28]

There is no record of weretiger stories of the western Indonesian type, but tigers abound in stories about the supernatural.[29] It is perhaps too far-fetched to regard the existence of the tiger motif in so many myths as proof of the tiger's former presence in Borneo, but it is also difficult to find a more satisfactory explanation for the existence of these stories (cf. Chapter 2).

Conclusion

Disregarding the léyak belief in Bali, which is a more generalized notion of shape shifting, there were two main types of weretiger beliefs in areas where tigers were present during historical times. One was the belief in shamans who had a tiger familiar (tiger spirit), who could turn themselves into tigers and would become tigers after their death. The function of shaman was hereditary, and so was the tiger spirit, who was in fact the dead shaman, who would come to the aid of his successor. Within the Malay world, this complex was to be found mainly among the tribal population of the Malayan Peninsula.

This set of beliefs is amazingly similar to beliefs regarding shamans and jaguars among the Amerindians of Central and South America. In Mexico, the term used for this complex is *nagualism,* a word derived from Nahuatl, the language of the Aztecs, denoting something hidden or disguised (Furst 1968, 167). This would make the jaguar from the Mexican stories a mock jaguar.

The macan gadhungan, the Javanese weretiger, was literally a mock tiger, and with that phenomenon comes the second type of weretiger beliefs. It comprises the harimau jadi-jadian of Malaya, the Cindaku people of Sumatra, the maung kajajadén of western Java, the macan gadhungan of central and eastern Java, and the macan dadèn-dadèn of Bali. The fairly extensive literature on this topic is ambivalent as to whether the weretiger is, in its essence, a human being, a tiger, or something that can assume either shape. Nevertheless, the last possibility is the one most supported by the sources, and it certainly differs from the classical European werewolf, who is definitely human. Other "Malay" weretiger characteristics also differ from the European model, such as its hereditary aspect, the existence of weretiger villages, and the physical features by which weretigers can be distinguished from normal people.

These features suggest that the origins of the second type of weretigers (macan gadhungan, and others) ultimately can be traced back to the first, shamanic type. The hereditary element, for instance, is clearly present in the Malayan stories about shamans and their familiars. Familiar spirits, who are at the same time dead shamans, have their own abode, often on an inaccessible mountain or in an impenetrable forest (e.g., Schebesta 1928a, 163; Endicott 1970, 16, 30). This conception seems to be the origin of the weretiger villages located on mountains (Malaya, Sumatra, and Java) or in forests (Java). Additional features support this hypothesis, including fasting, somersaulting, reciting incantations, and, possibly, the use of drugs. These activities had to be undertaken by Cindaku people or a macan gadhungan who wanted to assume the tiger form. The same activities are, however, also a very good description of a shamanic trance dance staged in order to attract the tiger familiar (during initiation rites, or to make the journey to the land of lost souls).[30] Furthermore, the Malayan and Sumatran weretiger stories (of the macan gadhungan type) feature the theme that men turn into tigers—and the other way around—when they cross a certain river or enter a certain area. It is likely that this element represents the border crossing in the shaman's journey to the land of the souls.

Another indication that weretiger beliefs may have had a shamanic origin is that weretigers were sometimes said to become tigers when they died.[31] This notion is alien to the concept of the European werewolf, but it agrees very well with the idea that a shaman who is able to turn himself into a tiger when in trance will also become a (spirit) tiger after his death, enabling him to give guidance to his son and successor as a shaman.

The Malayan people believed that hajis from Kerinci often were weretigers. This may sound rather odd, as one is not inclined to associate orthodox Muslims with weretiger stories. The local population, however, although nominally Muslim, had retained much of its pagan beliefs. Moreover, because they were Muslims they regarded a haji, by virtue of his pilgrimage to Mecca, as a spiritually powerful person. The idea that spiritually powerful people were able to turn themselves into tigers is probably related to the belief that such people had a tiger familiar and/or that they were tiger-charmers. Both beliefs are in all likelihood of shamanic origin.

The idea that "holy men" were weretigers is also to be found in India, where it was mentioned as early as the fourteenth century and as late as the 1930s. It is also present in a Thai folktale.[32]

In Java the shamanic origins of weretiger stories probably were all but forgotten by 1800 and perhaps even earlier. Belief in tiger-charmers—in fact, specialized shamans—locally survived somewhat later, but the link with weretigers was no longer made, unless the European reports missed this detail. There is no need, however, to suppose that the European reports got it wrong. There are other examples of shamanic elements that survived "in isolation," as witness the trance dances that can be observed to this very day.[33]

In Sumatra, shamanistic practices and experiences were—and sometimes are—much more part of everyday life. Nevertheless, the many European reports on Sumatra do not seem to link stories about tiger-charmers to weretiger beliefs.

European observers likely regarded shamanistic practices as typically rural or even tribal phenomena, whereas the weretiger stories have an urban or "commercial" ring to them. The oldest weretiger story from the Malay world was definitely urban, as it referred to markets in the fifteenth-century town of Malacca. In most other stories the weretigers were itinerant (cloth) peddlers, sellers of merchandise in markets, wage-laborers, poor people, or beggars. Although many of these people doubtless had a rural background, they all participated in and probably largely depended on urban and/or commercial, or at least extra-village, circuits. The weretiger is never the average field- or farm-owning peasant. Insofar as he or she is still part of the village community, it is in a marginal position.[34] Usually, however, he seems to be an outsider, a physically disfigured and poor vagrant, the occasional possession of gold dust—no doubt acquired by supernatural means—notwithstanding.

Weretiger beliefs, although originally in all probability of shamanic origin, had acquired a totally different connotation. In fact, they present a striking resemblance not so much to European werewolf beliefs but to European beliefs in witches (e.g., Levack 1995, 149–54). Such descriptions also feature poor, marginal, and sometimes disfigured people who were accused of employing supernatural means in order to improve their position, to the detriment of the better off.[35] According to many historians, accusations of witchcraft in Early Modern Europe were inspired by feelings of hate, resentment, guilt, and fear with regard to these poor wretches. We may safely assume that this was also the case with weretiger accusations.

The attitude toward witches in Europe differs in at least one respect from that toward weretigers in Indonesia: the absence of large-scale weretiger hunts comparable to the witch hunts in Europe. In the few remarks available on weretigers being captured and killed, it appears that a person—not a tiger—suspected of being a weretiger may have been occasionally executed. There is nothing similar to the prolonged and large-scale witch hunts reported in detail from Early Modern Europe. One can assume that the fear inspired by the Indonesian weretigers was more dominant than the resentment they engendered, a resentment that in Europe may be held responsible for so many deaths. In this respect the people whom the Dutch often described as witches—the suangi and the like from eastern Indonesia—were more comparable to the European witches, being much more persecuted by their countrymen than were the weretigers.

Far from being responsible for the deaths of large numbers of people or tigers, the belief in weretigers may have prevented people in Indonesia—particularly those in Sumatra—from going after tigers that they might have killed if such a belief had not existed. After all, the weretiger was a being with supernatural powers. In that sense, the belief in weretigers reinforced Indonesians' reluctance to go after tigers in general.

10

The Rise, Decline,
and Fall of the Tiger

The tiger has disappeared from Bali, has disappeared or is about to disappear from Java, and is becoming rare in Sumatra and the Malayan Peninsula. Half a century ago, tigers were plentiful in some of these regions, but less so in others. This chapter examines the reason tigers vanished where they did, the timing of their disappearance, and the development of tiger numbers during the period under consideration. Much of this discussion summarizes the quantitative evidence presented in earlier chapters.

Regarding numbers of tigers, only a rough estimate is available for the Malayan Peninsula c. 1950. In this chapter I apply the tiger densities found for the Malayan Peninsula to the other areas, compensating for differences in vegetative cover and population density and concentration. I also look at figures regarding people killed by tigers and tigers killed by humans in order to establish a trend (numbers up, down, or stable) for each of the four regions. I then establish a link between these sets of figures.

The Balance of Death

The data available on numbers of people killed by tigers are probably fairly reliable, although those for Sumatra have to be corrected for the area outside colonial control. However, the data on tigers killed by people doubtless underestimate the actual numbers, because many cases were not reported to the authorities. These data, together with other estimates, are summarized in Table 10.1 (figures were not available for Malaya).

The data presented here on people killed by tigers are rather straightforward, although a guesstimate appears for Sumatra in the 1850s. This last num-

Table 10.1. Average numbers of (real) tigers killed by people, and people killed by tigers, 1820s–1930s, Sumatra, Java, and Bali

	Killed	1820s	1850s	1870s	1900s	1930s
Sumatra	tigers	—	600	—	500	(500)
	people	—	(400)	175	75	(75)
Java	tigers	350	350	400	65	5
	people	400	200	100	50	(0)
Bali	tigers	—	—	5	(15)	3
	people	—	0	0	—	—

Note: Data shown in parentheses are estimates.

ber is based on Table 3.3, which presented data from the official reports for Palembang and Tapanuli. For the whole of Sumatra, therefore, the figure of people killed by tigers must have been much higher, but only if the estimates for Tapanuli and Palembang may be accepted as reliable, and this is less than certain. In the same table there are figures for two Sumatran Residencies around 1820 showing that 775 people were killed by tigers in Bengkulu and Lampung, but the figure for the latter is so incredibly high (675) that it is not used for Table 10.1. Nevertheless, the 1820 figures in Table 3.3 do suggest that the number of people killed by tigers around 1820 may have been even higher than in c. 1850. The more reliable figures for Java and Sumatra suggest that the numbers of people killed by tigers were dropping during the nineteenth century, and a figure for Sumatra in the 1820s higher than that of the 1850s would be in keeping with this trend.

I have found no data by region for the decades preceding World War II, but in Java the number of people killed by tigers surely had dropped to zero or nearly zero by the late 1940s. However, this was certainly not the case in Sumatra. Mary Bradley, who visited Sumatra in the late 1920s, wrote, "There were tigers enough, for in this Residency of the West Coast they killed a dozen people each year—only eight years ago fifty-one had been killed in one locality." Westenenk, writing about Sumatra in the 1920s and 1930s, mentioned a man-eater who alone was responsible for 22 deaths in a short period. Hazewinkel described the activities of man-eaters with even more dead people to their discredit. One of them killed 39 people; another one, 69 humans, a number he killed during half a year; and finally two tigers, mother and son, who together killed 33 people in about as many weeks.[1] Given such data, the number of people killed annually in the 1930s cannot have been much lower than the figure for the 1900s, which was 75.

As regards Bali, there are a few figures for the 1860s, and, except for one year when four people were reported to be killed, the annual number was zero (see 1850s column). Statistics collected for the years 1897, 1903, and 1904 show the number of people killed on the island of Bali as zero in all three years.[2] This supports what is sometimes said in the literature, namely that in Bali the tigers posed no threat to humans as the two lived in separate areas, the tigers in the mountains and the humans in the plains. In fact, around 1850 tigers were so rarely seen in the densely populated lowlands that the indigenous population said that a state where tigers did appear would soon succumb.[3] Perhaps this was meant as a metaphor, but it is also possible, and even likely, that tigers came down from the mountains only under the worst of circumstances, such as a prolonged drought, which might also topple a dynasty or at least a ruler.

Turning now to the figures of tigers killed by people, there are some difficulties. In the first place, the term "tiger" was ambiguous, often meaning "big cat" (tiger, leopard, or clouded leopard). For some years a breakdown by species is available, but not for other years, and it is unlikely that these proportions remained the same over time, if only because there were changes in the system of bounties.

In the second place, the data available only reflect the number of "tigers" caught or killed for which a bounty had been collected. Some groups of people were probably not interested in collecting the bounty, including professional European animal catchers who trapped animals for zoos and circuses and indigenous groups who lived too far away from a European official to bother. The proportion unreported may not be assumed to have been stable, either. However, this problem was limited to Sumatra, because professional animal catchers did not try trapping tigers in Java because these animals had become rather scarce when this particular group started its business (after 1885).

In Sumatra around 1860, on average 500 "tigers" had been registered as captured or killed per annum, of which approximately 400 were real tigers. These figures cover only the regions then under Dutch rule, or 60% of the surface area of the island. Correcting for this factor would yield a result of 650 tigers killed. However, as no bounties were being paid in the areas outside Dutch control, it seems reasonable to correct downward to about 550. With a modest upward correction for unregistered hunting and trapping, the 1850s figure would become 600. Around 1900, some 349 "tigers," of which approximately 300 were real tigers, were registered as caught or killed on average per year. The area not under Dutch control was then much smaller, but the unregistered killing by professionals had no doubt increased. This brings the total figure for 1900 up to 500.

Figures of tigers killed for bounties were no longer published after 1904 and were no longer collected after 1922. Nor were bounties automatically paid out, but it was left to local functionaries to decide on these matters. In various areas the payment of bounties continued, and private enterprises (such as plantations) often chipped in when the state was reluctant to do so. Nevertheless, the number of tigers captured or killed for a bounty probably decreased. It is also likely that an increase in professional European hunting compensated for this loss. Therefore, the number of tigers killed annually around 1930 probably was not much different from that of 1900, namely c. 500. Owing to the Great Depression of the 1930s tiger hunting may have slumped somewhat. Fewer tigers were caught in the Siak area, because the market in Singapore had more or less disappeared. In Rokan, bounties were no longer paid out after 1932, whereafter the number of tigers increased. Others apparently continued their crusade, and it is therefore not clear whether the Depression made more than a small dent in the figures.[4]

There is no information at all regarding the years around 1820, but the numbers of tigers killed per year would have been considerably lower than c. 1850, given the fact that European hunting was almost entirely absent then, while the availability of firearms was also much lower. Whatever the precise figure, it was surely lower than the number of people killed by tigers in the same year; this last number, as noted above, may have been much higher than the figure of 400 found in 1850. If that is true, it would be the only period in the table in which the number of people killed (perhaps 750) was higher than the number of tigers killed (possibly 500).

Turning now to Java, 1,100 "tigers" were registered as captured or killed at the end of the 1820s and 900 around 1850, of which the latter figure is certainly too low. I have assumed that the figures for these years were more or less the same, and that about one-third of the animals registered were real tigers. The rounded figures given in the table for these years, therefore, are 350 in both cases. The figure for the 1870s derives from an average number of 1,431 "tigers" having been registered as killed around this year. One-third of that figure would have been nearer 480 than the 400 given in the table, but the high bounties paid for leopards and the fact that tigers were becoming scarcer probably influenced the proportion of real tigers.

The proportion of real tigers to "tigers" is known for the years around 1900, and the number given in the table (65) is reliable. In all these cases there should probably be a slight upward correction due to European hunters who did not bother to collect the bounty for a dead animal. However, this has little effect, as the number of kills by European "Sunday" hunters was not much compared to the registered kills.

Finally, the estimate for the 1930s is based on the fact that the number of tigers had by then reached a very low level, and shot or trapped tigers had become something of a rarity. In the years 1938 up to and including 1941, there is information on eight tigers having died, of whom seven were killed by human interference (trapped, poisoned, or shot). This is probably a rather complete record, which implies that two tigers were killed per year on the eve of World War II (Hoogerwerf 1970, 242–43).

In sum, during the 1820s the number of people killed by tigers in Java was larger than the number of tigers killed, as was probably the case in Sumatra in the same period. In both regions this ratio would be reversed from the 1850s onward. From then on, people were a bigger threat to tigers than the other way around.

Numerical data for Bali are rare. Prior to the war between the colonial Government and Bali from 1846 to 1849, information on tigers is absent, and very few people even knew that there were tigers on the island of Bali. However, before 1882, when the Dutch established the Residency Bali and Lombok, the situation was not much better, and only after the final subjugation of Bali, between 1906 and 1908, would more detailed information become available.

From 1906 onward Bali became a favorite spot with big-game hunters, who were attracted by the largely uninhabited mountain areas of the island, abounding with deer and tiger. The holotype—that is, the tiger upon which the claim of the Bali tiger as a separate subspecies was based—was shot in 1909, one year after the final skirmishes between the Balinese and the Dutch. Many hunters made an annual trip to the island. Among these was the riflemaker E. Munaut, from Surabaya, who had brought down 20 Bali tigers by 1913. The well-known big-game hunters the Ledeboer brothers, from east Java, managed to shoot 11 Bali tigers before 1915. Another annual visitor, an Englishman living in Banyuwangi, had shot 11 Bali tigers by 1918. The table puts the annual loss of tiger lives owing to this kind of human interference at 15, a figure that includes indigenous trapping and hunting. It is probably a conservative estimate.

We can be more certain about the years around the turn of the century, when data for three years are available, yielding on average four tigers killed per year. One should probably add one tiger per year for (unreported) European hunting prior to the final colonial conquest. The result, five tigers, appears in the table under the 1870s column, reflecting the "precolonial" situation.

There is a rather precise figure for the mid-1930s. Zimmermann counted 14 tigers shot in the "empty" northwestern area between 1933 and 1937, or roughly 3 tigers on average per year. In 1937 there were still six tigers left in the area, and higher up in the mountains some more were supposed to be present. There was still some shooting going on around 1940, but the tiger disappeared here almost certainly in the 1940s.[5]

For the period dealt with in Table 10.1, only the data for Sumatra and Java are complete enough to discuss possible trends regarding tigers killed by humans. Killing tigers in Bali probably increased after 1906, only to drop off quite soon because almost all tigers had been killed in some 25 to 30 years. The data for Sumatra suggest a drop between the 1850s and the 1900s, after which a more or less stable level was reached. Numbers of tigers killed prior to the 1850s were probably lower. The data for Java suggest a rather stable level between the 1820s and 1870s, with perhaps an increase after 1850 and certainly a sharp drop after the 1870s because there were no longer all that many tigers.

Data prior to 1800 are not entirely absent, at least for Java, but there are so many uncertainties that it is impossible to establish a trend. As noted previously, 200 tigers were said to have been captured in a few months in central Java in 1620. If this figure is to be trusted—a very big if indeed—the figure for the entire island could have been 300 or even 400 in one year. Thus we would arrive at an estimate comparable to figures dating from the period 1820s–1870s. In 1747–48, 80 tigers were destroyed around Batavia, a figure, again, to be compared with similar levels in the early nineteenth century. However, the pre-1800 numbers may reflect extraordinarily bad years (drought, etc.), and the evidence is too weak for firm conclusions. One can say only that, occasionally and locally, nineteenth-century levels of tigers killed and captured may have been reached between 1600 and 1800.

One conclusion that can be drawn from these figures (and from this discussion) is that there is not one trend for the whole area during the period between the 1820s and the 1930s.

Reconstructing Tiger Population Numbers in the Past

Chapter 2 presented data on tiger densities in India and the Malay world. These varied from 1 to 17 tigers per 100 square km. Most of these ratios, however, refer to nature reserves and similar game-rich areas, and they cannot be applied to entire regions. Luckily, an estimate is available for the end of the colonial period regarding the Malayan Peninsula as a whole. The British hunter Locke estimated around 1950 that there were some 3,000 tigers to be found on the Peninsula. This would reflect a ratio of 2 tigers per 100 square

**Table 10.2. Estimated number of tigers in the four "Malay"
regions, 1820–1950**

	1820	1900	1950
Malaya	2,000	3,000	3,000
Sumatra	7,000	6,500	6,500
Java	2,500	500	25
Bali	150	125	0
Total	11,650	10,125	9,525

km. I will argue that a somewhat lower ratio (such as 1.5) obtains for Sumatra around the same time.

At that time Bali had already lost all or almost all of its tigers, and Java was not much better off. The ratio for Malaya in 1950 might apply to Java and Bali around 1820. Estimates based on these ratios are presented in Table 10.2.

The 1950 figure for Malaya is given in the literature. The other two figures are based on the following assumptions. Environmental change between 1900 and 1950 was partly negative for tigers (more wet rice lands and urban areas), and partly positive (more secondary forest taking the place of primary forest). This implies that, on balance, tiger densities may not have changed much, the more so as hunting pressure was fairly low. Between 1820 and 1900 densities may have increased, as there was a growth of typical tiger habitats (secondary forest, etc.). The estimated increase as given in Table 10.2 (1,000) is really pure guesswork and might err on the high side, so that a number of 2,500 tigers in Malaya in 1820 is perhaps equally likely.

Regarding Sumatra, I have applied a slightly lower ratio for 1950 than the Malayan one. This is based on the fact that, although population densities were roughly the same, a higher proportion of Sumatra's surface area was by then taken up by cities and towns, continuous stretches of permanently cultivated fields, and other tigerless areas, mostly in populous upland valleys (Batak, Minangkabau)—and had been so for a long time. As was shown in Chapter 6, Sumatra probably also had suffered more from tiger hunting, so a slightly lower tiger density is plausible. Around 1900, circumstances were probably somewhat better for tigers, particularly because population growth and land clearing for plantations had led to the creation of more tiger-friendly ecotones, but on the other hand hunting pressure was probably higher. Around 1820 there was still much primary forest, which was less attractive to tigers than forest fringes and disturbed forest. On the other hand there was probably less hunting pressure, so that on balance densities may have been slightly higher than around 1900, though by how much is anyone's guess.

Around 1820, Java had a much lower population density and fewer unbroken wet-rice plains and urban areas than it would have later on. Java's population density around 1820 (c. 45/km^2) was no doubt higher even then than Sumatra's was around 1950 (c. 20), and the proportion of the surface area under wet rice was also higher (some 10% versus 2%). But Java has a monsoon vegetation and therefore does not have the large expanses of climax rainforest vegetation shunned by tigers, as did Sumatra and Malaya. Therefore, application of Malaya's 1950 tiger density figure to Java in 1820 is appropriate.

Numbers for Bali are not easily reconstructed, as there is not much to go on. Bali was densely populated in the early nineteenth century, and applying the ratio of Malaya around 1950 to Bali in 1820 might seem to be overstating the case for Bali. This procedure would yield 120 tigers for the whole island. However, tigers survived in Bali at least until the 1940s, and, given the heavy hunting that went on from the 1900s onward, such a low figure for 1820 seems unlikely. The tigers were concentrated in the mountainous uplands of the island; conditions there might have been ideal for tigers. Taking these possibilities into consideration I have opted for a slightly higher number around 1820. It is still lower than the maximum number suggested by John Seidensticker, who stated that Bali could never have had more than 125 adult tigers. Figuring one juvenile for each adult would yield a maximum of 250 tigers, a number that may have obtained in a more remote past (Seidensticker 1987, 4). Around 1900, on the eve of higher hunting pressure owing to the final conquest, numbers may have dropped somewhat, perhaps not so much because of hunting, which was rather modest prior to 1906, but because of increased population density.

Comparing the Estimates

Under "normal" circumstances, tigers produce a surplus in terms of offspring. A modest level of hunting, therefore, would not be a threat to a stable tiger population. There is empirical evidence that among big cats densities will not be depressed if hunters remove less than 10–20% of the population annually (Karanth and Stith 1999, 108). Therefore, the data on hunting in Table 10.1 can be used as a check on the figures in Table 10.2.

Starting with Java, it can be said that the data for that region are consistent. Hunting pressure throughout the period was higher than 10%, and during the second half of the century higher than 20% of the hypothetical population; a continuously declining tiger population is, therefore, to be expected. The few figures we have for Bali also are consistent. Hunting pressure during the early years of this century was higher than 10% and probably higher than 20% of the population, and extinction around 1950 was the result. In Sumatra the comparison also largely supports the hypothetical population figures. If the numbers hunted in the 1850s also obtained in later decades, a percentage of more than 10 and a slight drop in total population, as is shown in Table 10.2, would then be the expected result. As hunting pressure after 1900 was certainly somewhat lower than 10%, the tiger population may have remained stable.

Other things being equal, one might expect that lower numbers of human tiger victims would correspond to lower numbers of tigers. This is, indeed, what can be observed in Java. It is also seen in Sumatra, although it is difficult to explain why the figure for human victims around 1900 is so much lower than the one for the 1870s, since a sharp drop in the number of tigers during those years is somewhat unlikely. The figure presented in Table 10.1 for the 1900s (6,500) is only slightly lower than that for the 1820s (7,000), and, unless the number of tigers peaked somewhere in the middle of the century (and then dropped off rather sharply), one would expect a gradual decline. The only explanation is that the pattern of land clearing and the growth of towns were increasingly keeping tigers and humans apart. This process created concentrations of humans on the one hand, and, on the other hand, concentrations of tigers in areas at quite some distance from the centers of civilization. Thus, a situation would have been created that already obtained naturally in Bali, where numbers of victims (of both species) had always been low because tigers and humans hardly ever met.

It has been assumed that between 3 and 10 tigers per thousand were man-eaters. Is it possible to check this supposition with the data in these tables? In the case of Java the answer can be affirmative. Tigers were killed there almost immediately when they had killed a human being. This implies that the number of people killed per year more or less equals the number of man-eaters. Thus, in the 1820s, 400 people killed per year imply 400 man-eaters, or 160 per thousand of the hypothetical number of tigers. That is a far cry from the 10 per thousand maximum suggested by the literature. If that figure were right, Java would have had 40,000 tigers in the 1820s, a figure that is totally impossible.[6] As regards Sumatra it is impossible to carry out such a check, as tigers could go "unpunished" for a long time and often killed various people before they were captured.

Even though the sets of data are compatible, the figures in Table 10.2 remain estimates. They give an impression of the order of magnitude of the numbers involved. The very least that can be said is that for Malay tigers as a whole, the period 1800 to 1950 was one of a very slow decline. If we base our calculations of the rate of decline on the figures given in Table 10.2, we get a rate of decline of 0.2% per year on average during the nineteenth century and an annual average of 0.1% for the first half of the twentieth century. Today there are not more than 1,200 Malay tigers left, which implies a much higher rate of decline since the 1950s, on average 4.2% per year.

Changes in the Distribution of Tigers over Time

No information is available on the distribution of tigers on the Malayan Peninsula. Around 1950 it had the highest tiger density of the four Malay regions, and it is not unlikely that tigers were still ubiquitous.

There is not all that much information on tigers in Bali either, although probably enough to get an impression of the extinction process. Pierre Dubois, who stayed on the island of Bali for quite some time around 1830, was the first European to provide information on the Bali tiger. He wrote that the mountainous areas of Bali—that is, roughly the northern part of the island—contained many more tigers than people. Friederich mentioned the nearly unpopulated state of Jembrana and the mountains of the states of Buleleng and Tabanan as tiger areas, which, taken together, cover the entire western half of Bali. About a decade later, the Swiss botanist H. Zollinger visited Bali, where he found tigers in the mountains of Bangli, eastern Bali. Together, therefore, Friederich and Zollinger confirm the presence of tigers in the entire northern half of Bali. Another ten years later, the American tourist A. S. Bickmore and the Dutchman R. van Eck mentioned tigers in the western half of the island. Jacobs, who came to Bali in 1881, named the state of Bangli explicitly as regards the presence of tigers. He was, however, the last one to do so, and it seems likely that the Bali tiger had been rare outside the western part of the island since the 1860s. Jacobs confirmed that they were to be found only in the mountains. During the last decades of his existence, the Bali tiger was probably confined to the western tip of the island.[7]

In Sumatra tigers were not confined to the mountainous areas. They were found from the mangrove belt to the upper slopes of the mountains, although they may have been scarce in the more swampy areas of the East Coast. This was equally true around 1850 as it was c. 1900, and also at the end of the colonial era. Nevertheless, there were some areas were they were very seldom seen. Such was the case in the entirely deforested Karo Batak and Toba Batak highlands around 1890, but probably much earlier; these plains had been stripped of their forest cover long ago, as witness Junghuhn's description dating from the 1840s. In the 1920s, tigers were no longer present in the area around Fort de Kock (Bukittinggi), and this may have been true for most of the rice-producing valleys in the Minangkabau uplands of central Sumatra. As these upland areas had been densely populated for quite some time, tigers may have vanished there much earlier, but this is not documented. Around 1930, game had become scarce in the Aceh lowlands, and tigers likely had followed the deer and wild boar to the mountains. A 1932 survey stated that tigers, though not yet rare, had shown a notable drop in numbers in the densely populated areas. Finally, around 1950 it was said that tigers had not been seen around the city of Bengkulu in living memory, and this may have been true for most of the cities.[8] At the end of the colonial period, then, tigers had disappeared from the more densely populated areas, but in terms of surface area this was not an impressive proportion.

Around 1820, tigers were mentioned in all Residencies of the island of Java that were ruled by the colonial government. It is important to specify "the island of Java" because the island of Madura, usually administratively regarded as part of Java, had no tigers, and none were mentioned at the beginning of the nineteenth century. However, an encyclopedia dating from the 1860s stated that according to some people there were no dangerous animals in Madura, but that others argued that there were tigers and leopards. A study dating from 1888 stated explicitly that tigers could be found occasionally in the island's teak forests. A zoogeographical map dated 1938 excluded Madura from the area where tigers could be found. I am inclined to side with the latter source and with the one from 1808. The leopards mentioned around 1860 could be a reference to a tiny archipelago, administratively part of Madura, called the Kangean Islands, where leopards were found around 1930 (and were still present c. 1980).[9]

In some of the government Residencies, even as early as 1820 tigers were rarely mentioned, namely in Batavia and Kedu. The first Residency comprises the city of Batavia and its Environs, an area outside the city limits that had been stripped of its original vegetative cover and was largely dedicated to estate agriculture. Small wonder that tigers were rare in this area. Kedu, in the southwestern part of central Java, had the highest population density of all government Residencies around 1820, with almost 170 people per square km, while the islandwide density was only 45. Apart from the mountainous fringes of the Residency, therefore, tigers could find no (forested) place to hide.

After 1830, at the end of the Java War, the central Javanese Residencies Banyumas, Bagelen, Madiun, and Kediri, until then part of the Principalities, were ceded to the Dutch. At the same time, information on the remaining Principalities, Yogyakarta and Surakarta, started to flow more abundantly. Tigers were to be found in all these areas, although little was reported from Yogya, as these animals were probably restricted to the mountains surrounding the central plain.

In 1830, tigers were still to be found in all Residencies of the island. They were also present at all altitudes, from the beaches to the highest upland valleys. In theory, a tiger could have walked from the Ujung Kulon peninsula in the extreme west to the Purwo peninsula in the extreme east of Java. They could have stuck to the mountain range that forms the spinal column of the island without coming across cultivated lands, thus easily avoiding the valleys and towns where the population was concentrated. In all likelihood, the Kedu-Yogya Valley was the first breach in this continuum, and the 1820s or 1830s may have been the last decades that tigers could be found in these lowlands.

The following story may illustrate this process. Around 1830 two parties visited the so-called Valley of the Dead, on the Dieng plateau, at the northern fringe of Kedu, where animals and people dropped dead because of the presence of a suffocating natural gas (carbon dioxide?). They saw the dead bodies of tigers, wild boar, deer, and humans. Junghuhn visited the same area 13 times between 1838 and 1845, but he only found a human body and a number of dead boar, but no longer tigers. The Dieng plateau, still largely uninhabited and covered with forests in 1828, had by 1838 been cleared from most of its original vegetation, and in its stead the area was now covered with meadows, market gardens, tobacco, and tea.

After 1830, we do not hear much about tigers in the Residency of Buitenzorg, to the south of Batavia, of which the town of Buitenzorg formed the core, located around the summer palace of the Governor-General. It was also an area of estates owned by Chinese and Europeans. Tigers could still be found in the mountains, from where they made occasional forays, but such occurrences were becoming exceptional.[10]

By 1855, tigers had become rare in a whole group of adjacent Residencies in central Java, including Banyumas, Bagelen, Kedu, and Yogyakarta, and they had more or less disappeared from there by 1870. In the two adjacent Residencies, Surakarta and Madiun, the tigers had virtually vanished ten years later, by 1880. Bagelen and Kedu had population densities way above the Java average, and, although this was not the case in the other Residencies, the valleys where the population was concentrated did reach high densities. Moreover, this was the region where tigers had been captured continuously for the tiger rituals at the courts. Therefore, it is not surprising that it was the first greater region—southern central Java—where the tiger was no longer found in the lowlands and on the lower slopes of the mountains. The rituals were no longer performed in the Principalities after 1882. One function of these rituals may have been to rid the countryside of troublesome tigers, and it seems that they had finally succeeded in doing so.

Between 1870 and 1880 tigers had become very rare in another group of neighboring Residencies those of Tegal, Pekalongan, and Semarang, all in the northwestern section of central Java. All three Residencies had a higher than average population density. By 1880, therefore, a broad tigerless corridor had been created, namely the entire western part of central Java, although some tigers have been lurking in the mountains. Between 1880 and 1895, tigers disappeared also from the adjacent Residencies of Jepara, Rembang, and Surabaya, in the northeastern part of central Java. Surabaya and Jepara had higher population densities than average. The tigers in Jepara, concentrated on Mount Muria, went out with a bang, killing 44 people in 1894, one of the last documented "tiger plagues" in Java.

By the eve of the twentieth century, tigers had become very rare in the whole central part of the island, again with the exception of the still forested upper slopes of some mountains, where small numbers probably survived. Tigers were now to be found only in western and eastern Java, two regions where population densities—apart from Batavia—were much lower than in central Java. From 1900 onward there were in fact two separate tiger populations that could no longer exchange genes. After 1905, tigers were no longer mentioned in Kediri, the border between central and eastern Java, and seldom in Cirebon, the border between central and western Java. Thus, tigers continued to become more and more concentrated in the western- and easternmost parts of the island. Just prior to World War II, tigers could be found only in the Residencies of Banten and Priangan in the west and Besuki and Banyuwangi in the east.

This concentration (or rather isolation and separation) process culminated after Indonesian independence, when, in the 1960s, tigers were still mentioned only in two nature reserves: Ujung Kulon in Banten and Meru Betiri in Besuki. By 1970 they were no longer spotted in Ujung Kulon.[11] It came as quite a surprise when tigers allegedly appeared in central Java in 1997 and 1999, outside any reserve and in an area where tigers were assumed to have vanished about a century earlier.

Why Did Tigers Disappear Where They Did?

A 1997 article on the present and future status of the tiger features the following passage: "Studies by Karanth, Sunquist, Seidensticker, and others suggest that density of suitable prey is the most reliable indicator of how a tiger population is likely to fare. And history bears them out. Tiger hunting and loss of habitat were once blamed for the loss of the Bali, Caspian, and Javan tigers—and both surely played a part in their decline. But the latest research suggests that it was the loss of their prey that finally made their lives literally insupportable."

In a 1998 article, "illegal poaching for economic gain" is seen as the major factor leading to the tiger's demise. The conservationist A. Hoogerwerf, writing in the late 1960s but mainly referring to the period 1920 to 1950 in Java, gave another opinion. According to him, most tigers had been killed because they had eaten poisoned carcasses of wild boar. Around 1880, when the Java tiger was already on its way out, Mohnike had yet another explanation, arguing that it was a combination of population growth and therefore deforestation and the loss of other "wild" areas, along with the bounties paid out by government, or, in other words, hunting and trapping.[12]

Why are these explanations so different? The most plausible answer is that each may have been valid in its own time but not necessarily in other periods or at other places. It is, therefore, not to be excluded that one can be unable to present an explanation that applies to all situations where tigers disappeared or were/are about to disappear. Here the emphasis is on Java, where the extinction process of the tiger is well documented, but a few words can be offered about Bali, where the explanation seems to be straightforward. Prior to 1900 humans and tigers lived in separate areas and both species kept largely to themselves. Tigers killed few humans, and as long as that was the case the Balinese were apparently not much interested in killing them. Population growth at the end of the nineteenth century may have led to a slight increase in the number of confrontations. Shortly after 1900, direct colonial rule was established and European hunting increased sharply. As the number of tigers in Bali had never been large, a sharp increase in hunting may have been solely responsible for the rather rapid extinction of the Bali tiger, who vanished some 40 years after European hunting started. However, disappearance of prey may have contributed to the tiger's demise (Paardt 1929, 55–56).

Turning now to Java, it is difficult to escape the conclusion that there was a link in the nineteenth century between the declining numbers of tigers and the high figures on tigers killed and captured. Weighing the evidence presented in Chapter 6, one must conclude that most tigers were trapped rather than hunted. It seems that the specific tiger-traps were particularly successful, but poison and spring-guns were also reported to be quite efficient. Hunting by Europeans was in all likelihood only marginally important, as there were not all that many tigers left when European hunting became popular, after the 1870s. Nevertheless, the presence of Europeans and European guns in indigenous hunting parties, in addition to the bounty system in the directly governed Residencies between roughly 1815 and the 1870s, must have had some influence.

Tigers disappeared first in densely populated Residencies, where large, often unbroken tracts of permanently cultivated agricultural land had rendered the area unattractive to tigers and other game owing to a lack of cover. Many of these Residencies had problems with wild boar because so many tigers had been killed in the most densely settled areas. This led to the launching of massive wild boar hunts, in which thousands were killed per Residency. The relatively few tigers that were still around would then have become more troublesome, because their normal quarries had vanished. As they started to bother livestock and humans on a larger scale than before, they would be hunted down even more relentlessly, and soon tigers would be so rare that even cattle-lifting and man-eating stopped.

By the 1930s, when a game census of sorts was undertaken and the tiger was no longer found in central Java, there was not much other game left, either. By then, hunting (in general) was strictly regulated, but in many areas it was too late, and even game that had once been so abundant that it was regarded as a nuisance, like wild boar, had become rare in many areas, while deer had often disappeared entirely. At best, the deer, counted in the thousands per Residency around the middle of the nineteenth century, were now to be found in the hundreds. However, the absence of game postdated the absence of the tiger. Around 1900, even though tigers had become rare by then, many central Javanese areas had been good hunting grounds for European sportsmen.

For Java, then, habitat loss and indigenous trapping had rid some areas of tigers before the Europeans started to intervene seriously. During the nineteenth century, European guns and hunters together with continuing indigenous trapping and hunting and—partly European induced—continuing loss of habitat chased the tiger from most of central Java. Locally, disappearance of prey (wild boar) made for increased tiger trouble and, therefore, increased hunting pressure.

But what about western and eastern Java, where, at the turn of the century, some 500 tigers were probably still alive? These areas were still frequented by European hunters, and game seems to have been relatively abundant. Unfortunately, the game census of 1934–35, when the number of tigers had dropped to 50 or so, is not at its most informative regarding these areas, probably because they were still too "wild" for a reliable estimate. Nevertheless, it is possible that there was occasionally barely enough prey for even rather small numbers of tigers (e.g., *JvNIVN* 1935, 51). Numbers of game of all types probably were dropping, including the number of tigers. And whereas most game received some protection (licenses, bag limits, closed season), this was not the case with the tiger, who was "fair game" until the very end of the colonial period. Again, hunting was more important in getting rid of the tiger than the absence of prey, even though around this time western and eastern Java were probably no longer as game-rich as they used to be.

So far we have two "models," the Balinese and the Javanese one. In the first model, tigers and humans hardly bothered each other, and indigenous hunting and trapping was probably unimportant. European hunters, who swiftly dispatched the rather small numbers of tigers present on the island, brought about the extinction of the Bali tiger. As the same hunters went also after other game, lack of prey may have speeded up the tiger's demise. I will call this the "sudden death model."

In the Javanese model, tigers were already quite troublesome to humans during the early seventeenth century, and humans were quick to return the favor. The VOC in and around Batavia and the state of Mataram in central Java stimulated tiger trapping by way of bounties and tiger rituals, respectively. Tiger numbers had already started to drop owing to indigenous hunting and trapping and to loss of habitat prior to serious European hunting. When that became more important the tiger had already been hunted to extinction in central Java. This I will call the "lingering death model."

The Sumatran model, in which the tiger was not hunted to the brink of extinction during the colonial period, contains elements of both the Balinese and the Javanese models. Although tigers and humans often did not coexist peacefully, human attempts to kill tigers had not made much of a dent in the tiger population prior to European hunting. Although there was a Minangkabau state of sorts, it did not have the numbers of people and the power that the central Javanese state of Mataram had, and there is no information on tiger rituals organized by the court. In the few areas where the tiger was no longer found in the nineteenth century, loss of habitat was probably as important as hunting, if not more important. However, tigers were so numerous, and there were so many areas where they could hide themselves, that even European hunting and European guns did not make much of a difference. At most, the Europeans kept the tiger population from growing. I will call this the "balance model."

The situation on the Malayan Peninsula probably did not differ much from that in Sumatra, and it seems likely that it followed the "balance model." In Sumatra and Malaya the real onslaught seems to have come after independence, as was the case in India (Greenough 1991, 10–11).

Conclusion

Theoretically, numbers of tigers must have grown when human populations were on the increase. In the Malay world, however, the Malayan Peninsula perhaps apart, the rise of the tiger predated the "proto-statistical" nineteenth century, which implies that the figures may never be at our disposal to illustrate this process. The first half of that century may have been a turning point in the relationship between tigers and humans, as it was for the last time in Sumatra and Java when more humans were killed than tigers. During the early decades of the nineteenth century, the tiger population had already started its decline in Java. On a much more restricted scale, it would also start in Sumatra later in the century. After 1900, tiger numbers probably stagnated in the Malayan area and Sumatra, but they fell sharply in Bali and Java.

Decline and fall were largely caused by loss of habitat, trapping, and hunting. Decline (or the absence of it) seems to have followed three different models, namely the sudden death, the lingering death, and the balance model.

Which model applied was determined in the first place by environmental givens. A sharp distinction can be drawn between mountains and plains (Bali); tropical rainforests, where humans came late and multiplied slowly (Malaya, Sumatra); and monsoon forests, where relatively high population densities obtained even at an early date (Java). Dense (Sumatra) versus relatively open forested areas (Java) was another relevant environmental factor, given that it influenced hunting behavior. In the second place, the presence or absence of large and powerful states influenced which model applied, partly determined by population densities. Variation in beliefs, as was shown between Java and Sumatra (see Chapter 8), seems to have reinforced environmentally induced differences in hunting behavior. Finally, the timing of serious European influence was important.

11

Living Apart Together

What was the historical relationship between tigers and people in the Malay world? The present chapter focuses on the main features of this relationship: fear of the tiger, the struggle for power between humans and tigers, and the tiger as a symbol of the frontier between nature and culture. At the same time we are confronted with the notion that people and tigers are somehow related. The current discussion explores whether that notion can be held simultaneously with ideas on fear and power struggles as main features in the tiger-human relationship. Finally, I discuss the mutual influences of the two species, and the influence of both on their environment.

Fear of the Tiger

In many areas in the Malay world the indigenous population had sufficient reasons to fear the tiger. In a demographic sense, the human death toll caused by tigers was, on average, not important, no matter how impressive the absolute figures, particularly the earlier ones, may seem. Locally the number of people killed by tigers could be quite high, and perhaps more importantly, in many districts and villages the man-eater threat was permanently present. In some areas, such as Batavia around 1625 and Singapore around 1850, tiger killings made a substantial contribution to the total death rate. In the case of Batavia, such a high proportion may have set the tone for decades and perhaps even centuries to come.

There are several manifestations of this fear of the tiger. The one probably most often mentioned was the refusal to use the word "tiger" when discussing

the animal. Also found in the reports is the phenomenon of deserted or stockaded villages. At least as impressive to the modern researcher is the refusal to
take measures against marauding tigers, who in some instances killed dozens
of people before they were captured or killed. Here it seems that fear of the
tiger's revenge, or perhaps fear of the revenge of the spirit that inhabited the
tiger, was stronger than all other considerations. There are also several descriptions of the atmosphere of joy and release from pent-up feelings of fear, rage,
and revenge when a tiger had been destroyed.

It is even possible to argue that the inclination of many Malays to regard the
tiger as the embodiment of a spirit represents fear, though it may not seem a
particularly compelling argument in view of the fact that animism has always
been a strong feature in Malay beliefs. However, various instances of spirit beliefs were highly elaborate complexes "constructed" around particularly life-
threatening occasions, such as certain illnesses (cholera, smallpox), and particular animals, such as the tiger. There are examples in the literature of villages
being struck by, for example, a cholera epidemic after a "tiger epidemic." The
villagers experienced this as the coming of one evil spirit after another, or even
the same spirit in various forms. I would argue that these instances reflect in-
tense feelings of fear.

Particularly regarding the belief in weretigers, such an interpretation seems
to be warranted. This is a rather complex phenomenon, in many respects similar to that of early modern European witchcraft beliefs. Fear of supernatural
powers of certain people seems to go hand in hand with feelings of hate, resentment, guilt, and fear toward poor people. On the other hand, it seems
likely that these emotions were being exploited by some itinerant beggars-
cum-bandits, who played on the fear they inspired in order to part the more
gullible from their money.

How can fear have been so important when many people from the Malay
world also looked upon tigers as ancestors? Many Malay people refused to capture or kill tigers because they regarded these animals as the embodiments of
the souls of ancestors who, far from harming their offspring, were supposed to
protect the villagers. In fact, there need not be a contradiction between the notion of the tiger as family and the feelings of fear inspired by these animals.

Fear of the tiger was also found in the writings of Europeans. Sometimes
this may have reflected indigenous opinions, but often it represented European fears. The distinction between European and indigenous fears is not always easily made, as many European or Indo-European children, born in the
Malay world, were brought up more by their *amah* or *babu* (indigenous nanny)

than by their own parents. These children were steeped in local folklore and beliefs and did not necessarily have typical European points of view regarding these matters.

The stories told by Europeans emphasize a number of behavioral elements, such as the fact that in many regions tigers operate mainly at night, they stalk and jump their quarries, and they return to decomposing kills, which are sometimes even unearthed if buried. Thus the tiger was mainly perceived as a nocturnal, ghoulish, carrion-eating, and cowardly danger, or, in other words, the perfect embodiment of evil.

It can be argued that the tiger, as the representation of evil, stands for much more than just himself. At the very least he represents the forest or jungle, which in turn stands for wild tropical nature. Wild tropical nature is a threatening environment that was (and is) feared by (most) Europeans and "Malay" alike. It was a colonial stereotype that the indigenous population "was close to nature." In reality many Malay peasants feared and hated wild nature, partly because forests are spiritually dangerous places. Only the nomadic and semi-sedentary groups felt at home in these surroundings. Generally speaking, however, the tiger was a magnificent symbol for the threat posed by wild nature.

Seen in an even broader perspective, it is tempting to argue that the tiger stands for the Orient as a whole. The Orient—of which the Malay area formed a part—was a dangerous place for Europeans, and not only because of the many forests to be found there. It is certainly possible that the dangers were overstated, but there is no doubt that many observers perceived the area to be quite dangerous. Europeans lived in constant fear of all kinds of diseases and of climatic and other environmental uncertainties. But people were seen as at least as dangerous as these natural phenomena. As the rulers in many parts of Asia, the Europeans were almost permanently alive to attacks by pirates, insurrections, peasant unrest, and all other manifestations of indigenous discontent. A silent killer who comes in the night seems to be an apt metaphor for such feelings of uncertainty. In fact, there were many parallels between hunting and capturing tigers on the one hand and hunting and catching criminals, pirates, and rebels on the other, including the fact that bounties were promised in both cases.[1]

One might even wish to take the tiger as a metaphor one step further. Europeans were warned, time and again, by their own spiritual and moral leaders that they were in danger of becoming morally degenerated if they "went native," yielding to the many temptations of the Orient. Although the threat appeared to come from the outside, it was the dark side of the human soul to which these temptations appealed, and thus it was the "evil from within" that was the real threat. After all, attempts to curb "the wild beast within us" (Plato) had been a concern of European philosophers, moralists, and theologians since the dawn of "high" European civilization (Thomas 1984, 36). Fear of this dark side may well be read into the European fear of the Orient; fear of the tiger as the epitome of evil arguably symbolized both. Therefore, tiger hunting and other ritual forms of killing tigers by Europeans and indigenous people have a symbolic meaning far beyond the actual killing of the animal.

During specific periods and under specific circumstances, tigers were no doubt dangerous to people. Nevertheless, it is also clear that many European writers stressed this point and often exaggerated the tiger threat, selecting those stories for a European audience that best reflected the frailty of indigenous human life. In this way they emphasized the need for European hunting and for protection of the local population in general, thus legitimizing colonial rule ("the white man's burden"). The big and brave white hunter as the savior of the Malays, as it were, and hunting as an essential element of the *mission civilisatrice*. It made an even better story that the tiger seemed to be afraid of Europeans but not of "natives."

Indigenous people also might have overemphasized the threat posed by the tiger and their fear of him. In such instances the tiger threat was used as a ruse, one of the many "weapons of the weak."

Finally, one of the features of the tiger that contributed considerably to the fear he inspired in Easterners and Westerners alike was his unpredictability. In the eyes of the Europeans, unpredictability was one of the main characteristics of the Oriental despot. Specialized hunters, who had thoroughly studied the tiger's behavior, could predict many of his moves, but in the end he remained an enigma and was thus again the perfect symbol of the Orient. To the Malay people the tiger's behavior was equally unpredictable, but in their eyes that was a typical feature of Europeans (together with rudeness and aggressiveness), which, at least in Java, gave rise to the symbolic role of the tiger as the European in the tiger-buffalo fights. It is remarkable to see that the tiger apparently reflected, in the eyes of both parties concerned, the worst features of "the other."

The Struggle for Power

There are some stories about people who met a tiger and lived to tell the tale, and it is true that tigers did not often kill Europeans. There is, however, also overwhelming evidence that tigers and people were often engaged in bloody confrontations. In fact, some areas seem to have been on a permanent war footing, with stockaded villages and all. From the earliest sources onward the dominant imagery, both verbal and visual and European and indigenous alike, is one of rival polities contending for power.

The tiger was called Lord or King of the Forest (*raja hutan*), and various Malay rulers, who saw themselves as the kings of the civilized (that is, nonforest) world, took this title quite seriously. Indeed, some rulers and noblemen were so impressed with the tiger that they styled themselves "tiger-kings" or added the word tiger in other ways to their title.[2] Tigers were housed at the court as honored guests of equal rank, although at the same time prisoners of war. They were also engaged in real or ritual battles with their adversaries from the nonforest world, be it people or buffaloes. In these encounters the tiger may be a king, but as the king of the forest he stands for wild nature in general and therefore for chaos, and, ultimately, evil. The Malay rulers, in turn, represented (agri)culture, civilization, order, and therefore good.

The tiger is also quite often the King of Beasts in fables. There are a great many fables, set in the world of animals, in which (King) Tiger is fooled by a much weaker animal, namely Goat and particularly Mousedeer. These trickster stories remind the European reader of the medieval fables with the Fox as main protagonist (*Van den Vos Reinaerde, Roman de Renart, Reinhart Fuchs*), in which the ruler and the nobility of the animal kingdom received the treatment to which the tiger was submitted in the Malay world.[3] Fables of this type are often interpreted as "weapons of the weak": it is only in these stories that the power struggle between the rich and mighty on the one hand and the poor and powerless on the other is played out in favor of the latter.

Rulers were not the only Malay people who regarded the tigers as rival kings. Those Indonesians who carried Government documents were convinced that the King of the Forest would grant them immunity as representatives of the Government.

Power over tigers—and tiger spirits—was also claimed by tiger-charmers and "holy" people, who supposedly were able to make the tigers do their bidding. In fact, spiritually powerful people had such a strong hold over tigers that the latter would even serve the former after their death, being the guardians of their graves.

In the eyes of the Europeans things were not so different. Raffles stated in so many words that he intended to resume the Empire of Man, which meant waging war on the Empire of Brute Beasts. This war was most impressively symbolized by the large-scale tiger hunt. These large-scale hunts were more typical for British India than for the Malayan Peninsula and the Indonesian Archipelago, but they took place nevertheless. It was in the tiger hunt that the European could play out, and could be seen to play out, feelings of superiority over the people of the Orient. These feelings implied protection of the indigenous population, but also submission. Taming the tiger stood for taming wild nature, and taming wild Oriental nature was a fitting metaphor for colonialism, of which submission was the core. As John MacKenzie (1988, 47), wrote about hunting and the British Empire, "Big-game hunting represented the striving and victory of civilized man over the darker primeval and untamed forces still at work in the world," and "It was as though the virile imperialist and the lion—in India the tiger—were locked in deadly combat for control of the natural world."

In the eyes of the European hunter of the nineteenth and twentieth centuries, killing the tiger was also a battle won in the war between the Empire of Reason and the Empire of Superstition. The European hunter, usually well provided with the best and most modern hunting equipment, was not afraid to kill even the most ferocious tigers, the *keramat* (haunted) ones included. Thus, in their view they had demonstrated that fear of spirits embodied in tigers was foolish superstition. In trying to establish the influence of these beliefs on the tiger population, it is worth remembering that European observers had a vested interest in exaggerating the extent to which the Malay people held such beliefs.

Getting rid of tigers was not only the self-imposed task of the individual white hunter; it was also seen as one of the obligations of the colonial state. In this respect the European rulers copied, consciously or not, the behavior of indigenous kings. From the early seventeenth century onward, rewards were given to those who captured or killed a tiger, and fairly soon the VOC offered standard bounties to the citizenry of Batavia and its Environs. In the nineteenth century, the destruction of tigers was one of the many official tasks of the European and the indigenous civil service. In Java, traditional rituals in which tigers were killed were strongly supported by the colonial state and even "invented" in areas where they had not been carried out before. Together, the colonial state and the European hunter were making the Orient safe for the Empire.

The colonial state was strongly anti-tiger, as was the indigenous state. Apart from the direct effects attained by the promise of bounties and the distribution of firearms, this attitude also influenced Malay behavior indirectly. When either state ordered its subjects to set tiger-traps, the spiritual burden of the tiger's death did not have to be shouldered by the individual or group of villagers who had constructed the trap. The state was responsible. It is possible that this had long-term effects on the mentality of those living near a court, as is perhaps demonstrated by the fact that the Acehnese and the people of northern Banten did not hesitate to go after tigers. It is also possible that the difference in response between the Javanese and the Sumatrans to tiger depredations ("massive retaliation" versus "flexible response") was partly related to the more pronounced role of the state in Java than in Sumatra.

Another example of Europeans trying to wield power over the tiger is their propensity to give names. This turned out to be, perhaps rather unexpectedly, a deadly power. Not only was it necessary to kill quite a number of tigers before it was possible to be certain about subspecies; in addition, the fact that the much less dangerous leopards and clouded leopards were often also called "tigers" led to much higher numbers of these animals being killed than otherwise would have been the case.

The tiger was not only involved in a struggle for power with the colonial and the indigenous states. The tiger as a spiritual force was also a contender for power with Islam. Muslims were not supposed to believe in ancestral tigers, weretigers, familiars, and other spirit tigers. The few indigenous professional tiger hunters mentioned in late-nineteenth- and early-twentieth-century sources were almost always orthodox Muslims, as they did not fear the spirit tiger. It is even likely that the predecessors of these professional hunters, the tiger-charmers, were also Muslim "priests." Here we may be confronted with a rare example of the *kafir* (un-Islamic) colonial state working hand in glove with orthodox Muslims at the destruction of tigers. The people were not always grateful for Islam's anti-tiger stand. Many a "priest" was killed because, as a spiritually powerful person, he was suspected of being a weretiger.

Nevertheless, it cannot be said that the rise of Islam was only a negative force as regards the tigers. As the consumption of pork was forbidden for Muslims, they stopped hunting wild boar. In theory, this would have been to the benefit of the tiger.

Finally, it should be mentioned that people and tigers sometimes coexisted peacefully. In the story of the *macan bumi,* the more or less tame village tiger, probably seen as an ancestor or even the village founder who was fed by the villagers and who did them no harm, there does not seem to be a struggle for power. However, this was probably rare, and even if the tiger may have been tame in his behavior toward the villagers, he was far from domesticated.

The Frontier between Nature and Culture

Where there are empires there are frontiers. The locus of the power struggle described above was the frontier between nature and culture. This was a manmade frontier. During the period under consideration the Empire of Culture grew to the detriment of the Empire of Nature, a rather slow process at first but one that sped up in the nineteenth century. Originally, this process led to the creation of more frontiers and to more tigers. The tiger, although he is the guardian of the forest (*penunggu hutan*), has a penchant for the border zone between the forest and arable lands, as this is also the preferred habitat of wild boar and deer. The frontier thus was created by humans, who were responsible for the creation of typical tiger areas and the multiplication of the tiger. Humans had themselves conjured up the (evil) spirit they lived in constant fear of and whom they tried to kill at the same frontier that had brought him into being.

Fire plays a remarkable role in all this. Next to the axe, fire is the mighty slayer of the forest. It was responsible for the creation and the upkeep of the alang-alang fields of the border zone and of the frontier itself, areas where the tiger feels very much at home. On the other hand, fire is one of the few things tigers are afraid of and that will make them keep their distance or even drive them away. Setting fire to the alang-alang fields at the beginning of the dry season was the only way that villages beleaguered by tigers could rid themselves of these enemies. As was the case with humans, then, fire was responsible for the creation of tiger-attracting frontiers, but once the tigers were there, fire was instrumental in chasing them away.

Although there is fire from heaven as well, most scholars assume that almost all fires in forests and grasslands in the Malay world are and presumably were manmade. Fire, therefore, is hardly an independent factor but mainly an extension of the role of humans. It has been argued that, in general, fire may have been an important element in shifting the balance between humans (or rather humanoids) and large predators in favor of the former (Goudsblom 1992, 41–45).

Not all frontiers between nature and culture were equally troublesome. When nature and culture were neatly separated, as was the case in Bali, there were very few conflicts between tigers and people. Although tigers were still perceived as dangerous, probably mostly in a spiritual sense, as long as the tigers stayed at their side of the border there was no need to go after them.

The highest incidence of violent confrontations occurred when borders were blurred and when one empire invaded the other on a permanent basis. The best example of the latter is the "creation" of the "specialized" man-eater in Java around 1875, when many European estates were established in the uncultivated areas of western and eastern Java, in the middle of the Empire of the Tiger.

Crossing borders was also a theme in the weretiger stories in the Malay world. Tiger-people were supposed to live in villages of their own, but occasionally they would leave these "imagined communities," traveling to the world of humankind. They then had to cross a river—arguably the border between nature and culture, but probably also the one between life and death—where they made the shift from tiger to human, or the other way around. This motif is one of the many indications that the Empire of Nature is not only also the empire of wildness, chaos, and evil but ultimately also the Empire of the Dead. The tiger is, then, a dead human soul.

The tiger on the *kayon.* In the *wayang kulit,* the Javanese shadow puppet play, the *kayon* demarcates the beginning and the end of the performance. It represents both the world tree and the holy mountain of Hinduism. On this *kayon* there is always a "big cat," often clearly a tiger. Kats 1923

The tiger's presence at the edge of so many real and imagined domains makes him the perfect symbol of the frontier, particularly the one between nature and culture. He is the epitome of dangerous nature, but he needs culture for the expansion of his empire.

This position seems to be represented admirably by the tiger's presence on the so-called *kayon*. In the *wayang kulit,* the Javanese shadow puppet play, the kayon is a "puppet" used to demarcate the beginning and end of the performance and to mark the major scene transitions. It is supposed to represent both the world tree and the holy mountain—both important elements in Hindu belief—and it always shows a number of large and small animals and flowers, together with the gate to the palace. Among the large animals there is always at least one "big cat," often clearly a tiger, usually confronting a water buffalo (as in the tiger-buffalo fights). However, sometimes there are two big cats and no buffalo. The kayon evidently represents the boundaries of the stage but arguably also the boundaries of the civilized world as the Javanese knew it.[4]

There must have been a time when there was no frontier to speak of. In the literature on the nomadic groups (Semang, Kubu) this situation still obtained, albeit on a small scale. People and tiger densities were low, and humans and tigers shared the same habitat. They even shared the spoils of the hunt. This does not mean that fear and conflict were absent, but the impression one gets from the admittedly rare sources is not one of a permanent struggle for power. It is tempting to suppose that when numbers of people increased, which entailed more and longer frontiers, the gap between humans and tigers widened not only in the physical sense but also in the perception of the people (and, who knows, also in that of the tigers).

People and Tigers as Kin

The idea that tigers and humans were somehow related could be found among most groups in the Malay world. Some clans recognized a tiger as one of their founding ancestors. According to other myths the tiger had preceded humans at the creation (he was sometimes called the First One), perhaps implying that humans were slightly improved tigers. In a sense, tigers indeed may have preceded humans in the Indonesian Archipelago, as they were already present when *Homo sapiens* came onto the scene.

There are many instances of belief in tigers as embodiments of dead human souls or tigers as reincarnated ancestors. Weretigers, who could assume the shape of tiger or human at will, were in fact tiger-people, combining the two species in one person. It is as if nature had refused to make a choice, which was all the more understandable as the two species were so closely related. Clearly, then, people and tigers were kin.

There seems to be a paradoxical situation, in which people are living in constant fear of their close kin. How do we explain the fear and hatred felt by many Malay people toward the tiger, so often described as a member of the human family? Four factors should be taken into account: Ancestors and other family members are not necessarily friendly; ghosts/spirits were (and are) always perceived as dangerous; there was a widening gap between tigers and people; perhaps fear of the tiger was also fear of the beast within oneself.

Close relatives killing each other is a well-known motif in mythology (Zeus and his father, Kronos, Cain and his brother Abel). In many human societies, relations between family members are often far from cordial and sometimes downright cold or even hostile. This is particularly true for several Malay societies such as the Javanese, in which relations between fathers and sons can be distinctly frosty. Although the ancestral tiger's behavior occasionally may be benign, he is not necessarily an object of warm feelings. On the contrary, these ancestors were stern disciplinarians who punished even minor infractions of the rules laid down by older generations. People brought them offerings, as was done all over the world by those who tried to atone for past crimes and misdemeanors and to propitiate the offended deity. Seen in this light, the refusal to go after "harmless" tigers perhaps reflects not grateful feelings toward the ancestral tiger but fear of revenge.

Death is feared in all societies, but some seem to fear the dead more than others. In the Malay world, *hantu* (ghosts, spirits, souls of dead people) have always been, and among many people still are, phenomena to be highly dreaded. This is particularly true of the ghosts of those people who died a "bad" (unnatural, premature) death (cf. Sell 1955), but in fact all souls of the dead are to be feared, as they are jealous of the living. So no matter how benign the spirit embodied in the tiger may be from time to time, he is still a ghost, and one would be well advised to look out for an unpleasant turn in his behavior.

As the physical distance between the two species increased, people may have experienced a growing spiritual rift from tigers as well, even though they still recognized the tiger as a relative. In the eyes of the sedentary peasants and the inhabitants of towns and cities the tiger was an alien presence, even if he was supposed to be an ancestor. Morally supported by the indigenous and the colonial state and by Islam, and in addition materially supported by the colonial state with bounties and guns, many Malay people no longer regarded killing a tiger as selling an ancestor. One could argue that the ancestral tiger might have been greatly feared or perhaps even hated, but that the nomadic and semi-sedentary groups probably did not regard him as evil. As the gap widened and the state became increasingly involved in ceremonial tiger killings, there must have been a very gradual shift toward the tiger as the embodiment of evil. As it was difficult to reconcile these notions (the tiger as an ancestor and the tiger as an evil force), the idea of the tiger as a member of the family weakened.

It is an irony of history that in the period when the gap between tigers and people widened in the perception of many Malay people, many Europeans were going through a reverse process. Around 1500, many Europeans probably shared a belief in were-animals with the people of the Malay world. Maintaining the boundaries between animals and people became a preoccupation of the leading moral authorities in Europe. However, from the eighteenth century onward a narrowing of the gap occurred (Thomas 1984, 36–39; 121–36). During the last two or three decades of colonial rule in Asia, a small elite of conservationists started to question the wisdom of killing all tigers and leopards on sight. In the eyes of the Malay people, then, the tiger gradually—and no doubt imperceptibly—changed from a stern and often dangerous ancestor into an evil being. At the same time, in the eyes of a supposedly more enlightened vanguard of Europeans the tiger came more and more to represent the beauty of unspoiled Oriental nature rather than its deadly and evil side.

Finally, for some indigenous people, fear of the tiger stood for fear of the beast within themselves. Just because the tiger was a close relative, he may have been perceived to mirror the darker side of humankind. The idea that one should beware of the tiger within oneself as a metaphor for the "evil within" is an important motif in the Indonesian author Mochtar Lubis's novel *Harimau! Harimau!* (1975). It is tempting, if unconventional, to see this supposition as a parallel to the hypothetical Western view of the tiger as the evil within.

People and Tigers in the Making of the Malay World

The shared history of humans and tigers in the Malay world differs from that in India, China, and Siberia, although there were many similarities. Even within the Malay world the four regions, Malaya, Sumatra, Java, and Bali, followed different paths as regards hunting, trapping, and the decline and fall of the tiger.

To say that humans and tigers have a shared history implies that tigers have a history, as humans do. The term "history" is used here as distinct from "past," since even inanimate objects have a past. To me, the term indicates that tigers learn from experience and that the lessons learned are transmitted from one generation to the other. For example, a Sumatran tiger around 1850 would be expected to behave differently from a Sumatran tiger around 1900. As experiences differ between places, there should also be different local changes in tiger behavior, hence different local histories. Tiger behavior, therefore, and the changes it undergoes, is specific as to time and place.

A good illustration of this statement is that the tiger, so often described as a nocturnal animal, adapted his diurnal rhythm to local circumstances. In areas where people were rare, he was reported to be an animal operating by day. In more densely settled regions he was indeed a nocturnal animal, probably partly in order to avoid humans. However, man-eaters were active in the daytime.

Humans adapted to the presence of the tiger in various ways. However, some features that have been described as adaptations to life in tiger country may have other origins. This could be the case with the elevated houses to be found particularly in Malaya and Sumatra, and to a much lesser extent in Java. This building style could have equally been adopted because flooding was thus avoided, refuse could be dropped through the floor, and mosquitoes did not occur at some distance from the ground. But in some areas it seems certain that construction styles were tiger inspired, namely when houses were built in trees or, as was often the case on ladang, at higher elevations then the usual few feet. Also, people seldom went unarmed when leaving the village, but was that in preparation for a tiger encounter or did they have other motives? Of course, humans made many adaptations to the presence of tigers. One of the most important adaptations may have been the flowering of all kinds of tiger beliefs, as reflected in myths, legends, fairy tales, and fables. Although it is possible to distinguish a restricted number of broadly formulated themes, of which examples were found in most of the areas of the Malay world, similar beliefs could vary between places. Differences in emphasis could mean life or death to the tiger. Such was the case with the notion of the tiger as a moral force and the related conviction that the right of revenge was severely limited or even absent. Of course, the same differences were also a matter of life and death to the people who held these beliefs.

Other possible consequences of these tiger beliefs are open to speculation. One wonders, for example, whether the quest for (spiritual) protection against tiger depredations may have predisposed people favorably toward the—indigenous or colonial—state. One also wonders whether it made people more submissive toward those in authority. On the other hand, in villages where the ancestral tiger was supposed to act as a moral force, the villagers may have felt that there was no need for a state, colonial or indigenous, because they had the tiger, who protected the village and punished those who had done wrong, charging only a moderate fee (livestock) for his services.

If there was no real tiger, as in Borneo, tiger beliefs were not absent but in several respects different. For example, the killing of a big cat (in this case the clouded leopard) seems to have been less of a problem in tigerless areas than in regions where real tigers were present, and where tiger beliefs also seem to have protected other big cats.

Humans must have known that the clearing of forest areas attracted tigers. Nevertheless, this did not stop them, and they created the ecotones attractive to tigers. Tigers, in turn, certainly influenced the hearts and minds of the Malay people. But were tigers equally responsible for the making of the (real) human world, as the Malay people were responsible for the creation of the tiger world? I think not. Nevertheless, they may have had some influence. One example is the supposition that tigers may have contributed to the conservation of relatively wild areas around tombs and (other) antiquities, particularly in Java (thus also contributing to their own survival).

Another area of speculation concerns the impact of tigers on economic and population growth in the Malay world. In the ecologically rather similar areas of Sumatra and Borneo, the one with real tigers and the other without, at least in historical times, there were remarkable differences in livestock densities during the nineteenth century. Sumatra, with only a slightly higher population density, had much higher numbers of livestock per capita. Is it possible that in Sumatra the tigers had taken away so much game that livestock had to be kept in compensation, whereas tigerless Borneo could do without it? The keeping of livestock implies the clearing of forest lands and some form of care and labor. Thus, the area with tigers may have generated more growth of the economy and the population than the area without tigers. If this is true, the tiger was indeed instrumental in the shaping of the human world. However, even then it would be difficult to argue that the expansion of the tiger population was a precondition for the further growth of the human population.

Although tigers had been imported into Europe as long ago as the early years of the Roman Empire (e.g., Stiles 1993, 160; Wiedemann 1995, 13, 61), Europeans did not come across tigers in their own territory until the sixteenth century. So here there was no shared past but an enormous distance. Only at a very late stage would this distance decrease, and some Europeans came to admire the animal with which they had shared the fringes of their world. Just before the European as a ruler vanished, the best among them actually started to regret ("penitent butchers")[5] that in some areas the tiger was about to vanish, too.

After having lived apart together for a long time, tigers and humans finally parted company in many areas of the Malay world.

Notes

Chapter 1. Introduction

1. Throughout the book, I will refer to a tiger as "he" unless the animal is clearly a tigress. This is in accordance with almost all the sources I have used, where the tiger is invariably regarded as male unless, of course, tigresses were referred to.
2. I will avoid the use of the anachronistic terms *Indonesia* and *Malaysia*, referring instead to the *Indonesian Archipelago* and the *Malayan Peninsula*.
3. Bruun and Kalland 1995; Grove 1995; Arnold 1996; Grove et al. 1998.
4. *Bataviasche Courant* 26 February 1820. The author stated that if people really put their mind to it, there would be no tigers left in Java by the year 1900. He was not much off the mark.
5. Thomas 1984; Hutterer and Rambo 1985; Ellen 1996.

Chapter 2. Meeting the Tiger and the Other Big Cats

1. On prehistoric climate, geography, flora, and fauna of the area, see, e.g., Bellwood 1985; Whitten et al. 1996.
2. Brongersma 1935, 71; Koenigswald 1935, 190; Bellwood 1985, 27; Bergmans and Bree 1986, 342–43; Whitten et al. 1996, 199.
3. Peranio 1959, 6; Harrisson 1984, 314; Mazák 1983, 49; Sellato 1983; King 1985, 91; Kitchener 1999, 21.
4. Bellwood 1985, 37; Whitten et al. 1996, 199.
5. Crawfurd 1820, vol. 2, 144; Raffles 1830b, vol. 1, 56; Temminck 1846–49, vol. 2, 88; Junghuhn 1853–54, vol. 1, 306; Cordes 1874, 333; Mohnike 1874, 141; *Catalogus* 1883, 88; Cordes 1881, 106; Balen 1914, 348; Koningsberger 1915, 422; Medway 1969, 96.
6. Perry 1964, 3; Ward (1997, 14) gives 5,000 to 7,000 as the present range, but Peter Jackson, a leading expert, gives 5,000 to 7,500 for 1997 (see website *http://www.5tigers.org*). In 1994 he had 4,400 as lower limit and 7,700 as upper

limit; Jackson, fax to author, 1 April 1994. In the recently printed version of this table (Seidensticker et al. 1999, xvii) the limits are given as 5,183 and 7,277.

7. Many sources are unclear about the subspecies to be found in Malaya, including the classic tiger study by Vratislav Mazák (1983, 143, 146). The correct classification is in *Carnivores* 1984, 30. That this is indeed correct is confirmed by Tilson and Seal 1987, viii, and by a 1994 table by Peter Jackson, then chairman of the Cat Specialist Group; Jackson, fax to author, 1 April 1994.

8. Zimmermann 1938, 50; Mazák et al. 1978, 112; Brink 1980, 286; Brink and Iongh 1980, 140; Seidensticker 1987, 3–4, 6–7; Becking 1989, 154; Whitten et al. 1996, 706.

9. Seidensticker and Suyono 1980, 16–17, 76; Hasanudin 1988; Becking 1989, 154; *Suara Pembaruan* 1 December 1994; *Kompas* 8 December 1994; *Kompas* 28 November 1996; Whitten et al. 1996, 707–9; *Antara News* 1 October 1997 and *Indonesia Times* 2 October 1997; *Jakarta Post* 7 July 1999. The information on camera traps is from Joe Maynard, the Cat Specialist Group (IUCN); Maynard, email to author, 8 June 2000.

10. Santiapillai and Widodo 1987, 86; *Kompas Online* 22 November 1996; *Antara* home page 2 October 1997; Ward 1997, 27–28.

11. Khan 1987, 81, 83–84; Peter Jackson, fax to author, 4 January 1994; Ward 1997, 15.

12. Other names for the Siberian tiger are Amur, Ussuri, North-East China, and Manchurian tiger.

13. Bois 1852, 326; McNair 1878, 122; Schwarz 1912, 324; Sody 1949, 169–70; Hoogerwerf 1970, 246; Seidensticker and Suyono 1980, 73; Mazák 1983, 147, 168, 172, 180; *Carnivores* 1984, 28; Khan 1987, 82; Whitten et al. 1996, 214, 706.

14. Batavia 1782–83, vol. 4, 69–70; Colenbrander 1911, 116; Lacombe 1937, 66.

15. Schwarz 1912; Koningsberger 1915, 421–22; Sody 1933; Hoogerwerf 1970, 241; Mazák 1983, 163–76.

16. E.g., Aylva Rengers 1844, 372–73; Davidson 1846, 30; Buddingh 1859–61, vol. 1, 64.

17. It seems that the white tiger is no longer considered an albino. It is now believed that its color is caused by a double recessive allele; see website *http://www.5tigers.org/white2.htm* (5 October 1998).

18. Brasser 1926, 130; Hoogerwerf 1970, 392; Mazák 1983, 37–40.

19. Temminck 1846–49, vol. 2, 88; Schwarz 1912; Schwarz 1913; Sody 1933; Mazák et al. 1978; Mazák 1983, 176. The Indo-Chinese tiger was not given subspecies status until 1968 (Khan 1987, 76).

20. Friederich 1849, 42; Banner 1927, 146; Whitten et al. 1996, 706.

21. Eck 1878, 129; *Catalogus* 1883, 88–89; Balen 1914, 362, 365; Hoogerwerf 1970, 392; "Report" 1979, 17–21; Brink and Iongh 1980, 140; McKinnon 1985, 24.

22. Koningsberger 1915, 421–22; Sody 1933, 233–34; Sody 1949, 166–170.

23. Occasionally (but rarely) I fall back on data on the Bengal tiger when data on the Malay tigers are not available.

24. "Vruchtbaarheid" 1855; Dippe 1911, 189; Koningsberger 1915, 422; Brasser 1926, 140; Locke 1954, 20–22; Bazé 1959, 30–33, 57–58; Kitchener 1961, 202; Medway 1969, 96–97; Hoogerwerf 1970, 269–70; Mazák 1983, 102–16; *Carnivores* 1984, 30; Khan 1987, 79–80; Sunquist & Sunquist 1988, 69, 160; Ward 1997, 12, 26.

25. Winter 1902, 85; Schneider 1905, 130–31; Dippe 1911, 189; Balen 1914, 357–60; Brasser 1926, 189; Locke 1954, 20; Bazé 1959, 57–58; Mazák 1983, 101–5; Khan 1987, 79.

26. Locke 1954, 44–45; Pieters 1955, 35; Bazé 1959, 17–19; Seidensticker and Suyono 1980, 80; Mazák 1983, 55–63; *Carnivores* 1984, 28–30; Sunquist and Sunquist 1988, 61–62; Ward 1997, 23.

27. Crawfurd 1820, vol. 2, 32–33; Müller 1839, 28; Junghuhn 1853–54, vol. 1, 363; Pigeaud 1967, vol. 1, 104–5; Seidensticker and Suyono 1980, 55; Boomgaard 1997, 187.

28. *Algemeen Rijks Archief* (National Archive, The Hague, ARA for short), *Archief Ministerie van Koloniën* (AMK for short) 1814–49, 3068: Report by F. Epp on Banyuwangi, c. 1845; Almeida 1864, vol. 1, 294; Vissering 1912, 112; Whitten et al. 1996, 539–43.

29. Crooke 1909–15, vol. 2, 72 (c. 1670s); Marsden 1811, 185–86; Mohnike 1874, 166; Cordes 1881, 104; Balen 1914, 350–51; Koningsberger 1915, 346, 423; Locke 1954, 31–33; Poser 1955, 187; Hoogerwerf 1970, 267; Seidensticker and Suyono 1980, 63–64; Mazák 1983, 55, 77–78; Santiapillai and Widodo 1987, 87; Ward 1997, 23.

30. Alang-alang is *Imperata cylindrica*, glagah is *Saccharum spontaneum*. Leschenault 1811, 434; Müller 1839, 28; Junghuhn 1853–54, vol. 1, 349, 410; Cordes 1874, 333; Otto 1903, 69; Volz 1912, 376; Brasser 1926, 130; Westenenk 1962, 67–68; Seidensticker and Suyono 1980, 55–59; McKinnon 1985, 56; Rambo 1985, 38; Santiapillai and Widodo 1987, 88.

31. Denis 1964, 54; Hoogerwerf 1970, 250; Mazák 1983, 97; *Carnivores* 1984, 31; Karanth 1987, 121; Ward 1997, 23; Sunquist et al. 1999, 13–14.

32. Cameron 1865, 91–94; Bradley 1929, 35; Locke 1954, 7–8; Denninghoff 1966, 98; Seidensticker and Suyono 1980, 79; Mazák 1983, 58–60; Karanth 1987, 121–24; Santiapillai and Widodo 1987, 88–89; Sunquist and Sunquist 1988, 61; Ward 1997, 23.

33. Bontius 1931, 217 (c. 1630); Saar 1930, 88 (c. 1650); *Daghregister* (henceforth, cited as D) 2.10.1657; Vogel 1704, 357–60; Kessel 1856, 92; Almeida 1864, vol. 2, 33; Martens 1864, 383–84; Cameron 1865, 97; Forbes 1885, 222; Leendertz 1890, 103; Martin 1905, 63; Balen 1914, 352; Bradley 1929, 62, 66; Locke 1954, 36, 135; Fraisse 1955, 151; Pieters 1955, 36; Schneider 1958, 267; Hoogerwerf 1970, 249–50; Mazák 1983, 84–94; *Carnivores* 1984, 31; Sunquist and Sunquist 1988, 118–22.

34. Cameron 1865, 103; McNair 1878, 123; Mohnike 1883, 411; Volz 1912, 241;

Munnecke 1931, 218; Hoogerwerf 1939, 12; Valk 1940, 228–29; Locke 1954, 45; Denninghoff 1966, 97; Hoogerwerf 1970, 258–59; Mazák 1983, 83–84; Sunquist & Sunquist 1988, 160.

35. Bontius 1931, 219 (c. 1630); Vogel 1704, 357–60; Rees 1863–65, vol. 3, 159; Leendertz 1890, 103; Martin 1905, 63; Moszkowski 1909, 111; Balen 1914, 350; Bünning 1947, 70; Locke 1954, 44; Bazé 1959, 37; Denis 1964, 51; Denninghoff 1966, 131; Hoogerwerf 1970, 247–48; Mazák 1983, 63–72.

36. Müller 1839, 29; Junghuhn 1853–54, vol. 1, 266, 306; Martens 1864, 419; Volz 1912, 374; Balen 1914, 350; Koningsberger 1915, 422–23; Brasser 1926, 130; Locke 1954, 17; Hoogerwerf 1970, 249; Mazák 1983, 74.

37. Although it is a well-worn phrase, I simply must quote here William Blake's "Tyger! Tyger! burning bright / In the forests of the night."

38. Bickmore 1868, 517; Innes 1885, vol. 2, 36–37; Bradley 1929, 61–62; Hoogerwerf 1939, 6–10; Bünning 1947, 70.

39. The terms date from the nineteenth century, and they do not imply that tigers did not eat women. Statistics on possible gender preferences are presented in Chapter 3.

40. Aylva Rengers 1846, 279; Brumund 1854, 186; Groneman 1874, 303–16; Mohnike 1874, 163–66; Schoebel 1882–83, 493; Hagen 1890, 86–87; Sandick 1892, 112; Breitenstein 1900, vol. 2, 79; Morin 1909, 118; Volz 1912, 375; Balen 1914, 350; Brasser 1926, 134; Buck and Anthony 1930, 136–37; Berg 1934, 71; Corbett 1944, xi; Schilling 1952, 37, 47; Poser 1955, 121; Westenenk 1962, 66; Perry 1964, 180; Mountfort 1969, 198–204; Mazák 1983, 124–37; De 1990, 27–39; Richardson 1992, 45. The most recent information on the Sundarbans is from the website *http:// www.5tigers.org/maneatin.htm* (5 October 1998).

41. S. Raffles 1830a, 636–37; Müller 1839, 28, 51–54; Junghuhn 1853–54, vol. 1, 306; Andrásy 1859, 61–62; Cordes 1874, 333; Mohnike 1874, 141; Veth 1875–82, vol. 1, 254; Hagenbeck 1924, 117–18; Hoogerwerf 1970, 389–400; *Carnivores* 1984, 36–39; Hinde 1992, x; Richardson 1992, 47–59.

42. Raffles 1830b, vol. 1, 56; Newbold 1839, vol. 1, 433–34; Temminck 1846–49, vol. 2, 88; Junghuhn 1853–54, vol. 1, 306; Crawfurd 1856, 431; *Catalogus* 1883, 88; Cordes 1881, 105–6; Medway 1969, 97.

43. Junghuhn 1853–54, vol. 1, 306; Hoogerwerf 1970, 389–400; *Carnivores* 1984, 36–39; Hinde 1992, 14–22, 176–88; Richardson 1992, 47–59.

44. Hoogerwerf 1970, 395; Hommel 1987, 158; Hinde 1992, 75; "Sita" 1997, 41. In the Indonesian Archipelago the only natural enemy of the tiger, humans apart, seems to have been the wild Asiatic dog (*Cuon alpinus*), but only when the latter hunt in packs are they a threat to the tiger.

45. Favre 1865, 146; Banner 1927, 147; Heynsius-Viruly and Heurn 1935, 62; Locke 1954, 13; Hoogerwerf 1970, 288.

46. The highest indigenous official in Java functioning under a European Resident was the *bupati*, called regent by the Dutch; his administrative unit was called a regency.

47. Aylva Rengers 1844, 372–73; Mohnike 1883, 408–9; Cordes 1881, 105–6;

Hagenbeck 1924, 58, 118, 301; Foenander 1952, 1; Schilling 1952, 156; Locke 1954, 13; Medway 1969, 97; Hoogerwerf 1970, 391; *Carnivores* 1984, 37; Richardson 1992, 55–56.

48. Junghuhn 1853–54, vol. 1, 306, 349; Couperus 1887, 302–4; Cordes 1881, 104–6; Koningsberger 1915, 326, 420–21; Hoogerwerf 1970, 391; Richardson 1992, 55.

49. Müller 1839, 53; Martens 1864, 383–84; Mohnike 1883, 408–9; Buck and Anthony 1930, 273; Corbett 1948, 8; Locke 1954, 13; Hoogerwerf 1970, 390, 400.

50. Horsfield 1825; S. Raffles 1830a, 636; Newbold 1839, vol. 1, 433–34; Temminck 1846–49, vol. 2, 408; Mohnike 1874, 141; Schneider 1905, 102; Mjöberg 1928, 22; *JvNIVN* 1936–38, 359; Medway 1969, 97; *Carnivores* 1984, 41; Richardson 1992, 110–17.

51. The clouded leopard was said to be lurking particularly from the aerial roots of the *Ficus benjaminica*.

52. Raffles 1821–23, 250; Horsfield 1825; S. Raffles 1830a, 636; Newbold 1839, vol. 1, 433–34; Crawfurd 1856, 431; Cordes 1874, 333; Hagen 1890, 92; Schneider 1905, 102; Shelford 1916, 27–28; Tideman 1922, 18; Mjöberg 1928, 22; Schilling 1952, 156; Medway 1969, 9.

53. Horsfield 1825, 550; Mohnike 1883, 407; Shelford 1916, 27–28; Mjöberg 1928, 22; Schneider 1905, 102; Tideman 1922, 18.

54. Brongersma 1935, 49–61; Vos et al. 1982, 208–9; Bellwood 1985, 38–43; Hemmer 1987, 30–31; Vos et al. 1994, 130–33; Storm 1995a, 27–29, 126–27; Storm 1995b, 7–8.

Chapter 3. The Tiger: Friend or Foe?

1. Kipling (1865–1936) was born and bred in India. The stories from *The Jungle Books* first appeared in magazines and were subsequently published as books in 1894 and 1895.

2. In Chapters 4 and 10 the numerical data are discussed in detail.

3. D 12.9.1657; 4.11.1668; 14.2.1671; 16.7.1679; Andriesz 1670, 8; Saar 1930, 88.

4. D 30.1.1644; 31.1.1644; 1.2.1644; 9.4.1644; 12.4.1644.

5. D 30.9.1636; 18.4.1644; 12–13.3.1659; 11.12.1678; Fayle 1929, 33, 188 (31.7.1676).

6. D 2.1.1633; 17.9.1657; 20.1.1659; 22.4.1659; 14.11.1670; 14.1.1671; 8.6.1671; Herport 1669, 113–19; Haan 1910–12, vol. 2, 148; Saar 1930, 87.

7. ARA, Coll. Schneither, 83: *Algemeen Verslag* Banten 1823; Philippus 1673, 198–99; Hesse 1690, 87–88; Aylva Rengers 1844, 382; Doren 1851, vol. 2, 25; Locke 1954, 22.

8. *Javasche Courant* 8 May 1839; Rigg 1850b, 131–33; Kussendrager 1861, 24; Forbes 1885, 103; Tricht 1929, 62.

9. *Bataviasche Courant* 22 January 1820; Verhuell 1835–36, vol. 2, 103; Roorda van Eysinga 1841–50, vol. 3, 98; Greiner 1875, 140.

10. *Javasche Courant* July 1827; Roorda van Eysinga 1841–50, vol. 3, 323–24; Doren 1851, II, 180–81.

11. Olivier 1836, vol. 1, 70–72; Roorda van Eysinga 1841–50, vol. 3, 97; "Tijger-jagt" 1843, 779–80; Kussendrager 1861, 109–10.

12. "Multatuli" is the pseudonym of the Indies civil servant Eduard Douwes Dekker (1820–1887).

13. *Javasche Courant* July 1827; Olivier 1836, vol. 1, 68–69; Roorda van Eysinga 1841–50, vol. 3, 96–97; Doren 1851, vol. 2, 180, 265; Kussendrager 1861, 108; Bastin 1973, 60.

14. *Bataviasche Courant* 27 May 1820; Epp 1852, 376.

15. Hageman 1853, 44; Buddingh 1859–61, vol. 1, 399–401; Rees 1863–65, vol. 2, 102. This theme is also found in the literature on British India (Greenough 1991,13).

16. Raffles 1830a, 618; Verhuell 1835–36, vol. 2, 102; Olivier 1836, vol. 1, 193; Almeida 1864, vol. 1, 294–95.

17. A *gubuk* is a small, elevated hut in a rice field, occupied day and night when the crop is almost ripe in order to prevent damage from animals and theft. Access is possible only with a ladder, and as the tiger is an indifferent climber, one assumes that those people who were caught in their *gubuk* had forgotten to remove the ladder.

18. Materials used for thatched roofs include *ijuk,* which comes from the *anau* or *aren*-palm (*Arenga pinnata); nipah*-palm (*Nipa fruticans*); alang-alang; and rice straw. A *bilik* door was made of plaited bamboo strips.

19. Aylva Rengers 1846, 277; Jukes 1847, vol. 2, 31; Junghuhn 1853–54, vol. 1, 430; Hoogeveen 1858, 502; Buddingh 1859–61, vol. 1, 75; Kussendrager 1861, 110; *Javasche Courant* 15 January 1862; *Javasche Courant* March 1863; Greiner 1875, 218; Groneman 1902, 26; Bastin 1973, 19, 62.

20. Olivier 1826–30, vol. 1, 428; Epp 1849, 247; Junghuhn 1853–54, vol. 2, 516; vol. 3, 1003; Teijsmann 1855, 22; AStWbk 1863–69, vol. 3, 379; Stöhr 1874, 13.

21. Leschenault 1811, 426; Olivier 1826–30, vol. 1, 428; Junghuhn 1853–54, vol. 3, 704; Rees 1865, vol. 3, 102; Greiner 1875, 218; Breitenstein 1900, vol. 2, 79; Bastin 1973, 19, 60.

22. Thunberg 1796, vol. 4, 194; Olivier 1826–30, vol. 2, 2–3; Jukes 1847, vol. 2, 32; Buddingh 1859–61, vol. 1, 403; Jagor 1866, 185; Stöhr 1874, 2; Heering 1886, 190; Bonneff 1986, 170.

23. Arsip Nasional (National Archive Jakarta, ARNAS for short), appendices to *Besluit* (decree)5.4.1854, 3; *Besluit* 29.5.1888, 20; *Besluit* 31.12.1895, 34; Junghuhn 1853–54, vol. 1, 288, 430.

24. Winter 1902, 85; Schilling 1952, 47. The tiger is not supposed to have a clearly marked rutting-season (Mazák 1983, 101–5), but a certain concentration in time is likely (cf. also Chapter 2).

25. Junghuhn 1853–54, vol. 1, 308; Hoogeveen 1858, 504; Breitenstein 1900, vol. 2, 71.

26. ARA, Coll. van Alphen/Engelhard, 1896, 30: Report survey Pekalongan, 12 Sept. 1803; idem, 1916, 104; report, regent Batang, c. 1806.

27. Leschenault 1811, 426; Olivier 1826–30, vol. 1, 447; *Javasche Courant* 14 Feb-

ruary 1835; Kussendrager 1841, 107; Aylva Rengers 1846, 268; Doren 1851, vol. 2, 72; Hoogeveen 1858, 502–4; Buddingh 1859–61, vol. 1, 111.

28. An "f." is the usual symbol for guilders. Around this time average annual income of an agricultural family was f. 144 (Boomgaard 1989, 135).

29. ARNAS, *Besluit* 29.5.1888, 20; ARNAS, Groot Bundel MGS (*Missive Gouvernements Secretaris*), Openbaar: answers of the Residents to MGS 12.9.1895, 1881 (Banten); ARA, AMK, *Memorie van Overgave* Banten, 1906; Sandick 1892, 112; *Adatrechtbundel* 1911, 8.

30. Vissering (1912, 43) mentioned a village at the foot of Mount Semeru (at the border between regency Malang, Pasuruan Residency, and Probolinggo) that had been largely deserted by its inhabitants on account of a tiger, who had made already nine victims. The exact year is uncertain. What was probably the very last "tiger plague" in Java occurred in 1946, when in 10 months 64 people fell victim to tigers in southern Banyuwangi (*Verslag* 1940–46, 143).

31. Kal 1910, 139; Brasser 1926, 138; *JvNIVN* 1932, 33; Hoogerwerf 1970, 11, 242.

32. ARNAS, MGS 28.12.1922, 3542/IIIB.

33. E.g., ARNAS, Groot Bundel MGS, Openbaar: answers of the Residents to MGS 12.9.1895, 1881 (Banten and Priangan).

34. ARA, Coll. van Alphen/Engelhard, 1900, 118: report, Commissioner P. Engelhard to Governor-General, 4 September 1802; ARA, Ministerie van Koophandel en Koloniën (MKK for short), 159: Report Overseer Parakanmuncang to Inspection Committee, 31 March 1807; letter, Inspection Committee to Governor-General, 14 April 1807; ARNAS, Groot Bundel MGS, Openbaar: answers of the Residents to MGS 12.9.1895, 1881 (Besuki); Heering 1886, 190; Boissevain 1909, 207–8.

35. ARNAS, *Besluit* 8 April 1895, 9; *Besluit* 31 December 1895, 34; *Gedenkboek Rotterdam* 1938, 24.

36. ARNAS, Boschwezen, 23: letter, Veeckens to von Winckelmann and Knops, Semarang, 29 October 1808; ARA, Coll. Baud, 40: report on teak forests, 1 November 1818, par. 59 and 83; Courier dit Dubekart 1872, 14; Cordes 1881, 105.

37. ARA, Coll. Baud, 40: report on teak forests, 1 November 1818, par. 59; Jachtmuseum Doorwerth, Collection Hardenbroek, letter dated 10 April 1922.

38. ARA, Coll. du Bus, 24: report, Commission of East Indies Affairs, 1803; ARA, Coll. van Alphen/Engelhard, 1896, 30: report, Survey of Semarang, 6 April 1803; report, survey of Pekalongan, 12 September 1803.

39. ARA, Coll. van Alphen/Engelhard, 1916, 104: report, Regent Batang, c. 1806; Hasskarl 1842, 250; Jukes 1847, vol. 1, 396; Epp 1849, 247; Buddingh 1859–61, vol. 1, 219.

40. ARA, AMK, *Verbaal* 3.12.1859, 20: report, Prof. de Vriese to Governor-General, 1859; Janssen 1835, 266; Junghuhn 1853–54, vol. 3, 633–36; Buddingh 1859–61, vol. 1, 158.

41. ARNAS, Arsip Daerah (AD for short) Kediri, 5/1: report, Resident, 1832; Roorda van Eysinga 1841–50, vol. 3, 147–50; Junghuhn 1853–54, vol. 3,

665, 704–6; Teijsmann 1856, 146–49; Kussendrager 1861, 262; Courier dit Dubekart 1872, 12–14; Ruzius 1905, vol. 2, 31; Sibinga Mulder 1944, 25; Bonneff 1986, 180.

42. ARA, Coll. Schneither, 98: *Algemeen Verslag* (AV for short) Besuki 1824; Jukes 1847, vol. 2, 31–33; Junghuhn 1853–54, vol. 3, 1119; Almeida 1864, vol. 1, 198.

43. *Bataviasche Courant* 20 October 1827; Junghuhn 1853–54, vol. 3, 894–896; Buddingh 1859–61, vol. 1, 393; Gevers Deynoot 1864, 123.

44. Jukes 1847, vol. 1, 396; Junghuhn 1853–54, vol. 3, 988; Greiner 1875, 218–20; Meister 1875, 47; Heynsius-Viruly and Heurn 1935, 60; *JvNIVN* 1936–38, 100; Baerveldt 1950, 18.

45. Leschenault 1811, 426; Olivier 1826–30, vol. 1, 447; Verhuell 1835–36, vol. 2, 101–3; Bleeker 1849, 134; Junghuhn 18535–4, vol. 3, 990; Teijsmann 1856, 172–73; Buddingh 1859–61, vol. 1, 399–403; AStWbk 1863–69, vol. 3, 379; Stöhr 1874, 6, 13; Greiner 1875, 218; Kern 1941, 295.

46. *Java Government Gazette* 27 August 1814; "Banjoewangi" 1845, 139; Zollinger 1846, 167–69; Doren 1851, vol. 2, 375; Junghuhn 1853–54, vol. 1, 634–38; idem, vol. 2, 380; idem, vol. 3, 704, 1082–1105; Teijsmann 1855, 67–70; Heering 1886, 88; Groneman 1902, 19; Bezemer 1906, 416; Vissering 1912, 105; Heynsius-Viruly and Heurn 1935, 60.

47. Teijsmann 1856, 113–14; AStWbk 1863–69, vol. 2, 500.

48. Andries de Wilde was not above exaggerating a bit, as witness his estimate, dated 1815, that in Java some 100 people were killed per month (Bastin 1973, 60). That would yield an annual average of 1,200 people, compared to my own estimate of 400 to 500 people in the 1820s.

49. Wilde 1830, 113; Roorda van Eysinga 1841–50, vol. 3, 323–24, 405; *Javasche Courant* 1 October 1851; Brumund 1854, 184; "Vruchtbaarheid" 1855, 522–523; *Javasche Courant* 15 March 1863.

50. ARNAS, *Besluit* 8.8.1862, 7 (appendices); Aylva Rengers 1844, 372–73; Mohnike 1883, 408–409.

51. ARNAS, *Besluit* 8.8.1862, 7 (appendices); Aylva Rengers 1846, 277–78; Martens 1864, 384; Banner 1927, 147, 186; *JvNIVN* 1929–31, 72.

52. Müller 1855, 195–96; Hagen 1890, 88–91; Brenner 1894, 13; Valk 1940, 232; Poser 1955, 171, 188; Hazewinkel 1964, 182.

53. Müller 1839, 29; Rosenberg 1878, 101; Hasselt 1882, 414; Brau 1884b, 310; Otto 1903, 69–70; Schneider 1905, 4; Morin 1909, 117; Volz 1912, 376; Westenenk 1962, 67 (see also Chapter 2).

54. Schneider 1905, 129–31; Dippe 1911, 189; Balen 1914, 357–60; Brasser 1926, 189; Schilling 1952, 47.

55. Marsden 1811, 184–85; Heyne 1814, 427; Bastin 1965, 149; Andaya 1993, 23.

56. Mohnike 1874, 162; Schneider 1958, 269; Westenenk 1962, 66; Hazewinkel 1964, 18.

57. ARA, AMK, 7161: *Besluit* 23 Sept. 1854, 9; ARA, AMK, 7165: *Besluit* 5 Jan. 1855, 3; S. Raffles 1830a, 314; Bois 1852, 320.

58. ARNAS, Groot Bundel MGS, Openbaar: answers of the Residents to MGS 12.9.1895, 1881; S. Raffles 1830a, 322–23; Leendertz 1890, 103; Bradley 1929, 120; Poser 1955, 72.
59. S. Raffles 1830a, 322; Müller 1855, 196; Bickmore 1868, 503; Mohnike 1874, 126, 162; Rosenberg 1878, 101; Hagen 1890, 88; Moszkowski 1909, 201; Tideman 1922, 17–18; Schneider 1958, 266.
60. S. Raffles 1830a, 314; Kessel 1856, 92; Mohnike 1874, 163; Forbes 1885, 222; Moszkowski 1909, 69.
61. Mohnike 1874, 161–62; Mohnike 1883, 409; Schneider 1905, 129–31; Volz 1912, 245, 374.
62. ARNAS, Groot Bundel MGS, Openbaar: answers of the Residents to MGS 12.9.1895, 1881; Buddingh 1859–61, vol. 3, 244; Bickmore 1868, 413; Volz 1912, 374; Brasser 1926, 186; Bradley 1929, 95, 124–25; Poser 1955, 8, 72–76.
63. ARA, AMK, 2587: *Besluit* 22 Oct. 1838, 2; ARA, AMK, 7165: *Besluit* 5 Jan 1855, 3; Müller 1855, 130; Buddingh 1859–61, vol. 3, 249; Rosenberg 1878, 14, 32, 101–2; Dijk 1884, 157; Neumann 1886–87, 237; Brasser 1926, 188.
64. ARNAS, Groot Bundel MGS, Openbaar: answers of the Residents to MGS 12.9.1895, 1881; S. Raffles 1830a, 325–26; Bickmore 1868, 503, 514–18; Mohnike 1874, 126, 162–63; Forbes 1885, 221.
65. ARNAS, Groot Bundel MGS, Openbaar: answers of the Residents to MGS 12.9.1895, 1881; Mohnike 1883, 407; Raedt van Oldenbarnevelt 1888, 186; Hagen 1890, 91; Schneider 1905, 102; Whitney 1905, 265; Tideman 1922, 17–18.
66. ARNAS, appendices to *Besluit* 5.4.1854, 3; Brasser 1926, 139; *JvNIVN* 1935, 145.
67. Dijk 1884, 156; Dongen 1910, 201; Schebesta 1928a, 229; Wiele 1930, 109.
68. Koninklijk Instituut voor Taal-, Land- en Volkenkunde (Leiden, KITLV for short), Coll. H 277: J. A. Stützer (1786–87); ARNAS, appendices to *Besluit* 5.4.1854, 3 (Yogyakarta, Kediri); Olivier 1827–30, vol. 1, 195–96.

Chapter 4. Man-Eating Tigers

1. Wiele 1930, 119; Berg 1934, 71; Perry 1964, 52; Mazák 1983, 81. These distinctions apply to leopards as well.
2. E.g., Berg 1934, 71; Perry 1964, 185.
3. Khan 1987, 94; McDougal 1987, 442–45; Mishra et al. 1987; Sanyal 1987; Sunquist and Sunquist 1988, 71–78; Bakels 2000.
4. Berg 1934, 73, 78; Corbett 1948, 9–10.
5. Data for this period can be found in the archives in the *Proceedings of the Government of India in the Home Department (Public)* and, in published form, in the *Gazette of India* and the *Statistical Abstracts*.
6. I have not used the figures for 1897 because they are obviously underestimates, probably because the premium system had just been changed.
7. Figures for 1833 (only Java) in ARA, Collection Baud, 407. Data on 1852 (Java alone) in *Javasche Courant* (the Netherlands Indies Government gazette),

5 November 1853. Figures for 1858–60 in ARNAS, appendices to *Besluit* 8 August 1862, No. 7. Data on 1897 and 1903–4 in ARNAS, appendices to MGS 28 December 1922, No. 3542/IIIB.

8. Joost 1983, 2 (1623–27); Colenbrander/Coolhaas 1919–53, vol. 7/2, 1098 (1625); Bontius 1931, 221 (1629); D 1644, 23 April.

9. *Plakaatboek* V, 14 January 1749; Bolling 1913, 329. Prior to the late nineteenth century, the term "tiger" almost always covered all three big cats of the Malay world.

10. The Javanese word for tiger is *macan*, pronounced "machan." It is intriguing that Scott used the words "tygar" and "matchan" for two different animals. His description of the "matchan" (stripes) is that of a real tiger, which probably means that he used the term "tiger" for a leopard.

11. D 1659, 20 January; 12 March; Colenbrander/Coolhaas 1919–53, vol. 7/2, 1098; Bontius 1931, 217–19; Foster 1967, 154–61.

12. If we assume a death rate of 40 per thousand, 240 people from Batavia's population died in 1624, of which tigers killed 60, or one-fourth.

13. Around 1800 the population of western Java did not number more than 1.5 million. If we accept an annual growth rate of not less than 0.1% and not more than 0.2%, we arrive at a population of 1.1 million around 1600.

14. Hesse 1690, 110–11; Vogel 1704, 129; Behr 1930, 42–43; Saar 1930, 36.

15. Brasser 1926, 133 (10 per 1,000); Perry 1964, 190 (3 or 4 per 1,000); Fend 1971, 136 (5 per 1,000); Hodges-Hill 1992, 20 (<10 per 1,000). It goes without saying that these figures are wild guesses.

16. Corbett 1944, xi–xii; Perry 1964, 57–59; Fend 1971, 146; Mazák 1983, 74.

17. Colenbrander 1911, 116 (1628); Wurffbain 1686, 32 (1632–46); *Generale Missiven* (GM for short) vol. 1, 444 (1634); D 1648, 27 June; Haan 1910–12, vol. 3, 7 (1701); Worm 1745, 185–86 (1710–20); Heijdt 1744, 120.

18. Colenbrander/Coolhaas 1919–53, vol. 7/2, 1098 (1624); Saar 1930, 87 (c. 1650); Nagel 1828, 18; Aylva Rengers 1846, 279; Morin 1909, 118; Munnecke 1931, 197–98.

19. Balen 1914, 350; Brasser 1926, 134; Schilling 1952, 37; Perry 1964, 180.

20. Corbett 1944, 1–27; Fend 1971, 147; Mazák 1983, 136–37; McDougal 1987.

21. Westenenk 1962, 64–77; Hazewinkel 1964, 127–202.

22. ARNAS, appendices to *Besluit* 8 April 1895, No. 9, and 31 December 1895, No. 34.

23. Hagenbeck 1924, 56; Corbett 1945, 20–22, 27; Perry 1964, 191; Anderson 1968, 135–37; Fend 1971, 46, 112; Sunquist and Sunquist 1988, 70.

24. Forbes 1885, 76; Bazé 1959, 34; Perry 1964, 54, 197–98; Mazák 1983, 132.

25. D 1624, 19 February, 21 March, 17 and 22 August, 7 September, 12 October; Jonge 1862–95, vol. 5, 42; Colenbrander/Coolhaas 1919–53, vol. 7/2, 1097–98.

26. See, e.g., Colenbrander/Coolhaas 1919–53, vol. 5, 90–99, and vol. 6, 442.

27. Jonge 1862–95, vol. 5, 263–64; GM vol. 2, 262–63.

28. D 1659, 11 January, 14 March, 16 April, 3 July; Jonge 1862–95, vol. 6, 82.

29. Data on Banten in ARA, Coll. Schneither, 83: Statistical Report 1820–22. Data

on Priangan in ARNAS, AD Priangan, 2/1: Annual Report 1829; ARNAS, appendices to *Besluit,* dated 8 August 1862, No. 7: advice from the Council of the Indies, 25 April 1862.

30. Krawang: Nagel 1828, 17–18. Probolinggo: ARA, Coll. Schneither, 98: General Report 1824; *Bataviasche Courant,* 20 October 1827. Chapter 10 presents a more detailed discussion of the distribution of tigers over Java.

31. ARA, MKK, 159; ARA, AMK (1850–1900), 5918/19; ARA, Coll. Van Alphen/ Engelhard, 1900, 118; ARA, Coll. Du Bus, 24; *Java Government Gazette,* 11 April 1812; Olivier 1826–30, vol. 1, 428; Nagel 1828, 63; Wilde 1830, 113; Olivier 1836, I, 70–72; Bastin 1973, 19–25, 60–62.

32. It is possible, however, that the reports on the infernal noises made by the "eastern" tigers were, by chance, based on observations during the mating period, when tigers are unusually noisy.

33. ARA, Coll. Baud, 40; ARA, Coll. Schneither, 98; *Bataviasche Courant,* 4 September 1819, 22 January 1820, 21 and 28 October 1820; Leschenault 1811, 426–37; Olivier 1826–30, vol. 1, 447, and vol. 2, 2–3; Verhuell 1835–36, vol. 2, 101–3; Aylva Rengers 1846, 268–79; Greiner 1875, 219.

34. *Ladang* is the term generally used for land under shifting (slash-and-burn) cultivation in Indonesia.

35. *Javasche Courant,* 14 February 1835, 8 May 1839; Hasskarl 1842, 250; Roorda van Eysinga 1842, vol. 3, 323–24; Doren 1851, vol. 2, 181; Epp 1852, 376; Junghuhn 1853–54, vol. 1, 265–66, 288–93, 308, 430, and vol. 3, 573; Teijsmann 1855, 22; Hoogeveen 1858, 495–504, 522; Buddingh 1859–61, vol. 1, 75, 111; Kussendrager 1861, 23; Jagor 1866, 185.

36. "Reisje" 1845, 121–23; Roorda van Eysinga 1850, vol. 3, 147; Junghuhn 1853–54, vol. 2, 472, 516, and vol. 3, 665; Kussendrager 1861, 262, 265; Deventer 1865–56, vol. 2, 430.

37. Perry 1964, 190; Mazák 1983, 128; McDougal 1987, 437.

38. ARNAS, AD Tegal, 16; *Javasche Courant,* 21 April 1858; Epp 1852, 357–63.

39. This is suggested by the data themselves. The ratio below 61.4 (Rembang) is 30.6 (Pasuruan). Of the 20 Residencies for which data are available, 11 are to be found within a very narrow range around the mean (18.7), namely between 14.0 and 30.6; three values are much lower and six much higher.

40. ARNAS, AD Rembang, 10/7; ARNAS, AD Madiun, 3/7; ARA, AMK, Comm. Umbgrove, 10; ARA, AMK, Comm. De Vriese, 269; *Javasche Courant,* 1 October 1851; Nagel 1828, 63; Almeida 1864, vol. 2, 8–12.

41. Courier 1872, 9–12; Huijser 1885, 20–25.

42. There is no universal definition of "tiger plague." For the purpose of this chapter I define it as any number that is at least twice as high as the average value for the surrounding years.

43. Sandick 1890, 109–16, and 1892, 29, 87; Breitenstein 1900, vol. 2, 68–69.

Chapter 5. Ancestors for Sale: Bounties for the Big Cats

1. Bontius 1931, 219–21 (1623–29); D 1644, 12 May; Behr 1930, 29–30 (1644); Merklein 1930, 13 (1645–53); D 1648, 20 January.

2. GM II, 467 (20 Jan. 1651); Valentijn 1724–26, vol. 4, 237–38; Schwarz 1751, 49–53; Bontius 1931, 221; Coolhaas 1962–63, vol. 1, 209.

3. The premiums are expressed in the sources in various monetary units (Spanish Reals, Rixdollars, ducatons, guilders), which I have converted—at the going rate—to guilders of 20 ("heavy") stivers.

4. Heijdt is exceptional in that he mentions tigers, leopards, and panthers (the latter two now regarded as one species), instead of calling them all tigers.

5. Heijdt 1744, 120. The official publication is in *Plakaatboek* V, 1 September 1747.

6. This calculation is based on a retail rice price of 7 *gantang* (or 70 *kati*) of average quality rice for 1 Rxs (D 1682, 13 March).

7. *Plakaatboek* V, 14 January 1749, and VII, 19 October 1762.

8. The circular letter in *Plakaatboek* XIV, 5 May 1808, question No. 21. English translations of the answers from various Residencies are in the India Office Library (IOL for short; London), Collection MacKenzie, Private, 3.

9. *Proclamations* 1813–16, I, 96 (No. 92, article 45).

10. ARA, AMK, 2437: *Besluit* 29.3.1817, No. 8.

11. As the Rixdollar ceased to be a unit of account in 1811, later conversion rates are not available.

12. The *Besluiten* are found in ARA, AMK, under the following inventory numbers: 2437: *Besluit* (B for short) 29.3.1817, 8; 2438: B 12.6.1817, 16; 2438: B 18.6.1817, 18; 2442: B 7.5.1818, 3; 2447: B 3.5.1819, 7; 2461: B 5.7.1821, 17; 2463: B 3.11.1821, 6; 2463: B 26.11.1821, 8; 2467: B 22.11.1822, 1; 2470: B 5.6.1823, 7; 2478: B 13.9.1824, 11; 2485: B 2.7.1825, 9.

13. Berlage (1931) has measured tree rings from a number of very old teak trees, thus constructing a series from the early sixteenth century up to 1929, which can be used as a proxy for data on rainfall. Index 100 indicates average rainfall, figures below 100 reflect dry years, above 100 wet years. For the years dealt with here see pp. 952–53.

14. ARNAS, AD Cirebon, 63/1: report, Resident.

15. Data on prices, harvest failures, famine, and epidemics in ARA, AMK, Coll. Schneither, Nos. 83–100: Statistical Reports of the Residencies, 1820–23. See also Boomgaard and van Zanden 1990, 45.

16. The bounty used to be 10 Rxs, a unit of account no longer in use when the request was written (1817). Prices of that order of magnitude were at the time of writing expressed in either guilders (f.) or Spanish dollars (Sp. $). The value of the Spanish dollar, expressed in guilders, had been fixed in 1816 at f. 2.2, which means that the equivalent of f. 22 was Sp. $10. In other words, the Resident had mixed up his dollars.

17. ARA, AMK, 2837: *Resolutie* 27.11.1830, 20; 2578: *Besluit* 22.1.1838, 2.

18. ARA, AMK, 2981: budget 1823; 2983: budget 1824; 2984: budget 1825; ARA, Collection Baud, 407: budget 1833.

19. ARA, AMK, 7146: *Besluit* 5.4.1854, 3; this was also printed as *Indisch Staatsblad* (IS for short) 1854, 22.

20. Data on weather, rice prices, harvests, etc., in Berlage 1931; Boomgaard and

van Zanden 1990; the (printed) *Koloniaal Verslag* and the (written) *Algemeen Verslag* (ARNAS: Arsip Daerah) of those years.

21. ARNAS, *bijlagen* (appendices) of *Besluit* 5.4.1854, 3.

22. ARA, AMK, 7332: *Besluit* 8.8.1862, 7; also printed as IS 1862, 84. The circular letter and the reactions of the Residents can be found in the appendices to the decree, in ARNAS.

23. MGS 9.11.1894, 2761, and letter, Dir. B. B. to Governor-General, 3.4.1895, in ARNAS, Groot Bundel MGS, Openbaar: BGS 28.12.1922, 3542/IIIB. On Banten and Jepara see also *Besluit* 29.5.1888, 20; *Besluit* 25.12.1888, 8; *Besluit* 8.4.1895, 9; and the answers of the Residents to MGS 12.9.1895, 1881, also under BGS 28.12.1895, 3542/IIIB.

24. MGS 12.9.1895, 1881 and all correspondence following this circular letter can be found in ARNAS, Groot Bundel MGS, Openbaar: BGS 28.12.1922, 3542/IIIB.

25. The *Besluit* was printed as IS 1897, 111.

26. ARA, AMK, 7441: *Besluit* 5.6.1867, 40.

27. The modern terminology was taken from *Carnivores* 1984, 44–45; and Melisch 1992, 22–23.

28. *Bijbladen* 6577, 7627, and 10228; ARA, AMK, *Memories van Overgave*, No. 1: Banten, April 1906.

29. ARA, AMK, 2587: *Besluit* 22.10.1838, 2.

30. ARA, AMK, 2688: *Besluit* 23.11.1846, 16.

31. ARA, AMK, 7161: *Besluit* 23.9.1854, 9; 7165: *Besluit* 5.1.1855, 3.

32. Hasselt 1882, 414; Dippe 1911, 175–176; Westenenk 1962, 107.

33. B. 1914, 432–433; Heynsius-Viruly and Heurn 1935, 60; Westenenk 1962, 64–65, 77.

34. Hamerster 1926, 39; Buck and Anthony 1930, 105–9; Coolhaas 1985, 206.

35. Barros 1727, 119; Temple 1928, 84; Mills 1970, 113.

36. ARA, AMK, 2984: Budget 1825.

37. Davidson 1846, 51; Keppel 1853, I, 9; Crawfurd 1856, 397; Cameron 1865, 83, 90–106. If we accept a death rate of 40 per thousand, tiger kills contributed 10% to 20% to total mortality.

38. Davidson 1846, 51; Martens 1864, 382; Cameron 1865, 83, 91–94; Vincent 1874, 104; Bird 1883, 110; Rupprecht 1923, 110.

39. McNair 1878, 82, 123; Bird 1883, 142; Innes 1885, vol. 1, 166, 262; Maxwell 1960, 51, 220.

40. *Blue Books* 1900–37; Martin 1905, 64; Locke 1954, 63–64.

41. In 1895 the Resident of Banten reported that no superstitious beliefs kept the local population from hunting leopards.

Chapter 6. Hunting and Trapping

1. Dames 1919–21, vol. 2, 194; Cortesão 1944, 168, 174–76; Pigeaud 1960–63, vol. 3, 57–62 and vol. 4, 145–49.

2. Haan 1910–12, vol. 4, 379; Keuning 1942, 35–36; Foster 1943, 161; Colenbrander/Coolhaas 1919–53, vol. 7/1, 608; Graaf 1958, 124.

3. Haan 1910–12, vol. 4, 379–80, 422–23; Boomgaard 1993a, 312–13.

4. *Tumenggung* is a high aristocratic-administrative title.

5. ARNAS, appendices to *Besluit* 5.4.1854, 3; Jonge 1862–95, vol. 10, 374–375; Rouffaer in ENI 1899–1905, vol. 4, s.v. *Vorstenlanden;* Schrieke 1957, vol. 2, 165–66.

6. GM III, 92 (4.12.1656); Haan 1910–12, vol. 4, 379; Foster 1934, 157; Unger 1948, 88; Lombard 1967, 143; Andaya 1979, 158, 196–197; Andaya 1993, 20.

7. Brown and Roolvink 1970, 137, 155; Andaya 1975, 47.

8. Buck and Anthony 1930, 38, 140–41, 207; Locke 1954, 11–12.

9. Olivier 1836–38, vol. 2, 208–10; Brau de Saint-Pol 1884a, 199; Poser 1955, 73.

10. ARNAS, *Besluit* 5.4.1854, 3, appendix (report, Pacitan); Olivier 1836–38, vol. 1, 187–88; "Reisje" 1845, 121–23; Teijsmann 1855, 79; Ritter 1872, 120–23; Leclercq 1898, 172.

11. IS 1867, 114, article 17 encouraged regents and district heads to catch and kill dangerous and other noxious animals. However, according to a list of duties drawn up by the regent of Bangil, dated 1843, killing tigers and wild boar was already part of the regent's obligations ("Opgave" 1863, 220).

12. ARNAS, *Besluit* 5.4.1854, 3, appendices; ARNAS, Groot Bundel MGS, Openbaar: answers of the Residents to MGS 12.9.1895, 1881; "Tijgerjagt" 1843, 779–81; Roorda van Eysinga 1841–50, vol. 3, 97–98; Groneman 1874, 170–72.

13. There is an extensive literature on some of these peoples, while other ones are poorly documented. On the Malaysian groups, see Newbold 1839; Favre 1865; Martin 1905; Skeat and Blagden 1906; Schebesta 1928a; 1928b; Evans 1937; Carey 1976; Endicott 1970; Rambo 1978; Endicott 1979; Rambo 1985. On the Kubu, see Boers 1838; Verkerk 1874; Winter 1901; Dongen 1906; Hagen 1908; Dongen 1910; Waterschoot 1915; Schebesta 1928b; Keereweer 1940; Sandbukt 1982; Persoon 1994. On the Lubu, see Müller 1855; Dijk 1884; Ophuijsen 1884; Kerckhoff 1890; Kreemer 1912. On the Sakai we have only Moszkowski 1909, and for the Mamak, Schneider (1905 and 1958) and Obdeyn 1929.

14. For literature comparing the use and efficiency of bows and arrows, blowpipes, spears, and guns, see Rambo 1978; Hames 1979; Yost and Kelley 1983.

15. D 9.2.1644 and 18.4.1644; D 4.5.1659; D 4.12.1677; Fayle 1929, 76–77; Bontius 1931, 219.

16. Wurffbain 1686, 32; Hesse 1690, 96; Fayle 1929, 76–77.

17. Salmon 1729–33, II, 173. The Dutch word used here, and in most texts about Java, is *strik*. This can be both "snare" and "noose." My impression is that in most cases the term "noose" is the best translation.

18. Other terms that appear in the literature are *grogol, pasangan,* and *srembong.* The latter term is not in Pigeaud's dictionary, but it may be a spelling variant of *srumbung* or *srombong.*

19. ARNAS, appendices to *Besluiten* 5.4.1854, 3, and 8.8.1862, 7; ARNAS, Groot Bundel MGS, Openbaar: answers of the Residents to MGS 12.9.1895, 1881;

Bataviasche Courant 21 & 28 Oct. 1820; Roorda 1830–32, vol. 3, 78; "Vruchtbaarheid" 1855, 522–23; Meister 1875, 59; *Catalogus* 1883, 89–90, 121–24; G. 1889, 186–87; Wormser 1941, 217.

20. ARNAS, appendices to *Besluit* 5.4.1854, 3 (reaction, Resident Tegal).

21. ARNAS, appendices to *Besluit* 5.4.1854, 3; *Bataviasche Courant* 21 & 28 Oct. 1820; *Javasche Courant* 20 Jan. 1829; Roorda 1841–50, vol. 3, 323–24; Teijsmann 1856, 114; Andrásy 1859, 61; G. 1889, 186.

22. ARNAS, appendices to *Besluit* 5.4.1854, 3; Olivier 1827–30, vol. 1, 164; Kussendrager 1861, 108; Gevers Deynoot 1864, 123; *Catalogus* 1883, 89–90; G. 1889, 187; Bastin 1973, 21.

23. ARNAS, appendices to *Besluiten* 5.4.1854, 3, and 8.8.1862, 7; *Catalogus* 1883, 89–90; Locke 1954, 50.

24. ARA, AMK, *Verbaal* 3.12.1859, 20: report, Prof. W. H. de Vriese to Governor-General, 1859; ARNAS, appendices to *Besluit* 5.4.1854, 3; ARNAS, Groot Bundel MGS, Openbaar: answers of the Residents to MGS 12.9.1895, 1881; Raffles 1830b, I, 387; "Vruchtbaarheid" 1855, 522–23; "Uitroeijing" 1858, 478; Kerkhoven 1879, 510; Cordes 1881, 107; *Catalogus* 1883, 89–90; G. 1889, 186.

25. ARNAS, appendices to *Besluit* 5.4.1854, 3; "Uitroeijing" 1858, 478; *Catalogus* 1883, 89–90; *DNIJ* 1939, 45; Hoogerwerf 1970, 244.

26. ARNAS, Groot Bundel MGS, Openbaar: answers of the Residents to MGS 12.9.1895, 1881; Gevers Deynoot 1864, 123; Buddingh 1859–61, vol. 1, 395; G. 1889, 187; *JvNIVN* 1936–38, 55.

27. ARA, Coll. Reinwardt, 17: Fischer; Salmon 1729–33, vol. 2, 173.

28. IOL, Coll. McKenzie, Private, 3: Statistical Queries, Daendels, May 1808 (question No. 21); Crawfurd 1820, vol. 1, 120; *Javasche Courant,* 20 Jan. 1829; Raffles 1830b, vol. 1, 387; Roorda 1841–50, vol. 3, 97–98, 323–24, 405, 426; "Tijgerjagt" 1843, 779–81; Jukes 1847, vol. 2, 41–42; Junghuhn 1853–54, vol. 1, 305; Waldeck 1862, 179–81; Wallace 1869, vol. 1, 168; Groneman 1874, 170–72.

29. *Aris* is a local name for the head of a group of villages.

30. ARNAS, appendices to *Besluit* 5.4.1854, 3; ARNAS, Groot Bundel MGS, Openbaar: answers of the Residents to MGS 12.9.1895, 1881.

31. ARNAS, Groot Bundel MGS, Openbaar: answers of the Residents to MGS 12.9.1895, 1881.

32. Vogel 1704, 360; Marsden 1811, 118, 184–85.

33. ARNAS, Groot Bundel MGS, Openbaar: answers of the Residents to MGS 12.9.1895, 1881; Müller 1855, 158; Buddingh 1859–61, vol. 3, 249; Mohnike 1874, 166; Toorn 1879, 453; Brau de Saint-Pol 1884a, 198; Helfrich 1889, 585; Schneider 1905, 98–101; Morin 1909, 117; Moszkowski 1909, 169; Volz 1921, 65–66; Poser 1955, 78, 189, 210.

34. ARNAS, Groot Bundel MGS, Openbaar: answers of the Residents to MGS 12.9.1895, 1881; Vogel 1704, 357; Mohnike 1874, 166; Neumann 1886–87, 274; Helfrich 1889, 585; Brau de Saint-Pol 1891, 211; Helderman 1891, 172; Bradley 1929, 126.

35. Raffles 1830a, 338; Steck 1862, 110; Martens 1864, 420; Hasselt 1882, 414;

Neumann 1886–87, 515; Warneck 1909, 129; Westenenk 1962, 28–29; Hazewinkel 1964, 18–19, 123.

36. ARNAS, Groot Bundel MGS, Openbaar: answers of the Residents to MGS 12.9.1895, 1881; Helderman 1891, 171–73; Volz 1921, 22; Brasser 1926, 139; *JvNIVN* 1935, 145–46; Hazewinkel 1964, 15.

37. Müller 1855, 103; Neumann 1886–87, 264; Weslij 1889, 284–85; Volz 1909, vol. 1, 31, 103; Volz 1912, 231, 245–46; Zentgraaff 1938, 218–20.

38. Brau de Saint-Pol 1884a, 200; Neumann 1886–87, 274; Brenner 1894, 338; Schneider 1905, 11; Volz 1912, vol. 2, 7.

39. Zentgraaff 1938, 218; Westenenk 1962, 107; Hazewinkel 1964, 36.

40. Newbold 1839, vol. 2, 190; Keppel 1853, vol. 1, 9; Winstedt 1911, 35–37; Locke 1954, 50.

41. Hubback 1905, 20; Winstedt 1911, 39; Locke 1954, 49–50. Gimlette (1923, 137–39) mentions poison used for dogs, cattle, and elephants, but does not refer to tiger poison.

42. Newbold 1839, vol. 2, 190–92; Innes 1885, vol. 1, 141, 166; Skeat 1900, 167–69; Martin 1905, 64; Locke 1954, 2.

43. Skeat 1900, 167; Winstedt 1911, 7; Maxwell 1960, 51.

44. Rigg 1850b, 84; Almeida 1864, vol. 2, 34; *Catalogus* 1883, 89–90; Neumann 1886–87, 264; Behr 1930, 42–43; Saar 1930, 36; Denninghoff 1966, 146; Cribb 1991, 178.

45. D 19.4.1637; D 4.9.1641; D 9.12.1663; Groeneveldt 1876, 79.

46. ARNAS, appendices to *Besluit* 8.8.1862, 7; *Bataviasche Courant,* 20 October 1827; Roorda 1830–32, vol. 3, 174; *Catalogus* 1883, 89–90; Brau de Saint-Pol 1891, 70; Moszkowski 1909, 169.

47. Bock 1882, 152–53; *Catalogus* 1883, 90–91.

48. Innes 1885, vol. 2, 45; Morin 1909, 110; Locke 1954, 182.

49. KITLV H 277: Stützer (1786–87); Rigg 1850b, 84; Bock 1882, 153; *Catalogus* 1883, 89–90; Hagen 1890, 90; Helderman 1891, 175; Moszkowski 1909, 169; Schilling 1952, 99.

50. Mohnike 1874, 208–10; Ruzius 1905, vol. 2, 31; Moszkowski 1909, 169; Mayer 1924, 97, 144–47; Buck and Anthony 1930, 144–45.

51. See, e.g., the title of a booklet by Wessing, *The Soul of Ambiguity.*

52. I deal with this topic in more detail in Chapter 8.

53. Jonge 1862–95, vol. 3, 155; Dames 1918–21, vol. 2, 193; IJzerman 1926, vol. 1, 113–14; Eredia 1930, 32; Cortesão 1944, 176.

54. The word *snaphaunce* is derived from the Dutch *snaphaan.* This is also the basis for the Indonesian word *senapan(g),* or even *salapang* (Borneo). For the Dutch terminology, see Puype 1993.

55. ARNAS, appendices to *Besluit* 5.4.1854, 3; ARNAS, Groot Bundel MGS, Openbaar: answers of the Residents to MGS 12.9.1895, 1881; *Javasche Courant,* 20 January 1829; Davidson 1846, 24; Doren 1851, vol. 2, 279; Ritter 1872, 123; Brau de Saint-Pol 1884a, 200; Stone 1961; Lenselink 1966, 14–23, 41–43; Dolínek and Durdík 1993, 176–266.

56. Valentijn 1724–26, vol. 4, 55, 156, 163; Radermacher 1781, 24, 79; Raffles

1830a, vol. 1, 330; Newbold 1839, vol. 2, 197; Junghuhn 1847, vol. 2, 170; Kessel 1856, 62; Jacobs 1883, 55, 94; Neumann 1886–87, 274; Volz 1912, vol. 2, 7; Voorhoeve 1940, 28–31; Remmelink 1994, 98.

57. Hornaday 1885, 89; Brenner 1894, 338; Volz 1912, vol. 2, 7; Schebesta 1928a, 108; Schilling 1952, 166.

58. IS 1822, 24; IS 1828, 58; IS 1829, 62; Couperus 1887, 317; Warren 1981, 129–30.

59. Dippe 1911, 187–89; Volz 1912, vol. 2, 7; Brasser 1926, 139; Denninghoff 1966, 26. For British India see MacKenzie 1988, 170.

60. D 1644, 4 and 8 February, 23 April; Merklein 1930, 40; Saar 1930, 36; Bontius 1931, 221; Joost 1983, 2. On the British Raj see MacKenzie 1988, 167–99; Ritvo 1990; Storey 1991; Rangarajan 1997.

61. Jukes 1847, vol. 2, 34; Whitney 1905, 212; Rupprecht 1923, 55.

62. Rhemrev 1884; Brasser 1926; Valk 1940; Voorhoeve 1940; Wals 1940; Baerveldt 1950; Schilling 1952; Denninghoff 1966.

63. The only moderately large-scale tiger hunt, with 800 beaters and lasting a number of days, took place in the regency Caringin, Banten, around 1887. It was organized by the Count de Bardi, who was not a Dutchman. Although Caringin was a tiger-stricken area, no tigers were sighted, but a tiger carried off one of the beaters during the night; see ARNAS, Groot Bundel MGS, Openbaar: answers of the Residents to MGS 12.9.1895, 1881.

64. Perry 1964, 9–10; Fend 1971, 169; Sunquist and Sunquist 1988, 41.

65. An exception was Charles te Mechelen, whose official career started in 1864 and who was appointed "Resident of the Sea" in 1885 and Chief Inspector of Opium Affairs in 1889. It may have played a role that he was the Indo-European son of a tobacco planter in Rembang (Mechelen 1879; Rouffaer 1917–18; Rush 1990, 159–78).

66. Brumund 1853–54, vol. 2, 185; Rees 1863–65, vol. 2, 94–97; Buddingh 1859–61, vol. 1, 393; Beauvoir 1873, 280; Jagt 1955, 208.

67. It is also possible that the highest estimate included leopards. Neither the Dutch nor the Indonesians were inclined to distinguish the two systematically.

68. Ms. Scholl 1881, 417 (private collection); Doren 1851, vol. 2, 273–75; Jagor 1866, 162–63; Greiner 1875, 141; Veth 1875–82, vol. 3, 524; Koningsberger 1915, 421–22; Campbell 1915, vol. 1, 413; Sody 1933, 233–34; Wormser 1941, 217; Sody 1949, 169; Hoogerwerf 1970, 242–44, 387; Bijl de Vroe 1980, 116.

69. Roy 1861, 248–53; Bickmore 1868, 291; Wallace 1869, 344; Mohnike 1874, 70–72, 142–56, 206–8; Rosenberg 1878.

70. Heering 1886, 190; Hagen 1890, 66–67, 71–72; Bemmelen 1895, 204; Weede 1908, 136, 151–56, 162; Boissevain 1909, 333; Morin 1909, 67–69, 117; Brasser 1926, 5–17; Feith 1940, 76–77; Wormser 1941, 190–91, 205; Bijl de Vroe 1980, 122, 130–34.

71. Weede 1908, 126; Boissevain 1909, 57–58; Brasser 1926, 59; Paardt 1929, 55. See also, mainly on India, Hagenbeck 1924, 66–67. On "respectability" and empire see Stoler 1990.

72. ARNAS, Groot Bundel MGS, Openbaar: answers of the Residents to MGS 12.9.1895, 1881; Rees 1863–65, vol. 2, 127; vol. 3, 36–37, 86–91; Weede 1908, 334, 341; Dippe 1911, 175–76; Zentgraaff and Goudoever 1947, 70; Sody 1949, 168; Poser 1955, 230; Denninghoff 1966; Anthonio 1990, 165–85.

73. Roorda 1830–32, vol. 3, 46–52; Wallace 1869; Hornaday 1885; Sliggers and Wertheim 1994.

74. Aylva Rengers 1846, 278; Brumund 1853–54, vol. 2, 186; Hornaday 1885, xi; Hagenbeck 1910, 89; Klös 1969, 19, 26–27; Nieuwendijk 1970, 17; Ritvo 1990.

75. Hornaday 1885, xvi, 8; Hagenbeck 1910, 21–53; Hagenbeck 1924, 309; Mayer 1924, 144; Buck & Anthony 1930, 272; Munnecke 1931, 96; Heynsius-Viruly and Heurn 1935, 61; Hammerstrom 1992.

76. Hagenbeck 1910, 75–78; Hagenbeck 1917, 66; Bradley 1929, 147–48; Munnecke 1931, 227; Valk 1940, 96.

77. Hubback 1905, vi; Weede 1908, 334, 344; Koningsberger 1915, 421–22; Banner 1927, 185; Heynsius-Viruly and Heurn 1935, 60–62; Foenander 1952, 92; Hoogerwerf 1970, 288.

78. ARNAS, MGS 28.12.1922, 3542/IIIB: appendix to letter, Director BB, 26.8.1896; Jachtmuseum Doorwerth, Collection Hardenbroek: letter, dated 1922; Schneider 1905, 101; Brasser 1926, 202–3; Hamerster 1926, 39; Bradley 1929, 116; Wormser 1941, 217; Poser 1955, 118, 227–29; Kitchener 1961, 203; Hazewinkel 1964, 127–28; Hoogerwerf 1970, 242.

79. Bradley 1929, 170; Locke 1954, 73, 97, 102; Fraisse 1955, 75–76; Poser 1955, 109, 163; Bazé 1959, 80.

Chapter 7. Tiger and Leopard Rituals at the Javanese Courts, 1605–1906

An earlier version of this chapter was published in *South East Asia Research* 2/2 (Boomgaard 1994). I acknowledge with thanks the permission to publish a rewritten version of my article.

1. The generic term in Javanese for a tiger/leopard is *macan*. The high Javanese term for tiger and leopard is *sima*.

2. The Javanese word for water buffalo is *kebo;* the high Javanese word is *maésa.*

3. Graaf 1958, 123; Pigeaud 1960–63, vol. 4, 519; Foster 1967, 161.

4. Regents are the highest local representatives of the ruler, or the highest local indigenous official in the areas under VOC rule.

5. Graaf 1956, 238; Moertono 1968, 96. The reference dating from the early fifteenth century is from Mills (1970, 94). For the fourteenth century see Pigeaud 1960–63, vol. 4, 519.

6. Teijsmann 1855, 78; Buddingh 1859–61, vol. 1, 241; Groneman 1900, 7; Morin 1909, 74; Zimmermann 1919, 318; Adam 1930, 150; Warnsinck 1930, 198.

7. Warnsinck 1930, 198; Foster 1967, 161; Fayle 1929, 77.

8. KITLV Coll. 1027/G 113; GM V, 349 (30 Dec. 1689); Valentijn 1724–26, vol. 4 no. 1, 58, 146; Fayle 1929, 72; Graaf 1958, 271–72.

9. Ricklefs 1993, 208 (1723); Remmelink 1994, 102–3 (1737); Stavorinus 1797–

98, vol. 1, 108 (c. 1775); Kumar 1980, 37(1780–90); Ricklefs 1974, 274, and Kumar 1980, 81 (1783 and 1789); Raffles 1830b, vol.1, 386–89 (c. 1800). *Mantri* is the title of an official.

10. Rouffaer 1899, 71–74; Natahamipradja 1931, 96–97; Remmelink 1994, 19, 110–11, 119.

11. Valentijn 1724–26, vol. 4 no. 1, 203–4; Olthof 1941, 267; Kumar 1980, 37.

12. Valentijn 1724–26, vol. 4 no. 1, 204; Remmelink 1994, 122. Remmelink states that it was a fight between a lioness and a banteng, but he explains banteng as wild buffalo, which is obviously wrong.

13. Thunberg 1796, vol. 4, 170; Stavorinus 1797–98, vol. 1, 106–9; Ricklefs 1974, 274–75; Kumar 1980, 81.

14. Rothenbühler 1882, 354–57, 331–34; Ricklefs 1974, 275, 303, 345–46; Kumar 1980, 37, 81, 85.

15. It is possible that Stavorinus had witnessed this around 1775, which might explain his garbled description.

16. Raffles 1830b, vol. 1, 388; Rothenbühler 1882, 332–34.

17. ARA, Coll. Reinwardt, 17: C.G. Fischer, "Beschrijvinge van Java's Noord Oost kust" (c. 1780); Kumar 1980, 38; Remmelink 1994, 123.

18. Groneman 1891, 65; Groneman 1895, 27, 35; Leclercq 1898, 161; Groneman 1900, 9; Morin 1909, 74; Petrus Blumberger 1917, 40 (photo); Zimmermann 1919, 318; Tirtokoesoemo 1931, 73, 102.

19. Wardenaar and du Puy 1804; Jonge 1862–95, vol. 10, 374–75; Schrieke 1957, vol. 2, 165–66.

20. Staged fights between animals are of all ages and places; the animals mentioned are specific for Asia around 1600.

21. On the Moghuls c. 1600 and their court rituals two references may suffice: Temple 1914, 127–28; Foster 1921, 17, 115, 184. On Aceh c. 1600 see Foster 1967, 52, 163, 168, 210; [D 10.12.1632]. See also Reid 1988, 141, 184–86.

22. Raffles 1830b, vol. 1, 387; Crawfurd 1820, vol. 1, 115, 121.

23. Kern 1941, 291 (1822); "Reis" 1859, 450–60 (1838); Fontanier 1852, 227–28 (1847); Houben 1994, 80 (1852); Gevers Deynoot 1864, 103–7 (1862).

24. Hoëvell 1840, 298–312; Junghuhn 1845, 205–22; Rigg 1850a, 75–84.

25. Olivier 1827–30, vol. 1, 148–51; Doren 1851, vol. 2, 386–89; Bastin 1957, 69–70.

26. Roorda van Eysinga 1830–32, vol. 3, 42; Roorda van Eysinga 1841–50, vol. 3, 96; ARA, Coll. Uhlenbeck, 163; "Reis" 1859, 481–82; Jagor 1866, 203–4; Meister 1875, 59–68; Huijser 1885, 7.

27. Martens 1864, 418–19; Jagor 1866, 203–4; Meister 1875, 59–68.

28. On the Dutch as "creators" of Javanese tradition see Pemberton 1994 and Sears 1996.

29. Gevers Deynoot 1864, 103–7; Meister 1875, 59–68; *Mataram* 3.7.1882; Barfus 1893, 253–68.

30. ARA, AMK, Mailrapport 1881, No. 875: Reports from the Residents of Solo and Yogya on the ceremonies at the courts; *Catalogus* 1883, 89–90.

31. Huijser 1885, 1–7. At the inauguration of the railway between Pasuruan and

Probolinggo (eastern Java) in 1884, a fight was staged in Probolinggo between a tiger and a *sapi* (cow or bull); it was a failure (*Nieuws-en Advertentieblad van Probolingo [sic] en Omstreken* 7.5.1884).

32. Jagt 1955, 177 (photo), 242–44; Campbell 1915, 1021; Rouffaer 1899, 75; Nieuwenhuys 1984, 9–16 (photos); Ruzius 1905, vol. 2, 22–31; Sibinga Mulder 1944, 20–25.

33. Raffles 1830b, vol. 1, 387. In at least one case, nature was lent a hand by burning the tiger's mouth (Waldeck 1862, 160).

34. Banner 1927, 67; Ricklefs 1993, 157. Pigeaud (1938, 179–80) suggested that sham fights between a tiger-masked person and someone masked as a buffalo—in his opinion imitations of the earlier tiger-buffalo fights—were indeed forbidden by the Government.

35. Pigeaud 1938, 424; Pigeaud 1940, 182; Anderson 1972, 32.

36. Lombard 1974, 478; Schefold 1988, 6; Wessing 1992, 296–97.

37. Ricklefs 1974, 275; Nieuwenhuys 1984, 9; Wessing 1992, 299–303.

38. It is probably not a coincidence that plantation owners figured prominently in the stories on the Kediri rampog macan.

Chapter 8. The Ancestral Tiger: From Protection to Punishment

1. KITLV, H 277: Stützer (1786–87).

2. Olivier 1827–30, vol. 1, 195–96; Roorda van Eysinga 1841–50, vol. 3 no. 1, 98.

3. ARNAS *Besluit* 5.4.1854, No. 3, appendices.

4. S. Raffles 1830a, 314; Wiele 1930, 109; Locke 1954, 170.

5. Whitney 1905, 281; Hagenbeck 1924, 58.

6. On "village crocodiles" see Olivier 1827–30, vol. 1, 163; Kussendrager 1843, 18; Mohnike 1874, 176; Wilken 1884, 68–71.

7. Pfyffer zu Neueck 1838, 56–57; Mohnike 1874, 176–78; Skeat 1900, 287.

8. About 160 years later there is another reference to a Javanese macan bumi who is an ancestor, namely the spirit of the village founder (Martin-Schiller 1984, 54).

9. Heyne 1814, 427–28; Olivier 1827–30, vol. 1, 163; Raffles 1830a, 314.

10. Toorn 1879, 447; Toorn 1890, 72–73; Loeb 1935, 124; Westenenk 1962, 28–29, 44–45; Bakels 1994, 42–43. Actually, Van der Toorn used the words *orang jadi-jadian*. In Malaya the expression *(harimau) jadi-jadian* was used for weretigers (cf. Chapter 9); Newbold 1839, vol. 1, 192; Abdullah 1970, 114.

11. Schebesta 1928a, 229; Evans 1930, 120; Maxwell 1960, 10.

12. ARNAS, *Besluit* 5.4.1854, No. 3, appendices; Wilsen 1857, 80–81; "Summier" 1859, 585; Hoogeveen 1858, 505; Wilken 1884, 71; Couperus 1887, 303; Knebel 1899, 568–87; Kruyt 1906, 197–98; Pleyte 1910, 132–42; Nieuwenhuis 1911, 12; Geise 1952, 62, 90. *Sima* is high Javanese for tiger; *leluhur* is ancestor.

13. Marsden 1811, 292; Jacobs 1894, vol. 1, 298; Kruyt 1906, 197–98; Volz 1909, 375; Warneck 1909, 74, 129; Volz 1921, 22; Schilling 1952, 81; Westenenk 1962, 28–29; Hazewinkel 1964, 14–15; Bakels 2000.

14. Wilken 1887, 24–25; Skeat 1900, 436–44; Skeat and Blagden 1906, vol. 2, 191, 227–29; Evans 1923, 162–63, 210; Schebesta 1928a, 226–27; Evans 1930, 120; Winstedt 1961, 11–13, 56–57; Endicott 1970, 16–22.

15. Newbold 1839, vol. 1, 192; Maxwell 1881, 23; Bird 1883, 353–54; Evans 1923, 246.

16. ARNAS, *Besluit* 5.4.1854, No. 3, appendices; Raffles 1830a, 314; Hageman 1853, 69; Heering 1886, 88; Snouck Hurgronje 1893–94, vol. 2, 408; Jacobs 1894, vol. 1, 297; Hazeu 1903, 291; Kruyt 1906, 197–98; Warneck 1909, 74, 129; Volz 1912, 375; Volz 1921, 22, 57; Schilling 1952, 49; Westenenk 1962, 68; Collins 1979, 61.

17. Newbold 1839, vol.1, 193; Maxwell 1881, 22; Schebesta 1928a, 82, 147; Fraisse 1955, 83; Bazé 1959, 6.

18. ARNAS, *Besluit* 5.4.1854, No. 3, appendices. "Outer Islands" or "Outer Provinces" were the usual terms for all Indonesian areas outside Java.

19. ARNAS, Answers of the Residents to MGS 12.9.1895, 1881, in Groot Bundel MGS, Openbaar: BGS 28.12.1922, 3542/IIIB; Marsden 1811, 185; Heyne 1814, 427–28; Presgrave 1822, 91; Martens 1864, 420; Schneider 1905, 101; Schneider 1958, 267–69.

20. Mohnike 1874, 163; see also Volz (1921, 22) on Palembang.

21. Müller 1855, 103; Helderman 1891, 171; Volz 1909, 31; Warneck 1909, 15.

22. *Bataviasche Courant,* 20 October 1827; Neumann 1886–87, 237, 264. In the early twentieth century, one did find tiger skins in the houses of Westernized Javanese regents.

23. Toorn 1879, 453; Hasselt 1882, 84; Hazewinkel 1964, 19–20.

24. The ratio for India was even lower, 1.8 to 1. See Chapter 4 for more detail on these figures.

25. Steck 1862, 110; Toorn 1879, 447; Toorn 1890, 73. On this phenomenon in Malaya see Skeat 1900, 163–64.

26. On Java see ARA, Coll. Schneither, 83, Statistical Report, Banten, 1821, La. D 1; ARNAS, *Besluit* 5.4.1854, No 3, appendices (Yogyakarta). On Sumatra see Steck 1862, 110; Mohnike 1874, 164–65; Toorn 1890, 74; Hazewinkel 1964, 14.

27. Toorn 1890, 77; Helderman 1891, 173; Hagen 1908, 108; Volz 1909, 348; Warneck 1909, 34; Loeb 1935, 48; Schnitger 1939, 192; Josselin de Jong 1951, 99–100; Persoon 1994, 158.

28. Rigg 1850b, 131–33; Hoogeveen 1858, 505–7; Hazeu 1899, 693–94; Soemå Sentikå 1902, 11; Kruyt 1906, 170, 388; Jasper 1928, 23; Hidding 1935, 129; Geise 1952, 62, 90.

29. Raffles 1830a, 332; Steck 1862, 110; Hasselt 1882, 414; Neumann 1886–87, 515; Warneck 1909, 129; Westenenk 1962, 28–29; Hazewinkel 1964, 123.

30. Martin 1905, 953; Schebesta 1928a, 189, 229; Evans 1930, 120; Locke 1954, 170.

31. The notion of "good" and "bad" tigers is explicitly mentioned by Almeida 1864, vol. 1, 199; Rees 1865, vol. 2 no. 1, 25. On "mad" tigers see Marsden 1811, 292.

32. ARNAS *Besluit* 5.4.1854, No. 3, appendices; Veth 1875–82, vol. 1, 230–231.

33. Helderman 1891, 171–73; Volz 1921, 22; Locke 1954, 170; Hazewinkel 1964, 15.

34. Broek 1835, 195–96; Jacobs 1894, vol. 1, 298; Crooke 1909–15, vol. 1, 94; Foster 1921, 324.

35. Wilsen 1857, 80–81; Moszkowski 1909, 173, 250; Hien 1933–34, vol. 1, 247.

36. Wilken 1884, 65–66; Helderman 1891, 170–71; Kruyt 1906, 185; Tideman 1922, 17–18. In 1924 Schebesta encountered similar stories among the "heathen" Jakun in Malaya (1928b, 199–200) and among the Kubu in Sumatra (244).

37. Snouck Hurgronje 1893–94, vol. 1, 332; Jacobs 1894, vol. 1, 295–96; Kroesen 1899, 275; see also Kruyt 1906, 185, 197–98.

38. ARA, Coll. Schneither, 85, La. D 1; ARA, AMK 1814–49, 3065: Rapport G.F. Scharten over Buitenzorg, c. 1840; Thunberg 1796, vol. 4, 194; Roorda van Eysinga 1830–32, vol. 2, 403; "Oorspronk" 1855, 266–70; Kussendrager 1861, 74–76; Banner 1927, 158; Wessing 1986, 31–32. Wessing incorrectly uses the term "weretigers."

39. GM V, 153 (23 Dec. 1687); Rigg 1850b, 131–33; Wilsen 1857, 80–81; Jacobs and Meijer 1891, 14; Pleyte 1910, 137–42; Tricht 1929, 51–52, 62; Hidding 1932, 74; Veldhuisen-Djajasoebrata 1984, 59–60; Wessing 1986, 31–32.

40. Wilsen 1858, 59; Coolsma 1881, 70–72; Rinkes 1910, 564–565; Veldhuisen-Djajasoebrata 1984, 59–60.

41. Roorda van Eysinga 1841–50, vol. 3 no. 1, 150–51; Epp 1852, 485–87; Stöhr 1874, 39–41; Rouffaer 1899, 75; Pigeaud 1933, 19; Pigeaud 1938, 432–34; Bonneff 1986, 173; Arifin 1995.

42. Niemann 1866, 275; Helfrich 1889, 632; Snouck Hurgronje 1893–94, vol. 1, 332; Jacobs 1894, vol. 1, 296; vol. 2, 47–48; Moszkowski 1909, 207–8; Zentgraaff 1938, 217; Hazewinkel 1964, 18–19.

43. Hagen 1886, 372–74; Neumann 1886–87, 294–95; Hagen 1890, 185; Snouck Hurgronje 1893–94, vol. 1, 333; Warneck 1909, 105, 129; Tideman 1922, 17–18.

44. Knebel 1899, 568–87; Skeat 1900, 61–71, 163–64; Skeat and Blagden 1906, vol. 2, 222; Hidding 1932, 80; Winstedt 1961, 12.

45. Elsewhere I have dealt with sacred places and the preservation of nature in more detail (Boomgaard 1993a, 317–18, 329; Boomgaard 1995, 55–56).

46. Neumann 1886–87, 295; Snouck Hurgronje 1893–94, vol. 2, 332; Rinkes 1910, 565; Zentgraaff 1938, 152; Schnitger 1939, 192; Westenenk 1962, 42; Hazewinkel 1964, 38–41, 84–103; Wessing 1986, 20.

47. Skeat 1900, 70, 163–64; Winstedt 1961, 11–13, 56–57; Endicott 1970, 16–17, 21–22.

48. KITLV, H 277: Ms. Stützer; ARNAS, *Besluit* 5.4.1854, No. 3, appendices; Hoogeveen 1858, 495; Almeida 1864, vol. 2, 35; Moestapa 1946, 170.

49. Hamilton 1727, vol. 2, 83; Toorn 1879, 453; Hasselt 1882, 84; Brau de Saint-Pol 1884a, 198; Moszkowski 1909, 207–8; Zentgraaff 1938, 218–19; Schnei-

der 1958, 267–69; Westenenk 1962, 44–49; Hazewinkel 1964, 19–25, 36, 69–79, 84–88; Bakels 2000.

50. Skeat 1900, 167; Mayer 1924, 144–45; Locke 1954, 163–64. For a similar case in Indochina see Bazé 1959, 51.

51. Müller 1839, 51; Maxwell 1960, 10; Westenenk 1962, 107.

52. Lindskog 1954, 157–78; Furst 1968, 145, 154, 167–69; Reichel-Dolmatoff 1972, 58; Taussig 1987, 77, 358–63; Saunders 1989, 108–32.

Chapter 9. Devouring the Hearts of the People: The Weretiger

1. On Europe, see Otten 1986; on Africa, Lindskog 1954; on Latin America, Penard 1928; Furst 1968; Reichel-Dolmatoff 1972; Reichel-Dolmatoff 1975, 43–60, 108–32; Fiedel 1987, 224; Saunders 1989, 34–41, 47, 70–75; on Asia (Indonesia excepted) see Groot 1898 (mainly China), Gibb 1929, 224–25 (India), Velder 1979, 68–70, and Boyes 1997 (Thailand).

2. *Harimau* is tiger; *(men)jadi* means "to become."

3. Newbold 1839, vol. 1, 192; Hervey 1879, 110; Swettenham 1896, 200–201; Clifford 1897, 63–77; Abdullah 1970, 114, 118–19; Mills 1970, 113.

4. Wilken 1887, 24–25; Skeat and Blagden 1906, vol. 2, 191, 227–29; Evans 1923, 162–63, 210; Schebesta 1928a, 226–27; Evans 1930, 120; Winstedt 1961, 11–13, 56–57; Endicott 1970, 16–22.

5. Wilken 1887, 24–25; Skeat 1900, 436–44; Eliade 1964, 344-46, 459-60.

6. See, however, the tigers guarding the tomb of the Tuan Putri Gunong Ledang, mentioned in Chapter 8.

7. Hervey 1879, 108–10; Maxwell 1881, 23; Skeat 1900, 157; Mayer 1924, 172; Locke 1954, 158–59; Anderson 1983.

8. Marsden 1811, 292; Presgrave 1822, 325–26; Mohnike 1874, 165.

9. Mohnike 1874, 192; Hasselt 1882, 68, 75–76; Bellwood 1985, 230, 293–95. Map no. 10b of the *Atlas* (1938) excellently visualizes the high concentration of prehistoric remains in the Besemah area.

10. Thomassen à Thuessink 1932, 19; Schnitger 1939, 192; Hazewinkel 1964, 38; Andaya 1993, 28.

11. In Mexico and Colombia sculptures have been found, dating roughly from the first millennium BC, representing jaguars copulating with women. Several scholars have proposed a link between the statues and beliefs in supernatural jaguars (werejaguars, ancestral jaguars, and jaguar "familiars"). Furst 1968, 144–48; Reichel-Dolmatoff 1972, 53–59; Saunders 1989, 69.

12. Snouck Hurgronje 1893–94, vol. 1, 291; Volz 1921, 67–68; Hazewinkel 1964, 45–46; Watson 1985, 169; Kathirithamby 1986, 40.

13. Klerks 1897, 51; Watson 1985, 170; Boomgaard 1993b, 207–8.

14. Volz 1921, 67; Hazewinkel 1964, 46–48, 54–55; Watson 1993, 203; Collins 1979, 62; Bakels 1994, 34–35.

15. Graafland 1889, 18–19; Toorn 1890, 59; Jacobs 1894, vol. 1, 292; Rouffaer 1921, 537–38, 560–64; Obdeyn 1929, 379–80.

16. Pigeaud 1933, 16, 63. I am indebted to Willem van der Molen, who translated

the relevant passages from the *Serat Centhini* for me (*Serat Centhini,* 1991, vol. 12, 121–37).

17. ARNAS, *Besluit* 5.4.1854, No. 3 (appendix); Dissel 1870, 274; Veth 1875–82, vol. 1, 332; "Vragen" 1881, 304–7; Wilken 1884, 21–22.

18. Hazeu 1899; Knebel 1899; Rouffaer 1899. Those who read Javanese may wish to consult the original manuscripts used by Hazeu for his article, still to be found in the University of Leiden Library (LOr 6305 and 6307; cf. Pigeaud 1967–70, vol. 2, 352–53).

19. This was repeated by Hien 1933–34, vol. 1, 242, and Wessing 1986, 101.

20. Raffles 1830b, vol. 2, 43; Roorda 1841–50, vol. 3 no. 1, 150–51; Kussendrager 1861, 262–65; Groneman 1891, 67; Rouffaer 1899, 71–73; Bonneff 1986, 180.

21. Raffles 1830b, vol. 2, 37, 43; Krom and Bosch 1915–23, vol. 2, 280, 342–47; Graaf 1954, 61–62.

22. See, e.g., Soemå Sentikå 1902, 16–18; Pigeaud 1938, 432–34; Sibinga Mulder 1944, 25.

23. Vleuten 1872, 10–12; Gericke/Roorda 1901, vol. 2, 610–11; Pigeaud 1938, 432.

24. Jacobs 1883, 161–62. The term is also in Van der Tuuk's dictionary (Tuuk 1899, vol. 2, 442), but as no source is given, it is possible that this is based on Jacobs. Men who could turn themselves into tigers were also mentioned by W. Dreesen, a German who visited Bali in the 1930s (Dreesen 1937, 28).

25. Friederich 1849–50, vol. 1, 43; Plate 1912, 458, 461–64; Kat Angelino 1921, 2.

26. Danckaerts 1859, 115 (1621); Ludeking 1868, 49–50; Kruyt 1899, 548–67; Kruyt 1906, 109–19; Adriani 1908, 61–62; Arndt 1929, 828–31.

27. Nieuwenhuis 1904–7, vol. 1, 63; vol. 2, 237; Kruyt 1906, 419; Shelford 1916, 28; Elshout 1926, 215–17, 318–22; Peranio 1959, 6; Schärer 1963, 89, 123–25; Harrisson 1984, 314; King 1985, 91–93.

28. Kühr 1897, 66; Elshout 1926, 510–11; Huijbers 1931, 177, 209, 242; Sellato 1983; King 1985, 51; Gomes 1992.

29. Hardeland 1859, 160–61, 412; Elshout 1926, 498–505; Schärer 1963, 20–21, 51.

30. For example, on Malaya, see Wilken 1887, 24–25; Winstedt 1961, 13, 56–57; Endicott 1970, 16–22; on Latin America, see Penard 1928, 625, 644; Furst 1968, 151, 154–64; Reichel-Dolmatoff 1972, 59–61.

31. ARNAS, *Besluit* 5.4.1854, No. 3, appendices (Yogyakarta); Hazeu 1899, 693–94; Knebel 1899, 578; Pigeaud 1938, 432–34; Hazewinkel 1964, 35–36.

32. Gibb 1929, 224–25; Berg 1934, 61–62; Corbett 1948, 20–22; Velder 1979, 68–70.

33. Pigeaud 1938, 437–45; Clara van Groenendael 1995; Marschall 1995.

34. They are, admittedly, often supposed to be living in villages of their own, but this only emphasizes their position as outsiders to "normal" villagers.

35. Most people accused of witchcraft were female, whereas most weretigers seem to have been male.

Chapter 10. The Rise, Decline, and Fall of the Tiger

1. Bradley 1929, 71; Westenenk 1962, 77; Hazewinkel 1964, 203–16.
2. The figure 0, calculated for three years between 1897 and 1904, was put in the table under 1870s, as it represents the preconquest situation.
3. Friederich 1849, 42; Schwarz 1913, 73.
4. Bradley 1929, 148; Heynsius-Viruly and Heurn 1935, 60–61; Valk 1940, 96; Zentgraaff and Goudoever 1947, 70.
5. Weede 1908, 334, 344; Schwartz 1913, 73; Koningsberger 1915, 421–22; Banner 1927, 185; Dreesen 1937, 27; Zimmermann 1938, 50; Baerveldt 1950, 59; "Death" 1998.
6. This figure (40,000) is often given as the number of tigers to be found in India around 1900.
7. ARA, AMK 1814–49, 3087: letter III by P. Dubois; Friederich 1849, 42; Zollinger 1866, 526; Bickmore 1868, 95; Eck 1878, 129; Jacobs 1883, 30; Brink 1980.
8. Junghuhn 1847; Mohnike 1883, 409; Brenner 1894, 278; Volz 1912, 373–74; Bradley 1929, 61; Heynsius-Viruly and Heurn 1935, 61; Poser 1955, 226; Hazewinkel 1964, 25.
9. IOL, Coll. McKenzie, Private, 3: Daendels, Statistical queries, May 1808 (query #22); *AStWbk* 1863, vol. 2, 403; Massink 1888, 29; *JvNIVN* 1929–31, 75; *Atlas* 1938, map 7b3; Bergmans and Bree 1986, 329.
10. ARA, AMK, *Besluit* 22.11.1822, 1 (Kedu); ARA, Coll. Schneither, 85: Statistical Survey, Buitenzorg, 1822; ARA, AMK, *Besluit* 13.9.1824, 11 (Buitenzorg); Junghuhn 1853–4, vol. 2, 258–71, 285, 302–20.
11. E.g., Hoogerwerf 1970; Schenkel 1970; Seidensticker and Suyono 1980.
12. Mohnike 1883, 409–10; Hoogerwerf 1970, 244; Ward 1997, 25–26; Baker 1998, 12.

Chapter 11. Living Apart Together

1. Regarding this parallel in India see Rangarajan 1997.
2. The best-known tiger king of the East, however, was not a Malay ruler but the Indian Tipu Sultan of Mysore (Brittlebank 1995).
3. Gonda 1947, 13; Pigeaud 1967, vol. 1, 261; Tinbergen and Dis 1964, 9–12; Klokke 1993, 67, 180–81, 216–17, 246.
4. Stutterheim 1926, 337–40; Aichele 1928, 28; Pigeaud 1938, 180; Long 1985, 198.
5. The term "penitent butchers" is from William Beinart, quoted in Storey 1991.

References

Abbreviations Used

BKI   Bijdragen tot de Taal-, Land-en Volkenkunde [van Nederlandsch Indië] (van het Koninklijk Instituut) (title varies)

JMBRAS   Journal of the Malay(si)an Branch of the Royal Asiatic Society

JSBRAS   Journal of the Straits Branch of the Royal Asiatic Society

NTNI   Natuurkundig Tijdschrift voor Nederlandsch-Indië

TBB   Tijdschrift voor het Binnenlandsch Bestuur

TBG   Tijdschrift voor Indische Taal-, Land- en Volkenkunde van het Bataviaasch Genootschap van Kunsten en Wetenschappen

T(K)NAG   Tijdschrift van het (Koninklijk) Nederlandsch Aardrijkskundig Genootschap

TNI   Tijdschrift van/voor Nederlandsch-Indië (title varies)

VBG   Verhandelingen van het Bataviaasch Genootschap van Kunsten en Wetenschappen

Books, Articles, and Papers

Abdullah bin Abdul Kadir, 1970, *The Hikayat Abdullah* (annotated translation by A. H. Hill). Kuala Lumpur: Oxford University Press (1st ed. 1954)

Adam, L., 1930, "Eenige historische en legendarische plaatsnamen in Jogjakarta," *Djåwå* 10, pp. 150–62

Adams, T., 1928, "Die Kubus, die Waldmenschen Sumatras," *Mitteilungen der Anthropologischen Gesellschaft in Wien* 58, pp. 290–99

(*Adatrechtbundel*), 1911, *Adatrechtsbundel IV: Java en Madoera*. 's-Gravenhage: Nijhoff

Adriani, N, (1908), *Het animistisch heidendom als godsdient*. Den Haag: Boekhandel van den Zendingsstudie-Raad

Aichele, W., 1928, "Oudjavaansche bijdragen tot de geschiedenis van den wen-schboom," *Djåwå* 8, pp. 28–40

Almeida, W. B. d', 1864, *Life in Java with Sketches of the Javanese.* London: Hurst & Blackett (2 vols.)

Andaya, B. Watson, 1979, *Perak, the Abode of Grace. A Study of an Eighteenth-Century Malay State.* Kuala Lumpur: Oxford University Press

Andaya, B. Watson, 1993, *To Live as Brothers. Southeast Sumatra in the Seventeenth and Eighteenth Centuries.* Honolulu: University of Hawaii Press

Andaya, L.Y., 1975, *The Kingdom of Johor, 1641–1728.* Kuala Lumpur: Oxford University Press

Anderson, B., 1983, *Imagined Communities. Reflections on the Origin and Spread of Nationalism.* London: Verso

Anderson, B. R. O'G., 1972, "The Idea of Power in Javanese Culture," in C. Holt (ed.), *Culture and Politics in Indonesia.* Ithaca: Cornell University Press, pp. 1–70

Anderson, K., 1968, *Der Tod im Dschungel. Tiger im Hinterhalt.* Hamburg: Paul Parey (translation from English original, 1967)

Andrásy, Graf E., 1859, *Reise in Ostindien. Ceylon, Java, China, Bengalen.* Pest: Giebel

Andriesz, G. (= J. Andersen), 1670, *De beschrijving der reizen van—deur Oostindiën (. . .) 1644 tot 1650.* Amsterdam: Rieuwertsz & Arentsz

Anthonio, W., 1990, *Tjalie Robinson: "Reflections in a Brown Eye."* (Ph.D. diss., University of Michigan)

Arifin, W. P., 1995, *Babad Sembar. Chroniques de l'est javanais* (Monographies 177). Paris: Presses de l'Ecole Française d'Extrême-Orient

Arndt, P. P., 1929, "Die Religion der Nad'a (West-Flores, Kleine Sunda-Inseln)," *Anthropos* 24, pp. 817–61

Arnold, D., 1996, *The Problem of Nature. Environment, Culture and European Expansion.* Oxford: Blackwell

(*AStWbk*), 1863–69, *Aardrijkskundig en Statistisch Woordenboek van Nederlandsch-Indië.* Amsterdam: Van Kampen (3 vols.)

(Atlas), 1938, *Atlas van Tropisch Nederland.* Batavia: Koninklijk Nederlandsch Aardrijkskundig Genootschap & Topographische Dienst Nederlandsch-Indië

Aylva Rengers, L. H. W. van, 1844–46, "Onuitgegeven dagboek geschreven gedurende een verblijf op Java, van het jaar 1827–1830," *Bijdragen tot de kennis der Nederlandsche en vreemde koloniën (. . .)* 1, pp. 363–85, and 3, pp. 260–83

B., O. P., 1914, "100 koningstijgers gedood in zes jaar tijds," *TBB* 46, 432–34.

Baerveldt, W., 1950, *Edelwild in de archipel.* Deventer: Kluwer

Bakels, J., 1994, "But His Stripes Remain. On the Symbolism of the Tiger in the Oral Traditions of Kerinci, Sumatra," in J. G. Oosten (ed.), *Text and Tales. Studies in Oral Tradition* (CNWS Publications, 22). Leiden: University of Leiden, Research School CNWS, pp. 33–51

Bakels, J., 2000, *Het verbond met de tijger. Visies op de relatie tussen mensen en mensene-tende dieren in Kerinci, Sumatra* (Ph.D. diss., University of Leiden). Leiden: CNWS

Baker, L., 1998, "The Siberian Tiger and the Country of Tiger Tales," *Education about Asia* 3/3, pp. 11–16

Balen, J. H. van, (1914), *De dierenwereld van Insulinde in woord en beeld. Vol. I: De Zoogdieren*. Deventer: Van der Burgh

("Banjoewangi"), 1845, "Banjoewangi en de zwavelberg aldaar in 1789 en 1790," *Indisch Magazijn* 2/1, 2/2, 134–47

Banner, H. S., 1927, *Romantic Java as It Was & Is*. London: Seeley, Service

Barfus, E. von, 1893, *Kriegsfahrten eines alten Soldaten im fernen Osten. Nach den Aufzeichnungen eines ehemaligen Offiziers der niederländisch-ostindischen Armee*. Stuttgart: Deutsche Verlags-Anstalt

Barros, J. de, 1727, "Helddadige scheepstogt van Alfonso d'Albuquerque, 1506 en volgende," in J. L. Gottfried (ed.), *De aanmerkenswaardigste en alomberoemde zee-en landreizen der Portugeezen, Spanjaarden, Engelsen (. . .) tot ontdekking van de Oost- en West-Indiën*. 's-Gravenhage: Boucqueet et al., vol. 1

Bastin, J. (ed.), 1957, "The Journal of Thomas Otho Travers 1813–1820," *Memoirs of the Raffles Museum* 4, pp. 9–156

Bastin, J. (ed.), 1965, *The British in West Sumatra (1685–1825). A Selection of Documents (. . .)*. Kuala Lumpur: University of Malaya Press

Bastin, J. (ed.), 1973, "The Java Journal of Dr. Joseph Arnold," *JMBRAS* 46/1, pp. 1–92

Bazé, W., 1959, *Tijgers, tijgers*. Utrecht: Spectrum (Dutch transl. of French original)

Beauvoir, le Comte de, 1873, *Voyage autour du monde. Australie, Java, Siam, Pékin, Yeddo, San Francisco*. Paris: Plon

Becking, J. H., 1989, *Henri Jacob Victor Sody (1892–1959). His Life and Work. A Biographical and Bibliographical Study*. Leiden: Brill

Behr, J. von der, 1930, *Reise nach Java, Vorder-Indien, Persien und Ceylon, 1641–1650*. (Reisebeschreibungen von deutschen Beamten, 4) Den Haag: Nijhoff (1st ed. 1668)

Bellwood, P., 1985, *Prehistory of the Indo-Malaysian Archipelago*. Sydney: Academic Press

Bemmelen, J. F. van, 1895, *Uit Indië; reisindrukken en herinneringen uit onzen archipel*. Batavia: Kolff

Berg, B., 1934, *Tiger*. København: Gyldendalske Boghandel, Nordisk Forlag (Danish translation of Swedish original dated 1933–34)

Bergmans, W., and P. J. H. van Bree, 1986, "On a collection of bats and rats from the Kangean Islands, Indonesia (Mammalia: Chiroptera and Rodentia)," *Zeitschrift für Säugetierkunde* 51/6, pp. 329–44

Berlage Jr., H. P., 1931, "Over het verband tusschen de dikte der jaarringen van djatiboomen (Tectona grandis L.f.) en den regenval op Java," *Tectona* 24:939–53

Bezemer, T. J., 1906, *Door Nederlandsch Oost-Indië; schetsen van land en volk*. Groningen: Wolters

Bickmore, A. S., 1868, *Travels in the East Indian Archipelago*. London: Murray

Bijl de Vroe, C. L. M., 1980, *Rondom de Buitenzorgse troon; Indisch dagboek—1914–1919* (edited by M. Schouten). Haarlem: Fibula van Dishoek

Bird, I. L., 1883, *The Golden Chersonese and the Way Thither*. London: Murray

Bleeker, P., 1849, "Fragmenten eener reis over Java," *TNI* 11/2, pp. 17–55, 117–45, 177–90, 266–70

(*Blue Book*), 1900–1937, *Blue Book for the Year—(Colony of the Straits Settlements)*. Singapore: Government Printing Office (published annually)

Bock, C., 1882, *The Head-Hunters of Borneo: A Narrative of Travel up the Mahakkam and down the Barito; also, Journeyings in Sumatra*. London: Sampson Low et al.

Boers, J. W., 1838, "De Koeboes," *TNI* 1/2, pp. 286–95

(Bois, J. A. du), 1852–57, "De Lampongsche distrikten op het eiland Sumatra," *TNI* 14/1, pp. 245–75, 309–33; 18/2, pp. 347–74; 19/1, pp. 1–49, 89–117

Boissevain, Ch., 1909, *Tropisch Nederland. Indrukken eener reis door Nederlandsch-Indië*. Haarlem: Tjeenk Willink

Bolling, F. A., 1913, "Oost-Indisch Reisboek (.) 1678," *BKI* 68, pp. 289–381

Bonneff, M., 1986, *Pérégrinations Javanaises. Les voyages de R. M. A. Purwa Lelana: une vision de Java au XIXe siècle (c. 1860–1875)*. (Etudes insulindiennes/archipel, 7) Paris: Editions de la Maison des sciences de l'homme

Bontius, 1931, *Tropische Geneeskunde/On Tropical Medicine*. (Opuscula Selecta Neerlandicorum de Arte Medica, 10) Amsterdam: Nederlands Tijdschrift voor Geneeskunde (translation of texts dated 1642 and 1658)

Boomgaard, P., 1989, *Children of the Colonial State. Population Growth and Economic Development in Java, 1795–1880* (CASA Monographs 1). Amsterdam: Free University Press

Boomgaard, P., 1993a, "Protection de la nature en Indonésie pendant la fin de la période coloniale (1889–1949)," in J. Pouchepadass (ed.), *Colonisations et environnement*. Paris: Société Française d'Histoire d'Outre-mer, pp. 307–44

Boomgaard, P., 1993b, "Illicit Riches. Economic Development and Changing Attitudes Towards Money and Wealth as Reflected in Javanese Popular Belief," in J. Th. Lindblad (ed.), *New Challenges in the Modern Economic History of Indonesia*. Leiden: Programme of Indonesian Studies, pp. 197–215

Boomgaard, P., 1994, "Death to the Tiger! The Development of Tiger and Leopard Rituals in Java, 1605–1906," *South East Asia Research* 2, pp. 141–75

Boomgaard, P., 1995, "Sacred Trees and Haunted Forests in Indonesia, Particularly Java, Nineteenth and Twentieth Centuries," in O. Bruun and A. Kalland (eds.), *Asian Perceptions of Nature. A Critical Approach*. Richmond, Surrey: Curzon, pp. 47–62

Boomgaard, P., 1997a, "Introducing Environmental Histories of Indonesia," in P. Boomgaard, F. Colombijn, and D. Henley (eds.), *Paper Landscapes. Explorations in the Environmental History of Indonesia* (Verhandelingen KITLV 178). Leiden: KITLV Press, pp. 1–26

Boomgaard, P., 1997b, "Hunting and Trapping in the Indonesian Archipelago, 1500–1950," in P. Boomgaard, F. Colombijn, and D. Henley (eds.), *Paper Landscapes. Explorations in the Environmental History of Indonesia* (Verhandelingen KITLV 178). Leiden: KITLV Press, pp. 185–213

Boomgaard, P., 1999, "Oriental Nature, Its Friends and Its Enemies: Conservation of Nature in Late-Colonial Indonesia, 1889–1949," *Environment and History* 5/3, pp. 257–92

Boomgaard, P., in press, "'Primitive' Tiger Hunters in Indonesia and Malaysia,

1800–1950," in J. Knight (ed.), *Wildlife in Asia. Cultural Perspectives.* London: Curzon

Boomgaard, P., and A. J. Gooszen, 1991, *Population Trends 1795–1942* (Changing Economy in Indonesia, 11). Amsterdam: Royal Tropical Institute

Boomgaard, P., and J. L. van Zanden, 1990, *Food Crops and Arable Lands, Java 1815–1940* (Changing Economy in Indonesia, 10). Amsterdam: Royal Tropical Institute

Borie, 1861, "Notice sur les Mantras, tribu sauvage de la Peninsule Malaise," *TBG* 10, pp. 413–43

Boyes, J., 1997, *Tiger-Men and Tofu Dolls: Tribal Spirits in Northern Thailand.* Chiangmai: Silkworm

Bradley, M. H., 1929, *Trailing the Tiger.* New York: Appleton

Brasser, J. C., 1926, *Jacht op groot wild in Nederlandsch Oost-Indië; verhalen uit verre wildernissen.* Zutphen: Thieme

Brau de Saint-Pol Lias, X., 1884a, *Ile de Sumatra. Chez les Atchés, Lohong.* Paris: Plon

Brau de Saint-Pol Lias, X., 1884b, *De France a Sumatra par Java, Singapour et Pinang; Les anthropophages.* Paris: Oudin

Brau de Saint-Pol Lias, X., 1891, *La côte du poivre. Voyage a Sumatra.* Paris: Lecène, Oudin

Breitenstein, H., 1900, *21 Jahre in Indien; aus dem Tagebuche eines Militärarztes.* Leipzig: Grieben (2 vols.)

Brenner, J. Freiherr von, 1894, *Besuch bei den Kannibalen Sumatras. Erste Durchquerung der unabhängigen Batak-Lande.* Würzburg: Woerl

Brink, J. van den, 1980, "The Former Distribution of the Bali Tiger, *Panthera tigris balica* (Schwarz, 1912)," *Säugetierkundliche Mitteilungen* 28/4, pp. 286–89

Brink, J. van den, and H. de Iongh, 1980, "Op zoek naar de (laatste) Indonesische tijgers," *Spiegel der natuur* 11/4, pp. 137–41

Brittlebank, K., 1995, "Sakti and Barakat: The Power of Tipu's Tiger. An Examination of the Tiger Emblem of Tipu Sultan of Mysore," *Modern Asian Studies* 29/2, pp. 257–69

Broek, H . A. van der, 1835, "Verslag nopens het eiland Bali," *De Oosterling* 1, pp. 158–236

Brongersma, L. D., 1935, "Notes on Some Recent and Fossil Cats Chiefly from the Malay Archipelago," *Zoölogische Mededeelingen* 18, pp. 1–89

Brown, C. C., and R. Roolvink (eds.), 1970, *Sejarah Melayu or Malay Annals.* Kuala Lumpur: Oxford University Press

Brumund, J. F. G., 1853–54, *Indiana. Verzameling van stukken van onderscheiden aard, over landen, volken, oudheden en geschiedenis van den Indischen Archipel.* Amsterdam: Van Kampen (2 vols.)

Bruun, O., and A. Kalland (eds.), 1995, *Asian Perceptions of Nature. A Critical Approach.* Richmond, Surrey: Curzon

Buber, M., 1965, *Between Man and Man.* New York: Macmillan

Buck, F., and E. Anthony, 1930, *Bring 'em Back Alive.* Garden City, N.Y.: Garden City Publishing

Buddingh, S. A., 1859–61, *Neêrlands Oost-Indië. Reizen over Java, Madura (. . .) gedaan gedurende het tijdvak van 1852–1857.* Rotterdam: Wijt & Zonen (3 vols.)

Bünning, E., 1947, *In den Wäldern Nord-Sumatras. Reisebuch eines Biologen.* Bonn: Dümmlers Verlag

Cameron, J., 1865, *Our Tropical Possessions in Malayan India: Being a Descriptive Account of Singapore, Penang, Province Wellesley, and Malacca (. . .).* London: Smith, Elder

Campbell, D. M., 1915, *Java: Past & Present; a Description of the Most Beautiful Country in the World, Its Ancient History, People, Antiquities, and Products.* London: Heinemann

Carey, I., 1976, *Orang Asli. The Aboriginal Tribes of Peninsular Malaysia.* Kuala Lumpur: Oxford University Press

(*Carnivores*), 1984, *All the World's Animals. Carnivores.* New York: Torstar

(*Catalogus*), 1883, *Catalogus der afdeeling Nederlandsche koloniën van de Internationale Koloniale en Uitvoerhandel Tentoonstelling van 1 Mei tot ulto. October 1883 te Amsterdam. Groep II.* Leiden: Brill

Clara van Groenendael, V. M., 1995, *Java en Madura in de uitvoerende kunsten. Th.G.Th. Pigeauds Javaanse volksvertoningen en latere studies 1817–1995* (Werkdocumenten, 7). Leiden: KITLV

Clifford, H., 1897, *In Court & Kampong; Being Tales & Sketches of Native Life in the Malay Peninsula.* London: Richards

Colenbrander, H. T., 1911, *Korte historiael ende Journaels aenteyckeninge van (. . .) David Pietersz. de Vries.* (Werken Linschoten-Vereeniging, 3). 's-Gravenhage: Nijhoff

Colenbrander, H. T., and W. Ph. Coolhaas (1st and 2nd eds.), 1919–53, *Jan Pietersz. Coen. Bescheiden omtrent zijn verblijf in Indië.* 's-Gravenhage: Nijhoff (for KITLV) (7 vols.)

Collins, W. A., 1979, *Besemah Concepts. A Study of the Culture of a People of South Sumatra.* (Ph.D. diss., University of California, Berkeley)

Coolhaas, W. Ph. (ed.), 1962–63, *Pieter van den Broecke in Azië.* 's-Gravenhage: Nijhoff (Werken Linschoten Vereeniging, 63 & 64) (2 vols.)

Coolhaas, W. Ph., 1985, *Controleur BB. Herinneringen van een jong bestuursambtenaar in Nederlands-Indië.* Utrecht: HES

Coolsma, S., 1881, *West-Java; het land, de bewoners en de arbeid der Nederlandsche Zendingsvereeniging.* Rotterdam: Dunk

Corbett, J., (1991), *Man-Eaters of Kumaon.* Delhi, etc.: Oxford University Press (1st ed. 1944, in *The Jim Corbett Omnibus*)

Corbett, J., 1948, *The Man-Eating Leopard of Rudraprayag.* London: Oxford University Press

Cordes, J. W. H., 1874–75, "Herinneringen aan Sumatra's Westkust. Bijdrage tot de kennis van de boschstreken over een gedeelte van Sumatra," *Tijdschrift Nederlandsche Maatschappij ter bevordering van Nijverheid,* 3rd series, 15, pp. 289–396, and 16, pp. 1–48

Cordes, J. W. H., 1881, *De djati-bosschen op Java; hunne natuur, verspreiding, geschiedenis en exploitatie.* Batavia: Ogilvie

Cortesão, A. (ed.), 1967, *The Summa Oriental of Tomé Pires. An Account of the East, from the Red Sea to Japan, Written in Malacca and India in 1512–1515*. London: Works Hakluyt Society, 2nd series. (1st ed. 1944, Nendeln: Kraus)

Couperus, G. W., 1887, "Le gibier et la chasse à Java," *Revue Coloniale Internationale* 2, pp. 299–334

Courier dit Dubekart, A. M., 1872, *Feiten van Brata-Yoeda of Nederlandsch-Indische toestanden*. Semarang: Van Dorp

Crawfurd, J., 1820, *History of the Indian Archipelago*. Edinburgh: Constable (3 vols.)

Crawfurd, J., 1856, *A Descriptive Dictionary of the Indian Islands & Adjacent Countries*. London: Bradbury & Evans

Cribb, R., 1991, *Gangsters and Revolutionaries. The Jakarta People's Militia and the Indonesian Revolution 1945–1949* (Asian Studies Association of Australia Southeast Asia Publication Series 20). Sydney: Allen & Unwin

Crooke, W. (ed.), 1909–15, *A New Account of East India and Persia Being Nine Years Travels, 1672–1681, by John Fryer*. London: Hakluyt Society (Works Hakluyt Society, 2nd series, 19, 20, 39). (3 vols.)

(*Daghregister*), 1888–1931, *Daghregister gehouden int Casteel Batavia vant passerende daer ter plaetse als over geheel Nederlandts-India*. Batavia: Landsdrukkerij/Nijhoff (30 vols., covering selected years 1624–1682)

Dames, M. L. (ed.), 1918–21, *The Book of Duarte Barbosa. An Account of the Countries Bordering on the Indian Ocean and Their Inhabitants, Written by Duarte Barbosa and Completed about the Year 1518 A.D.* London: Works Hakluyt Society, 2nd series, 44 & 49 (2 vols.)

Danckaerts, S., 1859, "Historisch ende grondich verhael van den standt des Christendoms int quartier van Amboina (. . .)," *BKI* 6, pp. 105–36

Davidson, G. F., 1846, *Trade and Travel in the Far East. Or Recollections of Twenty-one Years Passed in Java, Singapore, Australia, and China*. London: Madden & Malcolm

De, R., 1990, *The Sundarbans*. Calcutta: Oxford University Press

("Death"), 1998, "Death of a Bali Tiger," *Cat News* (Gland, Switzerland) 28, p. 7

Denis, A., 1964, *Cats of the World*. London: Constable

Denninghoff Stelling, L., 1966, *Langs tijgerpaden*. Den Haag: Tong Tong

Deventer Jzn, S. van, 1865–66, *Bijdragen tot de kennis van het landelijk stelsel op Java (. . .)*. Zalt-Bommel: Noman & Zn. (3 vols.)

Dijk, P. A. L. E. van, 1884, "Rapport over de Loeboe-bevolking in de Onderafdeeling Groot-Mandheling en Batang Natal," *BKI* 32, pp. 151–61

Dippe, G. von, 1911, *Auf Grosswild. Jagd- und Reiseabenteuer in den Tropen*. Strassburg: Singer

Dissel, J. A. van, 1870, "Eenige bijgeloovigheden en gewoonten der Javanen," *TNI* 3rd series, 4/1, pp. 270–79

DNIJ, 1937–1941, *De Nederlandsch-Indische Jager* (annual)

Dolínek, V., and J. Durdík, 1993, *The Encyclopedia of European Historical Weapons*. London: Hamlyn

Dongen, G. J. van, 1906, "Bijdrage tot de kennis van de Ridan-Koeboes," *TBB* 30, pp. 225–53

Dongen, G. J. van, 1910, "De Koeboes in de onderafdeeling Koeboestreken der residentie Palembang," *BKI* 63, pp. 181–336

Doren, J .B. J. van, 1851, *Reis naar Nederlands Oost-Indië of land- en zeetochten gedurende de twee eerste jaren mijns verblijfs op Java.* 's-Gravenhage: Van Langenhuysen (2 vols.)

Dreesen, W., 1937, *Hundert Tage auf Bali.* Hamburg: Broschek

Eck, R. van, 1878, "Schetsen van het eiland Bali; I, algemeene beschrijving van het eiland," *TNI* new series, 7/2, pp. 87–130

Eliade, M., 1964, *Shamanism. Archaic Techniques of Ecstasy.* Princeton: Princeton University Press

Ellen, R., 1996, "Introduction," in R. Ellen & K. Fukui (eds.), *Redefining Nature. Ecology, Culture and Domestication.* Oxford: Berg, pp. 1–36

Elshout, J. M., 1926, *De Kenja-Dajaks uit het Apo-Kajangebied. Bijdragen tot de kennis van Cemtraal-Borneo.* 's-Gravenhage: Nijhoff (for KITLV)

Endicott, K. M., 1970, *An Analysis of Malay Magic.* Oxford: Clarendon

Endicott, K. M., 1979, *Batek Negrito Religion. The World-View and Rituals of a Hunting and Gathering People of Peninsular Malaysia.* Oxford: Clarendon

(*ENI*), 1899–1905, *Encyclopaedie van Nederlandsch-Indië,* 's-Gravenhage: Nijhoff/ Brill (4 vols.)

Epp, F., 1841, *Schilderungen aus Ostindiens Archipel.* Heidelberg: Mohr

Epp, F., 1849, "Banjoewangi," *TNI* 11/2, pp. 241–61

Epp, F., 1852, *Schilderungen aus Holländisch-Ostindien.* Heidelberg: Winter

Eredia, G. E. de, 1930, "Description of Malacca, Meridional India and Cathay (1613) (transl. L.V. Mills)," *JMBRAS* 8, pp. 1–288

Evans, I. H. N., 1923, *Studies in Religion, Folk-Lore, and Custom in British North Borneo and the Malay Peninsula.* Cambridge: Cambridge University Press

Evans, I. H. N., 1930, "Schebesta on the Sacerdo-Therapy of the Semangs," *Journal of the Royal Anthropological Institute* 60, pp. 115–25

Evans, I. H. N., 1937, *The Negritos of Malaya.* Cambridge: Cambridge University Press

Favre, 1865, *An Account of the Wild Tribes Inhabiting the Malayan Peninsula, Sumatra, and a Few Neighbouring Islands.* Paris: Imperial Printing-Office

Fayle, C. E. (ed.), 1929, *Voyages to the East Indies. Christopher Fryke and Christopher Schweitzer.* London, etc.: Cassell & Co.

Feith, Jhr. J. (1940), *Sport in Indië.* Deventer: van Hoeve

Fend, W. (c. 1971), *De Tijgers van Aboetsjmar.* Den Haag: Scheltens and Giltay (translation from German original dated c. 1970)

Fiedel, S. J., 1987, *Prehistory of the Americas.* Cambridge, etc.: Cambridge University Press

Foenander, E. C., 1952, *Big Game of Malaya. Their Types, Distribution and Habits.* London: Batchworth Press

Fontanier, V., 1852, *Voyage dans l'Archipel Indien.* Paris: Ledoyen

Forbes, H. O., 1885, *A Naturalist's Wanderings in the Eastern Archipelago.* New York: Harper

Foster, W. (ed.), 1921, *Early Travels in India 1583–1619.* London, etc.: Oxford University Press

Foster, W. (ed.), 1967a, *The Voyage of Sir Henry Middleton to the Moluccas 1604–1606.* Nendeln: Kraus Reprint (1st ed. 1943, London: Works issued by the Hakluyt Society, 2nd series, 88)

Foster, W. (ed.), 1967b, *The Voyage of Thomas Best to the East Indies 1612–14.* Nendeln: Kraus Reprint (1st ed. 1934, London: Works issued by the Hakluyt Society, 2nd series, 75)

Fraisse, J., 1955, *Coups de Feu dans la jungle. Chasses Indochinoises.* Paris: La Toison d'Or

Friederich, R., 1849–50, "Voorloopig verslag van het eiland Bali," *VBG* 22, p. 11; 23, p. 13

Furst, P. T., 1968, "The Olmec Were-Jaguar Motif in the Light of Ethnographic Reality," in E. P. Benson (ed.), *Dumbarton Oaks Conference on the Olmec, October 28th and 29th, 1967.* Washington D.C.: Dumbarton Oaks Research Library and Collections, pp. 143–78

G., 1889, "De weleng," *TBB* 2, pp. 186–92

(*Gedenkboek Rotterdam*), 1938, *Gedenkboek N.V. Internationale Crediet- en Handels-Vereeniging "Rotterdam."* Rotterdam (no publ.)

Geertz, C., 1980, *Negara. The Theatre State in Nineteenth-Century Bali.* Princeton: Princeton University Press

Geise, N. J. C., 1952, *Badujs en Moslims.* Leiden: de Jong

(*Generale Missiven*), 1960–88, *Generale Missiven van Gouverneurs-Generaal en Raden aan Heren XVII der Verenigde Oostindische Compagnie* (edited by W. P. Coolhaas et al. RGP, grote serie. 's-Gravenhage: Nijhoff (9 vols.)

Gericke, J. F. C., and T. Roorda, 1901, *Javaansch-Nederlandsch handwoordenboek.* Amsterdam: Müller/Brill (2 vols.)

Gevers Deynoot, Jhr. W. T., 1864, *Herinneringen eener reis naar Nederlandsch-Indië in 1862.* 's-Gravenhage: Nijhoff

Gibb, H. A. R. (ed.), 1929, *Ibn Battuta: Travels in Asia and Africa 1325–1354.* London: Routledge

Gimlette, J. D., 1923, *Malay Poisons and Charm Cures.* London: Churchill (1st ed. 1915)

Gomes, E. H., 1992, "Danjai and the Were-Tiger's Sister," in *The Sea Dyaks and Other Races of Sarawak.* Kuala Lumpur: Dewan Bahasa dan Pustaka, pp. 221–31

Gonda, J. (ed.), 1947, *Letterkunde van de Indische Archipel.* Amsterdam: Elsevier

Goudsblom, J., 1992, *Vuur en beschaving.* Amsterdam: Meulenhoff

Graaf, H. J. de, 1954, *De regering van Panembahan Sénapati Ingalaga* (Verhandelingen KITLV 13). 's-Gravenhage: Nijhoff

Graaf, H. J. de (ed.), 1956, *De vijf gezantschapsreizen van Rijklof van Goens naar het hof van Mataram 1648–1654* (Werken uitgegeven door de Linschoten-Vereeniging, 59). 's-Gravenhage: Nijhoff

Graaf, H. J. de, 1958, *De regering van Sultan Agung, Vorst van Mataram 1613–1645 en die van zijn voorganger Panembahan Séda-ing-Krapjak 1601–1613* (Verhandelingen KITLV, 23). 's-Gravenhage: Nijhoff

Graafland, A. F. P., 1889, *Schetsen uit Indragirie.* Batavia: Kolff

Gray, A., and H.C. P. Bell (eds.), 1887, *The Voyage of François Pyrard of Laval to the*

East Indies, the Maldives, the Moluccas and Brazil; Volume I (Works Hakluyt Society, 76). London: Hakluyt Society

Greenough, P., 1991, *"Naturae Ferae:* Historical Notes on the Management of Wild Animals in Colonial and Post-colonial South Asia," paper presented at the Conference on Common Property, Collective Action and Ecology, Bangalore, India

Greiner, C. G. C. F., 1875, *Over land en zee. Herinneringen uit mijn verblijf in Indië.* Leiden: Noothoven van Goor

Groeneveldt, W. P., 1876, "Notes on the Malay Archipelago and Malacca, Compiled from Chinese sources," *VBG* 39, pp. 1–144

Groneman, J., 1874, *Bladen uit het dagboek van een Indisch geneesheer.* Groningen: Wolters

Groneman, J., 1891, *Uit en over Midden-Java. Onuitgegeven en uitgegeven brieven over opiumpacht, Chineezenwoeker, en andere Javaansche belangen.* Zutpen: Thieme

Groneman, J., 1895, *De Garebeg's te Ngajogyåkartå.* 's-Gravenhage: Nijhoff (for KITLV)

Groneman, J., 1900, *Reisgids voor Jogjakarta en omstreken.* Jogjakarta: Van der Hucht & Co.

Groneman, J., 1902, *Op het Jang-gebergte in Oost-Java.* Zutphen: Thieme

Groot, J. J. M. de, 1898, "De weertijger in onze koloniën en op het Oostaziatische vasteland," *BKI* 49, pp. 549–85

Grove, R. H., 1995, *Green Imperialism. Colonial Expansion, Tropical Island Edens and the Origins of Environmentalism, 1600–1860.* Cambridge: Cambridge University Press

Grove, R. H., Vinita Damodaran, and Satpal Sangwan (eds.), 1998, *Nature and the Orient. The Environmental History of South and Southeast Asia.* Delhi, etc.: Oxford University Press

Haan, F. de, 1910–12, *Priangan: De Preanger-Regentschappen onder het Nederlandsche Bestuur tot 1811.* Batavia: Kolff (4 vols.)

Hageman Jcz., J., 1853, "Schetsen van Malang en omstreken," *TBG* 1, 44–76

Hagen, B., 1890, "Die Pflanzen- und Thierwelt von Deli auf der Ostküste Sumatra's; naturwissenschaftliche Skizzen und Beiträge," *TKNAG* 2nd series, 7, pp. 1–280

Hagen, B., 1908, *Die Orang Kubu auf Sumatra.* Frankfurt am Main: Baer

Hagenbeck, C. (c. 1910), *Van dieren en menschen.* Amsterdam: Scheltens & Giltay (translation of German original)

Hagenbeck, J., (c. 1917), *Tussen olifanten en krokodillen; Jachtavonturen op Ceylon, het tropische paradijs.* Amsterdam: Scheltens & Giltay (translation of German original)

Hagenbeck, J., (c. 1924), *Au pays du tigre royal; voyages et aventures dans l'Hindoustan, a Java, a Sumatra et aux Iles Andaman.* Genève: Jeheber (translation of German original)

Hamerster, M., *Bijdrage tot de kennis van de Afdeeling Asahan.* Amsterdam: Oostkust van Sumatra-Instituut (Mededeeling 13).

Hames, R. B., 1979, "A Comparison of the Efficiency of the Shotgun and the Bow in Neotropical Forest Hunting," *Human Ecology* 7, pp. 219–52

Hamilton, A., 1727, *A New Account of the East Indies (. . .) 1688 to 1723*. Edinburgh: Mosman (2 vols.)

Hammerstrom, D. L., 1992, *Big Top Boss. John Ringling North and the Circus*. Urbana: University of Illinois Press

Hardeland, A., 1859, *Dajacksch-Deutches Wörterbuch*. Amsterdam: Muller

Harrisson, T., 1984, "The Prehistory of Borneo," in P. van de Velde (ed.), *Prehistoric Indonesia. A Reader* (Verhandelingen KITLV, 104). Dordrecht: Foris

Hartwig, G., 1860, *Die Tropenwelt im Thier- und Pflanzenleben*. Wiesbaden: Kreidel und Niedner

Hasanudin, L., 1988, "Tracking the Javan Tiger," *Voice of Nature* 58, pp. 51–55

Hasselt, A. L. van, 1882, *Volksbeschrijving van Midden-Sumatra* (vol. 3 of P. J. Veth (ed.), *Midden-Sumatra. Reizen en Onderzoekingen der Sumatra-Expeditie 1877–1879*). Leiden: Brill

Hasskarl, J. K., 1842, "Bijdrage tot de kennis van Zuid-Bantam," *TNI* 4/2, pp. 221–56

Hazeu, G. A. J., 1899, "Eenige mensch-dierverhalen uit Java," *BKI* 50, pp. 688–94

Hazeu, G. A. J., 1903, "Kleine bijdragen tot de ethnografie en de folklore van Java," *TBG* 46, pp. 289–309

Hazewinkel, J. C., (1964), *De tijger in het volksgeloof*. Den Haag: Tong-Tong

Heering, P., 1886, *Indische schetsen*. Leiden: Brill

Heijdt, J. W., 1744, *Allerneuester Geographisch- und Topographischer Schau-Platz von Africa und Ost-Indien*. Willhermsdorff: Tetschner

Helderman, W. D., 1891, "De tijger en het bijgeloof der Bataks," *TBG* 34, pp. 170–75

Helfrich, O. L., 1889, "Bijdrage tot de geographische, geologische en ethnographische kennis der Afdeeling Kroë," *BKI* 38, pp. 517–632

Hemmer, H., 1987, "The Phylogeny of the Tiger (*Panthera tigris*)," in R. L. Tilson and U. S. Seal (eds.), *Tigers of the World. The Biology, Biopolitics, Management, and Conservation of an Endangered Species*. Park Ridge, New Jersey: Noyes Publications, pp. 28–35

Herport, A., 1669, *Eine kurtze Ost-Indianische Reisz-Beschreibung*. Bern: Sonnleitner

Hervey, D. F. A., 1879, "A Trip to Gunong Blumut," *JSBRAS* 3, pp. 85–115

Hesse, E., 1690, *Ost-Indische Reise-Beschreibung oder Diarium (. . .)*. Leipzig: Günther (2nd ed.)

Heyne, B., 1814, *Tracts, Historical and Statistical, on India (. . .)*. London: Baldwin

Heynsius-Viruly, A., and Jhr. F. C. van Heurn, 1935, "Overzicht van de uit Nederlandsch-Indië ontvangen gegevens (. . .), met biologische aanteekeningen omtrent de betreffende diersoorten," *Mededeelingen Nederlandsche Commissie voor Internationale Natuurbescherming* 10, supplement, pp. 25–77

Hidding, K. A. H., 1932, "Het erfdeel der vaderen," *Djawa* 12, pp.71–86

Hidding, K. A. H., 1935, *Gebruiken en godsdiensten der Soendanezen*. Batavia: Kolff

Hien, H. A. van (1933–34), *De Javaansche geestenwereld*. Batavia: Kolff (2 vols.) (6th ed.; 1st ed. 1894)

Hinde, G., 1992, *Leopards*. London: Harper Collins

Hodges-Hill, E., 1992, *Man-Eater. Tales of Lion and Tiger Encounters*. Heathfield: Cockbird Press

Hoëvell, W. R. van, 1840, "Spelen en volksvermaken der Javanen, I. Het tijger-gevecht," *TNI* 3/1, pp. 298–312

Hommel, P. W. F. M., 1987, *Landscape-Ecology of Ujung Kulon (West Java, Indonesia)*. (Ph.D. diss., Wageningen; privately printed)

Hoogerwerf, A., 1939, "Uit het leven van den gevreesden 'gestreepte,'" *De Tropische Natuur* 28, pp. 3–12

Hoogerwerf, A., 1970, *Udjung Kulon. The Land of the Last Javan Rhinoceros*. Leiden: Brill

Hoogeveen, W. F., 1858, "Het distrikt Djampang-tengah (regentschap Tjiandjoer, Preanger-Regentschappen)," *TBG* 7, pp. 493–525

Hornaday, W. T., 1993, *The Experiences of a Hunter and Naturalist in the Malay Peninsula and Borneo*. New York: Scribner's (1st ed. 1885)

Horsfield, T., 1825, "Description of the Rimau-dahan of the Inhabitants of Sumatra (. . .)," *Zoological Journal* 5, pp. 542–54

Houben, V. J. H., 1994, *Kraton and Kumpeni. Surakarta and Yogyakarta 1830–1870* (Verhandelingen KITLV 164). Leiden: KITLV Press

Hubback, T. R., 1905, *Elephant & Seladang Hunting in the Federated Malay States*. London: Rowland Ward

Huijbers, H. J., 1931, "De Embaloeh-Dajak," *Koloniaal Missie-Tijdschrift* 14, pp. 174–81, 204–9, 237–43

(Huijser) Een Pionier (P. C. Huijser), 1885, *De Pioniers van Indië*. 's-Gravenhage: Nijhoff

Hutterer, K. L., and A. T. Rambo, 1985, "Introduction," in K. L. Hutterer, A. T. Rambo, and G. Lovelace (eds.), *Cultural Values and Human Ecology in Southeast Asia* (Michigan papers on South and Southeast Asia 27). Ann Arbor: Center for South and Southeast Asian Studies, University of Michigan, pp. 1–23

IJzerman, J. W. (ed.), 1926, *De reis om de wereld door Olivier van Noort 1598–1601* (Werken Linschoten Vereeniging 27). 's-Gravenhage: Nijhoff (2 vols.)

Indisch Staatsblad (officially *Staatsblad van Nederlandsch-Indië*) and its *Bijblad*, various years

Innes, E., 1885, *The Chersonese with the Gilding Off*. London: Bentley (2 vols.)

Jacobs, J., 1883, *Eenigen tijd onder de Baliërs. Eene reisbeschrijving met aanteekeningen betreffende hygiène, land- en volkenkunde van de eilanden Bali en Lombok*. Batavia: Kolff

Jacobs, J., 1894, *Het familie- en kampongleven op Groot-Atjeh. Eene bijdrage tot de ethnographie van Noord-Sumatra*. Leiden: Brill. (2 vols.)

Jacobs. J., and J. J. Meijer, 1891, *De Badoej's*. 's-Gravenhage: Nijhoff (for KITLV)

Jagor, F., 1866, *Singapore-Malacca-Java. Reiseskizzen*. Berlin: Springer

Jagt, M. B. van der, 1955, *Memoires van—Oud-Gouverneur van Soerakarta*. Den Haag: Leopold

Janssen, J. H., 1835, "Uittreksel uit aanteekeningen gehouden op een reize in Oost-Indië," *De Oosterling* 1, pp. 263–71

Jasper, J. E. (1928), *Tengger en de Tenggereezen*. Weltevreden: Kolff (n.d.)

Jonge, J. K. J. de (and M. L. van Deventer), 1862–95, *De opkomst van het Neder-*

landsch gezag in Oost-Indië. Verzameling van onuitgegeven stukken uit het oud-koloniaal archief (1595–1814). 's-Gravenhage: Nijhoff (17 vols.)

Joost, W. (ed.), 1983, *Die wundersamen Reisen des Caspar Schmalkalden nach West-und Ostindien 1642–1652.* Weinheim: Acta Humaniora

Josselin de Jong, P. E. de, 1980, *Minangkabau and Negri Sembilan. Socio-Political Structure in Indonesia.* 's-Gravenhage: Nijhoff (1st ed. 1951)

Jukes, J. B., 1847, *Narrative of the Surveying Voyage of H.M.S. Fly (. . .) during the Years 1842–1846; together with an Excursion into the Interior of the Eastern Part of Java.* London: Boone

Junghuhn, F., 1845, "Schetsen eener reis over Java in 1844; tiende schets," *TNI* 7/2, pp. 205–22

Junghuhn, F., 1847, *Die Battaländer auf Sumatra.* Berlin: Reimer (2 vols.)

Junghuhn, F. W., 1853–54, *Java, zijne gedaante, zijn plantentooi en inwendige bouw.* 's-Gravenhage: Mieling (3 vols.)

JvNIVN, 1912–38, *(Jaar)verslag Nederlandsch-Indische Vereeniging tot Natuurbescherming.* 11 issues

Kal, H. Th., 1910, "Het schiereiland Djoengkoelon," *TBB* 39, pp. 136–40

Karanth, K. U., 1987, "Tigers in India; A Critical Review of Field Censuses," in R. L. Tilson and U. S. Seal (eds.), *Tigers of the World. The Biology, Biopolitics, Management, and Conservation of an Endangered Species.* Park Ridge, New Jersey: Noyes Publications, pp. 118–32

Karanth, K. U., and B. M. Stith, 1999, "Prey Depletion as a Critical Determinant of Tiger Population Viability," in J. Seidensticker et al. (eds.), *Riding the Tiger. Tiger Conservation in Human-dominated Landscapes.* Cambridge: Cambridge University Press, pp. 100–113

Kathirithamby-Wells, J. (ed.), 1986, *Thomas Barnes' Expedition to Kerinci in 1818* (Occasional Paper, 7). Canterbury: University of Kent at Canterbury; Centre of South-East Asian Studies

Kats, J., 1923, *Het Javaansche Toneel. I. Wajang Poerwa.* Weltevreden: Volkslectuur

Keereweer, H. H., 1940, "De Koeboes in de Onderafdeeling Moesi Ilir en Koeboestreken," *BKI* 99, pp. 357–96

Keppel, H., 1853, *A Visit to the Indian Archipelago in H.M. Ship Maeander.* London: Bentley (2 vols.)

Kerckhoff, Ch. E. P. van, 1890, "Eenige opmerkingen betreffende de zoogenaamde 'orang loeboe' op Sumatra's Westkust," *TNAG* 2nd series, 7/2, pp. 576–77

Kerkhoven, E. J., 1879, "Het vergiftigen van verscheurende dieren door middel van wali kambing," *Tijdschrift Nijverheid & Landbouw Nederlandsch Indië* 23, pp. 503–17

Kern, R. A., 1941, "Met den Gouverneur-Generaal op reis in 1822," *BKI* 100, pp. 283–99

Kessel, O. von, 1856, "Reis in de nog onafhankelijke Batak-landen van Klein-Toba, op Sumatra, in 1844," *BKI* 4, pp. 55–97

Keuning, J. (ed.), 1940, *De tweede schipvaart der Nederlanders naar Oost-Indië onder*

Jacob Cornelisz. van Neck en Wijbrant Warwijck 1598–1600. Vol. 2 (Werken Linschoten Vereeniging 44). 's-Gravenhage: Nijhoff

Khan, M. A. R., 1987, "The Problem Tiger of Bangladesh," in R. L. Tilson and U. S. Seal (eds.), *Tigers of the World. The Biology, Biopolitics, Management, and Conservation of an Endangered Species.* Park Ridge, New Jersey: Noyes Publications, pp. 92–96

Khan bin Momin Khan, M., 1987, "Tigers in Malaysia: Prospects for the Future," in R. L. Tilson and U. S. Seal (eds.), *Tigers of the World. The Biology, Biopolitics, Management, and Conservation of an Endangered Species.* Park Ridge, New Jersey: Noyes Publications, pp. 75–84

King, V. T., 1985, *The Maloh of West Kalimantan. An Ethnographic Study of Social Inequality and Social Change among an Indonesian Borneo People* (Verhandelingen KITLV 108). Dordrecht: Foris

Kipling, R., 1966, *The Jungle Books.* New York: Airmont (1st ed. published 1894–95)

Kitchener, A. C., 1999, "Tiger Distribution, Phenotypic Variations and Conservation Issues," in J. Seidensticker et al. (eds.), *Riding the Tiger. Tiger Conservation in Human-dominated Landscapes.* Cambridge: Cambridge University Press, pp. 19–39

Kitchener, H. J., 1961, "The Importance of Protecting the Malayan Tiger," in J. Wyatt-Smith and P. R. Wycherley (eds.), *Nature Conservation in Western Malaysia, 1961 (Malayan Nature Journal,* Special Issue). Kuala Lumpur: The Malayan Nature Society, pp. 202–6

Klokke, M. J., 1993, *Tantri Reliefs on Ancient Javanese Candi* (Verhandelingen KITLV 153). Leiden: KITLV Press

Klös, H-G., 1969, *Von der Menagerie zum Tierparadies; 125 Jahre Zoo Berlin.* Berlin: Haude & Spener

Knebel, J., 1899, "De weertijger op Midden-Java, den Javaan naverteld," *TBG* 41, pp. 568–87

Koenigswald, G. H. R. von, 1935, "Die fossilen Säugetierfaunen Javas," *Proceedings Koninklijke Nederlandse Akademie van Wetenschappen* 38, pp. 188–98

Koloniaal Verslag, 1849–1930, Batavia (annual)

Koning, J. (ed.), 1919, *De Kloetramp van 20 mei 1919.* Soerabaia: Soerabaiasch Handelsblad en Drukkerijen

Koningsberger, J. C., 1915, *Java zoölogisch en biologisch.* Buitenzorg: Departement van Landbouw, Nijverheid en Handel

Kreemer, J., 1912, "De Loeboes in Mandailing," *BKI* 66, pp. 303–35

Kroesen, J. A., 1899, "Nota omtrent de Bataklanden (speciaal Simeloengoen)," *TBG* 41, pp. 253–85

Krom, N. J., and F. D. K. Bosch (eds.), 1915–23, *Inventaris der Hindoe-oudheden* (Rapporten van de Oudheidkundige Dienst). Batavia: Albrecht/Nijhoff (3 vols.)

Kruyt, A. C., 1899, "De weerwolf bij de Toradja's van Midden-Celebes," *TBG* 41, pp. 548–67

Kruyt, A. C., 1906, *Het animisme in den Indische archipel.* 's-Gravenhage: Nijhoff (for KITLV)

Kühr, E. L. M., 1897, "Schetsen uit Borneo's Westerafdeeling," *BKI* 47, pp. 57–82

Kumar, A., 1980, "Javanese Court Society and Politics in the Late Eighteenth Century: The Record of a Lady Soldier," *Indonesia* 29, pp. 1–46, and 30, pp. 67–111

Kussendrager, R. J. L., 1843, *Verzameling van oudheden en derzelver fabelachtige verhalen in de Residentie Passaroeang met eene geographische beschrijving dier Residentie.* Rotterdam: Dupain

Kussendrager, R. J. L., 1861, *Natuur- en aardrijkskundige beschrijving van het eiland Java.* Amsterdam: Weyting & Brave (1st ed. 1841)

L., C., 1913, "In welk wereldgedeelte vindt men thans nog de meeste gevaarlijke roofdieren?" *TBB* 45, pp. 141–43.

Lacombe of Quércy, J. de, 1937, *A Compendium of the East Being an Account of Voyages to the Grand Indies* (ed. A. Gibson). London: The Golden Cockerel Press (original manuscript dated 1681)

Leclercq, J., 1898, *Un séjour dans l'île de Java. Le pays—les habitants, le système colonial.* Paris: Plon

Leendertz, C. J., 1890, *Van Atjeh's stranden tot de koraalrotsen van Nieuw-Guinea. Schetsen uit Insulinde.* Arnhem: van der Zande

Lenselink, J., 1966, *Vuurwapens van 1840 tot heden.* Bussum: van Dishoeck

Leschenault (de la Tour), 1811, "Notice sur un Lac d'acide sulfurique (. . .) dans la province de Bagnia-Vangi (. . .)," *Annales du Muséum d'Histoire Naturelle* 18, pp. 425–46

Leupe, P. A., 1859, "Stukken betreffende het beleg en de verovering van Malakka op de Portugezen in 1640–1641 (. . .)," *Berigten van het Historisch Genootschap te Utrecht* 2nd series, 2/1, pp. 1–272

Levack, B. P., 1995, *The Witch-Hunt in Early Modern Europe.* Harlow: Longman (1st ed. 1987)

Lindskog, B., 1954, *African Leopard Men* (Studia Ethnographica Upsaliensia, 7). Uppsala: Almqvist & Wiksells

Locke, A., 1993, *The Tigers of Trengganu.* Kuala Lumpur: The Malaysian Branch of the Royal Asiatic Society (Monograph No. 23). (1st. ed. 1954, London: Museum Press)

Loeb, E. M., 1935, *Sumatra, Its History and People.* Vienna: Institut für Völkerkunde

Lombard, D., 1967, *Le Sultanat d'Atjéh au temps d'Iskandar Muda 1607–1636.* Paris: EFEO

Lombard, D., 1974, "La vision de la forêt à Java (Indonésie)," *Etudes rurales,* 53–56, pp. 473–85

Long, R., 1985, "People and Nature in Javanese Shadow Plays," in K. L. Hutterer, A. T. Rambo, and G. Lovelace (eds.), *Cultural Values and Human Ecology in Southeast Asia* (Michigan Papers on South and Southeast Asia 27). Ann Arbor: Center for South and Southeast Asian Studies, University of Michigan, pp. 195–204

Lubis, Mochtar, 1975, *Harimau! Harimau!* Jakarta: Pustaka Jaya (English translation, 1991, *Tiger!* Singapore: Select Books)

Ludeking, E. W. A., 1868, "Schets van de Residentie Amboina," *BKI* 15, pp. 1–272

MacKenzie, J. M., 1988, *The Empire of Nature. Hunting, Conservation and British Imperialism.* Manchester: Manchester University Press

Marks, S., 1976, *Large Mammals and a Brave People*. Seattle: University of Washington Press

Marschall, W., 1995, "Possession, *Barongan,* and Social Relief in a Central Javanese Village," *Indonesia Circle* 66, pp. 100–108

Marsden, W., 1811, *The History of Sumatra*. Kuala Lumpur: Oxford University Press. (Reprint of the third ed. [1811] introduced by John Bastin)

Martens, E. von, 1864, "Aus dem Tagebuch meiner ostasiatischen Reise," *Der Zoologische Garten* 5, pp. 382–85, 418–20

Martin, R., 1905, *Die Inlandstämme der Malayischen Halbinsel; Wissenschaftliche Ergebnisse einer Reise durch die Vereinigten Malayischen Staaten*. Jena: Fischer

Martin-Schiller, B.,1984, "Islam and the 'Earth Tiger': Religion in a Pesisir Village," in R. Hatley et al., *Other Javas away from the Kraton*. Clayton: Monash University, pp. 49–60

Massink, H., 1888, *Bijdrage tot de kennis van het vroeger en tegenwoordig bestuur op het eiland Madoera*. Arnhem: Van der Zande (Ph.D. diss., University of Leiden)

Maxwell, G., 1960, *In Malay Forests*. Singapore: Eastern Universities Press (1st ed. 1907)

Maxwell, W. E., 1881, "The Folklore of the Malays," *JSBRAS* 7/8, pp. 11–30

Mayer, C., 1924, *Jungle Beasts I Have Captured*. London: Heinemann

Mazák, V., 1983, *Der Tiger. Panthera tigris* (Die Neue Brehm-Bücherei 356). Wittenberg Lutherstadt: Ziemsen Verlag (1st ed. 1965)

Mazák, V., C. P. Groves, and P. J. H. van Bree, 1978, "On a Skin and Skull of the Bali Tiger, and a List of Preserved Specimens of *Panthera tigris balica* (Schwarz, 1912)," *Zeitschrift für Säugetierkunde* 43/2, pp. 108–13

McDougal, C., 1987, "The Man-eating Tiger in Geographical and Historical Perspective," in R. L. Tilson and U. S. Seal (eds.), *Tigers of the World. The Biology, Biopolitics, Management, and Conservation of an Endangered Species*. Park Ridge, New Jersey: Noyes Publications, pp. 435–48

McKinnon, K., 1985, *Indonesië; natuur en natuurbehoud*. Weert: Uitgeverij M & P (English original, 1984)

McNair, F., 1878, *Perak and the Malays: "Sarong" and "Kris."* London: Tinsley

Mechelen, Ch. te, 1879, "Eenige dagen het desaleven meegeleefd," *TBG* 25, pp. 165–95, 256–318

Medway, Lord, 1969, *The Wild Mammals of Malaya and Offshore Islands including Singapore*. Kuala Lumpur: Oxford University Press

Meister, H., 1875, *Bilder aus Java*. Zürich: Schmidt

Melisch, R., 1992, *Checklist of the Land Mammals of Java*. Bogor: PHPA/AWB-Indonesia

Merklein, J. J., 1930, *Reise nach Java, Vorder- und Hinter-Indien, China und Japan, 1644–1653* (Reisebeschreibungen von deutschen Beamten, 3). Den Haag: (1st ed. 1663)

Mills, J. V. G. (ed.), 1970, *Ma Huan: Ying-yai sheng-lan; "The Overall Survey of the Ocean's Shores" (1433)* (for the Hakluyt Society; Extra Series, 42). Cambridge: Cambridge University Press

Mishra, H. R., C. Wemmer, and J. L. D. Smith, 1987, "Tigers in Nepal: Management Conflicts with Human Interests," in R. L. Tilson and U. S. Seal (eds.), *Tigers of the World. The Biology, Biopolitics, Management, and Conservation of an Endangered Species.* Park Ridge, New Jersey: Noyes Publications, pp. 449–63

Mjöberg, E., 1928, *Forest Life and Adventures in the Malay Archipelago.* Singapore, etc.: Oxford University Press

Moertono, Soemarsaid, 1968, *State and Statecraft in Old Java: A Study of the Later Mataram Period, 16th to 19th Century* (Monograph Series, 8). Ithaca, New York: Modern Indonesia Project, Southeast Asia Program, Department of Asian Studies, Cornell University

Moestapa, H., 1946, *Over de gewoonten en gebruiken der Soendaneezen* (translated and edited by R.A. Kern) (Verhandelingen KITLV 5). 's-Gravenhage: Nijhoff

Mohnike, O., 1874, *Banka und Palembang nebst Mittheilungen über Sumatra im Allgemeinen.* Münster: Aschendorffschen Buchhandlung

Mohnike, O., 1883, *Blicke auf das Pflanzen- und Thierleben in den Niederländischen Malaienländern.* Münster: Aschendorff'schen Buchhandlung

Morin, H. (c. 1909), *Unter de Tropensonne. Streifzüge auf Java, Sumatra und Ceylon.* München: Isaria Verlag

Moszkowski, M., 1909, *Auf neuen Wegen durch Sumatra; Forschungsreisen in Ost- und Zentral-Sumatra (1907).* Berlin: Reimer

Mountfort, G., 1969, *The Vanishing Jungle. The Story of the World Wildlife Fund Expedition to Pakistan.* London: Collins

Müller, S., 1839, "Over de zoogdieren van den Indischen archipel," in C. J. Temminck (ed.), *Verhandelingen over de natuurlijke geschiedenis der Nederlandsche overzeesche bezittingen (. . .).* Leiden: no publ., vol. 1

Müller, S., 1855, *Reizen en onderzoekingen in Sumatra, gedaan op last der Nederlandsche Indische regering, tusschen de jaren 1833 en 1838, door Dr. S. Müller en Dr. L. Horner.* 's-Gravenhage: Fuhri (for KITLV)

Multatuli (Eduard Douwes Dekker), 1943, *Max Havelaar of de koffiveilingen der Nederlandsche Handelmaatschappij.* Amsterdam: Wereldbibliotheek (1st ed. 1860)

Munnecke, W. (1931), *Met Hagenbeck in het oerwoud.* Amsterdam: Scheltens & Giltay (translation of the German original, c. 1929)

N., N., 1866, "Over de uitroeiing der tijgers op Java," *TNI* new series, 4/1, pp. 492–94

Nagel, G. H., 1828, *Schetsen uit mijne Javaansche portefeuille.* Amsterdam: Sulpke

Nahuys van Burgst, H. G., 1852, *Herinneringen uit het openbare en bijzondere leven (1799–1849).* (Utrecht): privately printed

Natahamipradja, 1931, "Memoires van Pangeran Harja—, regent van Kendal, tevens dienende tot verhaal voor zijn nakomelingen," *Djåwå* 11, pp. 96–99

Neumann, J. B., 1886–87, "Het Pane- en Bila-stroomgebied op het eiland Sumatra (Studiën over Batahs en Batahsche landen)," *TKNAG* 2nd series, 3/2, pp. 1–99, 215–314, 459–543

Newbold, T. J., 1839, *Political and Statistical Account of the British Settlements in the Straits of Malacca (. . .) with a History of the Malayan States on the Peninsula of Malacca.* London: Murray (2 vols.)

Niemann, G. K., 1866, "Mededeelingen omtrent de letterkunde der Bataks," *BKI* 13, pp. 245–303

Nieuwendijk, J. G. (1970), *Zoo was Artis—zo is Artis*. Amsterdam: De Bussy

Nieuwenhuis, A. W., 1904–7, *Quer durch Borneo. Ergebnisse seiner Reisen in den Jahren 1894, 1896–97 und 1898–1900*. Leiden: Brill (2 vols.)

Nieuwenhuis, A. W., 1911, *Animisme, Spiritisme en Feticisme onder de volken van den Nederlandsch-Indischen Archipel*. Baarn: Hollandia-Drukkerij

Nieuwenhuys, R., 1984, "De rampokan," *Orion* 1/1, pp. 9–16

Nieuwenkamp, W. O. J., 1922, *Zwerftochten op Bali*. Amsterdam: Elsevier (1st ed. 1910)

Obdeyn, V., 1929, "De langkah lama der orang Mamak van Indragiri," *TBG* 69, pp. 353–425

Olivier Jz., J., 1827–30, *Land- en zeetogten in Nederland's Indië (. . .) gedaan in de jaren 1817 tot 1826*. Amsterdam: Sulpke (3 vols.)

Olivier Jz., J., 1836, *Tafereelen en merkwaardigheden uit Oost-Indië*. Amsterdam: Beijerinck (2 vols.)

Olthof, W. L. (ed.), 1941, *Babad Tanah Djawi in proza; Javaansche geschiedenis lopende tot het jaar 1647 der Javaansche jaartelling*. 's-Gravenhage: Nijhoff

("Oorspronk"), 1855, "Oorspronk van de eerste heerschappye ofte de beginselen van de Javaanse regeringen op het eijland Groot Java," *Biäng Lala* 4/1, pp. 262–81

("Opgave"), 1863, "Opgave van alle diensten, die van rijkswege verrigt werden in het regentschap Bangil, van 1825 tot 1843," *BKI* 10, pp. 216–20

Ophuijsen, C. A. van, 1884, "De Loeboes," *TBG* 29, pp. 88–100

Otten, C. F. (ed.), 1986, *A Lycanthropy Reader. Werewolves in Western Culture*. Syracuse, New York: Syracuse University Press

Otto, E., 1903, *Pflanzer- und Jägerleben auf Sumatra*. Berlin: Süsserott

Paardt, Th. van der, 1929, "Onbewoond Noord-West Bali," *TKNAG* 46, pp. 45–77

Pemberton, J., 1994, *On the Subject of "Java."* Ithaca: Cornell University Press

Penard, A. Ph., 1928, "Het pujai-geheim der Surinaamsche Caraiben," *BKI* 84, pp. 625–71

Peranio, R., 1959, "Animal Teeth and Oath-Taking among the Bisaya," *Sarawak Museum Journal* (new series) 9/13–14, pp. 6–13

Perry, R., 1964, *The World of the Tiger*. London: Cassell

Persoon, G. A., 1994, *Vluchten of veranderen; Processen van verandering en ontwikkeling bij tribale groepen in Indonesië*. (Ph.D. diss., University of Leiden)

Petrus Blumberger, J. Th., 1917, "In en om de kraton te Soerakarta," *Nederlandsch-Indië Oud en Nieuw* 2, pp. 39–46

Pfyffer zu Neueck, J. J. X., 1838, *Schetsen van het eiland Java en deszelfs onderscheidenen bewoners*. Amsterdam: van Kesteren (translation of German original, 1829)

Philippus, P., 1673, *Orientalische Raisebeschreibung*. Franckfurt: Schiele

Pieters, D., 1955, "Mislukte Tijger-Aanslagen," *Penggemar Alam* (sequel to *De Tropische Natuur*) 35, pp. 35–43

Pigeaud, Th., 1933, "De Serat Tjabolang en de Serat Tjentini; inhoudsopgaven, bewerkt door-," *VBG* 72/2, pp. 1–89

Pigeaud, Th., 1938, *Javaanse volksvertoningen; bijdrage tot de beschrijving van land en volk.* Batavia: Volkslectuur

Pigeaud, Th., 1940, "De noorder aloen-aloen te Jogjakarta," *Djåwå* 20, pp. 176–84

Pigeaud, T. G. T., 1960–63, *Java in the 14th Century. A Study in Cultural History* (KITLV Translation series, 4). The Hague: Nijhoff (5 vols.)

Pigeaud, T. G. T., 1967–70, *Literature of Java.* The Hague: Nijhoff (for KITLV) (3 vols.)

(*Plakaatboek*), 1885–1900, *Nederlandsch-Indisch Plakaatboek 1602–1811* (edited by J. A. van der Chijs). Batavia: Landsdrukkerij (16 vols.)

Plate, L. M. F., 1912, "Bijdrage tot de kennis van de lykanthropie bij de Sasaksche bevolking in Oost-Lombok," *TBG* 54, pp. 458–69

Pleyte, C. M., 1910, "Bantensch Folklore," *TBG* 52, pp. 131–52, 590–95

Poser, M., 1955, *Mit dem Tiger stirbt die Wildnis; 20 Jahre unter der Sonne Sumatras.* Radebeul: Neumann

Presgrave, E., 1822, "Account of a Journey from Manna to Pasummah Lebar and the Ascent of Gunung Dempo (. . .) in the year 1817," *Malayan Miscellanies* 2/2, pp. 1–93

(*Proclamations*), 1813–16, *Proclamations, Regulations, Advertisements, and Orders, Printed and Published in the Island of Java, by the British Government, and under Its Authority.* Batavia: Hubbard (3 vols.)

Puype, J. P., 1993, "Zeventiende-eeuwse termen met betrekking tot wapens, toebehoren en aanverwante onderwerpen," in J. P. Puype and M. van der Hoeven (eds.), *Het arsenaal van de wereld. De Nederlandse wapenhandel in de Gouden Eeuw.* Amsterdam: De Bataafsche Leeuw, pp. 64–70

Radermacher, J. C. M., 1781, "Beschrijving van het eiland Sumatra, in zoo verre hetzelve tot nog toe bekend is," *VBG* 3, pp. 1–89

Raedt van Oldenbarnevelt, H. J. A., 1888, "Tochten in het stroomgebied der Beneden-Ketaun, en een vierdaagsch uitstapje in de Lebong," *TKNAG* 2nd series, 5, pp. 178–211, 417–40

Raffles, S. (ed.), 1830a, *Memoir of the Life and Public Services of Sir Thomas Stamford Raffles (. . .).* London: Murray

Raffles, T. S., 1821–23, "Descriptive Catalogue of a Zoological Collection in Sumatra," *The Transactions of the Linnean Society of London* 13, pp. 239–74, 277–340

Raffles, T. S., 1830b, *The History of Java.* London: Murray (2 vols.) (1st ed. 1817)

Rambo, A. T., 1978, "Bows, Blowpipes and Blunderbusses; Ecological Implications of Weapons Change among the Malaysian Negritos," *Malayan Nature Journal* 32, pp. 209–16

Rambo, A. T., 1985, *Primitive Polluters. Semang Impact on the Malaysian Tropical Rain Forest Ecosystem* (Anthropological Papers Museum of Anthropology, University of Michigan). Ann Arbor, Michigan

Rangarajan, M., 1997, "The Raj and the Natural World; The War against 'Dangerous Beasts' in Colonial India," paper presented at the Workshop on Animals in Asia, IIAS, Leiden

Rees, W. A. van, 1863–65, *Herinneringen uit de loopbaan van een Indisch officier.* 's-Gravenhage: Visser/van den Heuvell & van Santen (4 vols. in 2 parts)

Reichel-Dolmatoff, G., 1972, "The Feline Motif in Prehistoric San Agustín Sculpture," in E. P. Benson (ed.), *The Cult of the Feline. A Conference in Pre-Columbian Iconography, October 31st and November 1st, 1970.* Washington D.C.: Dumbarton Oaks Research Library and Collections, pp. 51–68

Reichel-Dolmatoff, G., 1975, *The Shaman and the Jaguar. A Study of Narcotic Drugs among the Indians of Colombia.* Philadelphia: Temple University Press

Reid, A., 1988, *Southeast Asia in the Age of Commerce, 1450–1680. Volume I: The Lands below the Winds.* New Haven: Yale University Press

("Reis"), 1859, "De reis over Java, in 1838, van den Gouverneur-Generaal van Nederlandsch Indië," *TNI* 21/1, pp. 442–92

("Reisje"), 1845, "Reisje van Solo naar Patjitan," *TNI* 7/2, pp. 119–36

Remmelink, W. G. J., 1994, *The Chinese War and the Collapse of the Javanese State, 1725–1743* (Verhandelingen KITLV 162). Leiden: KITLV Press

("Report"), 1979, "Report of Larger Cats on Bali Island (.) (March-April 1979)." Bandung: WWF/PPA/Van Tienhoven

Rhemrev, J. L., 1884, *Serat Gurma Lelana.* Leiden: Brill

Richardson, D., 1992, *Big Cats.* London: Whittet Books

Ricklefs, M. C., 1974, *Jogjakarta under Sultan Mangkubumi 1749–1792. A History of the Division of Java.* London: Oxford University Press

Ricklefs, M. C., 1993, *War, Culture and Economy in Java 1677–1726. Asian and European Imperialism in the Early Kartasura Period* (Southeast Asia Publications Series, 24). Sydney: Allen & Unwin/Asian Studies Association of Australia

Rigg, J., 1850a, "Tiger Fight at Solo," *Journal of the Indian Archipelago and Eastern Asia* 4, pp. 75–84

Rigg, J., 1850b, "Gunung Dangka or a Paradise on Earth; a Tale of Superstition," *Journal of the Indian Archipelago and Eastern Asia* 4, pp. 119–33

Rinkes, D. A., 1910, "De heiligen van Java I. De maqam van Sjech 'Abdoelmoehji,'" *TBG* 52, pp. 556–89

Ritter, W. L., 1872, Java. *Tooneelen uit het leven (. . .).* Leiden: Sijthoff (1st ed. 1855)

Ritvo, H., 1990, *The Animal Estate. The English and Other Creatures in the Victorian Age.* Harmondsworth: Penguin

Roorda van Eysinga, P. P., 1830–32, *Verschillende reizen en lotgevallen van S. Roorda van Eysinga (. . .).* Amsterdam: van der Heij (4 vols.)

Roorda van Eysinga, P. P., 1841–50, *Handboek der land- en volkenkunde, geschied-, taal-, aardrijks- en staatkunde van Nederlandsch Indië.* Amsterdam: Van Bakkenes (3 vols. in 5 parts)

Rosenberg, H. von, 1878, *Der Malayische Archipel. Land und Leute in Schilderungen, gesammelt während eines dreissig-jährigen Aufenthaltes in den Kolonien.* Leipzig: Weigel

Rothenbühler, F. J., 1882, "Dagregister of dagelijksche aanteekeningen van . . . de reis (van) P.G. van Overstraten, 20 Maart—13 April 1792," *TBG* 27, pp. 295–362

Rouffaer, G. P., 1899, "Matjan gadoengan," *BKI* 50, pp. 67–75

Rouffaer, G. P., 1917–18, "Charles te Mechelen; In memoriam," *Nederlandsch Indië Oud & Nieuw* 2, pp. 305–12

Rouffaer, G. P., 1921, "Was Malaka emporium vóór 1400 A.D., genaamd Mala-joer?," *BKI* 77, pp. 1–172, 359–604

Roy, J.-J. E., 1861, *Quinze ans de séjour a Java et dans les principales iles de l'archipel de la Sonde et des possessions Néerlandaises des Indes Orientales.* Tours: Maine

Rupprecht, Kronprinz von Bayern, 1923, *Reise-Erinnerungen aus Ostasien.* München: Kösel & Pustet

Rush, J. R., 1990, *Opium to Java. Revenue Farming and Chinese Enterprise in Colonial Indonesia, 1860–1910,* Ithaca: Cornell University Press

Ruzius, J. B., 1905, *'Heilig Indië.'* Bussum: Van Dishoeck (2 vols.)

Saar, J. J., 1930, *Reise nach Java, Banda, Ceylon und Persien, 1644–1660* (Reisebeschreibungen von deutschen Beamten, 6). Den Haag: Nijhoff (1st ed. 1662)

Said, E. W., 1979, *Orientalism.* New York: Vintage Books

Salmon, Th., 1729–33, *Hedendaegsche historie, of tegenwoordige staet van alle volkeren.* (translation from English original) Amsterdam: Tirion (5 vols.)

Sandbukt, Ø., 1982, "Kubu Conceptions of Reality," paper presented at the Symposium on Southeast Asian Folklore, Denmark

Sandick, R. A. van (1890), *In het Rijk van Vulcaan. De uitbarsting van Krakatau en hare gevolgen.* Zutphen: Thieme & Co.

Sandick, R. A. van, 1892, *Leed en lief uit Bantam.* Zutphen: Thieme & Co.

Sankhala, K., 1993, *Return of the Tiger.* New Delhi, etc.: Lustre Press

Santiapillai, C., and S. R. Widodo, 1987, "Tiger Numbers and Habitat Evaluation in Indonesia," in R. L. Tilson and U. S. Seal (eds.), *Tigers of the World. The Biology, Biopolitics, Management, and Conservation of an Endangered Species.* Park Ridge, New Jersey: Noyes Publications, pp. 85–91

Sanyal, P., 1987, "Managing the Man-eaters in the Sundarbans Tiger Reserve of India—A Case Study," in R. L. Tilson and U. S. Seal (eds.), *Tigers of the World. The Biology, Biopolitics, Management, and Conservation of an Endangered Species.* Park Ridge, New Jersey: Noyes Publications, pp. 427–34

Saunders, N. J., 1989, *People of the Jaguar. The Living Spirit of Ancient America.* London: Souvenir Press

Schama, S., 1996, *Landscape and Memory.* London: Fontana Press

Schärer, H., 1963, *Ngaju Religion. The Concept of God among a South Borneo People* (KITLV Translation Series, 6). The Hague: Nijhoff (original in German, 1946)

Schebesta, P., 1973 (1928a), *Among the Forest Dwarfs of Malaya.* Kuala Lumpur: Oxford University Press (1st ed. London: Hutchinson)

Schebesta, P., 1928b, *Orang-Utan; Bei den Urwaldmenschen Malayas und Sumatras.* Leipzig: Brockhaus

Schefold, R., 1988, "De wildernis als cultuur van gene zijde; tribale concepten van 'natuur' in Indonesië," *Antropologische Verkenningen* 7/4, pp. 5–22

Schenkel, R. (1970), *Operatie neushoorn. "Operasi badak"; op het spoor van een der zeldzaamste dieren ter wereld.* Zwolle: La Rivière & Voorhoeve

Schilling, T., 1952, *Tijgermensen van Anai. Jacht op grof wild.* Amsterdam: Meulenhoff

Schneider, G., 1905, *Ergebnisse zoologischer Forschungsreisen in Sumatra. Erster Teil.*

Säugetiere (Mammalia). Jena: Fischer (Abdruck aus den *Zoologischen Jahrbüchern, Abt. für Systematik, Geographie und Biologie der Tiere* 23/1)

Schneider, G., 1958, "Die Orang Mamma auf Sumatra," *Vierteljahrsschrift der Naturforschenden Gesellschaft in Zürich* 103/5, pp. 213–86

Schnitger, F. M., 1939, *Forgotten Kingdoms in Sumatra*. Leiden: Brill

Schoebel, C., 1882–83, "Le tigre à Singapore et à Java," *Bulletin de la Société Académique Indo-Chinoise de France* 2nd series, 2, p. 493

Schrieke, B., 1957, *Indonesian Sociological Studies*. The Hague: Van Hoeve (2 vols.)

Schwarz, E., 1912, "Notes on Malay Tigers, with Description of a new Form from Bali," *The Annals and Magazine of Natural History (London)* 8th series, 10, pp. 324–26

Schwarz, E., 1913, "Der Bali-Tiger," *Bericht der Senckenbergischen Naturforschenden Gesellschaft* 44/1, pp. 70–73

Schwarz, G. B., 1751, *Reise in Ost-Indien (. . .)* Heilbronn: Eckebrecht

Scidmore, E. R., 1899, *Java, the Garden of the East*. New York: Century

Scott, J., 1985, *Weapons of the Weak. Everyday Forms of Peasant Resistance*. New Haven: Yale University Press

Sears, L. J., 1996, *Shadows of Empire. Colonial Discourse and Javanese Tales*. Durham: Duke University Press

Seidensticker, J., 1987, "Bearing Witness: Observations on the Extinction of *Panthera tigris balica* and *Panthera tigris sondaica*," in R. L. Tilson and U. S. Seal (eds.), *Tigers of the World. The Biology, Biopolitics, Management, and Conservation of an Endangered Species*. Park Ridge, New Jersey: Noyes Publications, pp. 1–8

Seidensticker, J., S. Christie, and P. Jackson (eds.), 1999, *Riding the Tiger. Tiger Conservation in Human-dominated landscapes*. Cambridge: Cambridge University Press

Seidensticker, J., and Suyono, 1980, *The Javan Tiger and the Meru Betiri Reserve. A Plan for Management*. Gland, Switzerland: World Wildlife Fund

Sell, H. J., 1955, *Der schlimme Tod bei den Völkern Indonesiens*. 's-Gravenhage: Mouton

Sellato, B., 1983, "Le Mythe du Tigre au Centre de Borneo," *Asie du Sud-Est et Monde insulindien* 14/1–2, pp. 25–49

(*Serat Centhini*), 1991, *Serat Centhini (suluk tambangraras)* (ed. Kamajaya) Yogyakarta: Yayasan Centhini (12 vols.)

Shelford, R. W. C., 1916, *A Naturalist in Borneo*. London: Fisher Unwin. (Reprint Singapore: OUP, edited by E. B. Poulton)

Sibinga Mulder, J., 1944, "Hoe het einde der vasten in vroegere jaren te Kediri werd gevierd; de groote rampok," *Cultureel Indië* 6, pp. 20–25

("Sita"), 1997, "Sita: Life of a Wild Tigress," *National Geographic* 192/6, pp. 36–45

Skeat, W. W., 1900, *Malay Magic. Being an Introduction to the Folklore and Popular Religion of the Malay Peninsula*. London: Macmillan

Skeat, W. W., and C. O. Blagden, 1906, *Pagan Races of the Malay Peninsula*. London: Macmillan

Sliggers, B. C., and A. A. Wertheim (eds.), 1994, *Een vorstelijke dierentuin; De menagerie van Willem V.* (n.p.): Walburg Press

Snouck Hurgronje, C., 1893–94, *De Atjèhers*. Batavia: Landsdrukkerij/Brill (2 vols.)

Sody, H. J. V., 1933, "The Balinese Tiger. *Panthera tigris balica* (Schwarz)," *Journal of the Bombay Natural History Society* 36, pp. 233–35

Sody, H. J. V., 1949, "Notes on Some Primates, Carnivora and the Babirusa from the Indo-Malayan and Indo-Australian Region," *Treubia* 20/2, pp. 121–90

Sody, H. J. V., 1959, "Das Javanische Nashorn *Rhinoceros sondaicus* historisch und biologisch," *Zeitschrift für Säugetierkunde* 24, pp. 109–240 (translation of Dutch original, 1941)

Soemå-Sentikå, 1902, *De geschiedenis van het rijk Kedhiri opgetekend in het jaar 1873* (transl. by P. W. van den Broek). Leiden: Brill

Statistical Abstracts Relating to British India, various years

Stavorinus, J. S., 1797–98, *Reize..naar Samarang..gedaan in de jaren 1774 tot 1778*. Leyden: Honkoop (2 vols.)

Steck, F. G., 1862, "Topographische en geographische beschrijving der Lampongsche Distrikten," *BKI* 8, pp. 69–113, 123–26

Stiles, D., 1993, "Hunter-Gatherer Trade in Wild Forest Products in the Early Centuries A.D. with the Port of Broach, India," *Asian Perspectives, the Journal of Archaeology for Asia and the Pacific* 32/2, pp. 153–67

Stöhr, E., 1874, *Die Provinz Banjuwangi in Ost-Java mit der Vulkangruppe Idjen Raun. Reiseskizzen*. Frankfurt am Main: Winter

Stoler, A. L., 1990, "Making Empire Respectable: 'The Politics of Race and Sexual Morality in 20th-Century Colonial Cultures,'" in J. Breman (ed.), *Imperial Monkey Business. Racial Supremacy in Social Darwinist Theory and Colonial Practice*. Amsterdam: VU University Press (CASA Monographs 3), pp. 35–70

Stone, G. C., 1961, *A Glossary of the Construction, Decoration and Use of Arms and Armor in All Countries and in All Times, Together with Some Closely Related Subjects*. New York: Jack Brussel (1st ed. 1934)

Storey, W. K., 1991, "Big Cats and Imperialism: Lion and Tiger Hunting in Kenya and Northern India, 1898–1930," *Journal of World History* 2/2, pp. 135–74

Storm, P., 1995a, *The Evolutionary Significance of the Wajak Skulls* (Scripta Geologica 110). Leiden: Nationaal Natuurhistorisch Museum

Storm, P., 1995b, "Animals and Man in Prehistoric Java," *Indonesian Environmental History Newsletter* 5, pp. 7–9

Stuers, Jhr. L. H. W. M. de, 1865–68, *De Indische Archipel, tafereelen uit de natuur en het volksleven in Indië*. 's-Gravenhage: Mieling

Stutterheim, W. F., 1926, "Oost-Java en de hemelberg," *Djåwå* 6, pp. 333–49

("Summier") 1859, "Summier Ziekenrapport der Civiel Geneeskundige Dienst over 1857," *Geneeskundig Tijdschrift Nederlandsch Indië* 6, pp. 469–667

Sunquist, F., and M. Sunquist, 1988, *Tiger Moon*. Chicago: University of Chicago Press

Sunquist, M., K. U. Karanth, and F. Sunquist, 1999, "Ecology, Behaviour and Resilience of the Tiger and Its Conservation Needs," in J. Seidensticker et al. (eds.), *Riding the Tiger. Tiger Conservation in Human-Dominated Landscapes*. Cambridge: Cambridge University Press, pp. 5–18

Swettenham, F. A., 1896, *Malay Sketches*. London/New York: Lane/Macmillan

Taussig, M., 1987, *Shamanism, Colonialism, and the Wild Man. A Study in Terror and Healing*. Chicago: University of Chicago Press

Teijsmann, J. E., 1855, *Uittreksel uit het dagverhaal eener reis door Midden-Java*. Batavia: Lange & Co.

Teijsmann, J. E., 1856, "Uittreksel uit het dagverhaal eener reis door Oost-Java, Karimon Java en Bali Boleling," *NTNI* 11, pp. 111–206

Temminck, C. J., 1846–49, *Coup-d'oeil général sur les possessions Neerlandaises dans l'Inde Archipélagique*. Leiden: Arnz (3 vols.)

Temple, R. C. (ed.), 1914, *The Travels of Peter Mundy in Europe and Asia, 1608–1667. Vol. II, 1628–1634*. London: Works issued by the Hakluyt Society, 2nd series, 35

Temple, R. C. (ed.), 1970, *The Itinerary of Ludovico di Varthema of Bologna from 1502 to 1508*. Amsterdam: N. Israel (1st ed. 1928, London: Argonaut Press)

Thomas, K., 1984, *Man and the Natural World. Changing Attitudes in England 1500–1800*. Hammondsworth: Penguin

Thomassen à Thuessink van der Hoop, A. N. J., 1932, *Megalithische oudheden in Zuid-Sumatra*. Zutphen: Thieme (Ph.D. diss., University of Utrecht)

Thunberg, C. P., 1796, *Voyages de—au Japon, par le Cap de Bonne-Espérance, les îles de la Sonde, etc.*. Paris: Dandré, etc. (4 vols.)

Tideman, J., 1922, *Simeloengoen. Het land der Timoer-Bataks in zijn vroegere isolatie en zijn ontwikkeling tot een deel van het Cultuurgebied van de Oostkust van Sumatra*. Leiden: Becherer

("Tijgerjagt"), 1843, "Tijgerjagt," *TNI* 5/2, pp. 779–81

Tilson, R. L., and U. S. Seal (eds.), 1987, *Tigers of the World. The Biology, Biopolitics, Management, and Conservation of an Endangered Species*. Park Ridge, N.J.: Noyes Publications

Tilson, R. L., and U. S. Seal, 1987, "Preface," in R. L. Tilson and U. S. Seal (eds.), *Tigers of the World. The Biology, Biopolitics, Management, and Conservation of an Endangered Species*. Park Ridge, New Jersey: Noyes Publications, pp. vii-x

Tinbergen, D. C., and L. M. van Dis (eds.), 1964, *Van den vos Reinaerde*. Groningen: Wolters

Tirtokoesoemo, Soedjono, 1931, *De Garebegs in het Sultanaat Jogjakarta*. Jogjakarta: Buning

Toorn, J. L. van der, 1879, "Verscheidene verhalen omtrent het bijgeloof van de Maleiërs in het land Minangkabau," *TBG* 25, pp. 441–59

Toorn, J. L. van der, 1890, "Het animisme bij den Minangkabauer der Padangsche Bovenlanden," *BKI* 39, pp. 48–104

Tricht, B. van, 1929, "Levende antiquiteiten in West-Java; 1e gedeelte: de Badoejs," *Djawa* 9, pp. 43–96

Tuuk, H. N. van der, 1897–1912, *Kawi-Balineesch-Nederlandsch Woordenboek*. Batavia: Landsdrukkerij (4 vols.)

("Uitroeijing"), 1858, "Uitroeijing van Tijgers door middel van walikambing," *NTNI* 15, pp. 478–81

Unger, W. S. (ed.), 1948, *De oudste reizen van de Zeeuwen naar Oost-Indië, 1598–1604* (Werken Linschoten Vereeniging, 51). 's-Gravenhage: Nijhoff

Valentijn, F., 1724–26, *Oud en nieuw Oost-Indiën*. Dordrecht: Van Braam/Onder de linden (5 vols. in 8 parts)

Valk, A. C. van der, 1940, *Vangen en jagen in Sumatra's wildernis*. Amsterdam: Meulenhoff

Velder, C. (ed.), 1979, *Märchen aus Thailand*. Düsseldorf: Eugen Diederichs

Veldhuisen-Djajasoebrata, A., 1984, *Bloemen van het heelal; de kleurrijke wereld van de textiel op Java*. Amsterdam: Sijthoff

Verhuell, Q. M. R., 1835–36, *Herinneringen van eene reis naar de Oost-Indiën*. Haarlem: Loosjes (2 vols.)

Verkerk Pistorius, A. W. P., 1874, "Palembangsche schetsen; Een dag bij de wilden," *TNI* new series 3/1, pp. 150–60

(*Verslag*), 1900–46, *Verslag van den Dienst van het Boschwezen in Nederlandsch-Indië* (published nearly annually)

Veth, P. J., 1875–82, *Java, geographisch, ethnologisch, historisch*. Haarlem: Boon (3 vols.)

Vincent, F., 1874, *The Land of the White Elephant. Sights and Scenes in South-Eastern Asia (. . .)(1871–72)*. New York: Harper

Vissering, C. M., 1912, *Een reis door Oost-Java*. Haarlem: Bohn

Vogel, J. W., 1704, *Zehen-Jährige Ost-Indianische Reise-Beschreibung*. Altenburg: Richter

Volz, W., 1909, *Nord-Sumatra. Bericht über eine im Auftrag der Humboldt-Stiftung der Königlich Preussischen Akademie der Wissenschaften zu Berlin in den Jahren 1904–1906 ausgeführte Forschungsreise. Band I: Die Batakländer*. Berlin: Reimer

Volz, W., 1912, *Nord-Sumatra. Bericht über eine im Auftrag der Humboldt-Stiftung der Königlich Preussischen Akademie der Wissenschaften zu Berlin in den Jahren 1904–1906 ausgeführte Forschungsreise. Band II: Die Gajoländer*. Berlin: Reimer

Volz, W., 1921, *Im Dämmer des Rimba: Sumatras Urwald und Urmensch*. Breslau: Hirt

Voorhoeve, R. (1940), *Inlandsche jagers*. Den Haag: De Hofstad

Vos, J. de, S. Sartono, S. Hardja-Sasmita, and P. Y. Sondaar, 1982, "The Fauna from Trinil, Type Locality of *Homo erectus*; A Reinterpretation," *Geologie en Mijnbouw* 61, pp. 207–11

Vos, J. de, P. Y. Sondaar, G. D. van den Bergh, and F. Aziz, 1994, "The *Homo* Bearing Deposits of Java and Its Ecological Context," *Courier Forschungs-Institut Senckenberg* 171, pp. 129–40

("Vragen"), 1881, "Vragen en mededeelingen," *TBG* 26, pp. 202–4

("Vruchtbaarheid"), 1855, "Vruchtbaarheid van tijgers," *NTNI* 9, pp. 522–23

Waldeck, P. F. (1862), *Oost-Indische reis (. . .) in de jaren 1826–1829*. No pl.: no publ.

Wallace, A. R., 1986, *The Malay Archipelago; The Land of the Orang-utan, and the Bird of Paradise. A Narrative of Travel, with Studies of Man and Nature*. Singapore, etc.: Oxford University Press (1st ed. 1869)

Wals, H. de (1937), *Jan en ik, de jagers van de brandsavannen*. Batavia: Kolff

Ward, G. C., 1997, "Making Room for Wild Tigers," *National Geographic* 192/6, pp. 2–35

Wardenaar, W., and P. Ph. du Puy, 1804, *Journaal der Reize van Mr. S.C. Nederburgh, gewezen Commissaris Generaal over Nederlands India, langs Java's Noordoostkust in 1798*. Amsterdam: Holtrop

Wardrop, A. E., and C. W. G. Morris, 1923, *Days and Nights with Indian Big Game*. London: Macmillan

Warneck, J., 1909, *Die Religion der Batak. Ein Paradigma für die animistischen Religionen des Indischen Archipels*. Leipzig: Weicher

Warnsinck, J. C. M. (ed.), 1930, *Reisen van Nicolaus de Graaff, gedaan naar alle gewesten des werelds, beginnende 1639 tot 1687 incluis* (Werken uitgegeven door de Linschoten-Vereeniging, 33). 's-Gravenhage: Nijhoff

Warren, J. F., 1981, *The Sulu Zone 1768–1898. The Dynamics of External Trade, Slavery, and Ethnicity in the Transformation of a Southeast Asian Maritime State*. Singapore: Singapore University Press

Waterschoot van der Gracht, W. A. J. M. van, 1915, "Eenige bijzonderheden omtrent de oorspronkelijke orang Koeboe in de omgeving van het Doewa-belas-gebergte van Djambi," *TKNAG* 32, pp. 219–25

Watson, C. W., 1985, "Islamization in Kerinci," in L. L. Thomas and F. von Benda-Beckmann (eds.), *Change and Continuity in Minangkabau. Local, Regional, and Historical Perspectives on West Sumatra*. Athens, Ohio: Ohio University Press, pp. 157–80

Watson, C. W., 1993, "Perceptions from Within: Malign Magic in Indonesian Literature," in C. W. Watson and R. Ellen (eds.), *Understanding Witchcraft and Sorcery in Southeast Asia*. Honolulu: University of Hawaii Press, pp. 191–211

Weede, Jhr. H. M. van, 1908, *Indische reisherinneringen*. Haarlem: Tjeenk Willink

Weslij, L. F., 1889, "De onderafdeeling Rawas (Residentie Palembang)," *TBB* 3, pp. 275–366

Wessing, R., 1986, *The Soul of Ambiguity: The Tiger in Southeast Asia* (Monograph Series on Southeast Asia; special report, 24). DeKalb: Center for Southeast Asian Studies, Northern Illinois University

Wessing, R., 1992, "A Tiger in the Heart; The Javanese *Rampok Macan*," *BKI*, 148/2, pp. 287–308

Westenenk, L. C., 1962, *Waar mens en tijger buren zijn*. Den Haag: Leopold (1st ed. 1927–32; the cited edition includes *Het rijk van Bittertong*)

Whitney, C., 1905, *Jungle Trails and Jungle People. Travel, Adventure and Observation in the Far East*. New York: Scribner's

Whitten, T., Roehayat Emon Soeriaatmadja, and Suraya A. Afiff, 1996, *The Ecology of Java and Bali* (The Ecology of Indonesia Series 2). (n. pl.): Periplus

Wiedemann, T., 1995, *Emperors and Gladiators*. London: Routledge

Wiele, H., 1930, *Indische Jagdabenteuer*. Leipzig: Verlag Deutsche Buchwerkstätten (1st ed. 1925)

Wilde, A. de, 1830, *De Preanger Regentschappen op Java gelegen*. Amsterdam: Westerman

Wilken, G. A., 1884, *Het animisme bij de volken van den Indischen Archipel*. Amsterdam: de Bussy

Wilken, G. A., 1887, *Het Shamanisme bij de volken van den Indischen Archipel*. 's-Gravenhage: Nijhoff

Wilsen, F. C., 1857–58, "Bijgeloovigheden der Soendanezen," *TBG* 6, pp. 75–96; 7, 45–66

Winstedt, R. O., 1911, *Malay Industries. Part II. Fishing, Hunting and Trapping*. Kuala Lumpur: Federated Malay States Government Press

Winstedt, R. O., 1961, *The Malay Magician: Being Shaman, Saiva and Sufi*. London: Routledge & Kegan Paul

Winter, 1901, "Ook onderdanen onzer Koningin (Een bezoek aan de tamme Koeboes)," *Indische Gids* 23/1, pp. 208–47

Winter, J. W., 1902, "Beknopte beschrijving van het hof Soerakarta in 1824," *BKI* 54, pp. 15–72

Wolf, E. R., 1982, *Europe and the People without History*. Berkeley, etc.: University of California Press

Worm, J. G., 1745, *Ost-Indian- und Persianische Reisen (. . .)*. Franckfurt: no publ. (2nd ed.)

Wormser, C. W. (1941), *Drieendertig jaren op Java. Deel II: in de bergen*. Amsterdam/ Bandoeng: Ten Have/Vorkink

Wurffbain, J. S., 1686, *Vierzehen Jährige Ost-Indianische Krieg- und Ober-Kauffmanns Dienste*. Sultzbach: Endter

Yost, J., and P. M. Kelley, 1983, "Shotguns, Blowguns and Spears; The Analysis of Technological Efficiency," in R. B. Hames and W. T. Vickers (eds.), *The Adaptive Responses of Native Amazonians*. New York: Academic Press, pp. 189–224

Zentgraaff, H. C. (1938), *Atjeh*. Batavia: De Unie

Zentgraaff, H. C., and W. A. van Goudoever, 1947, *Sumatraantjes*. 's-Gravenhage: Van Hoeve

Zimmermann, H. C. O., 1938, "Bali Bevindingen," *De Nederlandsch-Indische Jager* 8/3, pp. 49–50

Zimmermann, V., 1919, "De kraton van Soerakarta in het jaar 1915," *TBG* 58, pp. 305–36

Zollinger, H., 1846, "Bijdragen tot de kennis van de gebergte-sijstemen in het oostelijk Java," *TNI* 8/1, pp. 125–90

Zollinger, H., 1866, "Togt naar het gebergte Bator," *BKI* 13, pp. 497–535

Newspapers and Gazettes

Bataviasche Courant
Gazette of India
Indonesia Times (post-independence)
Jakarta Post (post-independence)
Java Government Gazette
Javasche Courant
Kompas (post-independence)
Mataram
Nieuws- en Advertentieblad voor Probolingo (sic) *en Omstreken*
Suara Pembaruan (post-independence)

Index

Page numbers followed by "f" or "t" denote figures or tables, respectively.

E. D. Smith
714 Walnut Court
No. 401
Darien, Illinois 60561